BILINGUAL EDUCATION AND BILINGUALISM 23
Series Editors: Colin Baker and Nancy Hornberger

Language, Power and Pedagogy

Bilingual Children in the Crossfire

Jim Cummins

MULTILINGUAL MATTERS LTD
Clevedon • Buffalo • Toronto • Sydney

Library of Congress Cataloging in Publication Data

Cummins, Jim
Language, Power and Pedagogy: Bilingual Children in the Crossfire/Jim Cummins
Bilingual Education and Bilingualism: 23
Includes bibliographical references and index
1. Education, Bilingual–Social aspects. 2. Minorities–Education–Social aspects. I. Title. II. Series
LC3719.C86 2000
370.117'5–dc21   00-030543

British Library Cataloguing in Publication Data

A CIP catalogue record for this book is available from the British Library.

ISBN 1-85359-474-1 (hbk)
ISBN 1-85359-473-3 (pbk)

Multilingual Matters Ltd

UK: Frankfurt Lodge, Clevedon Hall, Victoria Road, Clevedon BS21 7HH.
USA: UTP, 2250 Military Road, Tonawanda, NY 14150, USA.
Canada: UTP, 5201 Dufferin Street, North York, Ontario M3H 5T8, Canada.
Australia: P.O. Box 586, Artarmon, NSW, Australia.

Printed and bound in Great Britain by Cambrian Printers Ltd.

Language, Power and Pedagogy

BILINGUAL EDUCATION AND BILINGUALISM
Series Editors: Professor Colin Baker, *University of Wales, Bangor, Wales, Great Britain* and Professor Nancy H. Hornberger, *University of Pennsylvania, Philadelphia, USA.*

Other Books in the Series
Bilingual Education and Social Change
    Rebecca Freeman
Building Bridges: Multilingual Resources for Children
    Multilingual Resources for Children Project
Child-Rearing in Ethnic Minorities
    J.S. Dosanjh and Paul A.S. Ghuman
Curriculum Related Assessment, Cummins and Bilingual Children
    Tony Cline and Norah Frederickson (eds)
English in Europe: The Acquisition of a Third Language
    Jasone Cenoz and Ulrike Jessner (eds)
Foundations of Bilingual Education and Bilingualism
    Colin Baker
Japanese Children Abroad: Cultural, Educational and Language Issues
    Asako Yamada-Yamamoto and Brian Richards (eds)
Language Minority Students in the Mainstream Classroom
    Angela L. Carrasquillo and Vivian Rodriguez
Languages in America: A Pluralist View
    Susan J. Dicker
Learning English at School: Identity, Social Relations and Classroom Practice
    Kelleen Toohey
Language Revitalization Processes and Prospects
    Kendall A. King
Multicultural Children in the Early Years
    P. Woods, M. Boyle and N. Hubbard
Multicultural Child Care
    P. Vedder, E. Bouwer and T. Pels
Policy and Practice in Bilingual Education
    O. García and C. Baker (eds)
The Sociopolitics of English Language Teaching
    Joan Kelly Hall and William G. Eggington (eds)
Studies in Japanese Bilingualism
    Mary Goebel Noguchi and Sandra Fotos (eds)
Teaching and Learning in Multicultural Schools
    Elizabeth Coelho
Teaching Science to Language Minority Students
    Judith W. Rosenthal
Working with Bilingual Children
    M.K. Verma, K.P. Corrigan and S. Firth (eds)
Young Bilingual Children in Nursery School
    Linda Thompson

Other Books of Interest
Beyond Bilingualism: Multilingualism and Multilingual Education
    Jasone Cenoz and Fred Genesee (eds)
Encyclopedia of Bilingualism and Bilingual Education
    Colin Baker and Sylvia Prys Jones
A Parents' and Teachers' Guide to Bilingualism
    Colin Baker

Please contact us for the latest book information:
Multilingual Matters, Frankfurt Lodge, Clevedon Hall,
Victoria Road, Clevedon, BS21 7HH, England
http://www.multilingual-matters.com

Contents

Acknowledgments

The ideas presented in this volume have evolved over a 25-year period and have been shaped through feedback and discussion with many people. I owe a significant debt to educators throughout North America and elsewhere whose practice has informed and elaborated the theory outlined here. Colleagues who have influenced my work and who have provided inspiration and support over many years include Alma Flor Ada, Anna Uhl Chamot, David Corson, Stephen Krashen, Sonia Nieto, Dennis Sayers, Tove Skutnabb-Kangas, Merrill Swain, and Lily Wong Fillmore. Others who helped shape the initial formulation of these ideas in the late 1970s and early 1980s, as well as the 'field-testing' of the ideas in teacher preparation programs and in classrooms, include Margarita Calderón of Johns Hopkins University, and David Dolson, Norm Gold, Judy Lambert, Jan Mayer, Dennis Parker, Fred Tempes and their colleagues at the California State Department of Education.

Among those who provided very useful suggestions or feedback on the ideas that found their way into one or more chapters are: Lyle Bachman, Jasone Cenoz, Stacy Churchill, Elizabeth Coelho, Carolyn Cohen, Virginia Collier, Alister Cumming, Robert DeVillar, Viv Edwards, John Gibbons, Pauline Gibbons, Ulrike Jessner, John McCaffrey, Helen Moore, Brian Morgan, Bonny Norton, Carlos Ovando, Penny Poutu, Elana Shohamy, Wayne Thomas, Toni Waho, Burns Wattie, and Joan Wink.

I am also grateful to those who provided or brought my attention to resources, research information, or experiences that are reflected in the book: Zeynep Beykont, Michael Bostwick, Michael Breen, Chris Davison, Thalia Dragonas, Anna Frangoudaki, Debra Hopkins, Lloyd Houske, David Freeman, Yvonne Freeman, Elena Izquierdo, Carolyn Kessler, Shelley Kwock, Constant Leung, Stephen May, Penny McKay, Marcia Moraes, J. Michael O'Malley, Marla Pérez-Sélles, Naomi Silverman, Tom Scovel, Howard Smith, Lourdes Soto, Carmen Tafolla and Alice Weinrib.

I would also like to express my appreciation to Mitsuyo Sakamoto for assistance in preparing the bibliography. Two information resources that were invaluable were James Crawford's web site (http://ourworld.compuserve.com/homepages/

jwcrawford) and the work of Bob Peterson and his colleagues at Rethinking Schools (http://www.rethinkingschools.org).

For intense discussions of the relevance of the framework elaborated in the book for the Greek context, I would like to thank Eleni Skourtou and Vasilia Kazoullis.

To my wife Ioana I would like to say 'thank you' for your patience, support, love, and not least feedback, during the many phases of this project.

Colin Baker and Nancy Hornberger gave the kind of editorial guidance that one dreams about. They pointed to some pitfalls and omissions, insightfully demurred on certain points and waxed enthusiastic on others, and generally helped shape the final version towards greater coherence and clarity.

Finally, I would like to pay tribute to Mike and Marjukka Grover, and their colleagues at Multilingual Matters, for their conviction, commitment, imagination, and intense hard work over a 20-year period that have exerted such a positive impact on the lives of bilingual/multilingual children and communities around the world. It is a privilege to be part of the team.

Part 1
Theory as Dialogue

My purpose in writing this book is to link theory, research, policy, and practice as a means of contributing to the improvement of educational practice. I see the relationship between theory and practice as two-way and ongoing: practice generates theory, which, in turn, acts as a catalyst for new directions in practice, which then inform theory, and so on. Theory and practice are infused within each other. The role of researchers and policy-makers is to mediate this relationship. Research provides a lens through which practice can be seen and brought into focus for particular purposes and in particular contexts. Policy-makers interpret the research findings and set guidelines for practice on the basis of both the research and sociopolitical and fiscal realities.

Research can be carried out by 'insiders' or 'outsiders'. Teachers, as inside participants in educational relationships, have the potential to 'see inside' these relationships; their 'in-sights' cannot be duplicated by those who gaze at these processes from the outside (e.g. typical university researchers). At the same time there are dimensions of issues and problems that are not apparent to those in the middle of a situation but potentially identifiable to those who are somewhat distanced from it.

Both insider and outsider perspectives are essential for understanding particular organizational situations and relationships. Dialogue that brings together what is seen from outside and what is felt from inside is necessary to articulate understandings. These understandings are always partial, and subject to expansion and refinement through further dialogue. Theory expresses this ongoing search for understanding. *As such, theory itself is always dialogical.* Just as oral and written language is meaningless outside of a human communicative and interpretive context, so too theory assumes meaning only within specific dialogical contexts. Shared understandings, assumptions, and conventions underpin both the generation of theory and its elaboration and refinement through dialogue. In this sense, theory is *utterance* rather than *text* (to borrow David Olson's (1977) terms – see Chapter 3).[1]

So what?

The 'so what' resides in the fact that the theory articulated in this volume does not stand as autonomous text. It has been elaborated through extended dialogue with educators and researchers in response to issues that have emerged in educational policy and practice during the past 25 years. Popular conceptions of 'theory' view it either as standing alone, aloof from and superior to practice, or alternatively, as being irrelevant to practice and the 'real world'. It is common to hear ideas being dismissed as 'just theory' followed up by demands to just 'show me the facts'. By contrast, I argue that it is *theory* rather than research ('facts') that speaks directly to policy and practice (see Chapter 8). It is theory that integrates observations and practices ('facts') into coherent perspectives and, through dialogue, feeds these perspectives back into practice and from practice back into theory. Theory addresses educational practice not only in the narrow sense of what happens in the classroom but also in terms of how classroom interaction is influenced by the societal discourses that surround educational practices. Theory can challenge inappropriate or coercive policies, practices, and associated discourses by pointing both to inconsistencies with empirical data and also to internal logical contradictions within these discourses. It can also propose alternative understandings of phenomena and chart directions for change.

Because their roots are in educational practice, the theoretical constructs in the present volume of necessity range across, and draw from, a number of disciplinary perspectives. The keys to unlock the secrets of human learning, of achievement and underachievement, are not to be found exclusively within the disciplines of psychology or sociology any more than within anthropology or applied linguistics. But each disciplinary perspective may bring certain aspects into focus, particularly when both 'insider' and 'outsider' research is considered.

Thus, the theoretical frameworks proposed in this volume are deliberately hybrid. Educational policy and practice in linguistically diverse contexts may be based on semi-articulated assumptions about the nature of human learning, and second language learning in particular. Theory and research within the disciplines of psychology and applied linguistics can speak to the validity of these assumptions. These disciplines, however, may contribute little to understanding the social roots of patently false assumptions about language learning and bilingualism and how these assumptions coagulate into coercive discourses designed to exclude bilingual children from educational opportunities. Understanding of these processes requires a focus on societal power relations and how they determine forms of educational organization (e.g. English-only submersion programs) and influence the mindset of goals and expectations that educators bring into the classroom.

Readers will read the text in whatever way they choose. What I can do is make clear the interpretive context within which I wrote the text. In the first place, the theoretical constructs highlighted in this volume and in most of my previous work have derived from educational practice. They respond to issues and concerns articulated by educators. The purpose of articulating these constructs has been to contribute to understanding the nature of educational practice and hopefully to change problematic practices for the better. For example, the initial impetus for making the distinction between basic interpersonal communicative skills (BICS) and cognitive academic language proficiency (CALP) came from discussions with school psychologists who were concerned about the potential for bias in their own cognitive assessment practices with bilingual children. The analysis of more than 400 teacher referral forms and psychological assessments carried out by these psychologists revealed the consequences of conflating conversational fluency in English (L2) with proficiency in academic registers of English (Cummins, 1980, 1984).

A second consideration is that I make no claim regarding the absolute 'validity' of any of the theoretical constructs or frameworks in the book. I do claim that the theoretical constructs are consistent with the empirical data; however, they are not the only way of organizing or viewing the data. Theories frame phenomena and provide interpretations of empirical data within particular contexts and for particular purposes. They generate predictions that are, in principle, falsifiable. Thus, any theory or set of hypotheses must be consistent with the empirical data. If a theory is not consistent with the data, then it must be rejected, or refined to achieve that consistency. However, no theory is 'valid' or 'true' in any absolute sense. A theory represents a way of viewing phenomena that may be relevant and useful in varying degrees depending on its purpose, how well it communicates with its intended audience, and the consequences for practice of following through on its implications (its 'consequential validity'). The collaborative dialogue that I hope this book continues is with educators and those concerned with education in culturally and linguistically diverse contexts. The book is intended to generate critical and constructive 'talk back', and activist collaboration, in the context of the shared goal of reducing discrimination and promoting learning opportunities for students who have been excluded and silenced in our schools.

A third point concerns the sociopolitical context within which these theoretical constructs have been generated. As we enter what has optimistically been called the 'knowledge society', we are bombarded with contradictory discourses about virtually every aspect of education (see Berliner & Biddle, 1995; Cummins & Sayers, 1995). Yesterday's dogma is today's heresy. These contradictions have been very evident with respect to policies and practices regarding the education of culturally and linguistically diverse students. In the United States, for example, diversity has been constructed as 'the enemy within', far more potent than any external enemy in its threat to the fabric of nationhood. Within this xenophobic discourse, Spanish–English bilingual education is seriously viewed (by reasonably intelligent people) as a potential catalyst for Quebec-style separation. It is also viewed by these same reasonably intelligent people as *the* cause of underachievement among bilingual students (despite the fact that only a small proportion of English language learners are in any form of bilingual education, as documented by Gándara, 1999).

While xenophobic discourse is broadcast loudly across the United States, it should also be remembered that the United States has probably the strongest legal protections (on paper) regarding equity in education of any country in the industrialized world. These legal protections provide potent tools for community groups to challenge discrimination in various spheres of education. The United States also has some of the most imaginative and successful bilingual programs of any country in the world (see Chapter 8). Certainly, there is far more imagination at work in promoting linguistic enrichment in education for non-dominant groups in the United States than is evident in its northern neighbour which, behind the facade of its prized 'Canadian mosaic', has largely constricted its educational imagination to providing for the linguistic interests of its two dominant anglophone and francophone groups.

Discourses regarding diversity, bilingualism, multiculturalism and their implications for education constitute the social context for the present volume. Bilingual children are truly caught in the crossfire of these discourses. Xenophobic discourse is broadcast into every classroom and constitutes the primary means through which coercive relations of power are enacted. This discourse constricts the ways in which identities are negotiated between teachers and students and the opportunities for learning that culturally and linguistically diverse students experience. The potency of the indoctrination process can be appreciated when a historian as eminent as Arthur Schlesinger Jr. makes the following observations about bilingualism and its consequences:

> Bilingualism shuts doors. It nourishes self-ghettoization, and ghettoization nourishes racial antagonism. ... Using some language other than English dooms people to second-class citizenship in American society. ... Monolingual education opens doors to the larger world. ... institutionalized bilingualism remains another source of the fragmentation of America, another threat to the dream of 'one people'. (1991: 108–109)

The claims that 'bilingualism shuts doors' and 'monolingual education opens doors to the wider world', are laughable if viewed in isolation, particularly in the context of current global interdependence and the frequently expressed needs of American business for multilingual 'human resources'. There is also an inexcusable abdication of intellectual responsibility in the fact that Schlesinger feels no need to invoke any empirical data to support his claims. As the data reviewed in this volume and many others illustrate, far from 'shutting doors', bilingualism is associated with enhanced linguistic, cognitive and academic development when both languages are encouraged to develop. Schlesinger simply assumes that 'bilingualism' means inadequate knowledge of English despite the fact that a simple one-minute consultations of any dictionary could have corrected his assumption. He also blithely stigmatizes the victim rather than problematizing the power structure in American society which, he asserts, dooms those who use some language other than English to second-class citizenship. He is presumably not against the learning of 'foreign' languages by native speakers of English, but he evades the obvious question of why bilingualism is good for the rich but bad for the poor.

Schlesinger's comments become interpretable only in the context of a societal discourse that is profoundly disquieted by the fact that the sounds of the 'other' have now become audible and the hues of the American social landscape have darkened noticeably.[2]

Xenophobic discourses about linguistic and cultural diversity, exemplified in Schlesinger's *The Disuniting of America*, express themselves differently in different social contexts. However, beneath the surface structure differences, these discourses generally serve the purpose of limiting the educational options that are seen as 'reasonable' for bilingual students from non-dominant groups. They make it more difficult for policy-makers to appreciate what the research is actually saying and to imagine educational initiatives that view linguistic and cultural diversity as individual and societal resources. The theoretical constructs in the present volume, derived from a variety of disciplinary perspectives, attempt to talk back to this discourse. The theory aims to provide educators and policy-makers with intellectual tools to understand the nature of the discourse on the education of bilingual children, to identify obvious internal contradictions in this discourse, and to construct a counter-discourse that simultaneously transcends and undermines the *Us versus Them* framework upon which xenophobia depends (see Chapter 9).

In the first chapter, I provide a sketch or a collage of recent incidents, debates, and problems from around the world which illustrate the concerns and confusions of educators and policy-makers charged with educating bilingual children. All of the issues sketched in this chapter are addressed either directly or indirectly in the present volume. The problematic assumptions that are rampant in contexts around the world (among both opponents and advocates of bilingualism and bilingual education) highlight both the relevance of theory and the urgency of theoretical coherence for policy and practice.

The issues sketched in the first chapter can be roughly grouped into the three major themes of the book:

- the relevance of power relations for understanding policy and practice in culturally and linguistically diverse educational contexts (Chapter 2);
- the ways in which 'language proficiency' is conceptualized and assessed in multilingual contexts and how policies and practices with respect to language teaching and testing are rooted in patterns of societal power relations (Chapters 3–6); and finally,
- the ongoing controversies regarding bilingualism and educational equity, specifically the potential of various forms of bilingual instruction to promote a transformative pedagogy that challenges patterns of coercive power relations in both the school and society (Chapters 7–10).

These issues range across a wide variety of disciplinary perspectives, from applied linguistics and cognitive psychology to sociology and sociolinguistics. Few volumes have attempted to bring this range of issues together within a unified and coherent theoretical perspective. The attempt at theoretical coherence in the present volume derives from the fact that the basic unit of analysis across all of the issues sketched above is the immediate interpersonal interaction between educator and student. What educators bring into the classroom reflects their awareness of and orientation to issues of equity and power in the wider society, their understanding of language and how it develops in academic contexts among bilingual children, and their commitment to educate the whole child rather than just teach the curriculum. To educate the whole child in a culturally and linguistically diverse context it is necessary to nurture intellect and identity equally in ways that, of necessity, challenge coercive relations of power.

In short, the starting point for the analysis in the present volume is the claim that interactions between educators and students represent the direct determinant of bilingual students' success or failure in school. These interactions *can* be conceptualized coherently from within a single isolated disciplinary perspective (e.g. sociology); however, if change in educational practice is the goal of the analysis (a perspective implied by a dialogical approach to theory), an *adequate* conceptualization of teacher–student interactions requires an interdisciplinary analysis that draws on, and integrates, different disciplinary perspectives.

To illustrate, in Chapter 1, I note the fact that 'superstar' ice hockey goaltender Dominik Hasek announced his retirement (short-lived as it happened) in the summer of 1999, partly on the grounds that his son was forgetting his native Czech language as a result of growing up and being schooled in the United States. By itself, this may seem like a piece of trivia until it is placed in the context of research, such as that carried out by Lily Wong Fillmore (1991), showing that loss (or lack of continued development) of L1 is the norm among language minority children schooled through L2. Wong Fillmore's study showed that the resulting communicative difficulties in the family can result in significant alienation of children from parents as development progresses. In addition, such students do not reap the linguistic and cognitive benefits of bilingualism consistently highlighted by the research in cognitive psychology (see Chapter 7).

If first language loss, with its problematic personal and academic consequences, is extremely common among bilingual students, why is it that relatively few 'mainstream' teachers know anything about this issue? Why is it the exception rather than the rule that teachers take proactive steps to help bilingual children feel proud of their linguistic accomplishments rather than ashamed of their linguistic differences? Why are we as educators not more conscious of the fact that our interactions with bilingual students communicate powerful messages regarding what is accepted, respected, and seen as normal in the classroom community? It costs nothing to communicate strong affirmative messages regarding the linguistic accomplishments of bilingual students even when the instruction is totally through the dominant language (see Edwards, 1998, for multiple examples of how this can be implemented). Why is it still relatively uncommon for educators to encourage bilingual students to maintain and develop their home languages? Simply because teacher education programs and school systems have consistently ignored issues related to cultural and linguistic diversity, relegating them to 'footnote' or 'afterthought' status. The generic student that pre-service teachers are being prepared to educate is white, middle-class, monolingual and monocultural. In cities such as Toronto, Canada, where at least 60% of the student body does not fit this generic stereotype, the failure to ensure that *all* teachers are prepared to teach *all* students (particularly the non-white, non-middle-class, multilingual mainstream) represents a sociological phenomenon that can be analyzed only in terms of the persistence of coercive relations of power hiding behind meaningless multicultural rhetoric. However, the starting point for this analysis of how structural factors relating to pre-service and in-service teacher education affect student outcomes is the pattern of interactions between educators and students in the classroom.

The second chapter provides an overview of the interdisciplinary theoretical framework proposed in the present volume. It briefly reviews psycholinguistic data regarding (1) the differences between conversational and academic aspects of language proficiency, (2) the positive effects of additive bilingualism, and (3) the interdependence between academic development in L1 and L2. The second part of the chapter focuses on classroom interactions between educators and students as the most direct determinant of educational success or failure for culturally and linguistically diverse students. The ways in which identities are negotiated in these interactions can be understood only in relation to patterns of historical and current power relations in the broader society. Reversal of educational underachievement requires that educators actively challenge coercive relations of power and repudiate the discourse through which these power relations are expressed. This framework responds directly to the issues outlined in the first chapter. Subsequent chapters elaborate aspects of this framework with equal emphasis on the importance of identity negotiation and processes of knowledge generation (learning) for charting more imaginative and equitable educational opportunities for all children.

Notes

1. The notion of theory as dialogical resonates obviously with Bakhtinian perspectives on language and discourse (Bakhtin, 1986; Moraes, 1996). Although I have been very conscious of the collaborative nature of theory construction and the primacy of practice, the explicit notion of *theory as dialogue* gelled in my mind only in early December 1999 in discussion with Brian Morgan. Brian's doctoral dissertation, and his earlier book, *The ESL Classroom*, explored aspects of theoretical hybridity: specifically, the consequences of analyzing his own teaching practice in a community-based adult ESL program from the simultaneous perspectives of applied linguistics and post-structuralist theory. This theoretical hybridity and the constant two-way dialogue between theory and practice was seen as a means of grounding theory while simultaneously challenging both the hegemony of a single theoretical paradigm and the potential relativism of a theoretical pluralism and associated unanalyzed eclecticism (see Morgan, 1998, 1999).
2. The United States is not in any sense unique in its current flirtation with xenophobia. Most countries in Europe have experienced spasms of the same affliction during the past decade, ranging from attacks on Turks in Germany to anger at Albanians and other minorities in Greece.

Chapter 1
Issues and Contexts

Komotini, Greece, 2 October, 1999: Power Relations Past and Present

My feelings yesterday were almost surreal as I listened to Howard Smith of the University of Texas at San Antonio describe the history of educational oppression experienced by African American children in the United States. What was I doing sitting in an auditorium in the province of Thrace, near Turkey, at a conference focused on the education of the Muslim minorities in Greece, listening to the ugly history of racism on the other side of the globe, and how its residues still persist?

Today, I listened to Daphna Bassewitch Ginzburg and Anwar Dawod from Israel present Jewish and Palestinian perspectives on two different attempts to heal the wounds of the past (and present) through education. Both described settings at the preschool (Daphna) and elementary school (Anwar) where Jewish and Palestinian children are being educated together in the same classrooms, with the same curriculum, and using both Arabic and Hebrew as languages of instruction. I was struck by the courage of educators in these schools who saw education as a means of transforming the future rather than reproducing the past.

Maria del Socorro Leandro, Director of Bilingual Programs in the Edgewood School District in San Antonio, Texas, also spoke of the two-way bilingual immersion program in Edgewood that brings together English-dominant and Spanish-dominant students in the same classrooms with the goal of promoting fluent bilingualism and biliteracy for both groups of students. Here again was testimony about reclaiming dignity and voice from a people who had experienced subordination for more than 150 years. Educators who remembered the very recent past, up to the late 1960s, when Mexican-Americans were treated as an inferior species by all institutions of society, were using the power of language and education to repudiate that past and evoke a very different future.

Too often, the conflicts of the past pervade the classrooms of the present. This was illustrated vividly when Anna Frangoudaki and Thalia Dragonas of the University of Athens, organizers of the conference and directors of the project on the education of the Muslim minorities, spoke yesterday about the history of education in Thrace and the goals of their project. The Turkish-speaking population of Thrace became Greek citizens in May 1920 when western Thrace became part of Greece. The 1923 Treaty of Lausanne, which was referred to many times during the conference, still governs the education of the Muslim minorities in Greece. It provides for a separate education for the Muslim minorities with Turkish textbooks to be developed by the Turkish government. However, use of these textbooks is subject to approval by the Greek government. The curriculum in the Muslim minority schools is divided in two: half of the subjects are taught by Greek teachers and half by Turkish teachers. The school principal comes from the minority group and the vice-principal from the majority. The vast majority (99%) of the Muslim minority attend these segregated schools and have no contact with non-Muslim students until at least the age of 12 when they finish elementary school. More than 7000 students attend 300 minority schools, many of them in isolated mountainous areas.

The situation is complicated by the fact that among the Muslim minorities are small groups of Roma communities speaking the Roma language as well as Pomak communities who speak a Slavic dialect related to Bulgarian. Although their language is not Turkish, their education is viewed by the Turkish minority and by the Turkish government as being regulated by the Treaty of Lausanne as a result of their Muslim religion. Originally, this interpretation of the Treaty was also encouraged by the Greek government. Consequently, these groups attend the Turkish/Greek medium minority schools and learn through two languages which are not their mother tongues. The mutual suspicion that has characterized relations with the Greek government and Greek communities of Thrace, together with pressure from the more powerful Turkish minority, has resulted in a bizarre situation where many Pomaks deny that they speak a different language and claim Turkish as their home language.

For the past 70 years, it seems that the Muslim minority children in Thrace have been pawns to be sacrificed in a struggle for historical righteousness. Turkish textbooks prepared by the Turkish government have been rejected by the Greek government on the grounds that they were full of anti-Greek propaganda. Turkish textbooks prepared in the early 1990s by the Greek government were burned by the Turkish community because they violated the Treaty of Lausanne. Many Greek teachers have approached their duty of 'teaching the enemy' with a feeling of hostility to the language, culture, and traditions that children bring to school. Their expectations for student success have been extremely low and thus it was not difficult to rationalize the minimal literacy skills attained by the Muslim children in Greek (and even Turkish) as being due to their inherent inferiority. Contact between Greek and Muslim teachers in the school has tended to be minimal and characterized by the same hostility and suspicion.

The project that Anna Frangoudaki and Thalia Dragonas spoke about was funded by the European Union and has initiated extensive professional development for teachers in the minority schools over the previous two years. It has also developed attractive and culturally sensitive teaching materials for use in teaching during the Greek part of the day. Not the least of its achievements has been to bring

Greek and Muslim teachers into constructive dialogue, perhaps for the first time ever, regarding ways of improving the education of minority children. This conference itself seemed to represent a huge step forward. It was endorsed by both the 'majority' and 'minority' Primary Schools Teachers Associations in Thrace and the auditorium was filled with teachers from both communities,. The droning repetitious discourses of past hatreds were at least temporarily set aside, although their echoes could occasionally be heard in the reflections and recommendations of participants.

We started this morning at 9.30 and continued through the day until almost 9.00 in the evening. At the end of the conference, the auditorium was almost as packed as it was earlier in the day. My own intellectual and physical stamina exhausted, I remember thinking that I could imagine few settings in North America where educators or any other profession would give up their weekend for almost 12 straight hours of lectures and often passionate discussion. The devastating earthquakes that had struck both Turkey and Greece in the weeks prior to the conference, and the mutual assistance given by each country to the other, perhaps had contributed to shaking up old ways of thinking. Expansion of imaginative horizons could perhaps also be read into the rapt attention paid to accounts from both the United States and Israel of similarly conflictual and oppressive social relations, and the possibility that educators could transform these coercive social relations into collaborative ones. Even if this collaborative transformation were to occur only within the microcosm of the school, or in the interactions of individual educators with their students, it would nevertheless constitute what Noam Chomsky (1987) called 'the threat of a good example'. When schools and individual educators refuse to play their preordained part in the social order, education becomes dangerous. The discourses of national and religious identity, and the historical myths that sustain them, risk implosion when contact and dialogue replace isolation and monologue. When two languages are used in the school to affirm the experiences and cultures of the students and communities who speak those languages, this in itself challenges the discourse of superiority and devaluation that characterizes social relations between these communities in the wider society.

To create a future we need to rupture the past.

Northern Ireland comes to mind and the half-truths of history into which I was socialized as a child.

It is not surprising to hear Thalia Dragonas speak of the change in attitudes towards the project among some officials in the Greek Ministry of Education – initial support and enthusiasm have been replaced by ambivalence and concern. Enemies have their place – they are essential to national identity. If education transforms enemies into colleagues, is it serving the interests of our society or undermining its strength?

Ironically, the Muslim children in Thrace have received a bilingual education for the past 70 years, illustrating the fact that language of instruction itself is only surface structure. Coercive power relations can be expressed as effectively through two languages as through one. Change in the deep structure will come only when educators walk into their classrooms burdened not by the anger of the past and the disdain of the present, but with their own identities focused on transforming the social futures towards which their students are travelling.

Victims and victimizers: Turkish minority children in Thrace caught in the crossfire of historical antagonisms, but at least with access to mother tongue instruction (however inadequate) and no prohibition on private use of Turkish; Kurdish children in Turkey still denied access to mother tongue instruction in any form and restrictions even on private use of Kurdish:

> The only ban on the Kurdish language that has been lifted [by new legislation passed in 1991] is that on private use, provided it does not fall under the other paragraphs. Thus, Kurds are now allowed to speak Kurdish in their homes and sing Kurdish love songs in their gardens, but if a Kurdish child complains to a parent in a private garden, while picking beans, about not being allowed to speak Kurdish during the breaks in school, this act is still a terrorist crime. (Hassanpour, Skutnabb-Kangas & Chyet, 1996: 371)

Earlier today, during one of the breaks, I spoke with a young man who was teaching in a Pomak village. He had come from another part of Greece and had not been socialized into the immediacy of hostile relations between Christians and Muslims that many Greeks in Thrace had experienced. He described his frustration at his inability to connect with his students early in the year. Teaching the prescribed curriculum was going nowhere. Things began to change when he discarded the curriculum and asked his students to teach him some of their language. In my terms, he moved from transmission of a prescribed curriculum rooted in a coercive power structure to an attempt to establish genuine human relationships with his students and their parents. His efforts were so successful that the community assumed that he must be a Muslim. When he demonstrated to them that he was in fact Christian (by showing them the cross he carried on a chain around his neck), the community was angry and rejected him. The teacher contemplated resigning and leaving the community but after further discussion the community asked him to stay.

This teacher's experience brought to mind a quotation from Oscar Wilde which suggests that educators have both the responsibility, and the opportunity, to refuse complicity in the punishments inflicted by society on children, as demonstrated by this Greek teacher in a remote area of Thrace:

> A child can understand a punishment inflicted by an individual, such as a parent or guardian, and bear it with a certain amount of acquiescence. What it cannot understand is a punishment inflicted by society.[1]

******

Tokyo, 1–5 August, 1999: Measured Words and Dissenting Voices

Several items in the media caught my eye on this the first day of the International Applied Linguistics (AILA) Congress. An article in the Airport Limousine magazine which I had picked up the previous day en route from Narita airport was entitled 'Japan's Baby Bust: Young and Old Alike Feeling the Pinch' (Odani, 1999). It outlined the mostly bleak economic consequences of the drop in Japan's birthrate to 1.4 births per woman, far below the 2.1 births required to sustain the population at its current level. Rapid constriction in all levels of education is predicted as fewer young people come to school and go to university. Without a dramatic increase in fertility (which is highly unlikely) or massive increases in immigration (which is currently negligible – foreigners account for only 1% of the Japanese population), the economy will shrink and make it difficult to maintain social services to the rapidly increasing elderly population (aged 65+) which will make up 20% of Japan's population by 2005. Two days later, the *Asahi Evening News* elaborated on these trends (Kristof, 1999), pointing out that the working-age population of Japan will drop by about 650,000 a year over the next 50 years.

Dramatically increase immigration or face economic decline? Stark choices for a nation accustomed to viewing itself as homogenous and proud of it (leaving aside some blips on the homogeneity screen resulting from groups such as the Ainu, Koreans, and Burakumin (Maher & Yashiro, 1995)). To increase immigration in such a way that immigrants would want to settle and boost the population would entail significant social changes: reduce widespread discrimination against foreigners, implement effective Japanese L2 language learning programs, and possibly bilingual education in immigrant languages, and generally adjust a social and educational system to promote equity and academic advancement for second language learners. Not simple to do, or even to contemplate, because we are talking about fundamental changes to the culture and power structure of the society.

These issues are just beginning to appear on the horizon of public consciousness and, to its credit, the Japanese government has initiated research to address the educational issues faced by the inevitability of increasing diversity. Preliminary results from a large-scale study involving approximately 9000 teachers, 800 parents, and 1000 children from Portuguese-, Chinese-, Spanish-, and Vietnamese-speaking backgrounds led by Professor Suzuki Nishihara of Tokyo Women's Christian University were reported at the AILA Congress. Among the findings reported by Professor Toshio Okazaki (1999) is a significant positive relationship between parental attitudes favouring active maintenance of their children's home language and both L1 maintenance and L2 acquisition. A positive relationship or interdependence between L1 and L2 emerges after the L1 has reached a certain level of development. In other words, contrary to the views of many Japanese (and North American) educators, active promotion of the first language in the home appears to benefit not only development of L1 but also the L2.

****

The importance for families of L1 maintenance and the challenges involved in achieving this goal were apparent in a news clip in the 1 August *Asahi Evening News*. This article reported the retirement of the Buffalo Sabres' Dominik Hasek, five-time choice as the National Hockey League's best goalie, and quoted him as follows:

> We want our kids to go back to the Czech Republic and share a Czech background. Every year he (nine-year-old son) has more problems to speak Czech. ...The longer we stay in the United States, the harder it will be for our kids. (*Asahi Evening News*, 1 August, 1999: 5)

Obviously, affluence and privilege alone can't buy L1 maintenance in the face of the massive power of the dominant language in the environment.

I frequently hear sad anecdotes from international students enrolled in the University of Toronto about how their elementary school children are rejecting the home language and culture. After just two years in Canada, many children refuse to use the first language in the home and want to anglicize their names in order to belong to the culture of the school and peer group. I very rarely hear stories of how teachers communicate strong affirmative messages to students about the value of knowing additional languages. In the vacuum created by the absence of any proactive validation of their linguistic talents and accomplishments, bilingual students' identities become infested with shame. A psychological phenomenon, to be sure; but also sociological. Pre-service teacher education programs across North America typically regard knowledge about linguistic and cultural diversity as appropriate for 'additional qualification' courses rather than as part of the core knowledge base that all teachers should possess. As the discussions about assessment and pedagogy in Chapters 6 and 10 make clear, the contradictions that derive from viewing the generic student as monolingual, monocultural, white, middle-class, and heterosexual are becoming embarrassingly evident.

Dominik Hasek's predicament, and that of millions of other minority language parents around the globe, reminds me of the incident that happened a few years ago in Amarillo, Texas, where State District Judge, Samuel Kiser, ordered a bilingual Mexican-American mother (Marta Laureano) involved in a child custody dispute to refrain from speaking Spanish to her daughter. If you are from a group that has historically been subordinated rather than a Hockey superstar, even the home is not a safe haven for the mother tongue. The judge told Laureano that she was 'abusing' her five-year-old daughter by speaking Spanish to her and ordered Laureano to speak only English at home. The father of the child, Timothy Garcia, who was seeking unsupervised visitation rights with his daughter, had complained that she was not proficient in English. As reported in *Maclean's* magazine (11 September, 1995: 13):

> In court, Kiser told Laureano that she was relegating her daughter 'to the position of housemaid'. After a public outcry, Kiser backed down – a little. He apologized to housekeepers everywhere, 'since we entrust our personal posses-

sions and our families' welfare to these hardworking people'. But otherwise, Kiser stood by his statements. Excerpts from his comments:

'If she starts first grade with the other children and cannot even speak the language that the teachers and others speak, and she's a full–blooded American citizen, you're abusing that child and you're relegating her to the position of housemaid. Now, get this straight: you start speaking English to that child, because if she doesn't do good [sic] in school, then I can remove her because it's not in her best interest to be ignorant.

'You are real big about talking about what's best for your daughter, but you won't even teach a five-year-old child how to speak English. And then you expect her to go off to school and educate herself and be able to learn how to make a living. Now that is bordering on abuse.'

Despite Judge Kiser's ruling, few in Texas would contemplate imposing legal prohibitions on the use of Spanish outside of school (although its status within schools is not entirely secure). The situation of Mexican-Americans in Texas is a far cry from that of Kurds in Turkey. However, Judge Kiser inadvertently reminds us that only 30 years ago, any use of Spanish in the schools by teachers would result in a $100 fine, and students caught speaking Spanish would usually be physically punished or humiliated.

Is promoting bilingualism in the home child abuse, or is it child abuse to punish children for being bilingual? To what extent is it child abuse to send new teachers into classrooms (in multilingual cities such as Toronto, London, or New York) with minimal or no preparation on how to teach academic content to students who are in the process of learning English and whose cultural background differs significantly from that assumed by all of the structures of schooling (e.g. curriculum, assessment, and teacher preparation)?

I wonder if Judge Kiser would be interested in reading about the multilingual accomplishments of developmentally disabled adolescents in Kenya in an article written in 1996 by Jamie Candelaria-Greene, a special educator and student teacher supervisor from California. Candelaria-Greene documents the fact that these mentally handicapped students attending Jacaranda School in Nairobi

> were speaking an average of three languages at similar fluency rates. ... Thus, students spoke English as a second or third language as well as they might speak Kiswahili, Gujerati, or Kikuyu. As an instructor in both countries, I found that the Kenyan students, with Down Syndrome for example, demonstrated receptive and expressive language proficiency in their third language (English) equivalent to that of the US monolingual English students with Down Syndrome. (1996: 550)

In rural areas, the children's L1 (tribal language) would be used in the home and for the development of literacy skills in lower elementary classes. Kiswahili (the national language) would be used for initial instruction in lower elementary classes in mixed language areas where it serves as the lingua franca. English (the official language) is used for academic instruction from upper elementary on and there is also exposure through television and other media outlets.

Candelaria-Greene contrasts the favourable multilingual environment for children in Kenya with the fact that special education programming for similar children in the US is usually through English only. She notes that 'school professionals know little to nothing about their [limited English proficient] students' language use patterns in the home communities' (1996: 560). Judge Kiser might be interested to know that 'not once in two years [in Kenya] did I hear anyone blame academic failure or inappropriate behavior on the fact that a student's family spoke a second language at home or that the student came from another tribe' (p. 560). She goes on to conclude that where 'multilingualism and the various cultures they represent are valued by the society, and where there is a continued expectation and need for multilingualism to continue, students can and do manage second languages as well as they handle their first language, regardless of handicapping condition' (p. 560).

****

While in Tokyo, I read in a special August supplement to the *Asahi Evening News*, produced for the AILA congress, an article entitled 'Learning New Methods to Swim in English Ocean'. The article discusses efforts to improve what many Japanese regard as the country's dismal record in learning English. The article reports, for example, that despite its relative affluence, Japan ranks 150th out of 165 nations in TOEFL (Test of English as a Foreign Language) results and languishes near the bottom of Asian countries, performing little better than North Korea. The author concludes that 'without a command of English, Japan is being left behind by the rest of the world' (Hiraoka, 1999: 3). Statements such as this might evoke a heated response from those who advocate a more critical perspective on the spread of English (see for example the articles in *TESOL Quarterly*, 33: 3, Autumn 1999, edited by Alistair Pennycook, as well as Pennycook, 1998, and Phillipson, 1992, 1999).

Hiraoka raises the issue of what we mean by proficiency in English and how conceptions of proficiency relate to language pedagogy:

> Today, two types of English are taught in Japan-entrance-exam English, and conversational English. When these two streams are brought together, the Japanese will at last be poised to join the world community. (1999: 3)

Again, I cringe at the assumption that knowledge of English is the passport to 'join the world community'. However, the claim that what is assessed will determine what is taught and learned resonates with my perception of what is increasingly happening in ESL contexts in Britain and North America. As system-wide assessment schemes are introduced into more and more jurisdictions in the name of accountability, the tension is increasingly apparent between, on the one hand, performance assessments that reflect the full range of curriculum objectives (including critical thinking and creative writing) but which are costly and time-consuming to administer in a reliable way on a large-scale, and, on the other hand, standardized tests that are reliable and efficient to administer, but which typically reflect only a narrow band of easy-to-test curriculum objectives. Into this mix of unresolved issues, throw the rapid increase in linguistic diversity, with many students still in the process of learning the language of instruction and of testing, and you have a set of very high-stakes headaches for the czars of educational quality control.

The issues are surprisingly similar on both sides of the Atlantic, reflecting another aspect of globalization or, perhaps global homogenization. The 28 May, 1999 *Times Educational Supplement* reported that refugee and immigrant children arriving in Britain with little or no English would be given 'two years' freedom from curriculum tests' (Jackson, 1999: 1) under proposals being considered by government ministers. These children would no longer be counted in their school's test results thereby addressing an issue which was described as 'a major cause of complaint for many inner-city schools' (1999: 1). The report goes on to note that there are half a million pupils in England who do not speak English as their first language and the proposed change 'would give a considerable boost to schools' placing in league tables' (1999: 1), the system of publishing the rankings of schools as a means of identifying 'failing' schools and exerting pressures for improvement.

Exactly the same issue is being debated in both the United States and Canada (see Chapter 6) and in every case the one set of data that policy-makers want to hear nothing about is the fact that it typically takes immigrant children at least five years (often more) to catch up academically to native-speakers English. At the AILA conference, Professor Elana Shohamy of Tel Aviv University in Israel reported that in the Israeli context, a period of seven to nine years is typically required for immigrant students to catch up, a figure consistent with the range found in North American data (e.g. Cummins, 1981a; Hakuta, Butler & Witt, 2000; Klesmer, 1994; Thomas & Collier, 1997). If a period of five or more years is typically required to catch up, then delaying testing for two years, as proposed in the United Kingdom (UK), reduces the inequity only slightly. Including these students in the testing will still skew the results and undermine the whole accountability enterprise unless the data are disaggregated in intelligent ways. This intelligence has to date not been very evident in the North American context, where policy-makers have preferred to bury their heads in the sand rather than really come to terms with what I call in Chapter 6, 'the awkward reality' of English language learning (ELL) students.

It would not be difficult to disaggregate the data according to a variety of criteria (e.g. poverty/socioeconomic status, proportion of ELL students, etc.) so that the quality of school instruction would emerge more clearly. In fact, a recent analysis in the *Times Education Supplement* does exactly this for the General Certificate of Secondary Education (GCSE) national school examination results at the secondary level. According to the report, 'it shows huge variations in education authorities with apparently similar levels of deprivation' (Dean, 1999). Furthermore, some authorities with high poverty levels emerged as 'winners' rather than 'losers' when the data were disaggregated:

> Arguably, the best-performing authority is the London borough of Tower Hamlets, where more than two-thirds of pupils are on free school meals, making it the most deprived area in the country on this measure. Though its GCSE score of 32.8 puts it well below the national average of 38.1, on the TES [Times Educational Supplement] analysis its pupils scored 7.3 GCSE points above what might be expected ... (Dean, 1999)

The same kind of analysis could be carried out for the proportion of ELL students in different schools, weighted by length of residence in the country.

So where does the figure of two years come from as the criterion for including or excluding ELL students from national testing? Presumably from the 'common sense' notion that this is how long it takes students to 'learn English'. As the chapters in Part 2 of the present volume argue, this conception of the nature of English proficiency is either naive or perhaps cynical; it reflects typical time periods required to gain a reasonable degree of conversational fluency in English but not the length of time required to catch up to native speakers in academic aspects of English. This example, and many more that could be drawn from other contexts, illustrates how crucial it is for policy-makers and educators to have a clear conception of what they mean by 'language proficiency'. In an era of widespread linguistic and cultural diversity, educational policies on curriculum and assessment that relegate considerations regarding diversity and language to 'afterthought' or 'footnote' status are likely to produce discriminatory instruction and utterly meaningless accountability data.

******

The *Alice in Wonderland* nature of much of the 'accountability and standards' debate in North America was aptly pinpointed by well-known educational writer Gerald W. Bracey in an article in *USA Today* which appeared in early November 1999. Bracey (1999: 19A) points to the hypocrisy of the rhetoric of educational reform in light of the fact that politicians and policy-makers have shown minimal interest in addressing issues of child poverty which has a 'devastating impact' on school performance:

> Poor children get off to a bad start before they are born. Their mothers are likely to get prenatal care late, if at all, which can impair later intellectual functioning. They are more than three times as likely as non-poor children to have stunted growth. They are about twice as likely to have physical and mental disabilities, and are seven times more likely to be abused or neglected. And they are more than three times more likely to die.
> What these kids need are high standards, right? (1999: 19A)

Payne and Biddle (1999) have recently demonstrated the independent effects of school funding levels and child poverty on mathematics achievement in the United States. Together these variables accounted for 25% of the variance in achievement. Level of curriculum challenge (ranging from remedial to advanced algebra curriculum) was also significantly related to achievement. Payne and Biddle point out that despite continuous economic growth during the past decade, the child poverty level in the most affluent country in the world is still more than 20%, substantially higher than any other industrialized nation. They suggest a far more likely explanation for the relatively poor showing of US schools in international comparisons than the 'declining standards' usually invoked by politicians:

> Since poorly funded schools and communities with high levels of poverty are very rare in other industrialized nations, education in America is uniquely handicapped because of the singular tolerance for large numbers of poorly funded schools and massive amounts of child poverty in our country. And as long as this tolerance continues, *none* of the present programs being touted for 'reforming' American education – educational vouchers, 'setting high standards', 'accountability' schemes, charter schools – are likely to improve America's aggregate math achievement substantially. (1999: 12)

I find the educational standards debate (discussed in Chapter 6) particularly interesting because policy-makers and politicians are being forced to come to terms with the situation of ELL/bilingual students in order to implement their grand designs for higher standards (and often their own aspirations for political advancement). The blatant contradictions between the political rhetoric of higher standards and the tolerance for massive child poverty and hugely inequitable school funding exposes very clearly the discourse of coercive power relations.

These contradictions are also readily apparent in debates on bilingual education considered in the next section. The clear message being broadcast by the media in the United States is that bilingual education is a cause of further impoverishment for the poor but a potential source of further enrichment for the rich.

California, 13–16 December, 1999: Sorting Fact from Friction in Bilingual Education

At a workshop in San Francisco on 16 December, 1999, one participant, Anat Harrel, originally from Israel, expressed her outrage at the hypocrisy evident in many of the arguments against bilingual education. She shared with participants an advertisement that appeared in a local parent newspaper in July 1998 right in the aftermath of the Proposition 227 referendum that aimed to vote public school bilingual education out of existence. The advertisement was for a private school, the French–American School of Silicon Valley, and urged readers to 'Give your children a wonderful gift: A *bilingual education*' (emphasis original). The text, with the Eiffel Tower in the background, continued: 'The best of two educational worlds: The accurate planning of the French and the pragmatic openness of the American system'. (*Bay Area Parent*, July 1998: 105). What angered Anat was not the advertisement itself but rather the implicit assumptions that it pointed to in the broader educational discourse: French–English bilingual education is prestigious and legitimate whereas Spanish–English bilingual education is neither; bilingual education is 'the best of two educational worlds' for those whose parents are wealthy enough to pay for a private school, but it causes educational failure among low-income public school students. Bilingualism is good for the rich but bad for the poor.

******

The results of a recent study in ten US cities showed clearly that bilingualism is certainly not bad for the poor, financially speaking. A 2 February, 2000, report in the Latino Link section of *Yahoo! News* on the world wide web (http://dailynews.yahoo.com) highlighted the fact that in Miami 'fully bilingual Hispanics earn nearly 7000 dollars per year more than their English-only counterparts' (Latino Link, 2000). Dr Sandra Fradd, one of the authors of the study, noted that people are often opposed to bilingual education because 'they are unaware of the economic importance of being able to communicate in more than one language ... such opposition may not make good sense when the financial benefits of being bilingual are considered'. The same pattern of economic advantage associated with fluency and literacy in two languages appeared in most of the other US cities (e.g. San Antonio, Jersey City, etc.) (see also, Fradd & Lee, 1998).

****

The motivation of parents who send their children to the French–American School of Silicon Valley is presumably similar to those in other parts of the world who want their children to have the advantages of knowing two or more languages fluently. I was reminded of the article 'Learning New Methods to Swim in English Ocean' in the *Asahi Evening News* which I had read in August in Tokyo. This article highlighted the promising results that are emerging from Katoh Gakuen in Numazu, Shizuoka Prefecture, an English/Japanese bilingual school designed to develop fluent and literate bilingual skills. Instruction in the early grades is two-thirds in English (L2) and one-third in Japanese (L1). Thus, students spend the same amount of time on Japanese language arts as students in a typical Japanese elementary school, although all other academic content is taught through English. Hiraoka (1999) describes how some parents have moved their families into the neighbourhood specifically to enable their children to attend Katoh Gakuen. One such parent articulates her rationale for this move:

> 'In this day and age ... everybody needs a second language. The English they teach at most Japanese schools is useless. I wanted Maki [her daughter] to speak real English in a natural manner.' (1999: 3)

This parent's confidence in the school appears to be well-justified from the careful evaluation carried out by Michael Bostwick (1999), the deputy director of the school, for his doctoral dissertation. Grade 5 students acquire considerable proficiency in English (roughly to the level of Grade 3 native-speaker students in the United States and equivalent to Grade 9 Japanese-L1 students in Japan). Their Japanese L1 academic development and mastery of academic content taught through English progresses at the same rate as that of control students in a Japanese monolingual program.

******

On 14 December, I presented a workshop to educators of ELL students in Buena Park, a community on the outskirts of Los Angeles. I emphasized the potential for developing students' critical language awareness when we encourage them to focus on language and make connections between their L1 and L2. This can and should happen even in monolingual English-medium classes (see Chapter 10). In particular, the wealth of cognates in Spanish and English deriving from their origins in Latin and Greek (see Chapter 3, and Corson, 1995, 1997) provide opportunities for students to become 'language detectives' (Delpit, 1998) searching out connections between languages or varieties within the same language. Several participants noted that in their school districts, after the passage of Proposition 227, teachers were being instructed not to send Spanish books home for parents and children to read together. Furthermore, they were being told to discourage parents from reading to their children in Spanish and even from speaking to their children in Spanish. In these districts, bilingualism was clearly being constructed as part of the problem, rather than as part of the solution.

Yet just down the road from these districts were dual language programs such as the Korean–English program in Cahuenga School (see Chapter 8). These programs, also termed 'two-way bilingual immersion', serve both English-dominant and L1-dominant students with the goal of developing bilingualism and biliteracy among both groups. Despite the negative societal climate around bilingualism and bilingual education, these dual language programs have expanded significantly across the state during the past year, up from 95 in 1997–98 to 108 in 1998–99. According to the California Department of Education (1999b), these programs have increased 272% since 1990.

I spoke in one of the breaks with a group of educators from one of the districts that operated a Spanish–English dual language program which appeared to be functioning very successfully for both groups of students. These educators wondered how the focus on language connections could be put into practice in the context of their dual language program. Formal English literacy instruction was not introduced until Grade 3 and there was some pressure to postpone it for another year, until Grade 4, in order to provide even more 'psychological space' for the minority language to develop to a higher level.

The discussion highlighted concerns about French immersion programs in Canada that I have had for more than 20 years (Cummins, 1977) and they appear highly relevant now in the context of dual language programs in the United States. It appears to me that we have become captive to the doctrines that emerged from the original St. Lambert model of French immersion implemented in the mid-1960s near Montreal. Among these are the following problematic assumptions:

- The two languages of instruction in bilingual programs should be kept rigidly separate.
- Models that provide exclusive or near-exclusive emphasis on the minority language in the early grades are superior to those that have more equal

instruction in the two languages (e.g. 50/50 models) and/or introduce literacy in both languages in Grade 1.

- Transfer of literacy and concepts across languages will happen 'automatically' and thus as much instructional time as possible should be provided for the minority language to develop because the majority language will 'look after itself' and students will catch up rapidly after formal English instruction is introduced.

There is some substance to all three of these assumptions, but without qualifications they become dangerous half-truths. Certainly, languages of instruction should not be mixed in any kind of random way and it is important to provide students with appropriate oral and written models of each language. However, by not creating a context for bilingual language exploration in our classrooms we miss out on one of the most powerful tools that children in such programs have to develop their literacy and awareness of language. In French–English programs and Spanish–English programs, the cognate connections between the languages provide enormous possibilities for linguistic enrichment, but not if the program is set up to ensure that the two languages never meet.

The assumption that early exposure to the minority language should be maximized in the early grades is not in itself harmful. There are many highly successful 90/10 dual language programs in operation throughout the United States, and Canadian French immersion programs that follow a similar model have also been evaluated very positively. However, several 50/50 programs that develop literacy in both languages simultaneously or in quick succession in the early grades have also been highly successful (e.g. the Oyster Bilingual School in Washington, DC and the Amigos Program in Cambridge Massachusetts – see Chapter 8). Thus a strong case should not be made for the absolute superiority of one model over another.

It appears to me also that it is highly problematic to assume that transfer of academic skills across languages will always happen automatically. In French immersion programs where most children have experienced a strong culture of literacy (in English) in the home, 'automatic' transfer usually does happen in the Grade 1 or Grade 2 year, but parental reinforcement of English literacy in the home plays a major role in this transfer (e.g. Cashion & Eagan, 1990; Cummins, 1977).

The dangers of assuming that instructional time through the minority language should be maximized for as long as possible and that the academic genres and conventions of literacy in the majority language do not require explicit formal teaching were brought home to me by debates that have been going on recently in New Zealand in the context of Maori-medium programs (*kura kaupapa Maori*). A discussion paper written by John McCaffrey, Colleen McMurchy-Pilkington, and Hemi Dale and presented at a conference in Palmerston North in late September 1998 highlighted both the considerable success that Maori-medium programs have experienced in a short period of time but also some unresolved problematic issues. Among these is wide range of opinion and program implementations with respect to when and how English (students' L1) should be introduced into the program. The authors point out that some Maori educators want no English whatsoever from

Grades 1 through 8. However, they also note that many educators 'are now seeking assistance with English developments after finding that total immersion in Maori followed by total submersion in English is not leading to the high levels of Secondary school success they hoped for' (1998: 14). They also note that educators in some programs are concerned that 'English is sometimes being delayed to the point of never being done or being done very badly and children are exited to all English Secondary programmes quite lost' (1998: 17). They recommend that English literacy should be introduced somewhere between Grades 3 and 5 and that a Transition program to prepare students for the challenges of English-medium secondary school be implemented.

Both of these suggestions appear reasonable to me. When the introduction of English is delayed until secondary school, a number of questions must be addressed: What are students reading in the later grades of elementary school? The amount of Maori literature is limited (although great strides have been made in developing material for the early grades). Are students reading in English despite having received minimal (or no) formal English literacy instruction, or are they reading very little in either Maori or English, compared to children in English programs? If they are not engaged in extended reading (and writing), this to me would represent a major gap in their educational experience.

Another issue concerns the need for extensive opportunities to write in a wide variety of genres if students are to develop coherent and powerful writing proficiencies. Corrective feedback and guidance from teachers are also crucial in this process. Writing expertise may be a central cognitive ability, as suggested by Cumming's (1989) findings, but extensive reading and exposure to academic registers, in addition to authentic opportunities for use of these registers, are required to realize this expertise in any particular language. For example, if students are not reading extensively in English, it is doubtful that their ability to spell correctly in English will develop adequately (e.g. Krashen, 1993). It does not surprise me at all that students who have not been encouraged to read and write extensively in English during their elementary school years experience significant difficulties in English when they enter secondary school.

However, the concern among many Maori educators about the quality of the Maori language that students are learning is also legitimate. They are concerned that when English is introduced too early (i.e. prior to Grade 8) there is extensive anglicization of the language due to interference from English. Discussions in the Summer of 1999 (and subsequent correspondence) with Maori educators Toni Waho and Penny Poutu brought home to me the difficulties of developing what Toni Waho calls 'real Maori and not a mish-mash of English and Maori' (personal communication, 19 January, 2000). Similar concerns have been frequently expressed in the context of Welsh and Irish language revival efforts. Research on these issues is lacking and thus educators must carefully observe the outcomes of different program options in order to work towards optimal development of both languages. As Toni Waho observed 'I believe we are only part way there on the journey to create the best solution for true high quality bilingualism' (personal correspondence, 19 January, 2000).

In the context of programs that aim to develop a high degree of bilingualism and biliteracy in non-threatened languages, I feel more comfortable with a program that unambiguously embraces bilingualism and biliteracy and takes steps to develop both languages at an early age. The research of Cashion and Eagan (1990) in Canadian French immersion programs and of Verhoeven (1991a) among minority language students in the Netherlands shows that transfer across languages is two-way (from L1 to L2 and then back from L2 to L1) if the sociolinguistic and educational conditions are right. Furthermore, the possibilities for linguistic enrichment as a result of encouraging students to compare and contrast their languages and develop a critical language awareness can be pursued only if both languages are acknowledged in the program (see Chapter 10). There is nothing in either the threshold or interdependence hypotheses (see Chapter 7) that would support neglect of the majority language. In fact, the data reviewed in Chapter 7 suggest that both L1 literacy and knowledge of the L2 are important determinants of successful literacy development in L2. Development of academic knowledge and skills in the majority language will *not* 'just take care of itself;' it requires *explicit* teaching with a focus on the genres, functions, and conventions of the language itself in the context of extensive reading and writing of the language (see Chapter 10).

This is in accord with Hornberger's (1989) discussion of cross-lingual transfer in the development of biliteracy. She notes that 'highly efficient reading/writing ability in L1 does not make up altogether for lack of knowledge of L2' (1989: 286). Furthermore, she emphasizes that 'the findings that a stronger first language leads to a stronger second language do not necessarily imply that the first language must be fully developed before the second language is introduced. Rather the first language must not be abandoned before it is fully developed, whether the second language is introduced simultaneously or successively, early or late, in that process' (1989: 287). In short, some anxiety in relation to the strength of the majority language is certainly justified, but protection and development of the minority language can be better achieved by providing extensive and motivating opportunities for its oral and written use rather than focusing on erecting barricades against English.

******

The very positive media picture of bilingual education for affluent children in countries around the world is similar to the way French immersion programs have typically been depicted in the Canadian context. These programs serve the interests of dominant middle-class majority language children. By contrast, when bilingual education aims to serve the interests of marginalized students from minority groups, the media appear to have extreme difficulty understanding the rationale for these programs. This was brought home to me in a personal way in a *New York Times Magazine* article by James Traub entitled 'Bilingual Barrier'. The rationale for bilingual education was presented as follows:

> The idea of bilingual education is that students can learn a subject in their native tongue, and then 'transfer' their skills to English once they have gained English proficiency. Some bilingual theorists, like the linguist Jim Cummins, argue that children should not switch to English until they have attained academic mastery in their native tongue, which takes at least five to six years – a staggering idea given the speed with which young children attain verbal fluency. ... Students in bilingual classes study all their subjects – and often English, too – in their native tongue. (1999: 33)

In these three sentences the inaccuracies are legion. A trivial one is that I am not a linguist (my academic degrees are in the area of psychology). I have never specified that any particular time period is required to attain 'academic mastery' in children's native tongue – clearly academic development in L1 continues for as long as there are opportunities for engagement with academic language in school or outside school. For English-L1 speakers in North America, academic development in L1 will continue throughout schooling and for many of us throughout our lifetimes. For speakers of minority languages, academic development will continue for as long as the school or home provides opportunities and encouragement for development to continue. There is no five to six year 'cut-off' point. What I have said, and what the author and his informants have obviously confused, is that it typically takes at least five years for ELL students to catch up academically to their native-speaking peers in *L2* (English).

Another confusion is the assertion that the speed with which 'young children attain verbal fluency' (in English, presumably) implies that language learning occurs rapidly and therefore there is no need for bilingual education. Or if there is bilingual education, transition to an all-English program should occur as soon as students have attained 'verbal fluency'. Traub clearly has no conception of the distinction between conversational and academic aspects of language proficiency nor of the relevance of this distinction for understanding patterns of achievement among bilingual students (see Chapters 3–6).

Traub also asserts that instruction in bilingual programs is in L1-only, with minimal exposure to English until students are transitioned to English programs after five to six years. In fact, the vast majority of bilingual programs spend only a small proportion of instruction through the L1 (Wong Fillmore & Valadez, 1986). Traub appears to believe that the 'L1-only' pattern is what I have advocated. This is absolutely incorrect. What the research that I and many others have carried out does show is that there is a strong correlation between the attainment of literacy in the bilingual student's two languages. Those who have strong L1 academic and conceptual skills when they start learning English tend to attain higher levels of English academic skills. However, as noted above, access to comprehensible input in English, and opportunities to use oral and written English powerfully, are also crucial. The strong L1–L2 relationship (see Chapter 7) certainly does not mean that English-medium academic instruction should be withheld from bilingual/ELL children for at least five years. *I believe, and have strenuously argued, that a bilingual program should be fully bilingual with a strong English language arts (reading and writing) program together with a strong L1 (e.g. Spanish) language arts program.* There is no set formula as to how much of each language should be used at particular grade levels (research suggests that a variety of options is possible and the sociolinguistic context with respect to the status of, and students' exposure to, each language will be a major consideration – see Chapters 7 and 8). Similarly, there is no formula as to which language reading should be introduced in during the early grades. My personal belief is that there are significant advantages in aiming to have children reading and writing (or beginning to read and write) in *both* languages by at least Grade 2.

*****

The Ides of March, 2000

Julius Caesar ignored the warning to 'beware the Ides of March' to his cost, but for advocates of bilingual education two millennia later the Ides of March brought mixed messages. An article in *The Economist* (11–17 March, 2000) by John Micklethwait warned us that the 'One-Stop Disinformation' service operated by opponents of bilingual education in the United States was still functioning very smoothly, as was also evident in Traub's (1999) article ten months previously. During the same week, however, US Secretary of Education, Richard W. Riley, delivered a speech in which he strongly endorsed dual language programs aimed at developing full biliteracy among Latino/Latina and other students. He advocated that these programs should be quadrupled in the next five years. Take your pick from two diametrically opposed versions of reality.

Richard W. Riley (US Secretary of Education):

First, I want to address the promise of language. For many, language is at the core of the Latino experience in this country, and it must be at the center of future opportunities for this community and for this nation. Parents and educators want all children to learn English because it is essential for success. And we also know how valuable two languages can be.

It is high time we begin to treat language skills as the asset they are, particularly in this global economy. Anything that encourages a person to know more than one language is positive – and should be treated as such. ... Unfortunately, some have viewed those who use a foreign language with suspicion and their language itself as a barrier to success. In some places, even the idea of 'bilingual education' is controversial. It shouldn't be ...

Proficiency in English and one other language is something that we need to encourage among all young people. That is why I am delighted to see and highlight the growth and promise of so many dual-language bilingual programs across the country. They are challenging young people with high standards, high expectations, and curriculum in two languages ...

Our nation needs to encourage more of these kinds of learning opportunities, in many different languages. That is why I am challenging our nation to increase the number of dual-language schools to at least 1,000 over the next five years, and with strong federal, state and local support we can have many more. (2000: 3–4)

John Micklethwait (*The Economist*, 11–17 March):

New York is the next target for Ron Unz, a Silicon Valley millionaire who was the guiding force behind California's Proposition 227. This measure replaced bilingual education, which around half the students with poor English were receiving, with crash courses in English. Bilingual education, originally invented as a way to steer funds to poor people in the southwest, has always produced disappointing results. It is now merely a sop to the teachers' unions. Since bilingual education was banned in California about a year ago, test scores have risen. Even more tellingly, the students who were put on the English crash course or into mainstream classes are well ahead of those still stuck in bilingual ones (which a few students have waivers to continue). (2000:15)[2]

Out of the six sentences in this passage, the first is true; the other five are blatantly false. Going through them in order:

- Prior to Proposition 227, only 30% of English language learners in California were in any form of bilingual program and less than 20% were in classes taught by a credentialed bilingual teacher.
- Bilingual education was not originally 'invented' in the United States-these programs have been operating since Greek and Roman times. Furthermore, the spread of these programs in countries around the world, including the spread of dual language programs in the United States, is hardly consistent with the claim that they have 'always produced disappointing results' (see Baker & Prys Jones, 1998).
- Contrary to the claim that bilingual education is a 'sop' to teachers' unions, teachers unions in California and elsewhere have tended to be very ambivalent about bilingual education for the simple reason that only a small fraction of their members are in fact bilingual teachers.
- The implication that test scores rose in California as a result of the banning of bilingual education is without foundation. Changes in scores occurred in districts in ways that appeared to be completely unrelated to what kind of program a district implemented (Hakuta, 1999).
- There is absolutely no data to support the claim that students put into all-English classes made better progress than those who were 'still stuck in bilingual ones' (Hakuta, 1999).

The remainder of this volume addresses these issues in much more depth. At this juncture, it is sufficient to note that Micklethwait's sketch of bilingual education would receive an 'F' grade in any assessment of journalistic competence or responsibility. He has taken the views of Ron Unz, or one of his associates, and has reported them as 'fact' rather than attributing them as the particular perspective of his source (e.g. 'Ron Unz claims that bilingual education has always produced disappointing results, etc.). He has obviously not checked out any of the data that might back up his claims nor even bothered to note that there is any alternative viewpoints on these data other than those he reports as 'fact'. Even a five-minute excursion into the *Encyclopedia of Bilingualism and Bilingual Education* (Baker & Prys Jones, 1998) or into journalist James Crawford's web site on Language Policy (http://ourworld.compuserve.com/homepages/jwcrawford), would have indicated to him that the vast majority of academic analysis of bilingual education is at variance with what he reports as undisputed fact. In this regard, the gaps in his coverage unfortunately appear typical of journalistic efforts in this area (see Crawford, 1998, for analysis of media coverage of Proposition 227).

*****

Opponents of bilingual education in the United States have consistently distorted its rationale – the example of Traub's article could be multiplied thousands of times (see McQuillan & Tse, 1996 and also Jim Crawford's language policy web site: http://ourworld.compuserve.com/homepages/jwcrawford, for many examples). However, advocates of bilingual education have also sometimes failed to understand what is central and what is peripheral in bilingual programs. This was brought home to me when I made a presentation at a conference on 'Reading and the English Language Learner' in Sacramento, California in March, 1998. The conference atmosphere was tense because of the assault on bilingual education in the media in the lead-up to the Proposition 227 referendum to be held in June of that year. Many of the educators present were also strong believers in whole-language approaches to reading which were now being castigated by the State Board of Education as *the* cause of the state's poor academic showing in nationwide tests. Intensive and sustained phonics instruction was seen as the saviour of the next generation. The 'buzzword' of the conference was that we should adopt a 'balanced' approach to reading instruction – a sentiment few could disagree with – phonics and whole-language advocates alike claimed that their approach was 'balanced'.

In my presentation, I tried to make essentially the two points sketched above (a variety of options is possible regarding (1) the amount of time each language should be used instructionally and (2) the language in which reading should be introduced). These issues seemed to me to be 'surface structure' considerations that were less fundamental than 'deep structure' issues related to the ways in which identities were being negotiated in classroom interactions.

The response from some advocates of bilingual education was less than enthusiastic. I was seen as 'selling out' to the new status quo. Many in the audience had spent 20+ years passionately defending bilingual education against its critics and arguing for the importance of strongly developing students' L1. My work had served a useful role in this battle (e.g. Cummins, 1981a). Now I was perceived as saying that there is no 'best' proportion of L1 instruction in the early grades and that it may not matter much whether reading is introduced in English or in students' L1 (usually Spanish). Many advocates of bilingual education had interpreted my work as saying that we should strive for the maximum amount of L1 instruction in the early grades and that introducing reading in L1 was a crucial component of an effective program.

In discussion with some participants afterwards, I tried to point out that I had not in any sense changed my position or emphasis from when I first started writing about these issues in the late 1970s. I had always maintained that there should be a strong emphasis on maintaining and developing literacy in the L1. In most cases, it will make good sense to introduce reading in that language; Spanish, for example, has a more regular sound–symbol relationship than English and is the language Spanish-L1 speakers know better when they enter school, so it will make sense in most circumstances to use that as the language of initial reading instruction. However, the data show clearly that under some circumstances Spanish-L1 students can learn to read first in English or in both languages in quick succession, and reviews of the literature for more than 20 years have shown no clearcut or absolute superiority for introducing reading in L1 as compared to L2 (e.g. Cummins, 1979a; Engle, 1975; Fitzgerald, 1995; Wagner, 1998). To make initial literacy in the L1 central to the rationale for bilingual education placed the whole enterprise on very shaky empirical and theoretical grounds. Similarly, with respect to the amount of L1 instruction in the early grades, I suggested that there is no one 'best' solution that applies across particular sociolinguistic contexts.

There seemed to me to be a danger of focusing predominantly on promoting L1 literacy in the early grades with some 'oral ESL' accompaniment and then transitioning students in Grades 2 or 3 into all-English programs with no ongoing academic support in the mainstream classes. Under these circumstances where there has been little focus on helping students transfer the language and literacy knowledge gained in L1 to L2, students are likely to flounder in an English-only program. This is particularly the case when students' L1 literacy accomplishments are neither acknowledged nor further developed after transition to the 'mainstream'. Rather than being suspicious of English and delaying its introduction, my belief is that we should encourage the development of biliteracy where students are writing bilingual books (according to well-established whole-language procedures), reading them with parents and peers, and generally augmenting their awareness of language and how it works. Strong and uncompromising promotion of L1 literacy is a crucial component of this approach but we should adopt a *both/and* rather than an *either/or* orientation to L1 and L2. When promoted together, the two languages enrich each other rather than subtracting from each other. We can promote critical language awareness among bilingual students by providing them with opportunities to carry out projects on language and its relation to their own lives.[3]

Conclusion

These illustrations of disputes, debates, and power struggles surrounding bilingual education could be multiplied many times over. Among the high-stakes issues whose specifics are beyond the scope of this volume are the following:

- The intense public and policy debate in the Hong Kong context over the sequencing and intensity of Chinese- and English-medium instruction at elementary and secondary school levels (Johnson, 1997; Lin, 1997; Lin & Man, 1999).

- Debates regarding the instructional uses of mother tongue, regional/national languages, and former colonial languages in many African societies and other post-colonial contexts (e.g. Dutcher, 1995; Obando, 1996, 1997; Bunyi, 1997; Williams, 1996).

- Controversies surrounding bilingual education for Deaf children – specifically, the extent to which in the North American context, American Sign Language (ASL) should be used as a medium of instruction and the degree to which linguistic and conceptual transfer will occur from ASL to written English (Gibson, Small & Mason, 1997; Mahshie, 1995; Mason, 1997; Meyer & Wells, 1996).

- The implementation of bilingual education, and the proportion of L1 and L2 instruction, in a variety of indigenous contexts throughout the world; for example, in the territory of Nunavut in the Eastern Arctic in Canada (Arnaqaq, Pitsiulak & Tompkins, 1999; McGregor, Pitsiulak & O'Donoghue, 1999; O'Donoghue, 1998; Tompkins, 1998) or in Australian Aboriginal contexts (e.g. Devlin, 1997; Harris, 1990).

In all of these contexts (and clearly many more), the theoretical and empirical issues discussed in this volume intersect in complex ways. The controversies that characterize policy-making in contexts of linguistic diversity in education can be analyzed from a variety of perspectives; for example, with respect to how power is negotiated between dominant and subordinated groups, how 'language proficiency' is conceptualized and assessed with high-stakes consequences for students and groups, the extent to which different languages of instruction are incorporated in school systems and the academic outcomes of different models, and the types of pedagogy that are appropriate to develop language skills and high levels of academic achievement in different sociolinguistic contexts. These issues have often been seen as relatively independent of each other, with the consequence that theoretical analyses and empirical research have remained locked within different disciplinary perspectives (e.g. sociology, linguistics, psychology, etc.)

My goal in this volume is to bring these perspectives together. Every interaction between teachers and students can be analyzed from multiple perspectives (how effective is it pedagogically, what conception of language is implicated in the instruction, what messages related to status and power are being communicated, etc.). The development of coherent policies and effective instructional practices requires that the theory and research be re-integrated rather than remain isolated in discipline-based chunks. Thus, although the topics discussed in the following chapters may initially appear quite distant from each other (e.g. the focus on power relations in Chapter 2, academic and language assessment in Chapter 6, and pedagogy in Chapter 10), they are fused in educational interactions. If theory is going to inform practice, and in turn be informed by practice, then the theory must search for coherence through an integrated interdisciplinary perspective that brings disparate fields into dialogue with each other.

Notes

1. On a lighter note, Bryan MacMahon, in his wonderful autobiography, *The Master*, highlights the fact that the efforts of teachers will not always be appreciated by the wider society. Walking home from school on the day he retired after almost 50 years of teaching in rural Kerry, in Ireland, he had this encounter:

    A genteel old woman paused as she passed me by. 'Was it all boys you taught up there in the school?' 'Yes', I said. 'No girls?' 'None'. 'Ach, sure you're only half a schoolmaster', came her verdict on my lifetime of endeavour. (1992: 202)

2. I became aware of John Micklethwait's article as a result of a contribution by Gisele A. Waters, a doctoral candidate in Educational Psychology at Auburn University, to the BILING listserve on 26 March, 2000.

3. One reason that has been suggested as to why little English literacy is taught in the early grades of some bilingual programs is that the teacher is more comfortable in Spanish than in English. In such circumstances, it would make sense to consider a team-taught 50:50 program where the bilingual teacher teaches two classes exclusively in Spanish and an English-speaking teacher teaches the same classes exclusively in English. The alternation could be according to a morning/afternoon or alternate day schedule. In this type of model, close coordination between the two teachers is essential for adequate implementation and ideally the goal should be to develop literacy in both languages.

Chapter 2
Language Interactions in the Classroom: From Coercive to Collaborative Relations of Power

Introduction

In June 1998, California voters reversed almost 25 years of educational policy in that state by passing Proposition 227 by a margin of 61 to 39%. Proposition 227 was aimed at eliminating the use of bilingual children's first language (L1) for instructional purposes except in very exceptional circumstances. The origins of this controversy go back 25 years to the 1974 ruling of the Supreme Court in the *Lau v. Nichols* case. According to the Court judgment, the civil rights of non-English-speaking students were violated when the school took no steps to help them acquire the language of instruction:

> … there is no equality of treatment merely by providing students with the same facilities, textbooks, teachers, and curriculum; for students who do not understand English are effectively foreclosed from any meaningful education. Basic English skills are at the very core of what these public schools teach. Imposition of a requirement that, before a child can effectively participate in the educational program, he must already have acquired those basic skills is to make a mockery of public education. We know that those who do not understand English are certain to find their classroom experiences wholly incomprehensible and in no way meaningful. (cited in Crawford, 1992a: 253)

The Court did not mandate bilingual education; rather it mandated that schools take effective measures to overcome the educational disadvantages resulting from a home–school language mismatch. The Office of Civil Rights, however, interpreted the Supreme Court's decision as effectively mandating transitional bilingual education unless a school district could prove that another approach would be equally or more effective. The Office of Civil Rights' interpretation of the Supreme Court decision sparked outrage among media commentators and educators in school districts which, for the most part, were totally unprepared to offer any form of bilingual instruction. The controversy has raged unabated since that time.

The debate leading up to the Proposition 227 referendum in California crystallized all of the arguments that had been advanced for and against bilingual education in the previous quarter century. Both sides claimed 'equity' as their central guiding principle. Opponents of bilingual programs argued that limited English proficient students were being denied access to both English and academic advancement as a result of being instructed for part of the day through their L1. Exposure to English was being diluted and, as a result, it was not surprising that bilingual students continued to experience difficulty in academic aspects of English. Only maximum exposure to English (frequently termed 'time-on-task') could remedy children's linguistic difficulties in that language on entry to school. Early in 1998, former Speaker of the House, Newt Gingrich expressed the views of many conservative policy-makers: 'When we allow children to stay trapped in bilingual programs where they do not learn English, we are destroying their economic future' (Hornblower, 1998: 44). According to Hornblower, 'He and other Republicans call for a return to the traditional expectation that immigrants will quickly learn English as the price of admission to America' (p. 44).

Proponents of bilingual education argued that L1 instruction in the early grades was necessary to ensure that students understood academic content and experienced a successful start to their schooling. Reading and writing skills acquired initially through the L1 provided a foundation upon which strong English language development could be built. The research literature on bilingual development provided consistent evidence for transfer of academic skills and knowledge across languages. Thus, L1 proficiency could be promoted at no cost to children's academic development in English. Furthermore, the fact that teachers spoke the language of parents increased the likelihood of parental involvement and support for their children's learning. This, together with the reinforcement of children's sense of self as a result of the incorporation of their language and culture in the school program, contributed to long-term academic growth.

In the context of Proposition 227, bilingual advocates argued that bilingual education itself could not logically be regarded as a cause of continued high levels of academic failure among bilingual students since only 30% of limited English proficient students in California were in any form of bilingual education. Gándara (1999) points out that in 1996 'more than one-third of teachers in bilingual classrooms were not fully credentialed, and while little is actually known about these teachers, the likelihood is that many were relying heavily on one of the 29,000 bilingual paraprofessionals employed in California's schools' (1999: 2). Thus, even before Proposition 227, 70% of California's ELL students were either in an all-English program or not receiving any services at all. Advocates of bilingual education could thus logically argue that the academic difficulties of ELL students were more appropriately attributed to the *absence* of effective bilingual programs than to bilingual education in some absolute sense.

The educational arguments on both sides of the issue represent, to a considerable extent, a surface structure for more deeply rooted ideological divisions. Opponents of bilingual education frequently characterized the use of languages other than English in schools as 'unAmerican' and many also expressed concerns about the number of immigrants entering the United States and the consequent growth of cultural and linguistic diversity (Crawford, 1992b). To them, the institutionalization of bilingual education by federal and state governments constituted a 'death wish' (Bethell, 1979) that threatened to fragment the nation. This ideological opposition to bilingual education frequently resulted either in lukewarm implementation of bilingual education or outright attempts to sabotage the program (Wong Fillmore, 1992).

Underlying the educational arguments of many bilingual education advocates was the conviction that a history of oppressive power relations was a significant contributing factor to bilingual students' underachievement. For many generations, bilingual students had been punished for any use of their L1 in the school context and were discriminated against in virtually all areas of education, from segregated schools to biased curriculum and assessment practices. Schools traditionally had communicated a sense of shame in regard to children's language and cultural background rather than a sense of affirmation and pride. Thus, some degree of genuine recognition or institutionalization of children's language and culture in the schools was a prerequisite to reversing this legacy of coercive power relations.

This orientation was linked to the perceived desirability of adopting a pluralist rather than an assimilationist social policy in which the value of different cultures and groups was recognized and their contributions to American society respected (Banks, 1996; Ovando & McLaren, 1999; Nieto, 1996). Implementation of multicultural education in schools was the logical expression of this pluralist orientation to social policy. In the case of bilingual students, promotion of pride in students' language and culture through bilingual programs was frequently regarded as an integral component of a broader philosophy of multicultural education (Nieto, 1999).

This chapter attempts to provide a framework for understanding how the interactions that bilingual students experience in schools create the conditions for academic success or failure. The initial sections focus on linguistic and cognitive aspects of students' development while the subsequent sections attempt to place students' linguistic and cognitive development into a broader sociopolitical context.

Among the relevant linguistic and cognitive issues are the nature of language proficiency, the effects of bilingualism on children's cognitive and educational development, and the relationship between students' first and second languages (L1 and L2). Research focused on these issues can answer questions such as how long it typically takes English language learning (ELL) students to catch up academically in English as compared to gaining fluency in conversational English. The research can also address questions about the relationship between bilingual students' L1 and L2 and the outcomes of different kinds of bilingual programs. However, linguistic and psychological research provides few answers to questions regarding why some culturally diverse groups tend to experience persistent long-term underachievement, nor does it give us clear directions regarding the kinds of educational interventions that will be effective in reversing this underachievement.

For answers to these issues we need to shift to a sociological and sociopolitical orientation. We need to ask questions such as: Why is it that underachievement tends to characterize social groups that have experienced long-term devaluation of their identities in the broader society much more than social groups that have immigrated to the host country more recently? How are patterns of discrimination in the wider society reflected (or challenged) in the school context? To what extent do structures that have been set up in the school, such as the content of the curriculum, assessment practices, and the language of instruction, contribute to perpetuating discrimination and underachievement among certain groups of students? How can subtle and more obvious manifestations of bias be challenged by educators and communities working together? To what extent can we see our classroom instruction as 'neutral' with respect to relations of status and power in the wider society? For example, what messages are being communicated to students when we set out to do our jobs by 'just teaching the curriculum' as compared to teaching the curriculum in such a way that bilingual/ELL students' cultural and linguistic identities are affirmed?

The chapter argues that students' identities are affirmed and academic achievement promoted when teachers express respect for the language and cultural knowledge that students bring to the classroom and when the instruction is focused on helping students generate new knowledge, create literature and art, and act on social realities that affect their lives. Only a brief overview of these issues is provided in this chapter. The goal is to sketch a framework for understanding the causes of bilingual students' academic difficulties and the kinds of intervention that are implied by this causal analysis. Subsequent chapters address these issues in greater depth.

Psycholinguistic Principles

Conversational and academic proficiency

Research studies since the early 1980s have shown that immigrant students can quickly acquire considerable fluency in the dominant language of the society when they are exposed to it in the environment and at school. However, despite this rapid growth in conversational fluency, it generally takes a minimum of about five years (and frequently much longer) for them to catch up to native-speakers in academic aspects of the language (Collier, 1987; Cummins, 1981b; Hakuta *et al.*, 2000; Klesmer, 1994). Collier's (1987) research among middle-class immigrant students taught exclusively through English in the Fairfax County district suggested that a period of five to ten years was required for students to catch up. The Ramírez Report data illustrate the pattern (Ramírez, 1992): after four years of instruction, Grade 3 Spanish-speaking students in both structured immersion (English-only) and early-exit bilingual programs were still far from grade norms in English academic achievement. Grade 6 students in late-exit programs who had consistently received about 40% of their instruction through their primary language were beginning to approach grade norms. Further analysis of a subset of these data (from a late-exit program in New York City) showed that the rapidity with which bilingual students approached grade norms in English reading by Grade 6 was strongly related to their level of Spanish reading at Grade 3. The better developed their Spanish reading was at Grade 3, the more rapid progress they made in English reading between Grades 3 and 6 (Beykont, 1994).

Gándara (1999), in summarizing data from California, has noted the 'large discrepancy' between the developmental patterns for oral L2 skills (measured by tests) as compared to L2 reading and writing during the elementary school years:

> For example, while listening skills are at 80% of native proficiency by Level 3 (approximately 3rd grade), reading and writing skills remain below 50% of those expected for native speakers. It is not until after Level 5 (or approximately 5th grade) that the different sets of skills begin to merge. This suggests that while a student may be able to speak and understand English at fairly high levels of proficiency within the first three years of school, academic skills in English reading and writing take longer for students to develop. (1999: 5)

Hakuta *et al.*'s analysis of data from two California school districts in the San Francisco Bay area showed that 'even in two California districts that are considered the most successful in teaching English to LEP [limited English proficient] students, oral proficiency [measured by formal tests] takes three to five years to develop, and academic English proficiency can take four to seven years' (2000: iii). They label the one-year time period of 'sheltered English immersion' that Proposition 227 gives ELL students to acquire English 'wildly unrealistic' (2000: 13).

Outside of North America, Shohamy (1999) reports ongoing research being conducted in Israel that shows a time period of seven to nine years for immigrant students to arrive at similar achievements as native speakers in Hebrew literacy and slightly less in mathematics.

There are two reasons why such major differences are found in the length of time required to attain peer-appropriate levels of conversational and academic skills. First, considerably less knowledge of language itself is usually required to function appropriately in interpersonal communicative situations than is required in academic situations. The social expectations of the learner and sensitivity to contextual and interpersonal cues (e.g. eye contact, facial expression, intonation etc.) greatly facilitate communication of meaning. These social cues are largely absent in most academic situations that depend on knowledge of the language itself for successful task completion. In comparison to interpersonal conversation, the language of text usually involves much more low frequency vocabulary, complex grammatical structures, and greater demands on memory, analysis, and other cognitive processes (see Chapter 3).

The second reason is that English L1 speakers are not standing still waiting for English language learners to catch up. A major goal of schooling for all children is to expand their ability to manipulate language in increasingly abstract academic situations. Every year English L1 students gain more sophisticated vocabulary and grammatical knowledge and increase their literacy skills. Thus, English language learners must catch up with a moving target. It is not surprising that this formidable task is seldom complete in one or two years.

By contrast, in the area of conversational skills, most native speakers have reached a plateau relatively early in schooling in the sense that a typical six-year-old can express herself as adequately as an older child on most topics she is likely to want to speak about and she can understand most of what is likely to be addressed to her. While some increase in conversational sophistication can be expected with increasing age, the differences are not particularly salient in comparison to differences in literacy-related skills; compare, for example, the differences in literacy between a twelve and a six-year-old student in comparison to differences in their conversational skills.

Several obvious implications of these data can be noted. First, educating bilingual/ELL students is the responsibility of the entire school staff and not just the responsibility of ESL or bilingual teachers. The numbers of ELL students in many districts, together with the time periods typically required for students to catch up, means that 'mainstream' classroom teachers must be prepared (in both senses of the term) to teach all the students in their classrooms.

A related implication is that school language policies should be developed in every school to address the needs of *all* students in the school, and in particular, those students who require support in English academic language learning (Corson, 1998a). This also implies that administrators in schools should be competent to provide leadership in addressing issues of underachievement in culturally and linguistically diverse contexts.

A third set of implications concerns assessment issues. District-, state-, or nation-wide assessment programs that assess ELL students who are still in the process of catching up academically in English are likely to give a very misleading impression both of students' academic potential and of the effectiveness of instruction. Students who have been learning English for about three years in a school context perform about one standard deviation (the equivalent of 15 IQ points) below grade norms in academic English skills (Cummins, 1981b). If the interpretation of test results fails to take account of these data, highly effective schools with large numbers of ELL students will appear ineffective to parents and policy-makers. This perception is likely to reduce student and teacher morale. Similarly, assessment of bilingual students who are referred for special education assessment is likely to give distorted results if the assessment is conducted only in students' L2.

In short, the differences between conversational and academic proficiency and the length of time required to catch up academically have major consequences for a variety of curricular and assessment issues. In particular, these data suggest that we should be looking for interventions that will sustain bilingual students' long-term academic progress rather than expecting any short-term 'quick-fix' solution to students' academic underachievement in English.

The positive effects of additive bilingualism

There are close to 150 empirical studies carried out during the past 30 or so years that have reported a positive association between additive bilingualism and students' linguistic, cognitive, or academic growth. The most consistent findings among these research studies are that bilinguals show more developed awareness of language (metalinguistic abilities) and that they have advantages in learning additional languages. The term 'additive bilingualism' refers to the form of bilingualism that results when students add a second language to their intellectual tool-kit while continuing to develop conceptually and academically in their first language.

This pattern of findings suggests that the proficiency attained by bilingual students in their two languages may exert important influences on their academic and intellectual development. Specifically, I suggested in 1976 that there may be threshold levels of proficiency in both languages which students must attain in order to maximize the cognitive, academic, and linguistic stimulation they extract from social and academic interactions with their environment (Cummins, 1976, 1979a, 1981a). Continued development of both languages into literate domains (additive bilingualism) is a precondition for enhanced cognitive, linguistic, and academic growth. By contrast, when bilingual students develop low or minimal literacy in L1 and L2 as a result of inadequate instructional support (e.g. in submersion programs), their ability to understand increasingly complex instruction (in L2) and benefit from their schooling will decline. The causal factors here are instructional and sociopolitical, but students' L1 and L2 academic proficiency acts as a mediating or intervening variable which influences the quality and quantity of their classroom participation, and hence academic growth.

Diaz has questioned the threshold hypothesis on the grounds that the effects of bilingualism on cognitive abilities in his data were stronger for children of relatively low L2 proficiency (non-balanced bilinguals) (Diaz, 1985; Diaz & Klinger, 1991). This suggests that the positive effects are related to the initial struggles and experiences of the beginning second-language learner. This interpretation does not appear to be incompatible with the threshold hypothesis since the major point of this hypothesis is that for positive effects to manifest themselves, children must be in the process of developing literacy in both languages. If beginning L2 learners do not continue to develop both their languages, any initial positive effects are likely to be counteracted by the negative consequences of subtractive bilingualism.

Recent studies continue to support the idea of threshold levels of bilingual proficiency that influence students' academic and possibly cognitive growth (Lasagabaster, 1998; Ricciardelli, 1992). However, the hypothesis remains speculative and is not essential to the policy-making process (see Chapter 7). The central and well-supported finding is that the continued development of bilingual students' two languages during elementary school entails the potential of positive academic, linguistic and cognitive consequences.

The linguistic and academic benefits of additive bilingualism for individual students provide an additional reason to support students in maintaining their L1 while they are acquiring English. Not only does maintenance of L1 help students to communicate with parents and grandparents in their families, and increase the collective linguistic competence of the entire society, it enhances the intellectual and academic resources of individual bilingual students. At an instructional level, we should be asking how we can build on this potential advantage in the classroom by focusing students' attention on language and helping them become more adept at manipulating language in abstract academic situations.

Interdependence of first and second languages

The interdependence principle has been stated as follows (Cummins, 1981a):

> To the extent that instruction in Lx is effective in promoting proficiency in Lx, transfer of this proficiency to Ly will occur provided there is adequate exposure to Ly (either in school or environment) and adequate motivation to learn Ly. (p. 29)

The term *common underlying proficiency (CUP)* has also been used to refer to the cognitive/academic proficiency that underlies academic performance in both languages.

Consider the following research data that support this principle:

- In virtually every bilingual program that has ever been evaluated, whether intended for linguistic majority or minority students, spending instructional time teaching through the minority language entails no academic costs for students' academic development in the majority language (Baker, 1996; Cummins & Corson, 1997).

- An impressive number of research studies have documented a moderately strong correlation between bilingual students' L1 and L2 literacy skills in situations where students have the opportunity to develop literacy in both languages. It is worth noting that these findings also apply to the relationships among very dissimilar languages in addition to languages that are more closely related, although the strength of relationship is often reduced (e.g. Arabic–French, Dutch–Turkish, Japanese–English, Chinese–English, Basque–Spanish) (Cummins, 1991c; Cummins *et al.*, 1984; Genesee, 1979; Sierra & Olaziregi, 1991; Verhoeven & Aarts, 1998; Wagner, 1998).

A comprehensive review of US research on cognitive reading processes among ELL students concluded that this research consistently supported the common underlying proficiency model:

> ... considerable evidence emerged to support the CUP model. United States ESL readers used knowledge of their native language as they read in English.

This supports a prominent current view that native-language development can enhance ESL reading. (Fitzgerald, 1995: 181)

In short, the research data show clearly that within a bilingual program, instructional time can be focused on developing students' literacy skills in their primary language without adverse effects on the development of their literacy skills in English. Furthermore, the relationship between first and second language literacy skills suggests that effective development of primary language literacy skills can provide a conceptual foundation for long-term growth in English literacy skills. This does not imply, however, that transfer of literacy and academic language knowledge will happen automatically; there is usually also a need for formal instruction in the target language to realize the benefits of cross-linguistic transfer. The status of the interdependence principle is reviewed in more detail in Chapter 7.

Conclusion

This sketch of psycholinguistic data regarding bilingual academic development shows that a substantial research and theoretical basis for policy decisions regarding minority students' education does exist. In other words, policy-makers can predict with considerable confidence the probable effects of bilingual programs for majority and minority students implemented in very different sociopolitical contexts.

First, they can be confident that if the program is effective in continuing to develop students' academic skills in both languages, no cognitive confusion or handicap will result; in fact, students may benefit in subtle ways from access to two linguistic systems.

Second, they can predict that bilingual/ELL students will take considerably longer to develop grade-appropriate levels of L2 academic knowledge (e.g. literacy skills) in comparison to how long it takes to acquire peer-appropriate levels of L2 conversational skills, at least in situations where there is access to the L2 in the environment.

Third, they can be confident that for both majority and minority students, spending instructional time partly through the minority language will not result in lower levels of academic performance in the majority language, provided of course the instructional program is effective in developing academic skills in the minority language. This is because at deeper levels of conceptual and academic functioning, there is considerable overlap or interdependence across languages. Conceptual knowledge developed in one language helps to make input in the other language comprehensible.

These psycholinguistic principles by themselves provide a reliable basis for the prediction of program outcomes in situations that are not characterized by unequal power relations between dominant and subordinated groups (e.g. L2 immersion programs for students from dominant language backgrounds). However, they do not explain the considerable variation in academic achievement among culturally and linguistically diverse groups nor do they tell us why some groups have experienced persistent school failure over generations. The next section addresses these issues and elaborates a framework that combines a causal analysis of educational failure with an intervention framework for reversing this pattern of failure. The focus is on how unequal power relations are played out and can be challenged in the interactions between educators and students in the school context.

A Framework for Reversing School Failure

The starting point for understanding why students choose to engage academically or, alternatively, withdraw from academic effort is to acknowledge that *human relationships are at the heart of schooling*. All of us intuitively know this from our own schooling experiences. If we felt that a teacher believed in us and cared for us then we put forth much more effort than if we felt that she or he did not like us or considered us not very capable. A major study carried out in southern California in the early 1990s documented this 'common-sense' phenomenon:

> Relationships dominated all participant discussions about issues of schooling in the US. No group inside the schools felt adequately respected, connected or affirmed. Students, over and over again, raised the issue of care. What they liked best about school was when people, particularly teachers, cared about them or did special things for them. Dominating their complaints were being ignored, not being cared for and receiving negative treatment. (Poplin & Weeres, 1992: 19)

Teachers in these schools reported that their best experiences were when they connected with students and were able to help them in some way. However, they also reported that they did not always understand students who were culturally different from themselves. They also felt isolated and unappreciated inside schools by students, administrators, and parents as well as within the larger society.

What determines the kinds of relationships that educators establish with culturally diverse students? To answer this question we need to look at the relationships that exist between dominant and subordinated communities in the wider society and how these relationships (henceforth *macro-interactions*) influence both the structures that are set up in schools and the way educators define their roles within the school context.

When patterns of school success and failure among culturally diverse students are examined within an international perspective, it becomes evident that power and status relations between dominant and subordinated groups exert a major influence. Subordinated groups that fail academically have generally been discriminated against over many generations. They react to this discrimination along a continuum ranging from internalization of a sense of ambivalence or insecurity about their identities to rejection of, and active resistance to, dominant group values. At both extremes, alienation from schooling and mental withdrawal from academic effort have been a frequent consequence.[2] The international trends can be illustrated both with reference to the historical situation of minority francophone students in Canada and also in relation to John Ogbu's (1978, 1992) theoretical work.

Minority francophone students in Canada

Numerous studies have shown that disproportionate numbers of minority francophones in comparison to anglophones are characterized by the related phenomena of low educational levels and low levels of functional literacy (e.g. Baril & Mori, 1991; Gérin-Lajoie, Labrie & Wilson, 1995; Wagner, 1991). Various estimates put the rate of functional illiteracy among minority francophones at approximately double that of the majority anglophone population.

Wagner (1991) has provided an insightful analysis of the factors that combine to create the phenomenon that he terms *analphabetisme de minorité*, translated here as 'subordinated group illiteracy'. He argues that illiteracy among subordinated groups is not just quantitatively different from illiteracy among the general population; there is also a crucial qualitative difference. Two distinct forms of subordinated group illiteracy can be distinguished that have no counterpart in the general population. He terms these two phenomena *illiteracy of oppression* and *illiteracy of resistance*. Both derive from the basic problems of access to appropriate schooling and contact between minority and majority languages. He describes these two forms of subordinated group illiteracy as follows:

> Illiteracy of resistance, although caused by oppression, is to some extent instituted by the minority group itself which, wishing to safeguard its language and culture, and fearing assimilation, turns in on itself and rejects the form of education imposed by the majority group. At the extreme, the minority group would prefer to remain illiterate rather than risk losing its language. The group will cultivate the spoken word and fall back on the oral tradition and other components of its culture. By contrast, illiteracy of oppression is a direct consequence of the process of integration/assimilation at work in the public school and in the entire society; it results in the slow destruction of identity and of the means of resistance in the minority community; thus, it is brought about by the oppressive action of the majority society. (1991: 44–45; my translation)

Wagner's account of minority francophones' response to oppressive societal institutions is consistent with descriptions of the identity choices made by other marginalized groups in similar situations. The 'slow destruction of identity' brought about by remaining trapped in oppressive school and social situations echoes accounts of the ambivalence and insecurity in relation to identity that marginalized groups often experience. However, the preservation of identity, albeit an oppositional identity, through resistance often results in equally poor achievement (Fordham, 1990; Willis, 1977).

In the case of minority francophones in Canada, issues of identity and power have intersected both in classroom instruction and in school organization for most of the 20th century (see Duquette & Riopel, 1998 and Heller, 1994, 1999, for detailed reviews). Specifically, francophone communities have experienced long-term devaluation of their cultural identity and languages both in the school and wider society. In Ontario, for example, Regulation 17 passed in 1912 eliminated for more than 50 years the possibility for francophones to be educated in their own language.

Ambivalence in regard to cultural identity still emerges in debates about the proportion of French that should be included in French language schools. Wagner, for example, points out that in a context of societal oppression, education is often devalued and this can persist even when the minority controls its own schools:

> It can happen that the minority group devalues its own schools or refuses to have them because the group is ashamed of itself and its culture as a result of internalizing the critical or scornful views of the majority group. The fiercest adversaries of the 'French school' in Saskatchewan are francophones themselves. (Wagner, 1991: 41) (my translation)

Ogbu's (1978, 1992) theoretical framework

Another example that illustrates the influence of societal power relations on educational achievement is the case of Burakumin in Japan. Burakumin perform poorly in Japanese schools as a result of their low social status but perform well after immigration to the United States because educators are unaware of their low social status in their home country. Thus, educators tend to have the same high academic expectations of them as they do for other Japanese students (Ogbu, 1992). Ogbu distinguishes between voluntary or immigrant minorities, who tend to succeed academically, and involuntary minorities who tend to experience academic difficulties. The former have immigrated to the host country with the expectation of a better life and generally have a positive orientation to the host community and no ambivalence or insecurity in regard to their own identities. Involuntary minorities, by contrast, were originally brought into the society against their will, for example, through slavery, conquest, colonization, or forced labour, and were often denied the opportunity for true participation in or assimilation into the mainstream society. The four major groups that experience disproportionate academic failure in the United States (African Americans, Latinos/Latinas, Native Americans, and Hawaiian Americans) clearly match the profile of involuntary minorities. Similarly, in the Canadian context, First Nations (Native) and minority francophone students underachieve academically in ways that would be predicted from Ogbu's dichotomy.

However, Ogbu's distinction is undoubtedly oversimplified. It fails to explain the underachievement of some immigrant minority groups in the Canadian context (e.g. Afro-Caribbean, Portuguese-speaking, and Spanish-speaking students). Similarly, it does not account for considerable within group variance in academic achievement nor the effect of variables such as socioeconomic status (Cummins, 1997; Gibson, 1997). It is also likely that refugee students constitute a separate category that cannot easily be subsumed within the *voluntary–involuntary* distinction (Vincent, 1996).

In spite of its inability to account for the complexities of dominant–subordinated group relationships, Ogbu's distinction represents a useful starting point in conceptualizing the causes of underachievement among subordinated group students. It highlights important patterns of how coercive power relations operating in the broader society find their way into the structures and operation of schooling. The distinction must be conceived in dynamic rather than static terms. The status of groups may change rapidly from one generation to another in ways that a rigid dichotomy cannot accommodate.

For these reasons, I prefer to discuss the issues in terms of coercive and collaborative relations of power that encompass the important distinction that Ogbu has made as well as the other categories of difference that define inter-group power relations (e.g. racism, sexism, homophobia, discrimination based on language and/or cultural differences, etc.). This orientation also facilitates examination of how power relations in the broader society get translated into educational failure within the schools, and most importantly, how this process can be resisted and reversed.

The two diagrams (Figures 2.1 and 2.2) outline an analysis of the causes of school failure and the intervention model that forms the basis for the current theoretical

FIGURE 2.1 Coercive and collaborative relations of power manifested in macro- and micro-interactions

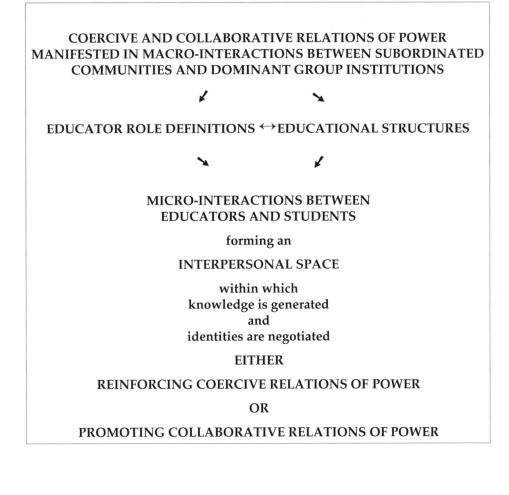

COERCIVE AND COLLABORATIVE RELATIONS OF POWER
MANIFESTED IN MACRO-INTERACTIONS BETWEEN SUBORDINATED
COMMUNITIES AND DOMINANT GROUP INSTITUTIONS

EDUCATOR ROLE DEFINITIONS ↔ EDUCATIONAL STRUCTURES

MICRO-INTERACTIONS BETWEEN
EDUCATORS AND STUDENTS

forming an

INTERPERSONAL SPACE

within which
knowledge is generated
and
identities are negotiated

EITHER

REINFORCING COERCIVE RELATIONS OF POWER

OR

PROMOTING COLLABORATIVE RELATIONS OF POWER

framework. The framework (Figure 2.1) proposes that relations of power in the wider society (macro-interactions), ranging from coercive to collaborative in varying degrees, influence both the ways in which educators define their roles and the types of structures that are established in the educational system. Role definitions refer to the mindset of expectations, assumptions and goals that educators bring to the task of educating culturally diverse students.

Coercive relations of power refer to the exercise of power by a dominant individual, group, or country to the detriment of a subordinated individual, group or country. For example, in the past, dominant group institutions (e.g. schools) have required that subordinated groups deny their cultural identity and give up their languages as a necessary condition for success in the 'mainstream' society. For educators to become partners in the transmission of knowledge, culturally diverse students were required to acquiesce in the subordination of their identities and to celebrate as 'truth' the perspectives of the dominant group (e.g. the 'truth' that Columbus 'discovered' America and brought 'civilization' to its indigenous peoples).

Collaborative relations of power, by contrast, reflect the sense of the term 'power' that refers to 'being enabled', or 'empowered' to achieve more. Within collaborative relations of power, 'power' is not a fixed quantity but is generated through interaction with others. The more empowered one individual or group becomes, the more is generated for others to share, as is the case when two people love each other or when we really connect with children we are teaching. Within this context, the term *empowerment* can be defined as *the collaborative creation of power*. Students whose schooling experiences reflect collaborative relations of power participate confidently in instruction as a result of the fact that their sense of identity is being affirmed and extended in their interactions with educators. They also know that their voices will be heard and respected within the classroom. Schooling amplifies rather than silences their power of *self*-expression.

Educational structures refer to the organization of schooling in a broad sense that includes policies, programs, curriculum, and assessment. While these structures will generally reflect the values and priorities of dominant groups in society, they are not by any means fixed or static. As with most other aspects of the way societies are organized and resources distributed, educational structures are contested by individuals and groups.

Educational structures, together with educator role definitions, determine the micro-interactions between educators, students, and communities. These micro-interactions form an interpersonal space within which the acquisition of knowledge and formation of identity is negotiated. Power is created and shared within this interpersonal space where minds and identities meet. As such, these micro-interactions constitute the most immediate determinant of student academic success or failure.

Micro-interactions between educators, students and communities are never neutral; in varying degrees, they either reinforce coercive relations of power or promote collaborative relations of power. In the former case, they contribute to the disempowerment of culturally diverse students and communities; in the latter case, the micro-interactions constitute a process of empowerment that enables educators, students and communities to challenge the operation of coercive power structures.

The relationships sketched in Figure 2.1 are elaborated in Figure 2.2. The term *Exclusionary/Assimilationist* refers to the general orientation to education characteristic of most countries prior to the 1960s and still characteristic of many today. The goal of education was either to exclude certain groups from the mainstream of society or assimilate them completely. The term *Transformative/Intercultural* refers to the orientation required to challenge the operation of coercive relations of power in the school and wider society. This form of pedagogy entails interactions between

FIGURE 2.2 Intervention for collaborative empowerment

COERCIVE RELATIONS OF POWER MANIFESTED IN THE MACRO-INTERACTIONS BETWEEN DOMINANT GROUP INSTITUTIONS AND SUBORDINATED COMMUNITIES	→	**AMBIVALENT/INSECURE OR RESISTANT SUBORDINATED GROUP IDENTITY**

EDUCATOR ROLE DEFINITIONS ↔ **EDUCATIONAL STRUCTURES**

MICRO-INTERACTIONS BETWEEN EDUCATORS AND STUDENTS

reflecting a

	TRANSFORMATIVE/ INTERCULTURAL ORIENTATION	**EXCLUSIONARY/ ASSIMILATIONIST ORIENTATION**
Cultural/Linguistic Incorporation	Additive	Subtractive
Community Participation	Collaborative	Exclusionary
Pedagogy	Transformative	'Banking'
Assessment	Advocacy	Legitimation
	↓	↓
	Academically and Personally Empowered Students	Academically Disabled or Resistant Students

educators and students that foster the collaborative creation of power; in other words, *empowerment*. Although *exclusionary* and *assimilationist* may appear to be opposites insofar as 'exclusionary' focuses on segregation of subordinated groups from the mainstream of schools and society while 'assimilationist' focuses on total integration into the society, in reality they are frequently two sides of the same coin: both orientations aspire to make subordinated groups invisible and inaudible. Minority groups constructed as 'racially different' have historically been subjected to exclusionary rather than assimilationist policies for the simple reason that 'disappearance' could not readily be achieved through assimilation. In addition, if assimilationist policies were applied to 'racial' minorities, it would imply inter-marriage across 'races' within the same 'melting pot'. This mixing of 'races' would implode the myths of racial superiority that have characterized most dominant groups in societies around the world.

It is easy to recognize the Exclusionary/Assimilationist patterns outlined in Figure 2.2 as characteristic of historical realities in many countries. The extent to which they still characterize educator–student interactions is a matter for debate and school-by-school analysis.[3]

By contrast, *Transformative/Intercultural* orientations are based on principles of racial and cultural equality and a commitment to educate students for full participation within a democratic society. This implies providing opportunities for students to develop a form of critical literacy where they become capable not only of decoding the words, but also reading between the lines in order to understand how power is exercised through various forms of discourse (advertisements, political rhetoric, textbooks, etc.). The focus is on understanding not only what is said but also whose perspectives are represented and whose have been excluded (see Chapter 10).

The macro-interactions between dominant and subordinated groups in the wider society give rise to particular forms of educational structures that are designed to reflect the priorities of the society. Since dominant groups, almost by definition, determine the priorities of the society, education has historically tended to reproduce the relations of power in the broader society.

Examples of educational structures that reflect coercive relations of power are:

- submersion programs for bilingual students that actively suppress their L1 and cultural identity;
- exclusion of culturally diverse parents from participation in their children's schooling;
- tracking or streaming practices that place subordinated group students disproportionately in lower-level tracks;
- use of biased standardized tests for both achievement monitoring and special education placement;
- teacher education programs that prepare teachers for a mythical monolingual monocultural white middle-class student population;
- curriculum content that reflects the perspectives and experiences of dominant groups and excludes those of subordinated groups.

These educational structures constitute a frame that sets limits on the kinds of interactions that are likely to occur between educators and students. They *constrict* rather than expand the interactional space.

Societal macro-interactions also influence the ways in which educators define their roles in relation to culturally diverse students and communities; in other words, they influence the mindset of assumptions, expectations and goals that educators bring to the task of educating students. The framework presented in Figures 2.1 and 2.2 argues that culturally diverse students are empowered or disabled as a direct result of their interactions with educators in the schools. These interactions are mediated by the implicit or explicit role definitions that educators assume in relation to four organizational aspects of schooling:

- The extent to which students' language and cultural background are affirmed and promoted within the school; this includes the extent to which literacy instruction in school affirms, builds on, and extends the vernacular literacy practices that many culturally diverse students engage in outside the context of school (see, for example, Hardman, 1998; Heath, 1983; Lotherington *et al.*, 1998; Martin-Jones & Bhatt, 1998; Vasquez, Pease-Alvarez & Shannon, 1994).

- The extent to which culturally diverse communities are encouraged to participate as partners in their children's education and to contribute the 'funds of knowledge' that exist in their communities to this educational partnership (Moll, Amanti, Neff & González, 1992; Schecter & Bayley, 1998).

- The extent to which instruction promotes intrinsic motivation on the part of students to use language actively in order to generate their own knowledge, create literature and art, and act on social realities that affect their lives. The alternative is what Freire (1983) termed a *banking education* where the teacher defines her role as depositing information and skills in students' memory banks.

- The extent to which professionals involved in assessment become advocates for students by focusing primarily on the ways in which students' academic difficulty is a function of interactions within the school context rather than legitimizing the location of the 'problem' within students.

These four dimensions namely, language/culture incorporation, community participation, pedagogy, and assessment represent sets of educational structures that will affect, but can also be influenced by, educators' role definitions.

It is important to note that students (and communities) do not passively accept dominant group attributions of their inferiority. Frequently, they actively resist the operation of the societal power structure as it is manifested in educational settings. An example is the three-day school boycott called by the Latino/Latina community in Santa Barbara when the school board voted to end the city's 25-year-old bilingual program in January 1998. Four hundred families set up their own alternative bilingual academy in a community centre (Hornblower, 1998).

For some students, resistance can contribute to academic development (Zanger, 1994); students work hard to succeed in order to repudiate their teachers' low expectations. However, more typically, resistance takes the form of mentally with-drawing from a coercive educational relationship. Unfortunately, this withdrawal usually entails severe costs with respect to academic success and upward mobility (Fordham, 1990; Willis, 1977). Students find affirmation on the streets rather than in the classroom. Armando Vallejo, director of the Casa de la Raza in Santa Barbara which housed the alternative academy set up by the parents who boycotted the school expressed his view that abolishing bilingual classes amounts to cultural genocide: 'Kids sit in the back of the classroom for a couple of years without under-standing, and they get disillusioned. That's when they join gangs' (cited in Hornblower, 1998).

In summary, a central principle of the present framework is that the negotiation of identity in the interactions between educators and students is central to students' academic success or failure. Our interactions with students are constantly sketching a triangular set of images:

- an image of our own identities as educators;
- an image of the identity options we highlight for our students; consider, for example, the contrasting messages conveyed to students in classrooms focused on collaborative critical inquiry (*transformative education*) compared to classrooms focused on passive internalization of information (Freire's *banking education*);
- an image of the society we hope our students will help form.

In other words, an image of the society that students will graduate into and the kind of contributions they can make to that society is embedded implicitly in the interactions between educators and students. These interactions reflect the way educators have defined their role with respect to the purposes of education in general and culturally diverse students and communities in particular. Are we preparing students to accept the societal status quo (and, in many cases, their own inferior status therein) or are we preparing them to participate actively and criti-cally in the democratic process in pursuit of the ideals of social justice and equity which are enshrined in the constitutions of most democratic countries?

This perspective clearly implies that in situations where coercive relations of power between dominant and subordinated groups predominate, the creation of interpersonal spaces where students' identities are validated will entail a direct challenge by educators (and students) to the societal power structure. For example, to acknowledge that culturally diverse students' religion, culture and language are valid forms of *self*-expression, and to encourage their development, is to challenge the prevailing attitudes in the wider society and the coercive structures that reflect these attitudes.[4]

In summary, empowerment derives from the process of negotiating identities in the classroom. Interactions between educators and culturally diverse students are never neutral with respect to societal power relations. In varying degrees, they either reinforce or challenge coercive relations of power in the wider society. Historically, subordinated group students have been disempowered educationally in the same way their communities have been disempowered in the wider society. In the same way as the attribution of inherent inferiority legitimated the brutalities of slavery, the slaughter of indigenous peoples, and the exploitation of colonized populations in countries around the world, definitions of subordinated group students as 'genetically inferior' (e.g. Dunn, 1987; Jensen, 1969), 'culturally deprived', or simply suffering cognitive confusion as a result of bilingualism have been used to explain their poor academic performance and justify their continued educational exclusion. It follows from this analysis that subordinated group students will succeed academically to the extent that the patterns of interaction in the school challenge and reverse those that have prevailed in the society at large.

Relationship Between the Intervention Framework and Psycholinguistic Principles

The analysis of power relations operating in educator–student interactions within the school context is intended to address a different, although complementary, set of questions than the analysis of psycholinguistic issues. Understanding how power relations operate in the process of identity negotiation between educators and students points to some of the causes of underachievement among subordinated group students and provides general directions for reversing this process. The intervention framework provides a lens through which the learning process can be observed and assessed. It allows us to look at the deep structure of learning. What matters is not whether a program is called 'bilingual', 'ESL' 'structured immersion' or 'mainstream;' much more significant is what is being transacted in the interactions between educators and students. Some 'bilingual' programs make little attempt to develop students' L1 literacy skills or to promote students' pride in their cultural and linguistic heritage. By contrast, some predominantly English-medium programs may operate largely on the *Transformative/Intercultural* end of the continua in Figure 2.2. One example is the International High School at La Guardia Community College in New York City (DeFazio, 1997) in which students' pride and competence in their first language is strongly promoted despite the fact that instruction is predominantly through English (see Chapter 6).

It is doubtless much easier to promote students' bilingualism, involve parents (who may speak little or no English), and build on students' background experience, in the context of a genuine bilingual program than in a monolingual program. A shared language between teachers, students, and parents clearly facilitates communication. However, use of students' L1 for instructional purposes is no panacea. To be truly effective bilingual education should encompass a transformative/intercultural orientation to instruction that challenges the operation of coercive relations of power.

Essentially, the psycholinguistic principles are links in the causal chain that relate societal power relations to student outcomes. If it were the case that knowledge of two languages resulted in cognitive confusion and linguistic retardation (as some still appear to believe – for example, Dunn, 1987; Schlesinger, 1991), then any positive impact of bilingual education on students' sense of cultural identity would have to be weighed against the potentially negative cognitive consequences of bilingualism. Similarly, if less instructional time through English exerted adverse effects on the development of students' English academic skills (as most opponents of bilingual education claim), then bilingual education would indeed be a risky educational strategy.

The research data (noted above and in Chapter 7), however, are unequivocal in demonstrating that additive forms of bilingualism are associated with positive linguistic and academic consequences. They also show clearly that literacy in two or more languages can be promoted by the school at absolutely no cost to students' academic development in English. Thus, the psycholinguistic research findings, and the theoretical principles that account for these findings, open up significant possibilities both for enriching the personal and academic lives of bilingual students and for challenging coercive relations of power in the wider society. Educators who encourage students to develop their L1 literacy skills are not only promoting learning in the narrow sense, they are also challenging the coercive discourse in the wider society which proclaims that 'bilingualism shuts doors' and 'monolingual education opens doors to the larger world' (Schlesinger, 1991: 109). The psycholinguistic research illuminates these views (and the discourse surrounding Proposition 227 in California) not only as factually wrong but as forms of racism designed to return the educational system to the exclusionary/assimilationist orientations characteristic of the pre-Civil Rights era in the United States.

Similarly, the distinction between conversational and academic language proficiency together with the time periods required to attain grade expectations in English academic tasks, refutes the assumption that most bilingual/ELL students can catch up within a year of starting to learn English (as Proposition 227 claims). Again, the psycholinguistic data lay bare the coercive sociopolitical agenda that is at work in the claims of groups such as *US English*.

In summary, although they were elaborated at different times and addressed to different questions, the psycholinguistic and sociopolitical theoretical constructs intersect in fundamental ways. Both sets of constructs are essential components of the theoretical framework, as Figure 2.1 suggests. The psycholinguistic constructs are focused more on *knowledge generation* (i.e. learning) while the sociopolitical constructs focus on *identity negotiation* and its rootedness in societal power relations. The point of the framework is that one dimension cannot be adequately considered without the other. They are two sides of the same coin.

Notes

1. In legal declarations submitted in the wake of the passage of Proposition 227 in California, Kenji Hakuta and Lily Wong Fillmore each reported data showing what level of English language proficiency might be expected after one year of intensive exposure. Wong Fillmore's (1998) study conducted with 239 limited English proficient students showed that more than 60% of them fell into Levels 1 and 2 of the Language Assessment Scales after one year of intensive exposure to English at school. These levels indicate minimal English proficiency on the five-point scale.

Hakuta (1998) examined data from the Westminister School District in Orange County California which has operated an all-English rather than bilingual education program. His conclusions are reproduced below:

> 37. Several things are noteworthy about Westminster's data, particularly the use of it to show that the district's all-English 'program is successful in overcoming language barriers' (Westminster declaration; para. 13).

> 38. The average LEP (limited English proficient) student in Westminster gains slightly more than one (1.1) language level per year of instruction. This means that if a student begins school in first grade at language Level A (i.e. a non-English speaker unable to function in English at any level), she or he will require *nearly 3 years* to be at Level D, which IPT test developers (IPT 1 Oral, Grades K-6, English forms C & D) designate as 'limited English speaking', and an additional *2 years* to become a fluent English speaker. Even on the face of it, Westminster's data appear to support the proposition that achieving English fluency requires approximately 5 years: A non-English speaker entering 1st grade will become 'limited English proficient' in late 3rd/early 4th grade and will not become a fluent English speaker until around the end of 5th grade (Hakuta, 1998).

In short, the presuppositions of Proposition 227 regarding the amount of time required to learn English for academic purposes are without empirical foundation.

2. The systematic devaluation of student identities within the school has been documented in contexts around the world that are characterized by coercive relations of power in the wider society. For example, Antti Jalava vividly describes the 'internal suicide' that he committed as a result of the rejection of his Finnish identity that he experienced in Swedish schools:

> When the idea had eaten itself deeply enough into my soul that it was despicable to be a Finn, I began to feel ashamed of my origins. ... To survive, I had to change my stripes. Thus: to hell with Finland and the Finns! ... A Swede was what I had to become, and that meant I could not continue to be a Finn. Everything I had held dear and self-evident had to be destroyed. ... My mother tongue was worthless – this I realized at last; on the contrary it made me the butt of abuse and ridicule. So down with the Finnish language! I spat on myself, gradually committed internal suicide. (1988: 164)

Gloria Morgan, a Caribbean-origin educator in Britain, similarly highlights the ambivalence that bicultural pupils often develop in relation to both their cultural backgrounds:

> I suggest that children of African-Caribbean heritage in Britain are caught up between two cultures, one of which they see devalued and the other with which they do not fully identify but which is seen as superior by society. Just coping with being black and watching and listening as society devalues us can be stressful and contribute to low self-esteem, poor motivation, depression and even anti-social behaviour. (1996: 39)

3. Despite Canada's official policy of *multiculturalism*, exclusionary practices that devalue students' identities are still extremely common in schools. This is illustrated in a case study of one ten-year-old African Canadian male student (James, 1994). Although Darren was a leader on the playground and in recreational activities, in the classroom he was seen by his teacher as 'emotionally flat'. He participated minimally in class activities and justified this on the grounds that they were boring. James describes the instructional context as follows:

> Every teacher in Darren's school is white, as is the principal, the secretary, the lunchroom supervisors, and even the man who puts on the 'Scholastic Book Fair' presentations ... The curricular materials to be found in Darren's classroom are textbooks that have been used since the 1960s and 70s. One of these, a reading comprehension book, presents 'Canadian history' as a collision of white Europeans

with 'primitive native tribes' who do such things as 'dance ceremoniously' ... If the images of blacks that Darren constantly encounters in classes are ones that present them as low achievers, 'primitive', and 'slum dwellers', and there are no discussions about these images, then this will operate to silence Darren. His experience is not acknowledged or validated; he is invisible; and moreover, he is powerless in challenging the teacher. No wonder then that Darren, like many other black students ..., finds his classes 'boring' and refuses to ask questions which would help him with classroom tasks'. (1994: 26–27)

It seems clear from this and many other accounts of black students' educational experiences (e.g. Dei, 1996) that issues related to the social construction of identity within schools play a significant role in the extent to which African Canadian students continue to engage academically. Considerable Canadian data suggest that African Canadian students and their parents perceive education as extremely important but are frustrated in their educational aspirations by the systemic racism underneath the facade of multiculturalism in Canadian schools (Brathwaite & James, 1996).

4.   The perspective presented here is consistent with other recent accounts of the centrality of identity issues in language learning, social adjustment, and academic achievement (e.g. Kanno, in press; Igoa, 1995, 1999; McKay & Wong, 1996; Peirce, 1995; Tse, 1999). In 1996, I attempted to express the reciprocal nature of identity negotiation and its academic implications by suggesting that 'if teachers are not learning much from their students, it is probable that their students are not learning much from them' (1996: 4). Cristina Igoa expresses the same idea more poetically: 'Uprooted children need a safe place to make mistakes; a warm and friendly environment with no fear of ridicule or shame to speak or be silent. The nest is a place where every child's culture is valued; a place that makes it safe for the child to break out of a shell. ... If we listen to immigrant children, they will teach us how to reach them' (1999: 6, 12).

Sheila Shannon (1995) has also documented the necessity for bilingual classrooms to become 'sites of resistance' (counter-hegemonic) if they are to be truly successful in promoting bilingualism. Teachers must recognize how the power of English as the high status language in the school and society undermines children's desire to speak Spanish and identify with their home culture. They must also take active steps to challenge and resist the unequal language status in bilingual classrooms by conveying an enthusiasm for Spanish and ensuring equity in materials and attention to each language. In Shannon's account of one bilingual classroom, we see how issues of power and identity are virtually inseparable from issues of language learning and academic achievement.

Part 2
The Nature of Language Proficiency

There are few areas in the social sciences that entail such far-reaching consequences as the conceptualization and assessment of 'language proficiency'. The vast majority of native speakers of any language come to school at age five or so fluent in the language of their homes. We spend an additional 12 years in school focused largely on expanding this linguistic competence into the areas of literacy and helping students acquire the technical language of various content areas such as Science, Mathematics, and Social Studies. Whether students go to university, the kind of employment they qualify for – in short, their life chances – depend very much on how successfully they acquire this specialized language required to gain academic qualifications and carry out literacy-related tasks and activities. Students' expanding language proficiency is constantly assessed either through examinations or standardized tests which focus on various dimensions and functions of academic language. Sometimes knowledge of grammar is assessed, sometimes vocabulary knowledge, or ability to read increasingly complex texts, or to write on complex topics in coherent and accurate prose.

Schools rarely assess dimensions of students' native language such as conversational fluency or pronunciation that most children have already mastered by the time they arrived in school. Yet, we spend enormous amounts of time and money elaborating on this basic linguistic competence in order to prepare students for the complex linguistic realities of the worlds of employment and citizenship. The formidable nature of this linguistic challenge even for native speakers can be appreciated from the constant public, corporate, and media concern that schools are failing to develop sufficient language and literacy skills to enable students to handle the language demands of the workplace. Clearly, the way we conceptualize 'language proficiency' and assess its development entails major consequences for virtually everyone in our society.

For those individuals who immigrate to a new country and learn the language of that country as adults, the difficulty of the challenge they face is all too obvious. Not only are they required to compete with native speakers of English (in English-speaking countries) with respect to academic or literacy-related language skills, they must also acquire the basic fluency and phonological competence in English that native speakers developed as a first language. The extent of their integration into the society and their employment prospects depend significantly on how successfully they acquire both of these broad dimensions of English proficiency. Thus, how we conceptualize and assess second language proficiency also clearly entails important consequences for the life chances of adult immigrants.

In view of the high stakes involved in the phenomenon, it is disconcerting to realize that there is still relatively little consensus on the theoretical nature of second (or first) language proficiency and its development in different contexts. Issues related to the nature of first and second language proficiency still fuel volatile debates among applied linguists (e.g. Edelsky, 1990; Oller, 1983, 1997) and empirical studies often appear to yield inconclusive results (e.g. Harley *et al.*, 1990).

These issues are explored in the next four chapters. Chapter 3 addresses the nature of the language proficiency we acquire in school. It suggests that we need to make a fundamental distinction between conversational aspects of proficiency in a language and academic aspects. This distinction is elaborated into a framework for examining the cognitive demands and contextual supports that underlie the relationship between language proficiency and academic development. I argue that failure to make this distinction has resulted in the creation of academic difficulties for ELL learners who typically require at least five years to catch up academically in their second language.

The conversational/academic language proficiency distinction has been controversial in the field, spawning accusations that it is a 'deficit theory' and constitutes an 'autonomous' perspective on language that ignores its sociopolitical dimensions. These issues are examined in Chapter 4. I argue that no deficit position has ever been implied by the conversational/academic distinction. Furthermore, the distinction is integrated within a broader framework that analyzes how language interactions in school can be conceptualized along a continuum reflecting the degree to which these interactions either reinforce or challenge coercive relations of power, as outlined in Chapter 2.

In Chapters 5 and 6, the issue of what constitutes proficiency in a language is broadened to include conceptualizations of proficiency within the broader field of applied linguistics. I specifically address the assessment of language proficiency for both adults (Chapter 5) and school-aged children (Chapter 6). In Chapter 5, the historical development of how language proficiency and its assessment have been conceptualized and investigated is initially reviewed and the assumptions underlying the current focus on 'communicative' language testing are examined.

Drawing on the distinction between those aspects of first language proficiency that continue to develop throughout our schooling and often throughout our lives (e.g. lexical knowledge) and those that reach a plateau relatively early in our chronological development (e.g. phonology, basic fluency), I suggest that language development is characterized by increasing differentiation according to particular contexts and tasks. Different contexts require access to specific linguistic registers for adequate or successful functioning, as illustrated in the different registers required for success in a university English literature course as compared to success as a stand-up comedian. An implication is that 'language proficiency' cannot be conceptualized outside of particular contexts of use and we can talk of different levels of accomplishment or expertise (or degrees of access) only with reference to specific contexts.

The context of the present discussion of academic language proficiency is, not surprisingly, education, and more specifically, education in industrialized societies at this particular historical juncture. There is no such thing as 'superior' or better developed language proficiency in a vacuum or in any absolute sense. We can, however, speak of greater access to particular registers or more expertise in using the particular registers that are required in schools in particular societies.

Education plays a major role in fuelling our continued language development along particular trajectories that are crucial to future employment status and life-chances. These dimensions of language development include acquisition of the predominantly Graeco-Latin lexicon of literacy, the specialized vocabularies of particular content areas, and ability to interpret and use more sophisticated syntax in oral and written modes. Other influences also play a significant role (e.g. the amount of free voluntary reading that individuals engage in) but these are usually also related to educational opportunities.

The consistent finding of strong relationships among those components of language proficiency that continue to develop in association with increasing literacy and schooling can be interpreted as evidence for the notion of a *general language proficiency* dimension, as proposed by John Oller (1979), or it can be seen as reflecting the construct of *cognitive academic language proficiency* (CALP), as proposed in the present volume. What makes such a construct *general* is its association with the content of mandatory schooling up to age 16 in most industrialized societies. Specialized lexical knowledge or performance abilities in spheres less related to schooling (e.g. expertise in effective use of 'street language', or joke-telling ability) may be no less sophisticated cognitively or linguistically than linguistic knowledge that is specific to the context of schooling and literacy. Such language uses are not in any way inferior to more conventional literacy-related uses of language. They are simply less relevant to the linguistic rules of the game as they have been established within typical educational contexts. Some of these linguistic rules of the game within schooling contexts may be contrived, unnecessary and an impediment to learning (e.g. learning phonics or grammatical rules by rote outside of meaningful contexts); others, however, are intrinsic to the nature of the relationship between language development and literacy (e.g. increasing ability to understand, articulate and discuss abstract concepts associated with social organization and spheres of knowledge (e.g. democracy, peace, human relationships, or photosynthesis in the Science curriculum).

It is worth noting that not all spheres of specialized lexical knowledge are related to the construct of CALP. For example, some individuals might have encyclopedic knowledge of the varieties of plants, shrubs, and flowers that exist throughout the world (or in their individual gardens). However, this degree of specialized lexical knowledge goes beyond what is expected in more general educational contexts and is thus unlikely to be of much value as an index of performance in these contexts.

This analysis of the construct of language proficiency is related to current trends in the assessment of adults and school-aged students in Chapters 5 and 6. While endorsing the trend towards more authentic, performance-based, assessment models for most purposes, I suggest that there is also a role for assessment of more limited indicators of cognitive academic language proficiency. Specifically, I argue that the most promising measures to assess this general academic dimension of proficiency are those that tap lexical knowledge. In addition, I suggest that, for certain purposes, authentic communicative measures are not necessarily more valid or useful than pragmatic/integrative or even discrete-point measures to assess this core general academic dimension of proficiency.

These perspectives challenge many of the current assumptions in the field. In particular, the claim that discrete-point measures of proficiency may be legitimate for some assessment purposes flies in the face of the current emphasis on communicative or authentic language testing. However, the psychometric research shows little support for distinguishing between communicative/authentic, integrative, and discrete-point measures with respect to their ability to assess the construct of academic language proficiency. In challenging current directions in the field, my goal is to promote further discussion of what exactly we are measuring with our language proficiency batteries and how can we assess proficiency effectively and in a way that is equitable to both adult and school-aged English language learners.

Chapter 3
Language Proficiency in Academic Contexts

A recurring issue for educational policy in many countries has been the extent and nature of support that second language learners require to succeed academically. Students must learn the language of instruction at the same time as they are expected to learn academic content *through* the language of instruction. An obvious issue that arises is 'How much proficiency in a language is required to follow instruction through that language?' Clearly, this is not just a matter of students' language proficiency considered in isolation; rather, proficiency will interact with the instruction that students receive. For example, less English proficiency will be required to succeed in classes that provide extensive comprehensible input than in classes where minimal accommodation is made for ELL students. The strategies that policy makers and teachers adopt to ensure academic participation by ELL students are inevitably based on assumptions regarding the nature of 'language proficiency' and its relationship to academic achievement.

A related issue concerns state-mandated standardized assessment. In an increasing number of educational jurisdictions, students at various grade levels are required to take tests designed to assess the adequacy of their academic progress. These results are frequently published in the media and are interpreted by the public as reflecting the quality of schools and, by implication, instruction. This interpretation is highly problematic in contexts where there is wide divergence in the proportions of ELL students in different schools. As noted in Chapter 2, a minimal period of five years is typically required for ELL students to catch up academically. Do we exempt these students from taking these state-mandated assessments for five years? This may communicate to educators that accountability towards ELL students' academic progress is not a concern. If we do not exempt ELL students, then when should they take such tests (after one year, two years, three years?) and what accommodations should be made to ensure that the test is as valid as possible? (Butler & Stevens, 1997; LaCelle-Peterson & Rivera, 1994).

In short, the question of how we conceptualize *language proficiency* and how it is related to academic development is central to many volatile policy issues in the education of ELL students. I have suggested that in order to address these issues we need to make a fundamental distinction between conversational and academic aspects of language proficiency (originally labelled *basic interpersonal communicative skills* (BICS) and *cognitive academic language proficiency* (CALP)) (Cummins, 1979b). The terms conversational and academic proficiency are used interchangeably with BICS and CALP in the remainder of this chapter.

This distinction has influenced policy and practice with respect to the assessment and instruction of ELL students in both North America and the United Kingdom (e.g. Cline & Frederickson, 1996) but it has also fuelled considerable controversy (e.g. Edelsky *et al.*, 1983; Martin-Jones & Romaine, 1986; Romaine, 1989; Wiley, 1996). In this chapter, I address the rationale and nature of the distinction in light of research evidence from a number of contexts. Chapter 4 reviews and responds to the critiques that have been made of the distinction. In the first section below I elaborate the rationale for the distinction and the evolution of the constructs during the past 20 years.

Evolution of the Conversational/Academic Language Proficiency Distinction

Skutnabb-Kangas and Toukomaa (1976) brought attention to the fact that Finnish immigrant children in Sweden often appeared to educators to be fluent in both Finnish and Swedish but still showed levels of verbal academic performance in both languages considerably below grade/age expectations. Similarly, analysis of psychological assessments administered to ELL students showed that teachers and psychologists often assumed that children had overcome all difficulties with English when they could converse easily in the language (Cummins, 1984). Yet these children frequently performed poorly on English academic tasks as well as in psychological assessment situations. The need to distinguish between conversational fluency and academic aspects of L2 performance was highlighted by the reanalysis of large-scale language acquisition data from the Toronto Board of Education (Cummins, 1981b). These data showed clearly that there was a gap of several years, on average, between the attainment of peer-appropriate fluency in L2 and the attainment of grade norms in academic aspects of L2. Conversational aspects of proficiency reached peer-appropriate levels usually within about two years of exposure to L2 but a period of five to seven years was required, on average, for immigrant students to approach grade norms in academic aspects of English.

The distinction between BICS and CALP (Cummins, 1979b) was intended to draw educators' attention to these data and to warn against premature exit of ELL students (in the United States) from bilingual to mainstream English-only programs on the basis of attainment of surface level fluency in English. In other words, the distinction highlighted the fact that educators' conflating of these aspects of proficiency was a major factor in the creation of academic difficulties for bilingual students.

The BICS/CALP distinction also served to qualify John Oller's (1979) claim that all individual differences in language proficiency could be accounted for by just one underlying factor, which he termed *global language proficiency*. Oller synthesized a considerable amount of data showing strong correlations between performance on cloze tests of reading, standardized reading tests, and measures of oral verbal ability (e.g. vocabulary measures) (see Chapter 5). I pointed out that not all aspects of language use or performance could be incorporated into one dimension of general or global language proficiency. For example, if we take two monolingual English-speaking siblings, a 12-year-old child and a six-year-old, there are enormous differences in these children's ability to read and write English and in the depth and breadth of their vocabulary knowledge, but minimal differences in their phonology or basic fluency. The six-year-old can understand virtually everything that is likely to be said to her in everyday social contexts and she can use language very effectively in these contexts, just as the 12-year-old can. In other words, some aspects of children's first language development (e.g. phonology) reach a plateau relatively early whereas other aspects (e.g. lexical knowledge) continue to develop throughout our lifetimes. Thus, these very different aspects of proficiency cannot be considered to reflect just one unitary proficiency dimension.

Another way of expressing this difference is to note that native-speakers of any language come to school at age five or so virtually fully competent users of their language. They have acquired the core grammar of their language and many of the sociolinguistic rules for using it appropriately in familiar social contexts. Yet, schools spend another 12 years (and considerable public funds) attempting to extend this basic linguistic repertoire into more specialized domains and functions of language. CALP or academic language proficiency is what schools focus on in this endeavour. It reflects the registers of language that children acquire in school and which they need to use effectively if they are to progress successfully through the grades. For example, knowing the conventions of different genres of writing (e.g. science reports, persuasive writing, etc.) and developing the ability to use these forms of expression effectively are essential for academic success. The characteristics of academic language registers are considered in more detail below.

The BICS/CALP distinction was elaborated into two intersecting continua (Cummins, 1981a) which highlighted the range of cognitive demands and contextual support involved in particular language tasks or activities (context-embedded/ context-reduced, cognitively undemanding/cognitively demanding) (see Figure 3.1, page 68). The BICS/CALP distinction was maintained within this elaboration and related to the theoretical distinctions of several other theorists. The terms used by different investigators have varied but the essential distinction refers to the extent to which the meaning being communicated is strongly supported by contextual or interpersonal cues (such as gestures, facial expressions, and intonation present in face-to-face interaction) or supported primarily by linguistic cues that are largely independent of the immediate communicative context. These linkages between conversational and academic proficiency and similar distinctions are sketched in the next section.

Related Theoretical Constructs

The conversational/academic language distinction addresses similar phenomena to distinctions made by theorists such as Vygotsky (1962) (spontaneous and scientific concepts), Bruner (1975) (communicative/analytic competence), Canale (1983a) (communicative/autonomous proficiencies), Donaldson (1978) (embedded and disembedded thought and language), Olson (1977) (utterance and text), Bereiter and Scardamalia (1981) (conversation and composition), Snow *et al.* (1991) (contextualized and decontextualized language) and Mohan (1986) (practical and theoretical discourse). The brief descriptions of these distinctions below help to elucidate significant aspects of how conversational registers of language differ from those typically used in academic contexts.

Spontaneous and scientific concepts (Vygotsky)

Vygotsky viewed both language and literacy as emerging from a social context. Interactions with more expert or knowledgeable members of their social groups enable children to internalize cultural tools such as language, literacy, and mathematics which have the power to transform higher psychological processes. The development of word meanings begins with everyday or spontaneous understandings which are tied to particular experiences and evolve through social mediation to scientific concepts which are more abstract and hierarchically organized in semantic networks. Kozulin expresses clearly the distinction that Vygotskian theory makes between spontaneous and scientific concepts:

> Spontaneous concepts emerge from the child's own reflections on immediate, everyday experiences; they are rich but unsystematic and highly contextual. Scientific concepts originate in the structured and specialized activity of classroom instruction and are characterized by systematic and logical organization. (1998: 48)

He goes on to note that the concepts themselves do not necessarily relate to scientific issues but their organization is 'scientific' in the sense of having a formal, logical, and decontextualized structure.

In the following quotation, Vygotsky expresses both the inseparability of concepts and words and the fact that word meanings develop and deepen in concert with intellectual development:

> At any age, a concept embodied in a word represents an act of generalization. But word meanings evolve. When a new word has been learned by the child, its development is barely starting; the word at first is a generalization of the most primitive type; as the child's intellect develops, it is replaced by generalizations of a higher and higher type – a process that leads in the end to the formation of true concepts. The development of concepts, or word meanings, presupposes the development of many intellectual functions: deliberate attention, logical memory, abstraction, the ability to compare and to differentiate. These complex psychological processes cannot be mastered through the initial learning alone. (1962: 83)

What differentiates scientific from spontaneous concepts is the degree of generalization that they embody. For example, *plant, flower*, and *rose* represent different levels of a particular conceptual hierarchy. According to Vygotsky, every concept is a generalization; he notes that 'concepts do not lie in the child's minds like peas in a bag, without any bonds between them' (1962: 110). As word meanings and concepts develop, they become increasingly embedded in a system or network of logical and semantic inter-connections. By contrast, spontaneous concepts are characterized by relatively undeveloped relations of generality, resulting in less ability on the part of younger children to recognize contradictions and other logical relations.

The process of instruction (understood as facilitative interaction with more expert representatives of the culture) is intimately intertwined with the development of concepts and word meanings. In other words, scientific concepts do not develop in a social or experiential vacuum; children are socialized into these ways of thinking and of using language in particular contexts of instruction. Kozulin (1998) suggests that Vygotsky's notion of the zone of proximal development (ZPD) can be conceptualized as a zone in which scientific concepts introduced by teachers interact with spontaneous concepts pre-existent in children.

Communicative and analytic competence (Bruner)

In discussing language as an instrument of thought, Bruner (1975) distinguished a 'species minimum' linguistic competence from both communicative and analytic competence. Species minimum competence implies mastery of basic syntactic structures (Chomsky, 1965) and semantic categories (Fillmore, 1968). Beyond the species minimum competence is communicative competence, which Bruner (following Hymes, 1971) defined as the ability to make utterances that are appropriate to the context in which they are produced and to comprehend utterances in relation to the context in which they are encountered. Analytic competence is made possible by the possession of communicative competence. It involves the 'prolonged operation of thought processes exclusively on linguistic representations' (p. 72) and is cultivated through formal schooling. Language in this sense is 'heavily metalinguistic in nature' (p. 72) and is used as an intrapersonal tool for thought and problem-solving. Schools promote the decontextualization of knowledge and demand the use of analytic competence as a feature of the communicative competence of their members (Davies, 1975: 148).

Bruner (1975) relates his emphasis on language as an instrument of analytic thought to Vygotsky's (1962) sociocultural theory of cognitive development. For example, there is an obvious link between Bruner's notion of *analytic competence* and his characterization of Vygotsky's contribution as tracing 'the manner in which the intellectual development of the child is given a classificatory structure that makes possible the use of language as a logical and analytic tool in thinking. Before that, in the absence of conceptual structures, language plays other roles, but not this one' (Bruner, 1962: viii).

Communicative and autonomous proficiency (Canale)

Canale (1983a) and Cummins (1983) have criticized Bruner's formulation because it implies that analytic competence is a 'higher' form of proficiency than either linguistic or communicative competence. Canale points out that the capacity for such intrapersonal language uses is universal although socialization within particular discourse communities (e.g. schools) will determine the range and contexts within which such functions will be used. Canale also points to problems with viewing any notion of language as 'context-free' or 'decontextualized', although clearly the types of contextual support will vary from one functional situation to another.

Canale's (1983a) proposed framework elaborates on and clarifies aspects of Bruner's distinctions. He distinguishes between *basic language proficiency, communicative language proficiency*, and *autonomous language proficiency*. Basic language proficiency is comprised of those language-related universals that are required for communicative and autonomous language uses. It includes not just universals of grammar but also sociolinguistic, discourse, and strategic universals as outlined in the communicative competence framework developed by Canale and Swain (1980) (see Chapter 5). Communicative language proficiency will typically involve grammatical, sociolinguistic, discourse, and strategic competencies but the focus is on the social meaning of utterances which draws primarily on sociolinguistic knowledge and skills. Autonomous language proficiency

> involves proficiency in less directly social, more intrapersonal uses of language such as problem-solving, monitoring one's thoughts, verbal play, poetry, or creative writing. Focus is less on social meaning than on grammatical forms and literal meaning. … The main language competence involved would seem to be grammatical (especially vocabulary and rules of sentence formation and literal meaning) with some contribution of discourse and strategic competencies and least demand on sociolinguistic competence. (1983a: 340)

The degree of socialization within a particular discourse community will determine the range of communicative and autonomous functions of language that an individual is able and willing to handle. Thus, socialization within particular schooling contexts promotes the acquisition of language registers that are valued within those contexts.

Embedded and disembedded thought and language (Donaldson)

Donaldson's (1978) distinction between embedded and disembedded modes of thought and language highlights the importance of context for any kind of cognitive or linguistic performance. She points out that young children's thought processes and use of language develop within a flow of meaningful context in which the logic of words is subordinated to perception of the speaker's intentions and salient features of the situation:

> The ease with which pre-school children often seem to understand what is said to them is misleading if we take it as an indication of skill with language *per se*.

> Certainly, they commonly understand us, but surely it is not our words alone that they are understanding – for they may be shown to be relying heavily on cues of other kinds. (1978: 72)

However, thinking and language that move beyond the bounds of meaningful interpersonal context make very different demands on the individual. In this case, it is necessary to focus on the linguistic forms themselves for meaning rather than primarily on the speaker's intentions. In re-interpreting Piaget's theory of cognitive development, she provides compelling evidence that children are able to manifest much higher levels of cognitive performance when the task is presented in an embedded context, or one that makes 'human sense'. She goes on to argue that the unnecessary disembedding of early reading instruction from students' out-of-school experiences contributes significantly to educational difficulties.

Utterance and text (Olson)

Olson's (1977) distinction between 'utterance' and 'text' relates to whether meaning is largely extrinsic to language (utterance) or intrinsic to language (text). In interpersonal conversational interactions the listener has access to a wide range of contextual and paralinguistic information with which to interpret the speaker's intentions. Thus, in these contexts the meaning is only partly dependent on the specific linguistic forms used by the speaker. However, in contrast to utterance, written text is an autonomous representation of meaning:

> Ideally, the printed reader depends on no cues other than linguistic cues; it represents no cues other than those represented in the text; it is addressed to no one in particular; its author is essentially anonymous; and its meaning is precisely that represented by the sentence meaning. (1977: 275)

Olson (1977) suggests that the ability to assign a meaning to a sentence per se, independent of its nonlinguistic interpretive context, is achieved only well into the school years. This view of text as autonomous has been critiqued on the grounds that it fails to represent the diverse forms and purposes of literacy in different contexts (e.g. Street, 1984). Words, written or uttered, are meaningless outside of particular interpretive contexts. This point is acknowledged by Olson in emphasizing the importance of socialization into a textual community:

> To be literate it is not enough to know the words; one must also learn how to participate in the discourse of some textual community. And that implies knowing which texts are important, how they are to be read and interpreted, and how they are to be applied in talk and action. (1994: 273)

While Olson's (1977) early representation of text as autonomous is problematic, the basic distinction he makes draws on the same differences between conversational and academic registers of language that have been emphasized by other investigators.

Conversation and composition (Bereiter and Scardamalia)

Bereiter and Scardamalia (1981) have analyzed the problems of learning to write as problems of converting a language production system geared to conversation over to a language production system capable of functioning by itself. They argue that the absence of normal conversational supports makes writing a radically different kind of task from conversation. Specifically, in writing the individual must:

- learn to continue to produce language without the prompting that comes from a conversational partner;
- learn to search his or her own memory instead of having memories triggered by what other people say;
- plan large units of discourse instead of planning only what will be said next;
- learn to function as both sender and receiver, the latter function being necessary for revision.

They suggest that the oral production system must be reconstructed to function autonomously rather than interactively if effective writing abilities are to develop. Furthermore, they suggest that as mastery increases there is progressive automatization of lower-level skills (e.g. handwriting, spelling of common words, punctuation, common syntactic forms) which releases increasingly more mental capacity for higher-level planning of large chunks of discourse.

Contextualized and decontextualized language (Snow)

Catherine Snow and her colleagues (e.g. Snow *et al.*, 1991) have shown that performance on highly contextualized language tasks (e.g. face-to-face communication) does not predict performance on less contextualized tasks such as defining the meanings of words. Snow *et al.* note that:

> definitions … constitute one example of what has been referred to as *decontextualized language use* – language used in ways that eschew reliance on shared social and physical context in favour of reliance on a context created through the language itself. … In order to give a good formal definition, one must analyze all one knows about a concept to separate the crucial from the irrelevant information. (1991: 90–91)

Their research suggests that although 'skills already acquired in a first language can ultimately be transferred to a second language, this transfer evidently does not occur until a relatively high level of proficiency in the second language is acquired' (p. 109). They conclude that the native language used in the home

> certainly enhances conversational skills, but does not appear to directly enhance those language skills that are called upon in the classroom context. It is those latter classroom skills (e.g. giving formal definitions, decontextualized picture descriptions, etc.) that are most predictive of successful literacy and school achievement. (1991: 110)

Practical and theoretical discourse (Mohan, 1986)

Mohan distinguishes between practical and theoretical discourse in discussing the optimal sequencing of language instruction. He points out that 'practical discourse is characteristic of everyday interactions in society; theoretical discourse is characteristic of language in school learning–academic discourse' (1986: 108). Formal educational settings, however, are not the only contexts where theoretical discourse occurs; it can also occur in informal settings whenever an expert conveys background knowledge to a learner.

Mohan highlights the distance that exists between the speaker and the topic and between the speaker and listener as dimensions along which discourses can be arranged. The school curriculum represents an arrangement of different forms of discourse from the least distant to the most distant along both these dimensions of distance. For example, 'show and tell' activities in the primary grades entail much less speaker–topic distance and speaker–listener distance than a research paper that a university student might write for a general audience. This dimension of *distance* is similar to the context-embedded/context-reduced continuum discussed later in this chapter.

Mohan relates practical and theoretical discourse to experiential and expository learning and to practical and theoretical content. The former distinction is between learning from experience and action as compared to learning from texts and teachers; the latter refers to the specific content that is close at hand as compared to general concepts and explanations. The three principles together provide for a sequencing of academic and language content that will expand from experiential learning of hands-on content and 'here-and-now' language to the learning of more abstract content presented in an expository way by means of language itself.

Conclusion

All of the theoretical constructs reviewed above make essentially one-dimensional distinctions between highly contextualized 'everyday' uses of language (and/or thought) and uses that are relatively less contextualized and more abstract. These different uses of language are associated with different contexts (e.g. everyday contexts versus academic contexts) and with differences in the degree to which verbal/conceptual structures are elaborated hierarchically. Recent research on depth of vocabulary illustrates this hierarchical organization of vocabulary knowledge (e.g. Paribakht & Wesche, 1997).

These distinctions are all addressing essentially the same dimension as the BICS/CALP distinction, although the theoretical contexts and purposes for elaborating the distinction differ from one version to another. However, there is a need to go beyond a simple dichotomy in mapping the underlying dimensions of linguistic performance in academic contexts. In the one-dimensional distinctions outlined above, as in distinctions between oral and literate forms of language, the degree of cognitive demand of particular tasks or activities is not represented. Thus there is no way to represent the fact that an intense intellectual discussion with one or two other people can be just as cognitively demanding as writing an academic paper, despite the fact that the former is relatively highly contextualized while the contextual support in the latter case lacks the same immediacy of 'human sense', in Donaldson's (1978) terms.

In order to provide a better basis for analyzing the language demands underlying academic tasks, the BICS/CALP distinction was elaborated into a framework that explicitly distinguished cognitive and contextual demands.

Cognitive and Contextual Demands

The framework outlined in Figure 3.1 is designed to identify the extent to which students are able to cope successfully with the cognitive and linguistic demands made on them by the social and educational environment in which they are obliged to function in school. These demands are conceptualized within a framework made up of the intersection of two continua, one relating to the range of contextual support available for expressing or receiving meaning and the other relating to the amount of information that must be processed simultaneously or in close succession by the student in order to carry out the activity. While cognitive demands and contextual support are distinguished in the framework, it is not being suggested that these dimensions are independent of each other. In fact, as Frederickson and Cline (1990) point out, increasing contextual support will tend to lessen the cognitive demands – in other words, make tasks easier.

Situating the framework

Before describing the framework, it is important to place it in an appropriate context of interpretation and to define some of the terms associated with it. In the first place, the framework, and the associated conversational/academic language proficiency distinction, focuses only on the sociocultural context of schooling. Thus, we are talking about the nature of language proficiency that is required to function effectively in this particular context. The framework was not intended to have relevance outside of this context.

Related to this is the fact that language proficiency and cognitive functioning can be conceptualized only in relation to particular contexts of use. Just as sociocultural or Vygotskian approaches to literacy emphasize that 'literacy is always socially and culturally situated' (Pérez, 1998a: 4) and cannot be regarded as content-free or context-free, language proficiency and cognitive functioning are similarly embedded in particular contexts of use or *discourses* which are defined by Pérez as the ways in which 'communicative systems are organized within social practices' (1998b: 23). Thus, the social practice of schooling entails certain 'rules of the game' with respect to how communication and language use is typically organized within that context. In short, in the present context the construct of *academic language proficiency* refers not to any absolute notion of expertise in using language but to the degree to which an individual has access to and expertise in understanding and using the specific kind of language that is employed in educational contexts and is required to complete academic tasks. Drawing on the categories distinguished by

Chapelle (1998), academic language proficiency can be defined as the language knowledge together with the associated knowledge of the world and metacognitive strategies necessary to function effectively in the discourse domain of the school.

As discussed in Chapter 5, this perspective is consistent with an interactionist perspective on language ability 'as the capacity for language use' (Bachman & Cohen, 1998: 18). Current theoretical approaches to the construct of language proficiency have shifted from viewing proficiency as a trait that individuals possess in varying degrees to seeing it as inseparable from the contexts in which it will be manifested. Thus, Bachman and Palmer (1996) use the term 'ability-task' to refer to the unity of ability and task (context) characteristics. Chapelle (1998: 44) similarly notes that a construct such as 'vocabulary size' 'cannot be defined in an absolute sense but instead is a meaningful construct only with reference to a particular context'. Thus, in the context of schooling, discussions of greater or lesser degrees of language proficiency or 'adequacy' of an individual's proficiency refer only to the extent to which the individual's language proficiency (CALP) is functional within the context of typical academic tasks and activities. As noted above and elaborated below, the characteristics of instruction (context) will determine the functionality or 'adequacy' of an individual's proficiency in the language of instruction as much as the degree of proficiency in any absolute sense.

In this regard, it is helpful to introduce the notion of *register* which will be elaborated further in subsequent sections. Register is defined in the *Concise Oxford Dictionary of Linguistics* (Matthews, 1997: 314) as 'a set of features of speech or writing characteristic of a particular type of linguistic activity or a particular group when engaging in it. … journalese is a register different from that in which sermons are delivered, or in which smutty stories are told'. Registers are the linguistic realizations of particular discourse contexts and conventions. Academic language proficiency thus refers to the extent to which an individual has access to and command of the oral and written academic registers of schooling.

In summary, as students progress through the grades, the academic tasks they are required to complete and the linguistic contexts in which they must function become more complex with respect to the registers employed in these contexts. Not only is there an ever-increasing vocabulary and concept load involving words that are rarely encountered in everyday out-of-school contexts but syntactic features (e.g. passive rather than active voice constructions) and discourse conventions (e.g. using cohesive devices effectively in writing) also become increasingly distant from conversational uses of language in non-academic contexts. The framework outlined in Figure 3.1 presents an analytic scheme for mapping in a general way how the construct of language proficiency can be conceptualized in terms of the intersections of cognitive (or information-processing) demand and contextual support in academic situations.

Description of the framework

The extremes of the context-embedded/context-reduced continuum are distinguished by the fact that in context-embedded communication the participants can

FIGURE 3.1 Range of contextual support and degree of cognitive involvement in language tasks and activities

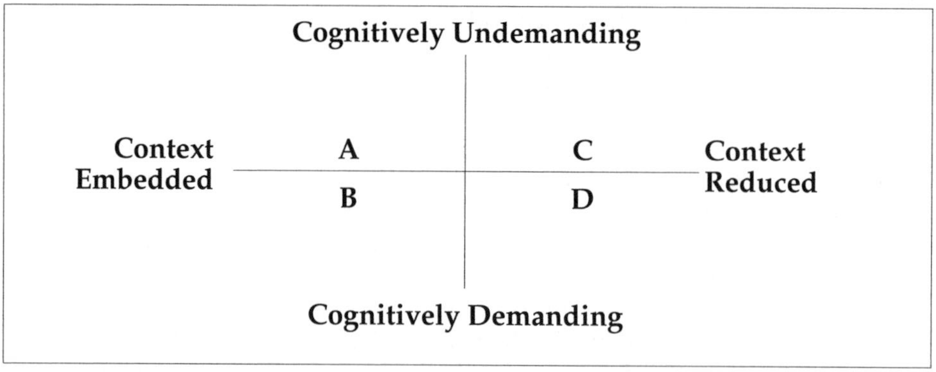

actively negotiate meaning (e.g. by providing feedback that the message has not been understood) and the language is supported by a wide range of meaningful interpersonal and situational cues. Context-reduced communication, on the other hand, relies primarily (or, at the extreme of the continuum, exclusively) on linguistic cues to meaning, and thus successful interpretation of the message depends heavily on knowledge of the language itself. In general, as outlined in the previous section, context-embedded communication is more typical of the everyday world outside the classroom, whereas many of the linguistic demands of the classroom (e.g. manipulating text) reflect communicative activities that are close to the context-reduced end of the continuum.

The upper parts of the vertical continuum consist of communicative tasks and activities in which the linguistic tools have become largely automatized and thus require little active cognitive involvement for appropriate performance. At the lower end of the continuum are tasks and activities in which the linguistic tools have not become automatized and thus require active cognitive involvement. Persuading another individual that your point of view is correct, and writing an essay, are examples of Quadrant B and D skills respectively. Casual conversation is a typical Quadrant A activity while examples of Quadrant C are copying notes from the blackboard, filling in worksheets, or other forms of drill and practice activities.

The framework elaborates on the conversational/academic distinction by high-lighting important underlying dimensions of conversational and academic communication. Thus, conversational abilities (Quadrant A) often develop rela-tively quickly among immigrant second language learners because these forms of communication are supported by interpersonal and contextual cues and make rela-tively few cognitive demands on the individual. Mastery of the academic functions of language (academic registers or Quadrant D), on the other hand, is a more formi-dable task because such uses require high levels of cognitive involvement and are only minimally supported by contextual or interpersonal cues. Under conditions of high cognitive demand, it is necessary for students to stretch their linguistic resources to the limit to function successfully. In short, the essential aspect of academic language proficiency is the ability to make complex meanings explicit in either oral or written modalities by means of *language itself* rather than by means of contextual or paralinguistic cues (e.g. gestures, intonation etc.).

As students progress through the grades, they are increasingly required to manipulate language in cognitively demanding and context-reduced situations that differ significantly from everyday conversational interactions. In writing, for example, as Bereiter and Scardamalia (1981) point out, students must learn to continue to produce language without the prompting that comes from a conversational partner and they must plan large units of discourse, and organize them coherently, rather than planning only what will be said next.

Evidence for the relevance and usefulness of the conversational/academic language distinction comes from observations made by Carolyn Vincent in an ethnographic study of a program serving second generation Salvadorean students in Washington DC:

> All of the children in this study began school in an English-speaking environment and within their first two or three years attained conversational ability in English that teachers would regard as native-like. This is largely deceptive. The children seem to have much greater English proficiency than they actually do because their spoken English has no accent and they are able to converse on a few everyday, frequently discussed subjects. Academic language is frequently lacking. Teachers actually spend very little time talking with individual children and tend to interpret a small sample of speech as evidence of full English proficiency. However, as the children themselves look back on their language development they see how the language used in the classroom was difficult for them, and how long it took them to acquire English. (1996: 195)

In this respect, Vincent notes on the basis of her classroom observations: 'It is clear that student achievement is promoted by instructional practices such as cooperative learning, the use of manipulatives, and project-based lessons' (1996: 201). These are activities that place a significant emphasis on Quadrant B insofar as they tend to be cognitively demanding but contextually supported.

Pauline Gibbons has similarly expressed the difference between the everyday language of face-to-face interaction and the language of schooling in outlining the distinction between what she terms *playground language* and *classroom language*:

> This playground language includes the language which enables children to make friends, join in games and take part in a variety of day-to-day activities that develop and maintain social contacts. It usually occurs in face-to-face contact, and is thus highly dependent on the physical and visual context, and on gesture and body language. Fluency with this kind of language is an important part of language development; without it a child is isolated from the normal social life of the playground …

> But playground language is very different from the language that teachers use in the classroom, and from the language that we expect children to learn to use.

The language of the playground is not the language associated with learning in mathematics, or social studies, or science. The playground situation does not normally offer children the opportunity to use such language as: *if we increase the angle by five degrees, we could cut the circumference into equal parts.* Nor does it normally require the language associated with the higher order thinking skills, such as hypothesizing, evaluating, inferring, generalizing, predicting or classifying. Yet these are the language functions which are related to learning and the development of cognition; they occur in all areas of the curriculum, and without them a child's potential in academic areas cannot be realized. (1991: 3)

Thus, the context-embedded/context-reduced distinction is not one between oral and written language. Within the framework, the dimensions of contextual embeddedness and cognitive demand are distinguished because some context-embedded activities are clearly just as cognitively demanding as context-reduced activities. For example, an intense intellectual discussion with one or two other people is likely to require at least as much cognitive processing as writing an essay on the same topic. Similarly, writing an e-mail message to a close friend is, in many respects, more context-embedded than giving a lecture to a large group of people.

It follows that cognitive academic language proficiency is not synonymous with *literacy*. It is manifested as much in oral interactions in academic contexts as in written interactions. For example, a classroom or small group discussion of the social consequences of industrial pollution will draw on participants' familiarity with features of academic registers (e.g. how to express cause–effect relationships linguistically) and will reveal the depth and richness of their understanding of words and concepts. In Aitchison's (1994) terms, the extent to which students have built extensive semantic networks will be evident in the way they use and relate words and concepts in such discussions. Thus, words are not just known or unknown; there is a continuum with respect to depth of vocabulary/concept knowledge (Paribakht & Wesche, 1997; Verhallen & Schoonen, 1998). One of the major functions of schooling is to deepen and broaden students' knowledge of words and their meanings and to develop what Norah McWilliam (1998) calls *semantic agility*. Oral classroom discussions do not involve reading and writing directly, but they do reflect the degree of students' access to and command of literate or academic registers of language. This is why CALP can be defined as *expertise in understanding and using literacy-related aspects of language*.

Skourtou has provided a particularly clear description of how the processing of experience through language transforms experience itself and forms the basis of literacy:

It seems to me that the entire process of language development both starts and ends with experience. This implies that we start with a concrete experience, process it through language and arrive at a new experience. In such a manner, we develop the main features of literacy, namely the ability to reconstruct the world through symbols, thus creating new experiences. Creating experiences through language, using the logic of literacy, whether speaking or writing, means that once we are confronted with a real context, we are able to add our own contexts, our own images of the world. (1995: 27)

Highlighted here is the fact that *context* is both internal and external, representing two sides of the same experiential coin; furthermore, the development of literate modes of thought cannot be separated from these experiential contexts.

Implications for pedagogy

A central implication of the framework in Figure 3.1 for instruction of second language learners is that language and content will be acquired most successfully when students are challenged cognitively but provided with the contextual and linguistic supports or scaffolds required for successful task completion. In other words, optimal instruction for linguistic, cognitive and academic growth will tend to move from Quadrant A, to B, and from Quadrant B to D. Quadrant C activities may be included from time to time for reinforcement or practice of particular points. This progression corresponds very closely to the stages that Gibbons (1995, 1998) observed in her research on classroom discourse in science teaching. She distinguished three stages:

- Small group work.
- Teacher guided reporting.
- Journal writing.

Thus, students initially participated in small-group learning experiences where the language used was clearly context-embedded. Gibbons notes that 'children's current understandings of a curriculum topic, and their use of familiar "everyday" language to express these understandings, should be seen as the basis for the development of the unfamiliar registers of school' (1998: 99).

The small-group exploration and discussion was followed by a teacher-guided reporting session, where each group described what they had done and offered explanations for what happened, while the teacher interacted with individuals from each group, clarifying, probing and recasting. Talking with the teacher about what had been learned, since this did not involve the use of the concrete materials, led to a mode shift towards more decontextualized language. When students reported back to the whole class the results of their 'hands-on' science explorations (e.g. with magnets), they were pushed to shift towards less context-embedded ways of expression than had been the case in their immediate small group discussion of the phenomena they observed. The teacher guided their reporting back and extended their linguistic resources by introducing more formal precise vocabulary to express the phenomena (e.g. introducing the term *repel* as equivalent to what the children described as *push away*). In responding to students' reporting back, the teacher will 'use new wordings and ways of meaning – a new register' (1995: 27) which is likely to be comprehensible to students because they have already gained some schematic knowledge about the topic. Through this interaction, students and teacher *co-construct* deeper understandings of the phenomena and students acquire the linguistic tools to express their observations in the more formal language of scientific discourse.

The reporting back phase provided a bridge into the writing, which was the final activity of the cycle and linguistically the most context reduced (1995: 11). Students wrote a response in their journals to the question 'What have you learned?' They described what they had learned as a personal and ongoing record of their learning rather than as a piece of formal writing. This third stage corresponds to Quadrant D in Figure 3.1. Gibbons suggests that the journals 'provide some evidence of second language 'uptake' in that they reflect wordings which occurred in the process of jointly negotiated learner–teacher interactions' (1998: 106). She also notes that there is a place for Quadrant C activities insofar as the teacher also spent some time rehearsing or practising the new words with students in order to consolidate their acquisition (personal communication, October, 1999).

Mackay (1992) has used the quadrants framework to document the consequences of requiring students to carry out tasks that are overly complex and insufficiently scaffolded for their linguistic level. He plotted the instructional task sequences in Grade 6 and Grade 7 classes taught in English to Inuktitut L1 students in the Canadian Eastern Arctic. The Grade 7 teachers initiated instruction with relatively complex tasks (Quadrant D) and then retreated to considerably less complex tasks (Quadrants B, C, and finally A, in that order) in response to evidence that the original task could not be performed adequately. The consequence of this 'task reduction' was that students were not being stimulated to advance academically or cognitively because they were carrying out only cognitively undemanding and context embedded tasks. In Mackay's words: 'By employing task-reduction, [teachers] unwittingly and unintentionally trap students into a learning environment which may permanently deprive them of the opportunity for developing the proficiency and skills they need to enjoy academic success' (1992: 162–163). By contrast, in the Grade 6 class, the instructional sequence of tasks was much more developmental, progressing from quadrants A to C to B and finally to D. In this way, students were enabled to carry out relatively complex tasks such as writing answers to questions about planets in their personal notebooks.

Internal and external context

As noted above, contextual support involves both internal and external dimensions. Internal factors are *attributes of the individual* that make a task more familiar or easier in some respect (e.g. prior experience, motivation, cultural relevance, interests, etc.). External factors refer to *aspects of the input* that facilitate or impede comprehension; for example, language input that is spoken clearly and contains a considerable amount of syntactic and semantic redundancy is easier to understand than input that lacks these features.

Douglas has similarly distinguished between external and internal aspects of context but suggests that these categories can be collapsed into 'an internal view of context as a cognitive construct created by language users for the interpretation and production of language' (1998: 146). In other words, what matters is how participants in a communicative event construct the context which is never static or 'external' but rather 'a dynamic social-psychological accomplishment' (p. 144).

The distinction between internal and external context parallels Chapelle's (1998) distinction between learner factors and contextual factors in determining language performance. Learner factors refer to the individual's knowledge of the world, knowledge of language, and strategic competence which, following Bachman (1990a) is defined as 'the metacognitive strategies required for assessing contexts, setting goals, constructing plans, and controlling execution of those plans' (1998: 44). Chapelle draws on Halliday and Hasan (1989) in describing *context* in terms of three overlapping theoretical components: field, tenor, and mode. 'Field' refers to the locations, topics, and actions present in a particular language use context (i.e. what is taking place). 'Tenor' includes the participants and the relationships among them (who is taking part), and 'mode' includes the channels (spoken/written) and genres involved in particular forms of language use (what part language is playing). She points out that even with the detailed description of context that these constructs permit, there is still the issue of how specific the description of context needs to be for particular testing purposes (e.g. all academic reading in university contexts as compared to science reading or research articles in chemistry, etc.).

This point highlights the fact that the degree of detail with which context is specified within any particular theoretical framework depends on the purpose of that framework. Thus, in the context of Figure 3.1, the continuum between context-embedded and context-reduced language is sufficient to capture the major underlying dimension that is relevant to language use and academic tasks in school contexts. Clearly, in different contexts or for different purposes (e.g. investigating sociolinguistic parameters of language use), a greater degree of specificity might be desirable.[1]

Clarifications of the Conversational/Academic Distinction

The distinction between BICS and CALP has been misunderstood or misrepresented by a number of commentators. For example, the distinction was criticized on the grounds that a simple dichotomy does not account for many dimensions of language use and competence, for example, certain sociolinguistic aspects of language (e.g. Wald, 1984). However, the distinction was not proposed as an overall theory of language but as a conceptual distinction addressed to specific issues concerning the education of second language learners. As outlined above, the distinction entails important implications for policy and practice. The fact that the distinction does not attempt to address all aspects of sociolinguistics or discourse styles or any number of other linguistic issues is irrelevant. The usefulness of any theoretical construct should be assessed in relation to the issues that it attempts to address, not in relation to issues that it makes no claim to address. To suggest that the BICS/CALP distinction is invalid because it does not account for subtleties of sociolinguistic interaction or discourse styles is like saying: 'This apple is no good because it doesn't taste like an orange'.

Another point concerns the sequence of acquisition between BICS and CALP. August and Hakuta (1997), for example, suggest that the distinction specifies that BICS must precede CALP in development. This is not at all the case. The sequential nature of BICS/CALP acquisition was suggested as typical in the specific situation of immigrant children learning a second language. It was not suggested as an absolute order that applies in every, or even the majority of situations. Thus attainment of high levels of L2 CALP can precede attainment of fluent L2 BICS in certain situations (e.g. a scientist who can read a language for research purposes but who can't speak it).

Another misunderstanding is to interpret the distinction as dimensions of language that are autonomous or independent of their contexts of acquisition (e.g. Romaine, 1989: 240). To say that BICS and CALP are conceptually distinct is not the same as saying that they are separate or acquired in different ways. Developmentally they are not necessarily separate; all children acquire their initial conceptual foundation (knowledge of the world) largely through conversational interactions in the home. Both BICS and CALP are shaped by their contexts of acquisition and use. Consistent with a Vygotskian perspective on cognitive and language development, BICS and CALP both develop within a matrix of social interaction. However, they follow different developmental patterns: phonological skills in our native language and our basic fluency reach a plateau in the first six or so years; in other words, the rate of subsequent development is very much reduced in comparison to previous development. This is not the case for literacy-related knowledge such as range of vocabulary which continues to develop at least throughout our schooling and usually throughout our lifetimes.

It is also important to point out that cognitive skills are involved, to a greater or lesser extent, in most forms of social interaction. For example, cognitive skills are undoubtedly involved in one's ability to tell jokes effectively and if we work at it we might improve our joke-telling ability throughout our lifetimes. However, our joke-telling ability is largely unrelated to our academic performance. This intersection of the cognitive and social aspects of language proficiency, however, does not mean that they are identical or reducible one to the other. The implicit assumption that conversational fluency in English is a good indicator of 'English proficiency' has resulted in countless bilingual children being 'diagnosed' as learning disabled or retarded. Their fluency and native-like phonology in English masks the fact that they are still a long way from grade norms in English academic knowledge. Despite their developmental intersections, BICS and CALP are conceptually distinct and follow different patterns of development among both native-speakers and second language learners.

An additional misconception is that the distinction characterizes CALP (academic language) as a 'superior' form of language proficiency to BICS (conversational language). This interpretation was never intended and was explicitly repudiated (Cummins, 1983), although it is easy to see how the use of the term 'basic' in BICS might appear to devalue conversational language as compared to the apparent higher status of *cognitive academic* language proficiency. Clearly, various forms of conversational language performance are highly complex and sophisticated both linguistically and cognitively. However, these forms of language performance are not necessarily strongly related to the linguistic demands of schooling. As outlined above, access to very specific oral and written registers of language are required to continue to progress academically and a major goal of schooling for all students is to expand students' access to these academic registers of language. However, the greater relevance of academic language proficiency for success in school, as compared to conversational proficiency, does not mean that it is intrinsically superior in any way. Nor does it mean that the language proficiency of non-literate or non-schooled communities is in any way inadequate within the contexts of its development and use. In fact, as noted in Chapter 2, one of the major reasons why non-middle class bilingual and monolingual children have tended to experience difficulty in school is that many schools have failed to acknowledge and build on the wide variety of culturally specific literacy events (oral and written) that children experience in their homes (e.g. Delpit, 1998; Martin-Jones & Bhatt, 1998). These literacy events (e.g. oral story telling) represent powerful occasions for learning particularly when classroom instruction integrates them with the learning of reading and writing in school (see, for example, McCaleb, 1994).

While all aspects of children's cultural and linguistic experience in their homes should form the foundation upon which literacy instruction in school builds, it is important not to romanticize the literacy and linguistic accomplishments of particular communities. These accomplishments form the basis for future development but in our current technologically oriented societies, specific forms of literacy and numeracy are required for educational success and career advancement. Instruction in school, as well as active engagement with books (Krashen, 1993), extends students' basic knowledge of syntax, semantics, and phonology, and their community-based literacy practices, into new functional registers or genres of language. Access to and command of these academic registers are required for success in school and for advancement in many employment situations beyond school.

Some investigators have also claimed that by 'the mid 1980s the dichotomy between CALP and BICS was largely abandoned by Cummins, although it has not ceased to influence subsequent research on second language acquisition and bilingual education' (Devlin, 1997: 82). This is inaccurate. I have tended to use the terms conversational and academic proficiency in place of BICS and CALP because the acronyms were considered misleading by some commentators (e.g. Spolsky, 1984) and were being misinterpreted by others (e.g. Romaine, 1989). However, the acronyms continue to be widely used in the field and from my perspective are still appropriate to use. Hence they are used interchangeably with conversational and academic proficiency in the present volume.[2]

A final point of clarification concerns the relationship of language proficiency to social determinants of minority students' academic development (e.g. Troike, 1984). The conversational/academic language proficiency theoretical construct is psychoeducational in nature insofar as it focuses primarily on the cognitive and linguistic dimensions of proficiency in a language. The role of social factors in bilingual students' academic success or failure was acknowledged in early work but not elaborated in detail. In 1986, I proposed a framework within which the intersecting roles of sociopolitical and psychoeducational factors could be conceptualized (Cummins, 1986). Specifically, the framework highlighted the ways in which the interactions between educators and bilingual students reflected particular role definitions on the part of educators in relation to students' language and culture, community participation, pedagogy, and assessment. It hypothesized that many groups of students have been educationally disabled in school in much the same way that their communities have historically been disabled in the wider society, and it pointed to directions for reversing this process. As outlined in Chapter 2, the framework argues that educational interventions will be successful only to the extent that they constitute a challenge to the broader societal power structure (Cummins, 1986, 1996).

Linguistic Evidence for the Conversational/Academic Language Distinction

To this point, two major sets of evidence have been advanced to support the conversational/academic language distinction:

- In monolingual contexts, the distinction reflects the difference between the language proficiency acquired through interpersonal interaction by virtually all six-year-old children and the proficiency developed through schooling and literacy which continues to expand throughout our lifetimes.
- Research studies since the early 1980s have shown that immigrant students can quickly acquire considerable fluency in the target language when they are exposed to it in the environment and at school but despite this rapid growth in conversational fluency, it generally takes a minimum of about five years (and frequently much longer) for them to catch up to native-speakers in academic aspects of the language.

In addition to the evidence noted above, the distinction receives strong support from three other sources: (1) Douglas Biber's (1986) analysis of a corpus of authentic discourse gathered from a wide range of communicative situations, both written and oral; (2) David Corson's (1995, 1997) documentation of the lexical differences between English everyday conversational language and textual language, the former deriving predominantly from Anglo-Saxon sources and the latter from Graeco-Latin sources; and (3) Snow and Hoefnagel-Hohle's (1979) longitudinal analysis of L1 and L2 development among English speakers learning Dutch in a naturalistic setting.

Biber's analysis of textual variation

Biber (1986) used psychometric analysis of an extremely large corpus of spoken and written textual material in order to uncover the basic dimensions underlying textual variation. Among the 16 text types included in Biber's analysis were broadcasts, spontaneous speeches, telephone conversation, face-to-face conversation, professional letters, academic prose and press reports. Forty-one linguistic features were counted in 545 text samples, totalling more than one million words.

Three major dimensions emerged from the factor analysis of this corpus. These were labelled by Biber as *Interactive v. Edited Text, Abstract v. Situated Content*, and *Reported v. Immediate Style*. The first dimension is described as follows:

> Thus, Factor 1 identifies a dimension which characterizes texts produced under conditions of high personal involvement and real-time constraints (marked by low explicitness in the expression of meaning, high subordination and interactive features) – as opposed to texts produced under conditions permitting considerable editing and high explicitness of lexical content, but little interaction or personal involvement. ... This dimension combines both situational and cognitive parameters; in particular it combines interactional features with those reflecting production constraints (or the lack of them). (1986: 385)

The second factor has positive loadings from linguistic features such as nominalizations, prepositions, and passives and, according to Biber, reflects a 'detached formal style v. a concrete colloquial one' (p. 396). Although this factor is correlated with the first factor, it can be empirically distinguished from it, as illustrated by professional letters, which, according to Biber's analysis, represent highly abstract texts that have a high level of personal involvement.

The third factor has positive loadings from linguistic features such as past tense, perfect aspect and 3rd person pronouns which can all refer to a removed narrative context. According to Biber this dimension 'distinguishes texts with a primary narrative emphasis, marked by considerable reference to a removed situation, from those with non-narrative emphases (descriptive, expository, or other) marked by little reference to a removed situation but a high occurrence of present tense forms' (p. 396).

It is clear that Biber's three dimensions provide a more detailed empirical analysis of the nature and contexts of language use than the conversational/academic distinction (as would be expected in view of the very extensive range of spoken and written texts analyzed). In this respect, they are similar to Halliday and Hasan's (1989) more detailed theoretical framework for describing contexts of language use in terms of field, tenor and mode. However, it is also clear that the distinctions highlighted in Biber's dimensions are consistent with the broad distinction between conversational and academic aspects of proficiency. For example, when factor scores were calculated for the different text types on each factor, telephone and face-to-face conversation were at opposite extremes from official documents and academic prose on Textual Dimensions 1 and 2 (Interactive v. Edited Text, and Abstract v. Situated Content). In short, Biber's research shows clearly that the general distinction that has been proposed between conversational and academic aspects of language has linguistic reality that can be identified empirically.

Corson's analysis of the English language lexicon

Corson (1993, 1995, 1997) has pointed out that the academic language of texts in English depends heavily on Graeco-Latin words whereas everyday conversation relies more on an Anglo-Saxon-based lexicon: 'most of the specialist and high status terminology of English is Graeco-Latin in origin, and most of its more everyday terminology is Anglo-Saxon in origin' (1993: 13). Graeco-Latin words tend to be three or four syllables long whereas the everyday high frequency words of the Anglo-Saxon lexicon tend to be one or two syllables in length.

Corson points out that

> Academic Graeco-Latin words are mainly literary in their use. Most native speakers of English begin to encounter these words in quantity in their upper primary school reading and in the formal secondary school setting. So the words' introduction in literature or textbooks, rather than in conversation, restricts people's access to them. Certainly, exposure to specialist Graeco-Latin words happens much more often while reading than while talking or watching television. … printed texts provided much more exposure to [Graeco-Latin] words than oral ones. For example, even children's books contained 50% more rare words than either adult prime-time television or the conversations of university graduates; popular magazines had three times as many rare words as television and informal conversation. (1997: 677)

To illustrate the difference, consider some of the most frequent Anglo-Saxon and Graeco-Latin nouns (from lists of the most frequent general and university-level words cited by Corson, 1997: 678–679, based on Nation (1990)):

Frequent Anglo-Saxon Nouns	*Frequent Graeco-Latin Nouns*
time	chapter
people	component
years	context
work	criterion
something	data
world	design
children	focus
life	hypothesis

All of the Anglo-Saxon nouns listed above are in the top category of the 6-point frequency band of the Collins Cobuild English Dictionary whereas the mean frequency of the Graeco-Latin nouns is 3.25, indicating that the most common Anglo-Saxon nouns occur considerably more frequently than is the case for the most common Graeco-Latin nouns.

Nation (1990) points out that most low-frequency vocabulary comes to English from Latin or Greek, often through Old French. He estimates that about two-thirds of the low-frequency words in English derive from these linguistic origins. He further points out that:

> High frequency vocabulary consists mainly of short words which cannot be broken into meaningful parts. Low-frequency vocabulary, on the other hand, while it consists of many thousands of words, is made from a much smaller number of word parts. The word, *impose*, for example, is made of two parts, *im-* and *-pose*, which occur in hundreds of other words – *imply, infer, compose, expose, position*. This has clear implications for teaching and learning vocabulary. (1990: 18)

To further illustrate the centrality of the Graeco-Latin lexicon to the comprehension of academic language consider the following passage from Edgar Allan Poe's *The Pit and the Pendulum* which appeared in a high school literature compendium:

> My outstretched hands at length encountered some solid obstruction. It was a wall, seemingly of stone masonry – very smooth, slimy, and cold. I followed it up; stepping with all the careful distrust with which certain antique narratives had inspired me. (Poe, 1997/1842: 256)

Among the more difficult words in this passage are the following: *outstretched, encountered, solid, obstruction, masonry, slimy, distrust, antique, narratives, inspired*. Few of these words are likely to be encountered in everyday conversational interactions (although in recent years *slime* and *slimy* have become commonplace in the lexicon of most North American four-year-olds). With the exception of *outstretched* and *slimy*, all of these words are Graeco-Latin in origin and have semantic relationships across the Romance languages. *Outstretched*, although deriving from Anglo-Saxon roots, has indirect cognate relationships with Graeco-Latin-based languages through its synonym *extended* (e.g. *extendido* in Spanish). In short, the lexicon used in English conversational interactions is dramatically different than that used in more literate and academic contexts.

An obvious implication of these data is that if second language learners are to catch up academically to native-speakers they must engage in extensive reading of written text because academic language is reliably to be found only in written text. The research on reading achievement also suggests, however, that in addition to large amounts of time for actual text reading, it is also important for students to have ample opportunities to talk to each other and to a teacher about their responses to reading (see Fielding and Pearson, 1994, for a review; also Chapter 10). Talking about the text in a collaborative context ensures that higher order thinking processes (e.g. analysis, evaluation, synthesis) engage with academic language in deepening students' comprehension of the text.

Snow and Hoefnagel-Hohle's (1979) analysis of individual differences in second-language ability

Snow and Hoefnagel-Hohle investigated the relationships among L1 (English) and L2 (Dutch) proficiencies among 51 participants aged from three years to adult at three different occasions during their first year of learning Dutch. They administered a variety of pronunciation, auditory discrimination, grammar, productive and receptive vocabulary and fluency measures to the sample including English vocabulary and fluency measures. The only standardized measures were English and Dutch versions of the Peabody Picture Vocabulary Test.

Three factors emerged in the first analysis. The first factor accounted for the bulk of the variance (76.2%). This factor had high loadings from both English and Dutch vocabulary measures as well as translation and morphology measures. The second factor was Dutch productive ability and the third English fluency. In the two subsequent factor analyses for performance at Sessions 2 and 3, the same first factor emerged, although it accounted for somewhat less of the total variance (70.5% and 65.2% respectively). In all analyses, Dutch phonological ability and both Dutch and English fluency were distinct from this first vocabulary factor.

Several aspects of these analyses are worth noting. First, the loading of Dutch and English vocabulary measures on the same factor is consistent with the interdependence hypothesis which predicts significant relationships between L1 and L2 cognitive/academic measures. Second, the fact that these cognitive/academic measures were distinct from conversational measures such as fluency (in both L1 and L2) and pronunciation in all three analyses supports the conversational/academic language proficiency distinction. Third, there was evidence of increasing differentiation of proficiency over time. As expressed by Snow and Hoefnagel-Hohle:

> The results suggest that there are separate components of second-language ability: control of grammatical skills and control of phonological skills. These two components become obvious only after speakers have achieved a fairly good control of their second language. (The subjects tested here were almost all functioning fairly well as bilinguals in Dutch school and work situations by the third test session). (1979: 157).

Snow and Hoefnagel-Hohle here include vocabulary knowledge within the category of 'grammatical skills'.

In summary, there is solid linguistic evidence for the reality of the conversational/academic language distinction in addition to the evidence of different time periods required to develop peer-appropriate levels of each dimension of language proficiency among second language learners. In the North American context, failure to take account of this distinction has led to inappropriate psychological testing of bilingual students and premature exit from bilingual or ESL support programs into 'mainstream' classes where students received minimal support for continued academic language development. In other words, the conceptual distinction between conversational and academic language proficiency has highlighted misconceptions about the nature of language proficiency that contributed directly to the creation of academic failure among bilingual students. This represents important evidence of its *consequential validity*, a construct that relates to the social consequences of a theoretical distinction or hypothesis (Chapelle, 1998).

Since the quadrants framework was initially elaborated, several investigators have related it to specific issues and problems in a variety of educational contexts. I briefly consider three sets of studies that have extended and clarified the nature of academic language in relation to the context-embedded/context-reduced continuum.

The Classroom Reality of Academic Language

Sociolinguistic perspectives

Solomon and Rhodes (1995, 1996), working in the United States, have conducted two studies aimed at clarifying the nature of academic language. One involved a survey of 157 ESL teachers which asked them to define and describe academic language. Most teachers viewed academic language either in terms of discrete aspects of language such as vocabulary or grammar or they focused on functions of language such as comparing and contrasting, categorizing, sequencing events, etc. Included in this latter functional category was the importance of students acquiring appropriate strategies for reading and writing effectively as well as concrete activities such as writing in journals, presenting findings to classmates, stating opinions, etc. Two-thirds of the sample (66%) stated that they explicitly teach academic language whereas 34% stated that they did not teach it explicitly. Solomon and Rhodes point out that teachers 'view academic language from a practical perspective – the language students need to understand the lesson or unit being studied' (1995: 9).

Solomon and Rhodes (1995) also carried out analyses of classroom transcripts which they related to Halliday's (1978) concept of register. As noted above, register reflects the fact that the language we speak or write varies systematically in lexical and syntactic features according to the context. Solomon and Rhodes' analysis of classroom interactions suggested that academic registers are associated with broad discourse levels of language rather than with discrete sentence-level linguistic features.

In Australia, John Gibbons and Elizabeth Lascar (1998) have also interpreted both Biber's work and the context-embedded/context-reduced framework in relation to Halliday's theory of systemic functional linguistics. They point to the fact that Biber's descriptions of different registers of language are consistent with the characteristics that Halliday (e.g. Halliday & Hasan, 1989) assigns to the concept of *Mode* 'which examines the linguistic effects produced by the distance (in terms of time, space and abstractness) between a text and the context to which it refers, and also the distance between listener/reader and speaker/writer' (p. 41). Gibbons and Lascar note that degree of context-embeddedness is a defining feature of this register parameter *Mode* and refer to it as the *literate register* on the grounds that 'it constitutes an important element of literacy' (p. 41). They point out that many minority language speakers often have a well-developed domestic or everyday register in their L1 but have not had opportunities to acquire many other registers in that language, particularly the academic or literate register.

Gibbons and Lascar's research with Spanish L1 speakers in Australia used multiple choice cloze procedures as a way of operationalizing cognitive academic language proficiency. They reported that extensive reading in the home (even of light material such as comics) and the oral discussion of serious topics such as history, science, and politics contribute to the development of the academic register in Spanish (Gibbons, 1999; Gibbons & Lascar, 1998).

Pedagogical perspectives

As noted above, Pauline Gibbons (1991, 1995, 1998) has elaborated on the implications of Halliday's model for pedagogy in the context of an analysis of science teaching in Australian classrooms. The advantage of Halliday's model is that it 'systematically relates language to meaning and to the context in which it is used' (1995: 9). She illustrates how the language used in classroom interactions changes in predictable ways as language shifts from the 'here-and-now' of face-to-face contacts and becomes increasingly less situationally embedded and closer to written forms. Teachers and students jointly construct academic discourse. She suggests that pedagogical activities can be structured to reflect points along this mode continuum, starting with small group interaction which permits students to gain some understanding of key concepts, followed by teacher-guided reporting back to the class, and finally some independent written work such as journal writing.

Gibbons contrasts the kinds of instructional opportunities for student-initiated talk within this cycle with the traditional *teacher initiation, student response, teacher feedback* sequence. She suggests that this type of classroom interaction 'may actually deprive learners of just those features which are enabling factors in language learning' (1995: 12). At a theoretical level she suggests that the construct of the mode continuum

> provides a linguistic rationale to the sequencing of tasks, suggesting a logical teaching sequence from context embedded through to more context reduced tasks which required students to use more unfamiliar registers. Within this sequence, teacher guided reporting can provide a 'bridge' into written language, a vital and sometimes missing step between experientially-based and literacy-focused classroom tasks. (1995: 27–28)

In the United Kingdom (UK) context, Leung (1996) has provided a useful elaboration of the concepts of contextual support and cognitive demand. He points out that the process of providing contextual support 'can be seen as an attempt to render cognitively demanding academic content and language more like everyday communication' (1996: 38). However, 'comprehension of meaning in context does not always automatically lead to language learning … [and] is not sufficient for the learning of complex and decontextualized language use (1996: 27–28). In order for contextual support to contribute to academic language learning it must start with the learners' background knowledge both about the content of a lesson and the forms of learning that are expected. At that point, drama, visuals, and concrete demonstrations should be used to make abstract concepts comprehensible (e.g. by evoking universal emotions such as humour, sorrow, happiness) and to scaffold content learning and language use. In addition, the teacher's language should be adjusted to the needs of the learner. Teachers should ensure that learners have comprehended relevant information and task requirements and they should provide learners with timely feedback. In addition, Leung emphasizes the importance both of high expectations for all learners and of sensitivity to their preferred learning styles.

Hall describes how the quadrants framework has been used in the Tower Hamlets school district in London to plan learning experiences that would move secondary level bilingual students 'from context embedded conversation to context reduced discussion as efficiently as possible to increase their chance of good academic qualifications' (1996: 58). Most challenging for teachers was designing activities that embedded the learning in sufficient context to enable students to acquire more complex concepts and stretch them cognitively (Quadrant B). Hall outlines the way in which instructional activities related to teaching both Romeo and Juliet and a Life Science unit were mapped onto the quadrants and used as a discussion tool in collaborative workshops with both primary and secondary teachers. She highlights the heuristic value and 'street credibility' of the framework for work with teachers by noting that 'the level of debate generated in the process of collaborative planning during the workshops means that teachers are considerably raising their own awareness of the needs of several groups of pupils' (1996: 70).

Assessment perspectives

The appropriate sequencing of instructional tasks and the implications of the quadrants framework for assessment of bilingual students has been a focus of psychologists and linguists working in the UK context (Cline & Frederickson, 1996; Frederickson & Cline, 1990; Hall, 1995; Robson, 1995).[3]

Frederickson and Cline (1990), for example, in discussing the applicability of the framework for curriculum-based assessment of bilingual children have correctly pointed out that in practice, the contextual and cognitive dimensions are not totally independent of each other. Many context-reduced activities tend to be more cognitively demanding than context-embedded activities. They note:

> In observing and analysing classroom tasks, instructions and performances, we have often found it difficult to disentangle the 'cognitive' from the 'contextual'. In some cases, movement along the contextual dimensions has actually been represented on the model as a diagonal shift, as it was found in practice that making tasks or instructions more context embedded also made them somewhat less cognitively demanding. Similarly, changes in cognitive demand may result in tasks actually being presented with greater context embeddedness. (1990: 26)

Despite the fact that there is clearly likely to be a correlation between degree of decontextualization and cognitive demand, I believe it is important to maintain the conceptual distinction between the two dimensions. They are not reducible to each other and both dimensions should be considered in any analysis of academic tasks. For example, it is important in teaching ELL students to keep up the cognitive challenge but to provide sufficient contextual supports to enable them to complete these challenging tasks successfully. In the one-dimensional distinctions proposed by other investigators reviewed above, the degree of cognitive demand of particular tasks or activities is not represented and consequently they are less useful for both task analysis and instructional planning.

Robson has summarized some of the ways the framework has been used in the UK context:

> We found that the Cummins model was particularly relevant as a tool for formative assessment in that it could offer a framework for ongoing assessment, evaluation of tasks set and the planning of further teaching programmes and tasks for bilingual pupils. ... With reference to a bilingual pupil who may have learning difficulties, the Cummins model offers a framework for assessing progress over time, taking into account context, cognitive demand and language ability in relation to the tasks set. (1995: 41 & 43).

Conclusion

This chapter has described the rationale for the conversational/academic language proficiency distinction and its elaboration into the underlying dimensions of contextual support and cognitive demand. The conversational/academic distinction addresses a variety of policy, instructional, and assessment issues related to ELL/bilingual students. For example, it helps account for the longer time periods typically required for ELL students to catch up academically in English as compared to acquiring fluent conversational skills in English. It also draws attention to the potential for discriminatory assessment of bilingual students when their L2 conversational fluency is taken as an index of academic L2 acquisition.

The general framework outlined here has proven compatible with detailed analyses of the linguistic dimensions underlying a wide variety of authentic oral and written texts in English (Biber, 1986). It is also consistent with the different lexical realities of everyday conversational English as compared to literate forms of English (Corson, 1995, 1997). In addition, it has been used, in combination with Halliday's linguistic model, to interpret instructional sequences in science teaching (Gibbons, 1995, 1998). Both Gibbons and various British researchers have used the framework as a tool for analyzing academic tasks and for designing learning experiences for bilingual students.

Finally, the framework has been used productively in various contexts by teachers as a means of discussing the sources of difficulty within various academic tasks for bilingual students and for individualizing instruction for these students. In this regard, it should be noted that tasks cannot be mapped in any precise way onto the quadrants because degree of both contextual support and cognitive demand are a function not just of the tasks themselves but of the characteristics and background experience of individual learners. Thus, e-mail communication for a beginning learner of English may be highly cognitively demanding and context reduced but for a more advanced learner it may be relatively undemanding cognitively and much more contextually supported than writing an essay.

The quadrants essentially represent a visual metaphor that encourages discussion of task difficulty and task sequencing for particular groups of students by teachers who are familiar with their needs and characteristics. It is an interpretive and planning tool that attempts to address some of the ways in which language proficiency relates to academic achievement. As noted in the Introduction to Part I, no theory is 'valid' or 'true' in any absolute sense. While a theory must be logically coherent and consistent with the empirical evidence, it should be judged primarily according to criteria of usefulness in elucidating phenomena and the 'real-life' consequences of carrying through on its implications. The quadrants framework and the BICS/CALP distinction can claim to have met these criteria to some extent but there are clearly many theoretical and practical issues related to bilingual students' language and academic development that are beyond their scope.

The next chapter addresses the serious concerns that a number of critics have raised in relation to the conversational/academic language proficiency distinction and its elaboration in the quadrants framework.

Notes

1. Pauline Gibbons (personal communication, October 1999) has raised the issue of whether the notion of context-*reduced* is compatible with the dynamic notion of context associated with neo-Vygotskian theory. She suggests that *less situationally embedded* is a preferable term. Clearly, terms have different connotations which will change over time but the essential meaning is very similar, as the discussion of related theoretical constructs suggests.
2. On a lighter note than some of the other misinterpretations of the acronyms, Dr Tom Scovel shared with me the response of a student to an examination question in a Second Language Acquisition class that went as follows:

    'Bilingual Education is a controversial topic, largely due to politics. BICS, an organization that does not believe in bilingual education, feels that children can pick up language very easily but don't necessarily have to attend bilingual education classes.'
3. The British researchers have inverted the vertical axis of the quadrants so that 'cognitively demanding' is on top and 'cognitively undemanding' is on the bottom. Clearly, the configuration of the quadrants is largely an arbitrary decision but I have noted the different configuration here to draw attention to the fact that the quadrant labels (A, B, C, D) as they are used in the British work will refer to different combinations of contextual support and cognitive demand than is the case for the quadrants layout presented here.

Chapter 4
Critiques of the Conversational/ Academic Language Proficiency Distinction

Early critiques of the conversational/academic distinction were advanced by Carole Edelsky and her colleagues (Edelsky *et al.*, 1983) and in a volume edited by Charlene Rivera (1984). These critiques were responded to and will not be discussed in depth in this chapter (see Cummins, 1984; Cummins & Swain, 1983). Edelsky (1990) later reiterated and reformulated her critique and other critiques were advanced by Martin-Jones and Romaine (1986) and Romaine (1989). More recently, Terrence Wiley (1996) and Jeff MacSwan (1999, 2000) have critiqued aspects of the conversational/academic language distinction, particularly the conception of literacy implied by the distinction and the relationship posited between 'language proficiency' and literacy.

The major criticisms in these and other critiques are as follows:

- The conversational/academic language distinction reflects an autonomous perspective on language that ignores its location in social practices and power relations (Edelsky *et al.*, 1983; Romaine, 1989; Troike, 1984; Wald, 1984; Wiley, 1996).
- CALP or academic language proficiency represents little more than 'test-wiseness' – it is an artifact of the inappropriate way in which it has been measured (Edelsky *et al.*, 1983; MacSwan, 1999, 2000).
- The notion of CALP and the threshold hypothesis promote a 'deficit theory' insofar as they attribute the academic failure of bilingual/minority students to low cognitive/academic proficiency rather than to inappropriate schooling; in this respect they are no different than notions such as 'semilingualism' (Edelsky, 1990; Edelsky *et al.*, 1983; Martin-Jones & Romaine, 1986; MacSwan, 1999, 2000).

I will outline in more detail the points raised by Edelsky (1990) and Wiley (1996) as representative of the general orientation of these critiques. The construct of 'semilingualism' will be considered in the second part of the chapter.

Edelsky's (1990) Critique

Consistent with her previous critique (Edelsky *et al.*, 1983), Edelsky disputes the legitimacy of the constructs of cognitive academic language proficiency (CALP) and basic interpersonal communicative skills (BICS). She argues that CALP consists of little more than test-taking skills and the construct encourages skills-oriented instruction, thereby impeding the literacy development of bilingual students who will thrive only in meaning-oriented whole-language instructional contexts. The tone and substance of her critique can be gauged from the following extracts:

> The fundamental problem with all versions of Cummins' THEORY is that it is premised on an erroneous, psychologically derived 'theory' of the nature of reading – a conception of reading as consisting of separate skills with discrete components of language. What counts as either reading-in-action or as evidence of reading ability is 'reading skills'. These are demonstrated by performance in miscontextualized tasks (performed for the sole purpose of either demonstrating proficiency or complying with the assignment) or on tests whose scores are presumed to represent some supposedly context-free reading ability. (1990: 60–61)

> Despite Cummins' occasional use of 'whole language' terminology (e.g. 'inferring', 'predicting' 'large chunks of discourse'), his underlying skills orientation shows through. (1990: 61) …

> He uses a discourse of empowerment and puts forward a set of suggestions that implicitly contradict his 'theory' of reading as consisting of separate skills (Cummins, 1986). … And Cummins uses the right rhetoric. He talks of students setting their own goals and generating their own knowledge and he mentions congruent educational practice (e.g. he refers to reports by Graves and the Bullock Report). Even so, the separate skills 'theory' slips out and he contradicts his own message. For example, for empirical support, he relies heavily on test score data that can only provide evidence of how well students perform on skill exercises. He applauds and describes at length programs that operate according to a skills 'theory'. For instance, he talks of two programs that make language or cultural accommodations which benefit minority language children by helping them attain readiness or success. Readiness for what? For the academic tasks of the traditional kindergartens the children will enter in California. Success at what? Success in doing reading exercises in tests and basal reading lessons in Hawaii. (1990: 62)

Edelsky is referring here to two programs that incorporated many of the characteristics that I postulated were necessary to challenge coercive power structures in school (Cummins, 1986). One was the bilingual preschool program in Carpinteria that used Spanish as the predominant language of instruction and attempted to incorporate children's cultural background experience into the design of the program which was strongly child-centred (Campos & Keatinge, 1988). The other was the Kamehameha Early Education Program in Hawaii that dramatically improved native Hawaiian children's reading performance by incorporating culturally familiar communal story-construction patterns into reading instruction (Au & Jordan, 1981).

Edelsky dismisses as suffering from internal contradictions any reference to the sociopolitical determinants of academic outcomes as well as advocacy of pedagogical models that create contexts of empowerment for bilingual students: 'Because of the contradictions he fails to see (e.g. juxtaposing Graves' pedagogy with test-score evidence), he is forced into another kind of contradiction: his entire THEORY does not fit his proposals for an empowering kind of education' (p. 62).

According to Edelsky the theory 'gained popularity so fast and was so effective in influencing policy' (p. 63) because it reinforced ideas that 'undergird predominant thinking about education in North America' namely 'that written language consists of separate skills, that curriculum should teach those skills, that tests can assess them' (p. 63).

Edelsky points out that in disputing the constructs of CALP and BICS, she is not claiming that all children are equally competent. She also points out that she does not believe that proficiency with *any* language variety, in either oral or written modes, enables one to do *everything* humanly possible with language:

> Though *potentially* equal, at any given historical moment different language repertoires (including literate repertoires) of particular speech communities are unequally efficient for all purposes and even then, unequally assigned to members. ... However, the nature of those repertoires, their functions, their meanings, and their inequalities must be determined by ethnographies of speaking and of literacy, not by differential performance in one (testing) context that is subject to criticism on multiple grounds. (1990: 65)

She is explicit about how she views the construct of cognitive academic language proficiency: it is nothing more than 'test-wiseness' (p. 65) or what she terms 'skill in instructional nonsense (SIN, if another acronym is needed)' (p. 69). Any research that has used any form of 'test', whether standardized reading measures or non-standardized measures of any kind of cognitive performance is dismissed. For example, in referring to Gordon Wells' (1986) documentation of the relation between exposure to literacy at home and subsequent literacy performance in school she notes: 'In fact, from the use he makes of Wells' research, Cummins seems to interpret the social grounding of CALP to mean no more than a correlation between test scores and certain kinds of home interactions' (p. 68). It is not surprising to her that support for the theoretical constructs of CALP and BICS would come

> ... almost entirely from studies using tests of separate so-called reading skills. (No wonder. His small parts, psychometric orientation that views all human

activity as first divisible into atomized skills and then measurable would certainly lead him to prefer such evidence). (1990: 61)

Edelsky concludes her critique by rejecting theories that locate 'failure in children's heads (in their IQ, their language deficits, their cognitive deficits, their learning styles, their underdeveloped CALP)'.

Response to the Critique

Let me first note that the vehemence of Edelsky's critique is clearly related to her strong beliefs regarding the importance of a whole-language pedagogical orientation that promotes reading and writing for authentic purposes. She has articulated this perspective effectively on many occasions and, as I document below and in Chapter 10, I concur with this general orientation to literacy instruction, with some qualifications similar to those articulated by Delpit (1988) and Reyes (1992). Edelsky has also highlighted the damaging effects of the increasing use of standardized tests to assess students' educational progress and the fact that what is measured on these tests typically represents only a small fraction of literacy and general educational objectives. I share her concerns regarding the inappropriate uses of standardized tests and have expressed this perspective on numerous occasions (e.g. Cummins, 1984, 1986, 1989; Cummins & Sayers, 1995). In fact, the BICS/CALP distinction arose from a study documenting the prejudicial nature for bilingual students of standardized IQ tests (Cummins, 1980, 1984). The reality of teachers teaching to the test rather than promoting extensive reading and writing for authentic purposes is evident in educational jurisdictions throughout North America that have fallen victim to 'knee-jerk accountability', as elaborated in Chapter 6.

Where I diverge from her position is that I am not prepared to reject any use of any test for any purpose, as she seems to advocate. Under some conditions, and properly interpreted, there are potentially appropriate and useful applications of some language testing procedures. These points are elaborated in Chapters 5 and 6. Below I address the specific claims made by Edelsky.

A first point to note is that there is nothing new in the Edelsky (1990) critique that was not already in the Edelsky *et al.* (1983) paper. The only difference is that she rejects any elaboration of the sociopolitical determinants of students' academic difficulties as suffering from internal contradictions. The same charge is levelled against any explication of the pedagogical implications of the theoretical framework that build on the quadrants framework and the sociopolitical analysis to advocate transformative or critical pedagogy (Cummins, 1986, 1996).

To set the record straight, the sociopolitical and instructional implications of the theoretical framework which Edelsky dismisses as internally contradictory were expressed in 1986 as follows:

Sociopolitical perspective:
Minority students are disabled or empowered in schools in very much the same way that their communities are disempowered in interactions with societal

institutions. … This analysis implies that minority students will succeed educationally to the extent that the patterns of interaction in school reverse those that prevail in the society at large. (Cummins, 1986: 24)

Given the societal commitment to maintaining the dominant/dominated power relationships, we can predict that educational changes threatening this structure will be fiercely resisted. (1986: 34)

Instructional perspective:
A central tenet of the reciprocal interaction model is that 'talking and writing are means to learning' (Bullock Report, 1975, p. 50). … This model emphasizes the development of higher level cognitive skills rather than just factual recall, and meaningful language use by students rather than correction of surface forms. Language use and development are consciously integrated with all curricular content rather than taught as isolated subjects, and tasks are presented to students in ways that generate intrinsic rather than extrinsic motivation. In short, pedagogical approaches that empower students encourage them to assume greater control over setting their own learning goals and to collaborate actively with each other in achieving these goals. (1986: 29)

In terms of the quadrants outlined in Figure 3.1, these approaches fall into Quadrant B (cognitively demanding, context embedded). In later work, I have emphasized the importance of going beyond whole-language or liberal/progressive pedagogy as illustrated in the quotation below:

Transformative pedagogy uses collaborative critical inquiry to enable students to relate curriculum content to their individual and collective experience and to analyze broader social issues relevant to their lives. It also encourages students to discuss ways in which social realities might be transformed through various forms of democratic participation and social action.

Thus, transformative pedagogy will aim to go beyond the sanitized curriculum that is still the norm in many schools. It will attempt to promote students' ability to analyze and understand the social realities of their own lives and of their communities. It will strive to develop a critical literacy … (1996: 157).

So how do these perspectives and the theoretical framework elaborated in Chapter 2 'implicitly contradict' the constructs of conversational/academic language proficiency and their relationship to cognitive demands and contextual support (Figure 3.1)? The reality is that *they are not in any way contradictory*. The construct of academic language proficiency does not depend on test scores as support for either its construct validity or its relevance to education. The evidence cited in Chapter 3 makes minimal reference to test scores. The obvious differences between six-year-old and 16-year-old monolingual students in multiple aspects of literacy-related knowledge (assessed by *any* criterion) illustrate this reality as does Corson's (1995) analysis of the lexicon of English, Biber's (1986) analysis of more than one million words of English speech and written text, Vincent's (1996) ethnographic observations of ELL students' language functioning in school, and Gibbons' (1995) ethnographic study of language interactions in science instruction.

Also, for the record, I have *never* advocated nor endorsed any theory of reading as consisting of separate skills. It is significant that despite her strongly expressed claims to this effect, Edelsky's evidence seems to consist of little more than the fact that I have occasionally referred to 'reading skills' and I am not willing to reject all tests used for any purpose in any context as measuring only 'skill in instructional nonsense'.

Edelsky's (1990) vehement dismissal of any test used for any purpose in any context and her adamant endorsement of only one way of collecting data on language proficiency (through ethnographies of speaking and literacy) might appear to some researchers as extreme and one-dimensional. There are very few educational researchers who, on ideological grounds, have refused to even cite research that derived from 'a small-parts, psychometric orientation' (p. 61) (i.e. used statistics) or that involved formal testing of academic progress; yet this is the logical implication of Edelsky's position.

It is worth noting that Edelsky (1990) makes no attempt to respond to the rebuttals of the Edelsky *et al.* (1983) position advanced by Cummins and Swain (1983). We made three basic points in response to the arguments that the CALP/BICS distinction entailed a 'deficit position' that blamed the victim by attributing school failure to 'low CALP' and furthermore that it promoted a 'skills' approach to pedagogy that would further victimize minority group students. We suggested that:

- Rational discussion of which theories constitute 'deficit theories' require *explicit criteria* of what constitutes a 'deficit theory'; for example, does it constitute a 'deficit theory' to note, as many researchers and theorists have done (e.g. Corson, 1997; MacSwan, 2000; Wells, 1981), that middle class children tend to have more experience of books than low-income students when they come to school and that this gives them access to a greater range of language functions and registers that are relevant to the ways schools tend to teach initial literacy? In this case, children's linguistic experience and the consequent earlier access to certain registers of language are seen as intervening variables that interact with patterns of instruction at school. Does any positing of learner attributes and linguistic experience as intervening variables constitute a deficit theory? As noted above, Edelsky herself claims that 'at any given historical moment different language repertoires (including literate repertoires) of particular speech communities are unequally efficient for all purposes and even then, unequally assigned to members' (1990: 65). Is she saying here that the language and literate repertoires of particular speech communities are less well developed that those of other speech communities? Does this constitute a 'deficit' position?
- Universal condemnation of all formal test situations is simplistic and fails to account for considerable data documenting strong positive relationships between reading test scores and 'authentic' assessment measures such as

miscue analysis and cloze procedures (see Chapter 5). We pointed out that 'if cloze tests are to be dismissed as 'irrelevant nonsense' then this surely merits some comment in view of their widespread use and acceptance among applied linguists' (1983: 28) including Sarah Hudelson, one of the co-authors of the Edelsky *et al.* (1983) critique.

- When language proficiency or CALP 'is discussed as part of a causal chain, it is *never* discussed as an isolated causal factor (as Edelsky *et al.* consistently depict it) but rather as *one of a number* of individual learner attributes that are determined by societal influences and which interact with educational treatment factors in affecting academic progress' (Cummins & Swain, 1983: 31). In other words, language proficiency was always seen as an *intervening variable* rather than an autonomous causal variable; it develops through social interaction in home and school.[1]

To deny this essentially Vygotskian perspective on language and academic development, one has to either adopt an extreme Chomskian perspective that identifies 'language proficiency' as Universal Grammar and immune from virtually all social interactional and environmental influence (which appears to be MacSwan's (1999, 2000) position) or claim that a student's language proficiency in a particular language has no relationship to that student's ability to benefit from instruction in that language.

In short, Edelsky (1990) fails to define what she means by a deficit position. She also fails to respond to the data we cited illustrating that 'authentic' measures of reading are closely related to measures of what she terms 'skill in instructional nonsense'. And finally, she fails to discuss the extent to which she believes that there is a place for any construct of 'language proficiency', and if so how it relates to academic progress and literacy (is it an intervening variable, a 'causal' variable, or totally unrelated?).

A less one-dimensional approach would admit that there is no contradiction between the conception of 'language proficiency' outlined in Chapter 3 and a theoretical framework that

- identifies coercive power relations as the causal factors in the underachievement of subordinated group students; and
- promotes transformative pedagogy as a central component in challenging these coercive relations of power in the classroom.

In fact, the distinction between conversational and academic dimensions of proficiency has been instrumental in highlighting both how standardized tests (e.g. IQ tests used in psychological assessment) and premature exit from bilingual programs on the basis of conversational rather than academic development in English have contributed to the perpetuation of coercive power relations in the educational system. A balanced critique would have acknowledged the impact of the conversational/academic distinction in highlighting these realities and in elucidating how standardized psychological tests were being used as a discriminatory force within the school system (see Cummins, 1980, 1984, 1986).

A final issue concerns Edelsky's dismissal of the efforts of innovative educators in the Carpinteria preschool program and in the Kamehameha Early Education Program (KEEP) in Hawaii (and countless other programs that have used standardized tests as one way of documenting student progress and establishing credibility to skeptical policy-makers and the general public). While the offensive tone of this dismissal is probably unintended, it illustrates the consequences of adopting a one-dimensional perspective on the contradictions encountered by educators attempting to create contexts of empowerment in the real world of classrooms and schools. It is certainly *not* the case that the theoretical orientation or significant academic achievements of these programs is adequately or fairly described as operating 'according to a skills "theory"' (Edelsky, 1990: 62). For the record, I described the KEEP program as follows: 'When reading instruction was changed to permit students to collaborate in discussing and interpreting texts, dramatic improvements were found in both reading and verbal intellectual abilities' (Cummins, 1986: 25). A focus on collaboration in discussing and interpreting texts is not usually what one associates with a 'skills theory' approach to reading.

Wiley's (1996) Critique

Wiley's critique forms a chapter in his useful volume *Literacy and Language Diversity in the United States*. The critique derives from a basic distinction he makes between different orientations to literacy. Specifically, following Street (1984, 1993), he contrasts the *autonomous approach* with the *ideological approach*. The former is described as follows:

> The autonomous approach to literacy tends to focus on formal mental properties of decoding and encoding text, excluding analyses of how these processes are used within social contexts. The success of the learner in acquiring literacy is seen as correlating with individual psychological processes. … Those operating within the autonomous approach see literacy as having 'cognitive consequences' at both the individual and societal level … An autonomous perspective largely ignores the historical and sociopolitical contexts in which individuals live and differences in power and resources between groups. (1996: 31)

By contrast, in the ideological approach advanced by Street and critical pedagogy theorists (e.g. Freire, 1970) 'literacy is viewed as a set of practices that are inextricably linked to cultural and power structures in the society' (Wiley, 1996: 32). From this perspective, literacy problems are seen as related to social stratification and to gaps in power and resources between groups. The role of schools in reinforcing this stratification is expressed as follows:

> Because schools are the principal institutions responsible for developing literacy, they are seen as embedded within larger sociopolitical contexts. Because some groups succeed in school while others fail, the ideological approach scrutinizes the way in which literacy development is carried out. It

looks at the implicit biases in schools that can privilege some groups to the exclusion of others. Finally, the social practices approach values literacy programs and policies that are built on the knowledge and resources people already have. (1996: 33)

Wiley's major concern is that constructs such as BICS/CALP or conversational/academic language and the contextual and cognitive dimensions outlined in Figure 3.1 appear to invoke an autonomous orientation to language and literacy that isolates language and literacy practices from their sociocultural and sociopolitical context. He concurs with the critiques of Edelsky *et al.* (1983) that the construct of CALP relies on inauthentic test data and cites Martin-Jones and Romaine that the distinction between CALP and BICS is suspect

> … if both are seen as independent of rather than shaped by the language context in which they are acquired and used … The type of literacy-related skills described by Cummins are, in fact, quite culture-specific: that is, they are specific to the cultural setting of the school. (1986: 30)

Wiley is also concerned about the higher status supposedly assigned to academic as compared to conversational language:

> Notions of academic language proficiency and decontextualization, as they are often used, are particularly problematic because they confound language with schooling and equate a higher cognitive status to the language and literacy practices of school. Academic language proficiency seems to equate broadly with schooling. Schooling is not a neutral process. It involves class and culturally specific forms of socialization. (1996: 183)

Finally, Wiley criticizes the 'simplistic' but 'well-intentioned' ways in which practitioners have attempted to operationalize the kinds of language tasks/activities that would fall into the four quadrants of Figure 3.1. He gives one set of examples of such tasks/activities used for professional development in California which he describes as 'value laden and arbitrary' with categorization of tasks which is 'confused and inaccurate'. He points out that 'professional development materials such as these illustrate the limitations of applying constructs in practice that have not been fully elaborated at the theoretical level'.

Wiley concludes that it is 'necessary to rid the framework of those constructs that are compatible with an autonomous view of language use. … It would require focusing more on social than on cognitive factors affecting language development (Troike, 1984) and on the cultural factors that affect language and literacy practices in the schools' (p. 178).

Response to the Critique

Wiley's analysis suffers from a rigid 'either–or' perspective on what forms of inquiry are appropriate in the area of literacy and schooling. Either an approach is autonomous or it is ideological but it can't be both, or draw from each tradition in order to address different kinds of questions. The complex manifestations of literacy practices in bilingual contexts described in Hornberger's (1989) *continua of biliteracy* illustrate the limitations of this 'either–or' perspective. Linked to Wiley's 'either–or' perspective is a prescriptivism which, although much less strident than Edelsky's (1990), suggests that only questions deriving from an ideological perspective can and should be asked.

This rigid dichotomy leads him to largely ignore the fact that the theoretical constructs associated with the notion of language proficiency have been integrated since 1986 with a detailed sociopolitical analysis of how schools construct academic failure among subordinated groups. This framework, summarized in Chapter 2, analyzes how coercive relations of power in the wider society affect both educational structures and the ways in which educators define their roles. These dimensions, in turn, have resulted in patterns of interactions between educators and subordinated group students that have constricted students' academic language development and identity formation. The framework documents educational approaches that challenge this pattern of coercive power relations and promote the generation of power in the interactions between educators and students.

This framework, however, does not regard subordinated group students' opportunities to gain access to academic registers, and their consequent expertise in using these registers, as irrelevant to their schooling or life chances. In order to analyze how power relations operate in the real world of schooling, it is crucial to ask questions such as 'How long does it take second language learners to gain sufficient control of the academic registers of school to participate in class on an equal basis with native speakers?' The data showing that five years are minimally required to bridge this gap continue to provide bilingual educators with a powerful rebuttal to efforts to deny students access to bilingual programs or exit them rapidly from support services whether bilingual or English-only. Yet, Wiley would presumably classify this question as deriving from an 'autonomous' perspective.

I also believe that it is legitimate to ask 'What forms of proficiency in English do bilingual students need to survive academically in all-English classrooms after they have been transitioned out of bilingual programs?' This question would also fall into the 'autonomous' category of the artificial either–or dichotomy that Wiley constructs. The conversational/academic language proficiency distinction has been instrumental in helping educators understand why students transitioned on the basis of conversational fluency in English frequently experience severe academic difficulties in all-English mainstream classrooms.

The same issue surfaces with respect to the assessment of bilingual children for special education purposes. The BICS/CALP distinction highlighted the fact that psychological assessment in English was considered appropriate by psychologists and teachers when students had gained conversational fluency in English but frequently were far from their native English-speaking peers in academic English development (Cummins, 1980, 1984).

Wiley's rigid interpretation of the autonomous/ideological dichotomy would also consign any question regarding how language and cognition intersect (in either monolingual or multilingual individuals) to the garbage heap of scientific inquiry. All of the research studies documenting that acquisition of bilingualism in childhood entails no adverse cognitive consequences for children and, in fact, is associated with more advanced awareness of language and ability to analyze language (see Chapters 2 and 7) would also be castigated as reflecting an 'autonomous' perspective.

It is also legitimate, I believe, to ask how linguistic interactions in home and school, and interactions related to print, affect children's linguistic, cognitive, and academic development. These interactions take place within a sociocultural and sociopolitical context but their effects are still linguistic, academic, and cognitive. Students from bilingual backgrounds who do not understand the language of instruction in school, and receive no support to enable them to do so, are unlikely to develop high levels of academic proficiency or literacy knowledge in either first or second languages (e.g. Verhallen & Schoonen, 1998).

The list of questions could go on. The point I want to make is that within the framework I have proposed, 'language proficiency' is seen as an *intervening variable* that mediates children's academic development. It is not in any sense 'autonomous' or independent of the sociocultural context. As should be clear from the discussion in Chapter 3, I fully agree with Martin-Jones and Romaine's point that the conversational and academic aspects of proficiency are 'shaped by the language context in which they are acquired and used' and that academic language is 'specific to the cultural setting of the school'. This is why it is called 'academic language'.

A central aspect of the framework, in fact, is that language proficiency is shaped by the patterns and contexts of educator–student interaction in the school and will, in turn, mediate the further outcomes of schooling. Thus the framework constructs academic success or failure as *social* rather than psychological. Learners' achievements can never be seen as solely the result of their abilities, whether innate or developed. Learning reflects the nature of the interactions that learners have experienced with educators and the adequacy of the linguistic and cultural frameworks in which these interactions have taken place.

The claim that the BICS/CALP distinction ascribes a superior status to academic language as compared to conversational has been addressed in Chapter 3. No form of language is cognitively or linguistically superior to any other form of language in any absolute sense outside of particular contexts. However, within the context of schooling, knowledge of academic language (e.g. the Graeco-Latin lexicon of written English text, the discursive conventions of academic genres, etc.) is clearly relevant to educational success. Wiley, like Martin-Jones and Romaine, takes a conceptual distinction that was addressed only to issues of schooling, and criticizes it on the grounds that this distinction is 'specific only to the cultural setting of the school'. These critics seriously misrepresent the distinction when they label it 'autonomous' or 'independent' of particular contexts.

An inconsistency in Wiley's attitude to 'inauthentic test data' should be noted. He suggests (p. 167) that there is a major concern regarding the authenticity of using school-test data as a means of determining language proficiencies. I would agree. School-test data attempt to assess certain kinds of language proficiencies but often do it very inadequately without regard to cultural and linguistic biases in the test instruments, as the study of psychological test data demonstrated (Cummins, 1984). However, in view of Wiley's dismissal of school-test data as even a partial basis for constructing theory, it is surprising to see him invoke exactly this type of data to assert that 'there is an ever-growing body of evidence that bilingual education is effective in promoting literacy and academic achievement among children when adequate resources are provided' (p. 153). Virtually all of this evidence derives from 'inauthentic' standardized test data. For example, among the references Wiley cites to back up this claim are Ramírez (1992) and Krashen and Biber (1988) who relied almost exclusively on standardized test data to support their claims for the effectiveness of bilingual education.

A final point concerns Wiley's unease with the 'simplistic', 'confused and inaccurate' interpretations by some practitioners of what kinds of language task or activities would fall into the four quadrants of Figure 3.1. He fails to appreciate that the quadrants represent a visual metaphor that incorporates hypotheses about the dimensions underlying various kinds of language performance. It makes linkages between the theoretical literature on the nature of proficiency in a language and specific instructional and policy issues faced on a daily basis by educators working with bilingual learners (e.g. how much 'English proficiency' do children need to participate effectively in an all-English classroom?). It attempts to provide tentative answers to certain questions such as why certain kinds of 'English proficiency' are acquired to peer-appropriate levels relatively quickly while a longer period is required for other aspects of proficiency. However, it was also intended as a heuristic tool to stimulate discussion regarding the linguistic and cognitive challenges posed by different academic tasks and subject matter content. As noted in the previous chapter, it has been effective in this regard in a number of international contexts (e.g. Australia, the United Kingdom, North America). Thus, it risks appearing condescending to dismiss as 'simplistic' the efforts of educators to use the framework as a tool to discuss, and attempt to better understand, the linguistic challenges their students face.

In summary, Wiley's basic point is that the theoretical construction of language and literacy and prescriptions regarding how they should be taught are never neutral with respect to societal power relations. An 'ideological' approach is fundamental to understanding literacy development, particularly in linguistically and culturally diverse contexts. I am in full agreement with this perspective and have attempted to highlight how coercive power relations affect the development of language and literacy among bilingual students (e.g. Cummins, 1986). However, there are also many important and legitimate questions regarding the nature of language proficiency, the developmental patterns of its various components, and the relationships among language proficiency, cognitive development, and academic progress, that cannot be totally reduced to 'ideological' or sociopolitical questions. To dismiss these issues as reflecting an 'autonomous' orientation and to demand that any traces of such an orientation be purged from theoretical approaches to literacy would eliminate much of the entire disciplines of psychology and applied linguistics. It also reflects a profound misunderstanding of the nature of intervening or mediating variables. There is absolutely no internal inconsistency in asking questions about the nature of the relationships between language, bilingualism, cognition, and academic achievement within the broader context of a sociopolitical causal model.

Conclusion

My primary goal in the preceding rebuttal has been to clarify misconceptions regarding the constructs of conversational and academic language proficiencies so that policy-makers and educators can re-focus on the issue of how to promote academic language development effectively among bilingual children. If academic language proficiency or CALP is accepted as a valid construct then certain instructional implications follow. In the first place, as Krashen (1993) has repeatedly emphasized, extensive reading is crucial for academic development since academic language is found primarily in written text. If bilingual students are not reading extensively, they are not getting access to the language of academic success. Opportunities for collaborative learning and talk about text are also extremely important in helping students internalize and more fully comprehend the academic language they find in their extensive reading of text.

Writing is also crucial because when bilingual students write about issues that matter to them they not only consolidate aspects of the academic language they have been reading, they also express their identities through language and (hopefully) receive feedback from teachers and others that will affirm and further develop their expression of self.

In general, the instructional implications of the framework can be expressed in terms of the three components of the construct of CALP:

Cognitive – instruction should be cognitively challenging and require students to use higher-order thinking abilities rather than the low-level memorization and application skills that are tapped by typical worksheets or drill-and-practice computer programs;

Academic – academic content (science, math, social studies, art etc.) should be integrated with language instruction so that students acquire the specific language or registers of these academic stubjects.

Language – the development of critical language awareness should be fostered throughout the program by encouraging students to compare and contrast their languages (e.g. phonics conventions, grammar, cognates, etc.) and by providing students with extensive opportunities to carry out projects investigating their own and their community's language use, practices, and assumptions (e.g. in relation to the status of different varieties and power relations associated with language policies and practices).

In short, instruction within a strong bilingual (or English-only) program should provide a *Focus on Meaning*, a *Focus on Language*, and a *Focus on Use* in both languages (see Chapter 10). We know our program is effective, and developing CALP, if we can say with confidence that our students are generating new knowledge, creating literature and art, and acting on social realities that affect their lives. These are the kinds of (Quadrant B) instructional activities that the conversational/academic language distinction is intended to foster.

'Semilingualism', Deficit Theories, and the BICS/CALP Distinction

Introduction

The critique by Edelsky *et al.* (1983) claimed that the BICS/CALP distinction is essentially identical to the semilingualism thesis which they interpret as arguing that bilingual students fail academically because they have low proficiency in both languages. There are two aspects to this issue: (1) the question of whether some students from linguistic minority backgrounds can legitimately be characterized as 'semilingual' (sometimes termed 'doubly semilingual'), a condition that implies inadequate development of both first and second languages; (2) the related question of whether such alleged linguistic and/or cognitive deficits may be regarded as causal factors in explaining the poor academic performance of some bilingual students (Cummins and Swain, 1983; Edelsky *et al.*, 1983; Hansegard, 1972; Kalantzis *et al.* 1989; Martin-Jones and Romaine, 1986; Paulston, 1982; Skutnabb-Kangas, 1984; Stroud, 1978).

These questions can be combined and rephrased as 'Does the construct of 'semilingualism' have any theoretical value in describing and/or explaining the poor school performance of some bilingual students?' My unequivocal answer to this question is: '*No – the construct of 'semilingualism' has no theoretical value in describing or explaining the poor school performance of some bilingual students.*' However, this denial of the theoretical utility of the construct of 'semilingualism' does not imply that the academic language proficiency (CALP) that bilingual students develop in their two languages is irrelevant to their academic progress. In fact, there is overwhelming evidence that for both monolingual and bilingual students, the degree of academic language proficiency they develop in school is a crucial intervening variable in mediating their academic progress. The vast majority of those who have argued that 'semilingualism does not exist' have failed to realize that theoretical constructs are not characterized by existence or non-existence but by characteristics such as validity and usefulness, or their opposites. Most have also declined to engage with the question of how language proficiency is related to academic achievement and how individual differences in academic language proficiency should be characterized. In short, their critiques of the construct of 'semilingualism' have failed to contribute much to our understanding of the underlying issues.

My personal involvement in this debate derives from the fact that in three articles in the late 1970s, I used the term 'semilingualism' in the context of the threshold hypothesis (see Chapters 2 and 7). I suggested that the levels of proficiency that bilingual students attained in their two languages might mediate the consequences of their bilingualism for cognitive and academic development (Cummins, 1976, 1978, 1979a). The term 'semilingualism' was used to characterize the reality that, as a result of discriminatory schooling, some bilingual students fail to attain strong academic proficiency in either their L1 or L2. The term was adopted from the work of Skutnabb-Kangas and Toukomaa (1976) and was intended to highlight the consequences of inappropriate forms of educational provision such as lack of L1 instruction/submersion in L2. Under these conditions, bilingual students in some contexts have failed to gain access in either L1 or L2 to the kinds of language registers (or proficiencies or functions) that are required to participate effectively in schooling. When schools deny bilingual students opportunities to access literacy and comprehensible academic language in both L1 and L2 (as they have historically done in many countries), students are denied the cognitive and linguistic benefits of additive bilingualism and frequently they tend to fall progressively further behind grade expectations in their functional command of academic registers.

Students fall behind for the simple reason that they do not sufficiently understand the language of instruction. This is illustrated by Hakuta, Butler and Witt (2000: 1) in their analysis of how long it takes English learners (EL) to catch up academically. They note that the 'analysis also revealed a continuing and widening gap between EL students and native English speakers'. While many students do catch up academically when the instructional conditions are favorable, the gap between learners and native speakers may widen in classroom contexts where students' English language proficiency is not sufficient to comprehend poorly delivered instruction. The *causes* of this are clearly sociopolitical and instructional but it is also legitimate to ask how students' proficiency in the language of instruction functions as an intervening variable in mediating the effects of these sociopolitical and instructional causal factors.

Controversy in Sweden over the construct of 'semilingualism' (e.g. Stroud, 1978) demonstrated that the term was potentially pejorative and did not contribute to productive debate of the issues. Consequently, in 1979, I repudiated my own and others' use of the term and argued that it should no longer be used (Cummins, 1979b). I noted, however, that there was still a legitimate issue regarding how we conceptualize individual differences in language proficiency in academic contexts and how these individual differences are related to educational outcomes. Certainly, in early papers outlining the threshold hypothesis, my own use of terms such as 'linguistic competence' and 'native-speaker competence' lacked precision and clarity. This was also true for most other investigators who explored issues related to how language proficiency related to academic achievement (e.g. see the articles in Oller, 1983). The BICS/CALP distinction and the quadrants framework (Figure 3.1) articulated in articles between 1979 and 1981 were an attempt to attain greater clarity and precision in the characterization of the construct of 'language proficiency'.

The evolution of the broader debate on the construct of 'semilingualism' is outlined below.

Evolution of the Debate on 'Semilingualism'

Hansegard (1972) provided an elaborated description of the construct of 'double semilingualism' based on his extensive observations among Finnish and Sami communities in Northern Sweden. The six characteristics outlined by Hansegard are as follows:

(1) Size of the repertoire of words, phrases, etc. understood or actively available in speech.
(2) Correctness with respect to syntactic, phonemic and discoursal aspects of language use.
(3) Degree of automatism in use of the language.
(4) Ability to create or neologize in the language.
(5) Mastery of the cognitive, emotive and volitional function of language.
(6) Degree of richness in the semantic networks available to the individual through the language.

It should be noted that Hansegard's observations were based on a lifetime of living in these communities rather than on any kind of test performance. They conform in many respects to Edelsky's (1990) requirement that descriptions of language repertoires and proficiencies be derived from 'ethnographies of communication'.

Edelsky *et al.* (1983: 2) characterized Hansegard's description as 'a confused grab-bag of prescriptive and descriptive components' and argued that to attribute minority students' academic difficulties to 'semilingualism' even as one link in a causal chain constitutes a deficit theory that 'blames the victim'. In a somewhat contradictory fashion, they did, however, admit that 'semilingualism might mean something more substantial (e.g. an inability to use language in its ideational or representational function ...)' (1983: 11) and they acknowledged that variation in language proficiency does exist, although they did not elaborate much further on what this might mean for bilingual students' academic development. They draw back, however, from addressing whether there are any differences between 'an inability to use language in its ideational or representational function' (which they suggest is a legitimate characterization of some individuals) and Hansegard's sixth characteristic 'Degree of richness in the semantic networks available to the individual through the language'.

Paulston (1982) also argued that there is no empirical evidence for the construct and she deplored its use in the Swedish debate as an argument for Finnish home language classes. Martin-Jones and Romaine (1986) similarly disputed the existence of 'semilingualism'. They attributed apparent inadequacies of linguistic competence among bilinguals to the normal processes of language contact and language shift.

Skutnabb-Kangas (1984), in response to criticism of the construct, made the point that most of the studies that claim not to have found evidence for inadequate command of two languages have focused on *syntax*, whereas many of those that support the construct have focused on range of vocabulary. She furthermore argued that semilingualism cannot be regarded as a deficiency inherent in the individual but should be treated as one result of the societal and educational discrimination to which minority groups are subjected. In other words, it is a political as much as an educational construct. Semilingualism can be avoided when minority children receive intensive L1 instruction through 'language shelter' (i.e. L1 immersion) programs.

Several authors have adopted an intermediate position with respect to this debate. McLaughlin (1985), for example, suggests that 'if the concept of semilingualism is defined as meaning that bilingual children do not perform as well as native speakers in either language, then there is some agreement that in fact this may be the case at certain points in the development of their languages' (1985: 33).

Kalantzis *et al.* similarly point to the situation 'in which the home language is not continued with growing sophistication past entry to formal schooling either at home or at school, and in which the initial experience of formal schooling does not adequately prepare students for proficiency in their second language' (1989: 30). They suggest that the consequence of this situation can be that 'children's ability to express themselves and manipulate the world around them through language is hampered' (1989: 31).

A lack of academic sophistication in both L1 and L2 is described empirically by Verhallen and Schoonen (1998) who investigated the lexical knowledge of Turkish elementary school students in the Netherlands. These investigators examined both range and depth of Grades 3 and 5 students' vocabulary knowledge in Turkish and Dutch based on interviews where students were required to give as many meanings as they could think of to six stimulus words. Previous research in the Netherlands had shown that Turkish background children had significantly lower levels of Dutch (L2) vocabulary knowledge than their Dutch L1 peers. Verhallen and Schoonen reported that 'bilingual children not only know fewer words in their L1 than in their L2, they also have a less profound knowledge of the L1 words they seem to have acquired (1998: 465). They suggest that the L1 (Turkish) lexical knowledge of the bilingual children does not compensate for their poor lexical knowledge in Dutch compared to their Dutch monolingual peers. They interpret their findings as support for the hypothesis that 'there is a 'serious break' in the lexical development of bilingual children in general (L1 and L2) due to a mismatch of L1 home experience (cf. Vygotsky's *spontaneous everyday concepts*) and L2 education (*academic concepts*)' (1998: 466).

Clearly, findings such as those reported by Verhallen and Schoonen are not generalizable beyond a specific context. As noted in Chapter 6, linguistic mismatch, in itself, does not account for the variability in findings associated with instruction through a second language. The roots of the particular pattern of lexical development they observed are more likely to be found in patterns of dominant-subordinated group macro-interactions in the wider society and the associated micro-interactions in the school context rather than in linguistic mismatch considered in isolation (see Chapter 2).

Verhallen and Schoonen do not use the term 'semilingualism' to describe their findings and they attribute children's pattern of bilingual lexical development to inappropriate schooling. However, their documentation of variation in L1 and L2 lexical knowledge is not at all surprising in contexts where L1 literacy and academic skills are not promoted in the school and L2-medium instruction in the early years of schooling fails to provide adequate comprehensible input and affirmation of students' identities.

Finally, Appel and Muysken (1987) make the point that the bilingual's verbal repertoire can be viewed as different and not deficient even though at some point in their development they may know less of each of their languages than monolingual children. For example, bilinguals' code-switching abilities give them the opportunity to convey messages in subtle and sophisticated ways not available to monolinguals. Appel and Muysken also point out that comparisons with monolinguals may not be justified since bilinguals use their two languages in different domains and for different purposes (see also Cook, 1992; Grosjean, 1989; Herdina & Jessner, 2000). These perspectives should be taken into account in interpreting the Verhallen and Schoonen data. Assessment of L1 and L2 in isolation from each other may misrepresent and underestimate the totality of the bilingual's conceptual and lexical repertoire when both languages are considered together (Muñoz-Sandoval, Cummins, Alvarado & Ruef, 1998).

Burying the Construct

The issues in the 'semilingualism' debate may be less complex than suggested by the heated controversy that surrounds the use of the term. In the first place, virtually all theorists on both sides of this issue agree that the major causal factors in linguistic minority students' underachievement are sociopolitical in nature: specifically, the coercive pattern of dominant–subordinated group relations in the wider society and the ways in which these coercive relations of power are manifested in the micro-interactions between educators and students in school.

Secondly, if one admits that there are individual differences in access to and command of literate/academic registers of language used in the social context of the school among monolingual populations, then there is no reason to deny the existence of similar individual differences among bilingual populations in their two languages. It is clear that there are major individual differences in literacy attainment and in certain aspects of oral language skills among the general population in their first languages. Not everybody is capable of reading and writing at the same level nor does everybody have identical oral repertoires (e.g. oratorical skills, joke telling ability). For example, Nobel Laureate for literature Toni Morrison has, in some legitimate sense of the term, 'more' functional language proficiency with respect to literate/academic registers than a six-year-old child even though the child has attained basic competence (in a Chomskian sense) in her language. In the same way, bilingual children and adults vary in their degree of mastery of different registers and functions of their two languages. For example, some students who drop out of school have much greater competence in 'street language' or writing rap (or other forms of) music than many who remain in school.

If we allow that individual differences exist among both monolinguals and bilinguals in access to and command of different registers of language, then it follows that certain bilinguals will have relatively limited access to academic or literate registers in both their L1 and L2, while others will have relatively high levels of literacy in both languages. Certainly some subordinated group students born in the host country who do not receive L1 instruction at school gain only limited access to literate/academic registers in their L1. Frequently, sibling and peer interaction is conducted largely through the dominant language within the first year or two of schooling. L1 speaking skills atrophy through disuse by the middle of elementary school (or earlier), although receptive skills may maintain themselves for a longer period (Cummins, 1991b; Wong Fillmore, 1990).

These children will also vary in the degree of formal L2 academic skills that they develop at school. The extent of mastery of these formal language skills is directly linked to future educational and economic opportunities. As Kalantzis *et al.* point out, 'in the modern world, formal language skills of speaking, reading and writing are the means to certain sorts of futures and power' (1989: 31). They suggest that all children should have the opportunity to develop mastery of these formal language skills. Furthermore, academic researchers 'who have mastered the pinnacle of mainstream language' (p. 31) should not view as unproblematic the fact that a disproportionate number of minority students fail to realize the full range of options in their two languages.

In short, the issue does not seem to revolve around the existence of individual differences in academic language knowledge among bilingual (and monolingual) populations. The issue is rather whether it is theoretically legitimate or useful to label some of these bilingual children 'semilingual' or 'doubly semilingual' or 'deficient' as a means of characterizing their relatively limited repertoires in literate aspects of their two languages.

There appear to be compelling scientific and sociopolitical reasons to avoid using such labels and to bury the construct of 'semilingualism'. First, as the debate clearly shows, there has been no precise linguistic or cognitive operationalization of the construct 'semilingualism'. In other words, there is no scientific rationale for choosing one arbitrary cut-off point over another as the level below which an individual supposedly becomes 'semilingual'. Thus, the term has no explanatory or predictive value but is rather a restatement of the equally ill-defined notion of 'limited proficiency in two languages'.

At a sociopolitical level the term has assumed pejorative connotations and may be misinterpreted as suggesting that linguistic deficits are a primary cause of bilingual students' academic difficulties, despite denials to the contrary. Furthermore, the futile debates to which use of the term has given rise suggest that its continued use is counterproductive.

In summary, there is no justification for continued reference to the construct of 'semilingualism'. The construct has no theoretical value and confuses rather than clarifies the issues. However, liberating the field of applied linguistics from the construct of 'semilingualism' does nothing, by itself, to resolve the issue of how should we conceptualize the nature of 'language proficiency' and its relationship to academic achievement in monolingual and bilingual contexts. The fact that the term 'semilingualism' potentially stigmatizes the victims of inappropriate schooling and coercive power relations in the society is good enough reason to drop it from the lexicon. However, we are still left with the reality that many subordinated group bilingual students tend to gain less access to literate/academic registers in both L1 and L2. The real issue is how do we challenge the coercive social and educational structure that gives rise to this pattern.

In this regard, just simply stating that 'semilingualism does not exist' evades rather than resolves the issue of how to conceptualize 'language proficiency' and its relationship to academic development. As noted above, theoretical constructs do not 'exist' in any material sense so the statement is essentially meaningless. However, there appears to be relatively little dispute about the 'existence' of the phenomenon to which the term 'semilingualism' was inappropriately applied, namely, limited access to academic/literate registers in both L1 and L2 among some bilingual groups who experienced the effects of long-term coercive relations of power both in schools and society. Simply to attribute academic underachievement in L2 (and L1) to the perfidies of inappropriate standardized testing (e.g. Edelsky, 1990) avoids rather than addresses the issue of how we should characterize individual differences in language proficiency. The experiences of countless bilingual adults and children in the United States, Europe, and elsewhere, who have been schooled exclusively through an L2 attest to the difficulties of gaining access to L1 academic registers in the absence of sustained exposure to them. Guerrero, for example, makes the point that 'it stands to reason that the acquisition and development of academic language proficiency is contingent upon being exposed to such language and having the social motivation to internalize its structure' (1997: 68). Prospective bilingual teachers in the United States generally have not had this opportunity, with the result that their academic proficiency in their L1 (Spanish) is limited in comparison to their academic proficiency in English:

> Generally, the prospective bilingual education teacher has managed to develop an oral ability in the Spanish language but one that better serves language domains (e.g. home, church, entertainment) other than schooling and academics. This is not a criticism of their abilities but simply the sociolinguistic outcome of an educational system that values and perpetuates only English monolingualism. (1997: 72)

Historically, many bilingual children in discriminatory school systems failed to gain significant access to academic registers in either L1 or L2. This is the reality that academics who used the unfortunate term 'semilingualism' focused on. They have always been explicit that they were not talking about *speech* or language in general; their focus was on structures (e.g. vocabulary range and depth) and functions (e.g.

reading and writing for academic purposes) of the very specific academic registers of language that are associated with literacy and schooling.

So exactly what construct of 'language proficiency' and individual differences in language proficiency is held by those who have characterized the notion of CALP and/or the threshold hypothesis as representing a 'deficit' position?' Most do not even consider this issue but there appear to be three possibilities:

> (1) *Language development is essentially complete for all children (except those with pathological conditions or extreme social deprivation) by the time they arrive in school at age 5; therefore, by definition, there is only minimal variation in language proficiency that is educationally relevant.*

This is the position adopted by MacSwan (1999, 2000) in claiming that the threshold hypothesis represents a deficit theory. He acknowledges that there is a 'middle-class advantage' when 'features of literary discourse (peculiar vocabulary, impersonal author, distant setting, special order of events, etc.) are present in the oral language of children' (p. 18) but this does not mean that their oral language is in any way superior to that of other children. It is simply a matter of the 'special alignment of their particular home experiences and speech registers with those encountered in school' (p. 18).

There is absolutely nothing in the threshold hypothesis that is inconsistent with this position. The threshold hypothesis certainly does not claim that any child's language is intrinsically 'superior' to any other's in some context-free sense. It simply claims that access to academic and literacy-related registers is relevant to students' understanding of instruction and ability to engage in academic tasks such as reading and writing. If students have not developed sufficient access to academic registers in either of their two languages, and if the instruction does not provide the support that students need to develop this access, then their academic, linguistic, and cognitive development will not be stimulated through their classroom interactions.

As far as I can judge, for MacSwan, the threshold hypothesis crossed the boundary into a 'deficit' position because it talked in terms of 'levels of language proficiency' rather than in terms of 'access to academic registers'. The aspects of 'language proficiency' that act as intervening variables were specified as 'vocabulary–concept knowledge, metalinguistic insights, and knowing how to process decontextualized language' (Cummins, 1979a: 242), all of which clearly fall within the scope of academic or literacy-related registers. However, MacSwan views 'language development' as entirely separate from literacy and academic development and thus, for him, any specification of 'language proficiency' as an intervening variable is problematic. He notes, for example, that 'language is independent of literacy and content area knowledge' (1999: 268) and elaborates on this position as follows:

> Why should [literacy] be regarded as a component of our knowledge of language any more than a component of our visual system? ... school literacy is viewed as one among many ways that language may be used to satisfy human

> purposes but is itself not useful in assessing a person's knowledge of language, *per se*. (2000: 25)

This perspective on the relation between literacy and language proficiency derives from an extremely narrow interpretation of the Chomskian theoretical perspective that language development is essentially complete before children come to school. I characterize this interpretation as 'narrow' because it appears to equate 'language proficiency' with the ability to produce largely correct and appropriate syntactical constructions in everyday conversational contexts. It ignores the fact that although most features of syntax may be largely acquired by age five, our lexical knowledge continues to expand throughout our lifetimes and schools *do* play a special role in expanding our lexical knowledge. MacSwan, however, sees only 'peripheral' aspects of language developing into the school years:

> As human beings, we acquire languages by virtue of our biological make-up (Chomsky, 1959), and the task of acquisition is essentially complete by the time we reach school for the first time. ... Nonetheless, there are peripheral aspects of language that children continue to develop into the school years, manifested in the use of creative errors like 'goed' (for 'went') ... and sometimes more subtle aspects of syntax. (2000: 18)

Clearly, if 'language proficiency' is essentially fully developed by the time children come to school (apart from some 'peripheral' aspects), then schooling will play very little role in developing students' language proficiency. Furthermore, a student's level of 'language proficiency' will have very little relevance to success in school. This position defines, *a priori*, literacy-related knowledge (e.g. range and depth of vocabulary, ability to understand and use formal discourse patterns, reading and writing expertise) as having minimal relationship to language proficiency.

Thus, MacSwan's argument essentially claims that the threshold hypothesis represents a 'deficit position' because it suggests that the level of academic *language proficiency* that children acquire in school acts as an intervening variable in mediating further educational outcomes. The claim that bilingual students' command of the language of instruction can affect their level of classroom understanding and participation, and consequently their rate of cognitive and academic growth in school, represents a 'deficit position' according to MacSwan because it posits a relationship between level of *language proficiency* and academic development. The fact that the *causal* variables were always posited as instructional and social (e.g. Cummins, 1979a) is dismissed as being irrelevant.

MacSwan seems to acknowledge that *literacy* or literacy-related knowledge could play a role as an intervening variable but not *language proficiency* which varies only minimally and in 'peripheral' ways across individuals after the start of school. Thus, if the threshold hypothesis had left out any reference to 'language proficiency' and instead explicitly posited variables such as 'access to academic or literacy-related registers' as intervening variables, it apparently would not have represented a 'deficit position'. MacSwan's (2000: 18) own explanation of what he calls the 'middle-class advantage' appears to posit access to literacy-related registers as an intervening variable that interacts with inappropriate schooling to produce school failure among many non-middle-class students.

To view literacy and language proficiency as largely unrelated and to see schooling as having minimal or no impact on the development of students' 'language proficiency', can best be described as idiosyncratic. Faltis and Hudelson, colleagues of MacSwan at Arizona State University, express a perspective that the vast majority of educators would see as considerably more defensible than MacSwan's position that 'knowledge of content and skills is independent of knowledge of language' (1998: 268):

> Language and literacy cannot be separated. Put another way, both spoken language and written language are language. They are different sides of the same coin. Central to both is the creation and construction of meaning. Both are socially constructed. Both are developed in and through use, as learners generate, test, and refine hypotheses. (Faltis & Hudelson, 1998: 101–102)

Thomas and Collier have expressed clearly the progression of language development in both oral and written modes that continues throughout schooling:

> Children from ages 6 to 12 continue to acquire (without being formally taught) subtleties in the phonological system, massive amounts of vocabulary, semantics (meaning), syntax (grammar), formal discourse patterns (stretches of language beyond a single sentence), and complex aspects of pragmatics (how language is used in a given context) in the oral system of the English language (Berko Gleason, 1993). Then there is the *written* system of English to be mastered across all of these same domains during the school years. Even an adolescent entering college must continue to acquire enormous amounts of vocabulary in every discipline of study and ongoing development of complex writing skills. (1997: 41)

The argument that language development is largely complete by age five essentially claims that Nobel Literature Prize laureate Toni Morrison has no more language proficiency than a five-year-old child. By its own admission, it has nothing to say to educators about the relationship between language and academic achievement since they are conceptualized *a priori* as unrelated. Most of the rebuttals to the construct of 'semilingualism' focus only on speech and on demonstrating that bilinguals have command of the *basic syntactic structures* of at least one of their two languages. As noted above, there is no dispute regarding this issue and there is no dispute regarding the inappropriateness of the construct of 'semilingualism'.

(2) *Variation in command of academic registers does exist between individuals but not across groups (e.g. between 'minority' and 'majority' groups).*

This position might acknowledge the legitimacy of academic registers of language but claim that it is illegitimate to view linguistic minority groups as lacking in these registers or as having 'low CALP'.

As Ogbu's (1978) work and considerable other research (e.g. Gibson, 1997) has demonstrated, there is huge variation within and across culturally and linguistically diverse groups in educational achievement. Thus, it is illegitimate to make *any* statement that applies to linguistic minority groups in general. However, it is also clear that groups that have been subjected to a sustained experience of coercive power relations tend to underachieve academically in comparison to other groups (e.g. Ogbu's involuntary versus voluntary minorities). Unequal access to academic registers (in comparison to dominant groups) in both L1 and L2 is often the result. This is caused by discriminatory schooling, not by any inherent characteristics of the group itself. In short, as a result of coercive power relations, there *are* group differences, in addition to individual differences, in access to academic registers (academic language proficiency).

Schooling that focuses on transformative pedagogy and student and teacher empowerment, as defined in Chapters 2 and 10, frequently reverses the pattern of underachievement in dramatic ways. To claim that there are no systematic group differences in access to, and command of, academic registers is to turn one's back on the consequences of coercive relations of power operating in societal and school contexts. Intervention to reverse this pattern of group differences in academic language proficiency requires a focus on language as a tool for empowerment (see Chapter 10).

(3) *Variation in command of academic registers does exist within and between groups. Between group differences are the result of coercive relations of power operating in both school and society. However, it is inappropriate to conceptualize these differences in terms of 'semilingualism' because the construct is theoretically vacuous and focuses attention on individual students rather than on the ways in which bilingual students are denied access to academic registers of language in L1 and L2 in the school context.*

This third position is the one that appears most defensible to me. Its goal is to reverse academic underachievement rather than deny that it exists. It acknowledges that variation in access to, and command of, academic registers (or variation in academic language proficiency or CALP) does exist and that subordinated groups have been, and still are, systematically denied access to the language of power within our society.

Conclusion

There is still considerable scope for debate on the nature of language proficiency and its relationship to academic achievement. The perspective presented in this and the preceding chapter attempts to bridge disciplinary gaps and provide a theoretical framework for thinking about how access to different registers of language relates to bilingual students' success or failure in school. The issues that stimulated the original development of these ideas were issues of policy and practice: specifically, discriminatory psychological assessment of bilingual students and premature exit from ESL or bilingual support programs into submersion 'mainstream' programs. The intent of elaborating the framework further is to feed the theory back into practice in order to augment the tools that educators have to challenge coercive relations of power in the school system. The most effective way in which educators and students together can challenge coercive power relations is to co-construct interactions that fuel the generation of students' proficiency in academic registers of language.

In the next two chapters I continue to explore the construct of language proficiency as it has been used and operationalized in contemporary educational contexts. The focus shifts to what we can learn about the nature of proficiency from research conducted on language testing and assessment. I also review the current debates on the role of authentic performance-based assessment of language proficiency (as opposed to standardized discrete-point testing) in both adult learning and school-based contexts. These issues have assumed considerable importance with the implementation of explicit curriculum standards in many countries around the world. For example, how we conceptualize 'language proficiency' and 'literacy' has major consequences for the assessment and advancement of second language learners in school systems internationally.

Note

1. Davies, Grove and Wilkes (1997), in an otherwise valuable review of the literature, totally misrepresent the theoretical status of language proficiency and medium of instruction that I have proposed. They interpret my position as claiming that CALP is an independent variable rather than an intervening variable. They concur with Paulston (1994: 6) that 'One reason there is no conclusive answer in the research on bilingual education of the seemingly simple question of whether a child learns to read more rapidly in a second language if first taught to read in his primary … is that medium of instruction in school programs is always an intervening variable rather than the independent variable it is always treated as.' Davies *et al.* make a linkage between this point and Martin-Jones and Romaine's (1986) critique of the BICS/CALP distinction. They suggest that CALP 'assumes a cross-linguistic dimension of competence that, once acquired, can be transferred to any language. On this basis, the school failure of minority children is attributed to lack of L1-medium instruction' (p. 54).
   It is extremely surprising to me that they see no inconsistency between this representation of my position, which they label the 'orthodox Cummins-type position' (e.g. p. 59), and the (accurate) way they represent my position two pages later as claiming that 'minority students will succeed educationally to the extent that the patterns of interaction in school reverse those that prevail in society at large' (Cummins, 1986: 24) and that 'an additive orientation [to students' L1] does not require the actual teaching of a minority language' (Cummins, 1986: 25).
   Davies *et al.* ignore the fact that the central point of the literature review and attempt at theoretical synthesis that I wrote in 1979 (Cummins, 1979a) was precisely that language variables and medium of instruction were intervening rather than independent variables. This point was also made explicit in many subsequent publications (e.g. Cummins, 1984; Cummins & Swain, 1983). I have also never argued that language minority children will inevitably fail if they are not taught through their L1 – the academic success of countless bilingual children taught primarily or exclusively through their L2 immediately refutes this type of strong position. Cummins (1984), for example, reports data from the Toronto Board of Education showing considerable variation among language minority groups in academic achievement but also many groups showing superior academic

performance in comparison to native English-speaking students despite having been taught exclusively through L2. What I have suggested, drawing on Ogbu's (1978) work among others, is that medium of instruction is one variable that both reflects and interacts with patterns of power relations in the wider society to create academic failure among groups that have historically been subjected to coercive relations of power in the wider society.

Chapter 5
Assessing Second Language Proficiency Among Adults: Do We Know What We Are Measuring?

One of the most pressing issues in the field of foreign language testing at present is that of defining the construct 'communicative competence' precisely enough to permit its assessment. A related issue involves defining what we mean by a 'communicative' or 'authentic' test and determining whether test takers perform differentially on 'communicative' and 'noncommunicative' language tests. (Bachman, Davidson & Foulkes, 1993: 41)

A review of the recent literature on proficiency and communicative competence demonstrates quite clearly that there is nothing even approaching a reasonable and unified theory of proficiency. (Lantolf & Frawley, 1988: 186)

Introduction

As suggested in the quotations above, and obviously in the two preceding chapters, there is considerable debate among applied linguists as to the nature of the constructs *language proficiency* and *communicative competence*. Clarification of these constructs is clearly important to ensure coherence and validity in the assessment of proficiency. If we are not clear about what we are attempting to assess, the resulting assessment instruments are likely to reflect this lack of clarity. These concerns are particularly important in view of the pervasiveness of language assessment in many spheres of human endeavour.

In a world where knowledge of and academic credentials in English are increasingly seen as the key to upward mobility and increased life chances both in the English-speaking world and internationally, the assessment of English proficiency has become a game with very high stakes for both adults and school children. The spread of English is hardly a neutral or value-free process, as theorists such as

Pennycook (1998), Phillipson (1992, 1999), Tollefson (1991) and others have convincingly pointed out. The sociopolitical dimensions of the spread of English are beyond the scope of this chapter which focuses on assessment issues and their relation to constructs of language proficiency. However, the spheres of language testing and linguistic imperialism clearly intersect insofar as language testing and teaching are embedded in a similar web of competing ideologies and social agendas (Moore, 1996; Shohamy, 2000).

My goal in this and the next chapter is to examine issues of construct validity in language assessment in an international context where assessment of English language proficiency (of both children and adults) plays an increasingly prominent gate-keeping role in the rationing of access to educational and employment opportunities. The issues for both adults and school-aged children with respect to the assessment of language proficiency are similar in many respects. However, the contexts and consequences of assessment are sufficiently different to warrant separate treatment.

In the first section of this chapter, I survey the contexts and assumptions underlying the assessment of adults' English language proficiency both in the context of immigration and university study in English-speaking countries. A recurring issue for language assessment specialists concerns the construct of language proficiency (what are English language tests designed to measure?). For example, in her introduction to a 1997 *Encyclopedia of Language and Education* volume on *Language Testing and Assessment*, Clapham notes that the 'search for a deeper understanding of language constructs is a common theme running throughout this volume' (1997: xvii). Obviously, the construct of language proficiency has been discussed in the previous two chapters but here I want to approach the issue from the perspective of the concerns of applied linguists involved in both language testing and second language assessment theory. In particular, I want to revisit and re-evaluate notions such as John Oller's (1979) *global language proficiency* in light of both psychometric research and theoretical developments in the field. The pendulum of language testing fashion has swung rapidly from discrete-point, to integrative, to communicative/authentic measures but many of the underlying issues remain theoretically unclear.

In the context of this and the next chapter, I interpret the research in ways that differ from current trends in the field. I suggest that for second language learners in the early stages of acquisition there is evidence to support the legitimacy of a core 'general language proficiency' dimension. As proficiency increases, conversational and academic language skills will become increasingly differentiated. With increasing differentiation, 'general language proficiency' is more adequately conceptualized as 'academic language proficiency' in view of the fact that as proficiency increases, language proficiency measures increasingly assess literacy-related aspects of language (e.g. knowledge of less frequent vocabulary and complex grammatical constructions). I see this *not* as a unitary dimension that accounts for most of the variance in proficiency measures but rather as a dimension that can reliably be identified in L1 and L2 contexts and which is related to academic or literacy-related performance. I argue that the most promising measures to assess this general or academic dimension of proficiency are those that tap lexical knowledge. Also, I suggest that, for certain purposes, authentic communicative measures are not necessarily more valid or useful than pragmatic/integrative or even discrete-point measures to assess this core general academic dimension of proficiency.

Trends in the Assessment of English Proficiency Among Adults

Assessment of English second language proficiency among adults has become a major focus for businesses operating in the international arena, for universities concerned that prospective students have sufficient English proficiency to pursue degree programs successfully, and for countries such as Australia, Canada, and the United States that continue to attract large numbers of immigrants. Both Australia and New Zealand have recently instituted English language requirements for prospective immigrants and their families who must demonstrate proficiency on tests such as the International English Language Testing System (IELTS) or face significant financial penalties. For example, in New Zealand, as of 1995, principal applicants had to meet IELTS Band Level 5 (on a 9-band scale) (5 = *modest user* – should be able to handle basic communication in own field). This requirement was revised downwards to Level 4 in 1997 (4 = *limited user* – basic competence is limited to familiar situations). If accompanying family members do not meet this standard, the principal applicant must pay a bond of NZ$20,000 per person which will be refunded in total if the non-principal applicant meets the English standard within three months of arrival. If the non-principal applicant meets the standard within one year of arrival, NZ$14,000 will be refunded, but no money will be refunded if the non-principal applicant fails to meet the standard within a year (Centre for Language Training and Assessment, 1998; Grove, 1998). Clearly, this is high-stakes testing and it illustrates the importance of theoretical clarity in the constructs being assessed.

As in the case of recent assessment initiatives in the educational systems of many countries, a clear distinction can be discerned between context-reduced formal tests of English language proficiency such as the IELTS and TOEFL, to name just two, and context-embedded benchmark or performance assessments that are more closely tied both to real life and instructional contexts. One of the issues that arises is the extent to which the formal tests are measuring the same constructs as the more 'authentic' benchmark assessments which also tend to be considerably more time-consuming and expensive.

I will review the development and theoretical assumptions underlying the development of the Canadian Language Benchmarks (CLB) and Canadian Language Benchmarks Assessment (CLBA) in order to illustrate both the practical and theoretical considerations in designing such instruments. Of particular concern is the construct validity of such performance assessment procedures and their relationship to theories of language proficiency and communicative competence. I want to sound a skeptical note regarding the assumed superiority and greater construct validity of communicative language assessment procedures as compared to more traditional context-reduced measures (integrative or discrete-point). I do not wish to advocate a return to context-reduced testing procedures in any general way nor do I wish to undermine the important applications of context-embedded performance assessment procedures. However, I do want to promote greater clarity about the theoretical constructs being assessed by different kinds of assessment procedures and the appropriateness of different procedures for different kinds of questions and contexts.

Development and Theoretical Foundations of the Canadian Language Benchmarks

Background

The Canadian Language Benchmarks (CLB) were developed as an initiative of Citizenship and Immigration Canada (CIC) as a means of providing a common set of standards to assist in the measurement and description of English language skills. As expressed by CIC:

> Governed by adult learning principles, the benchmarks would provide consistency of outcome for learners across the country, a common basis for both learner and program assessment and a concrete statement of language competencies to all stakeholders including learners, educators, employers and community and settlement agencies. (1996: 1)

The Benchmarks describe learners' English language competence along a 12-part continuum for each of three skill areas: Listening/Speaking, Reading, and Writing. Learners' progress is divided into three proficiency stages:

Stage I: Benchmarks 1–4, Basic Proficiency:
At this stage the learner is in the process of acquiring basic proficiency in English. S/he can communicate in predictable everyday contexts and on familiar topics of immediate personal relevance.

Stage II: Benchmarks 5–8, Intermediate Proficiency:
At this stage the learner has attained basic functional proficiency in English and can communicate in some unpredictable contexts and function independently in most familiar situations of daily social, educational, and work-related life experience.

Stage III: Benchmarks 9–12, Advanced Proficiency:
At this stage the learner is approaching the level of full functional proficiency in English. The learner can communicate effectively, precisely, appropriately, and fairly accurately in unpredictable contexts and can function independently in unfamiliar situations (CIC, 1996: 3).

With respect to employment possibilities, a person at Stage I would have difficulty in following instructions (spoken or written) and would be unable to follow safety procedures or heed warnings. At Stage II (Benchmarks 5–8), an individual has sufficient proficiency to enter the Canadian work force in areas where the requirement for English is not advanced. At Stage III, individuals are capable of studying in English at the tertiary level and can function in employment situations where the requirement for English is advanced (Jones, 1998).

A standardized criterion-referenced assessment procedure (the Canadian Language Benchmarks Assessment (CLBA)) has been established since 1996 for Benchmarks 1–8 (Stages I and II) for the purpose of placing adult learners in the ESL programs most suited to their needs (Norton Peirce & Stewart, 1997; Norton & Stewart, 1999). Separate task-based instruments are available for Listening/ Speaking, Reading, and Writing. The assessment focuses on the individual's ability to perform a variety of communicative tasks presented in a meaningful context. Analytic or structural features of the language (e.g. grammar, pronunciation, vocabulary) are taken into account only to the extent that they impede the individual's ability to carry out these communicative tasks successfully.

Benchmarks can also be established by using the Benchmarks Proficiency Checklist which is a detailed list of competencies that learners at each benchmark can be expected to carry out. This does not yield the kind of reliable standardized assessment that the CLBA provides but is useful for monitoring students' progress as their English skills increase (Jones, 1998).

Theoretical Foundations of the CLB/CLBA

The CLB Working Document (Citizenship and Immigration Canada, 1996) identifies three dimensions of language and language use that underpin the development of the CLB:

(1) Language is for communication;
(2) Proficiency in a second language means communicative competence and performance; and
(3) Spoken and written language draw from the same system but also differ in significant ways.

Language as communication

The first dimension highlights the fact that communication is always purposeful and meaningful. Meaning derives from 'the relationships between language functions, forms and context, including the intentions of the speaker and the expectations of the hearer' (1996: 12). Language functions are seen as more fundamental to the communication of meaning than language forms in isolation, and thus sociolinguistic considerations are of primary importance in the articulation of language benchmarks.

Although the CLB Working Document points out that 'an adequate model of the development of adult second language acquisition or learning on which to base

proficiency descriptions of communicative competence has not been fully developed' (p. 14), the development of the CLB was based on the assumption that
learning a language is learning to communicate through it. Thus, language development was described in terms of increasingly demanding contexts of language
use, including increasingly complex performance conditions.

Communicative competence

The second dimension views communicative performance as reflecting the individual's underlying communicative competence. The term 'communicative
competence' was originally coined by Hymes (1971) but became pivotal in the areas
of second language teaching and assessment largely as a result of the theoretical
framework proposed by Canale and Swain (1980). Following Canale and Swain
(1980) and Canale (1983b), the CLB Working Document (1996: 13) identifies
communicative competence as comprising:

(1) *Linguistic code competence*: grammatical accuracy at the sentence level including
    'lexical items and rules of word formation, sentence formation, literal
    meaning, pronunciation and spelling' (Canale, 1983b: 339).
(2) *Discourse competence*: mastery of how to use cohesion devices and coherence
    rules to combine (and interpret) meanings and forms into functional and effec-
    tive texts in both oral and written modes.
(3) *Sociolinguistic competence*: mastery of appropriate use and understanding of
    language in different sociolinguistic contexts (e.g. formal interview versus
    casual conversation).
(4) *Strategic competence*: mastery of verbal and non-verbal strategies to avoid
    potential difficulties in communication or repair communication breakdown.

The CLB Working Document links these levels of competence to their 'psychological representation', namely, John Oller's notion of a *pragmatic expectancy
grammar* which he defines as 'a psychologically real system that sequentially orders
linguistic elements in time and in relation to extralinguistic contexts in meaningful
ways' (1979: 34). In other words, the levels of linguistic competence outlined above
are integrated into a system that enables us to use our knowledge both of language
and the world to make predictions regarding the semantic and syntactic elements
that will come next in any given linguistic sequence. The more developed our
knowledge of language, the more efficiently our pragmatic expectancy grammar
operates. This perspective points to the integrative nature of language learning and
use in contrast to more traditional perspectives that view language as composed of
discrete skills and competencies. Oller's theoretical position is considered in more
detail in a later section.

Oral and written language

The CLB Working Document points out that speaking and listening are almost
always integrated simultaneously in oral discourse situations. The only significant
exceptions to this are broadcast and lecture situations. However, reading and

writing do not have to occur simultaneously for communication in the written medium to take place. These considerations justified the combination of Speaking/ Listening as one skill domain in the Benchmarks whereas Reading and Writing were kept separate.

The theoretical underpinnings of the CLB are generally consistent with most current conceptions of the constructs of language proficiency and communicative competence (see Cumming, 1995, 1997). The first dimension (*language as communication*) appears to emphasize what McNamara (1996) terms *ability for use* while the second (*communicative competence*) focuses on the *language knowledge* that underlies effective communicative performance.

Despite the fact that the CLB/CLBA framework is in the mainstream of current thinking on the nature of communicative competence, examination of the recent theory and research in this area reveals considerable complexity and many unresolved issues.

Historical Trends in the Conceptualization and Assessment of Language Proficiency

Although aspects of language proficiency have been assessed formally since the beginnings of standardized ability and achievement testing in the early years of this century, sustained consideration of the nature of the construct came only after the birth of the discipline of applied linguistics in the 1970s. Prior to this in the 1950s, Noam Chomsky (1959) had distinguished between linguistic competence and performance. Children in the first five or six years of life master the complex systems of their language in similar ways and according to similar schedules, reflecting what Chomsky later termed *Universal Grammar*, the child's innate linguistic endowment. Situational conditions will affect how the child or adult manifests his/her linguistic competence, but the basic structure is present from birth and actualized in the early years of the child's life.

Neither Chomsky nor his followers were particularly concerned with how this basic linguistic competence related to the forms of language proficiency that continue to develop through schooling as the child matures. However, these issues came to the fore in the 1970s as standardized language testing was mandated by the courts and by policy-makers for a variety of functions in schools in the United States. For example, schools were required in both the United States and several Canadian provinces to identify and assess students who were 'exceptional' (e.g. 'learning or language disabled' or 'gifted and talented') and would benefit from specialized intervention. Similarly, entry and exit criteria (determined by language testing) were mandated in the United States to control and monitor the provision of bilingual and ESL programs for English language learning students.

It soon became evident that different tests of 'language proficiency' were measuring very different aspects of the construct. For example, of the 46 tests examined by DeAvila and Duncan (1978), only four included a measure of phoneme production, 43 claimed to measure various levels of lexical ability, 34 included items assessing oral syntax comprehension, and nine attempted to assess pragmatic aspects of language. Many of these measures showed minimal relationship to each other, raising the question of what underlying traits were actually being assessed by these tests, all of which purported to measure 'language proficiency' (Ulibarri, Spencer & Rivas, 1981). A more recent review of six language proficiency tests similarly found major differences in what they purport to test and how they attempt to do so (Zehler, Hopstock, Fleischman & Greniuk, 1994).

The confusion in the area at this time is evident also at a theoretical level. Hernandez-Chavez, Burt and Dulay (1978), for example, proposed a model of language proficiency comprising 64 separate components, each of which, hypothetically at least, was independently measurable. By contrast, Oller (1979) synthesized a considerable amount of data showing strong correlations between performance on cloze tests of reading, standardized discrete-point reading tests, and measures of oral verbal ability (e.g. vocabulary measures). He suggested that language proficiency could be conceptualized as a unitary global dimension that was largely indivisible from intelligence as measured by both verbal and non-verbal IQ tests. Although Oller (1983) later distanced himself from the strong version of the unitary global language proficiency hypothesis, he still maintained the existence of a strong general or global proficiency dimension, claiming that the amount of additional variance accounted for by other components of proficiency was modest. More recently, he has again made a strong case for the close relationship between language proficiency and what IQ tests measure (Oller, 1997).

A major development in the field occurred with the publication of the Canale/Swain theoretical framework of communicative competence (Canale & Swain, 1980; Canale, 1983b), As outlined above, this framework distinguished grammatical (termed *linguistic* in the CLB documents), discourse, sociolinguistic, and strategic competencies. Research and theoretical work that pursued the orientation initiated by the Canale/Swain framework has evolved into the framework developed by Bachman (1990) and Bachman and Palmer (1996) which is considered in more detail below. Shohamy (1997), in a 'state-of-the-art' review of second language assessment, suggests that the Bachman language competence model 'has been accepted as the definition of language competence used by testers that is often used as a basis for test construction' (p. 143). However, she also notes that 'in the theoretical domain there is still no evidence for the validity of the Bachman model and its revised version in spite of its wide acceptability' (p. 146).

At around the same time, the BICS/CALP distinction was proposed (Cummins, 1979b) as a qualification to Oller's (1979) claim that all individual differences in language proficiency could be accounted for by just one underlying factor. It was argued that not all aspects of language use or performance could be incorporated into one dimension of global language proficiency. Specifically, the distinction suggested that what Oller (1979) termed *global language proficiency* was in fact a specific dimension of language proficiency that developed in tandem with academic and cognitive abilities.

Considerable psychometric research was conducted in the 1980s to investigate alternative constructs of language proficiency (see Harley *et al.*, 1990, and Oller 1983, for reviews of this research). One major set of studies was conducted in the Modern Language Centre of the Ontario Institute for Studies in Education and was designed on the basis of both the Canale/Swain and Cummins frameworks. Harley *et al.* (1990) note that when they started their research, two stages were evident in the way the construct of language proficiency had been conceptualized and investigated. The first stage, beginning with John Carroll's work on verbal abilities in the 1940s, was a continuation of exploratory factor-analytic research carried out since the 1920s by pioneers of psychometrics such as Thurstone and Burt. As noted above, during the 1970s, John Oller was a principal figure associated with this first stage. Oller's findings were consistent with previous psychometric research in showing evidence of a strong general proficiency/intelligence factor. In contrast to previous research, however, Oller interpreted his findings within a coherent theoretical framework derived from applied linguistics with an emphasis on the pragmatic or functional dimensions of language (e.g. the notion of a pragmatic expectancy grammar).

The second stage of research into the nature of language proficiency was characterized by a shift from exploratory factor analysis to the much more powerful form of confirmatory factor analysis that permitted the explicit testing of theoretical models. Bachman and Palmer's (1982) research, for example, used confirmatory factor analysis to show that more than just one general factor could be extracted from language proficiency data; specifically, both underlying proficiency trait and assessment method factors could be distinguished.

The Harley *et al.* (1990) confirmatory factor-analytic study failed to provide clear support for the hypothesized distinctions between grammatical, discourse and sociolinguistic competence in a sample of Grade 6 students in French immersion programs. A general proficiency factor and a written method factor emerged, although other (non-factor analytic) analyses of the data provided some support for the distinctiveness of the three proficiency constructs.

Despite the apparent inconclusiveness of the results, an important insight emerged from the Harley *et al.* study. It became clear that language proficiency and its components cannot be conceptualized in isolation from the contexts of their use and the experience of the individuals whose proficiency is being assessed. The authors expressed this perspective as follows:

> It is not sufficient to rely exclusively on confirmatory factor analysis, partly because of the difficulty of operationalizing constructs, and partly because of the fact that different groups of learners will have had a different array of language learning experiences. The relationship between components of proficiency is likely to be a function of these different experiences. Particular factor structures that emerge with adult second language learners are not necessarily applicable or replicable within a sample of young students who have had a different pattern of experiences. ...

An overall conclusion from the studies of the nature of language proficiency is that language proficiency must be conceptualized within a developmental context as a function of the interactions that students or learners experience in their languages. ... even though [traits] may not always be empirically distinguishable in certain samples, they are conceptually distinct and relevant to educational contexts. (1990: 24–25)

Bachman (1990b), commenting on this study, suggested that the Harley *et al.* (1990) research may have spurred the onset of a third stage in which the interpretation of language performance will be marked explicitly in terms of how different aspects of communicative competence have developed as a function of specific language acquisition/learning experiences. This stage will draw on both abstract models of language use and theories of language acquisition/learning and will utilize a much wider range of research approaches and analytic procedures. He concluded by noting that the Harley *et al.* (1990) study provides a sobering reaffirmation of the complexity of language proficiency at a time when overly simplistic views have gained ground in both language acquisition research and in language testing.

The three stages of research on the construct of language proficiency outlined above correspond in a general way to stages in the history of language testing distinguished by Shohamy (1997). She distinguishes three periods, the discrete point, the integrative, and the communicative, each of which reflected different conceptions of second language competence.

The discrete-point period was influenced by the tenets of structural linguistics and resulted in tests that 'focused on isolated and discrete elements, decontextualized phonemes, grammar and lexicon and used multiple-choice, true–false, and other types of objective items' (Shohamy, 1997: 141).

The integrative era which followed in the 1970s viewed language in a holistic and contextualized manner and was strongly influenced by Oller's (1979) claim that there was 'a unitary notion of language that underlies the learner's pragmatic grammar of expectancy which was believed to be the chief mechanism underlying the skills of understanding, speaking, reading and writing' (Shohamy, 1997: 142).

The third 'communicative' period began in the 1980s and was based on the notion that language is interactive, direct, and authentic. Thus, assessment procedures that emerged tended to be not only integrative but also required test takers to produce and comprehend language that replicated, as far as possible, real interaction using authentic oral and written texts and tasks. In discussing the characteristics of communicative language testing, Bachman (1998: 180) notes that 'authenticity generally refers to the extent to which the tasks required by the test involve the test taker in communicative language use, or the negotiation of meaning'. Linguistic samples derived from authentic communicative assessment are typically rated according to scales or benchmarks that define hierarchical levels of proficiency. The CLBA falls into this category of communicative assessment.

It should be noted that the historical trends identified by Shohamy (1997) are overlapping; integrative and discrete-point tests are still widely used both in research and practice despite the fact that they have fallen out of favour among

TABLE 5.1 Characteristics of three types of assessment procedure

Communicative	*Integrative*	*Discrete-Point*
Tasks involve processing of authentic language that reflects language use in real-life contexts (e.g. CLBA; performance assessments)	Tasks involve processing of authentic language but in a contrived (test) context (e.g. dictation, cloze)	Tasks involve processing of contrived language in a contrived (test) context (e.g. standardized multiple-choice tests)

many applied linguists. Table 5.1 displays the characteristics of these three types of assessment procedures.

These three types of assessment procedures are better seen as a continuum rather than as discrete categories. For example, a cloze-type procedure that requires learners to fill in missing words in discrete sentences (such as the active version of the Vocabulary Levels Test (Laufer & Nation, 1995)) is considerably less 'integrative' than a cloze procedure based on a coherent passage.

What do these developmental trends in language proficiency research and assessment tell us in the context of conceptualizing and assessing second language proficiency? Basically, they suggest that the 'language proficiency pie' can legitimately be sliced in a wide variety of ways. There is no one universal or absolute 'structure of language proficiency' that can be identified across domains of use or experiences of learners, nor is there one preeminent investigative approach to uncover this mythical structure of language proficiency. Thus, it is likely that psychometric research among Grade 12 students would uncover a general dimension of CALP defined by aspects of proficiency such as vocabulary knowledge. However, similar research conducted among graduate students specializing in Science and Humanities respectively, would likely be able to distinguish two distinct vocabulary factors reflecting knowledge of scientific vocabulary and literary vocabulary if the items were selected to tap these dimensions. Students who have strong knowledge of scientific vocabulary may have minimal knowledge of literary vocabulary and vice-versa as a result of their particular instructional experiences and readings during their university studies.

In short, the relationships among different components of language proficiency are a function of a variety of factors such as the contexts of acquisition, characteristics of the research participants (sample), variability in degree of proficiency among the sample which strongly affects the strength of psychometric relationships, developmental level of participants with respect to proficiency, etc. All of these factors will affect the degree of differentiation of the underlying structure of proficiency. Any theoretical construct, such as CALP, strategic competence, etc., therefore does not exist 'in reality' but rather is constructed to address particular issues in a limited set of contexts (e.g. schooling).

This is not to imply, however, that conceptualizations of proficiency are arbitrary

or all equally plausible. On the contrary, the way we conceptualize language proficiency will exert a profound impact both on how we assess and attempt to develop
proficiency among learners. What *is* implied by the previous analysis is that the
criteria for valid and appropriate conceptualizations of language proficiency, and
assessment of proficiency, must be based on considerations such as the purpose of
distinguishing different components, the internal coherence of the distinctions
made, and the consistency of the distinctions with available empirical evidence. For
example, a framework developed for instructional purposes might legitimately
distinguish between vocabulary knowledge and reading comprehension and see
these as distinct, albeit overlapping, constructs that can be taught in isolation from
each other. The fact that a wide array of research studies suggests that standardized
vocabulary tests assess essentially the same underlying trait as reading comprehension tests (e.g. Oller, 1979; Read, 1997) does not invalidate the legitimacy of
distinguishing between these traits for this particular purpose. A psychometric lens
provides only one partial perspective on the nature of language proficiency. Similarly, despite the currency of 'communicative' approaches to language proficiency
assessment, testing of specific components (e.g. vocabulary knowledge) in isolation
may be justified for particular purposes.

In the following section, I outline in more detail the Bachman and Palmer (1996)
framework which, as noted above, occupies a central place in the field.

The Bachman/Palmer Model of Communicative Competence

Bachman (1990) and Bachman and Palmer (1996) are explicit about the need, for
language testing purposes, to consider language ability within an interactional
framework of language use. Traits or attributes of learners cannot be viewed independently of the contexts within which these traits will be manifested.

They divide communicative language ability into *language knowledge* and *strategic competence* or metacognitive strategies. Language knowledge includes both
organizational knowledge and *pragmatic knowledge*, as outlined in the following listing
(Bachman & Palmer, 1996):

(1) **Organizational Knowledge (= how utterances or sentences and texts are
    organized)**
    Grammatical knowledge: Knowledge of vocabulary, syntax, phonology/
    graphology.
    Textual knowledge: Knowledge of cohesion, coherence, and rhetorical or conver-
    sational organization.

(2) **Pragmatic Knowledge (= how utterances or sentences are related to the
    communicative goals of the language user and the features of the language
    use situation)**
    Functional knowledge: Knowledge of ideational, manipulative, heuristic, and
    imaginative functions of language; in other words, using language to
    exchange ideas, exert an impact on the world around us, extend our knowl-

edge of the world, and create an imaginary world characterized by humorous or aesthetic expression.

Sociolinguistic knowledge:

Knowledge of dialects/varieties, registers, idiomatic expressions, and cultural references or figures of speech.

Bachman and Palmer reject, for purposes of language testing, the division of language proficiency into the four skill areas of speaking, listening, reading and writing. They see these traditional skill areas rather as combinations of language ability and task characteristics and use the term 'ability-task' to refer to the inseparability of ability and task. They cite two major reasons for disputing the usefulness of four separate abstract language skills:

> First, these features fail to capture important differences among language use activities that are within the same 'skill' (for instance, engaging in an oral conversation and listening to a radio newscast). Second, this approach to distinguishing the four skills treats them as abstract aspects of language ability, ignoring the fact that language use is realized in specific situated language use tasks. Thus, rather than attempting to distinguish among four abstract skills, we find it more useful to identify specific language use tasks and to describe these in terms of their task characteristics and the areas of language ability they engage. (1996: 79)

Bachman and Palmer distinguish two overlapping general types of target language use domains within which tasks are located: (1) situations in which the target language is used for purposes of communication in *real-life domains* and (2) situations in which the target language is used for the purpose of teaching and learning language, referred to as *language instructional domains*. The similarity to conversational and academic dimensions of proficiency (Cummins, 1984) is obvious. Thus, conversational and academic dimensions of proficiency cannot be conceived as traits that are independent of or isolated from their particular contexts of use. They represent particular constellations of ability-task associated with everyday face-to-face and academic/instructional language use domains respectively.

The Bachman/Palmer model of language proficiency should be seen as a conceptual scheme that maps out significant components of proficiency that will enter into the performance of specific language tasks. Its insistence on the integration of language ability and task characteristics is clearly consistent with the CLB's task-based focus in which language competence is integrated with specific performance and situational conditions. It is also consistent with Chapelle's (1998) analysis of interactionist perspectives which insist on the inseparability of attributes or traits of the individual (e.g. language knowledge, world knowledge) and the contextual configurations within which these traits are manifested. Within this orientation, performance is seen as a reflection of both underlying traits and the context within which performance occurs. Performance on a particular task therefore represents a sample of behaviour that can be generalized to similar contexts. Metacognitive strategies mediate between traits and context:

> For example, the language user's metacognitive strategies (e.g. 'assessing the context') would intervene between the context of language use and the user's knowledge during performance to assess the relevant features of context (e.g. level of formality) and decide which aspects of knowledge (e.g. which words) were needed. (Chapelle, 1998: 43).

Within the Bachman/Palmer model, the rationale for grouping components of proficiency together is based on linguistic categorizations rather than on psychological or psychometric considerations. The model makes no claims of psychometric relationships within particular components of the model such as Grammatical or Sociolinguistic. For example, it does not suggest that mastery of phonology and knowledge of vocabulary will be related to each other just because each is grouped within Grammatical Knowledge. This is clearly not the case in a first language context where phonological development reaches a plateau early in a child's life whereas vocabulary knowledge continues to grow throughout our lifetimes. In a second language context, these dimensions likewise typically show very different developmental patterns for both children and adults. Thus, the model does not address the psychological reality of the clusters identified in the model, although some of Bachman and Palmer's previous research does speak to these issues (e.g. Bachman & Palmer, 1982).

In short, there is little information in the model that would identify the extent to which its different components are psychometrically or developmentally related to each other. There is also little discussion regarding which aspects of the construct of 'language proficiency' are predictive of the development of other aspects. For example, if an individual has developed strong L2 vocabulary knowledge (as revealed in oral and written assessments of this component), is he or she also likely to have developed strong L2 grammatical skills or perhaps strong functional knowledge of the L2 in particular contexts?

These questions are not intended as criticisms of the Bachman/Palmer model. Rather they are intended to highlight the intent and uses of the model and also what the model does not purport to address. The Cummins framework considered in previous chapters also attempts to address the sources of variation in the performance of language tasks but in a way that explicitly takes into account psychological and developmental relationships among components of proficiency. The relationship between the two frameworks is considered in the next section.

Relationship between the Bachman/Palmer and Cummins Frameworks

These two frameworks were developed in different contexts and addressed different sets of issues. Both frameworks reject the organization of 'language proficiency' into the four traditional skills of speaking, listening, reading and writing; they attempt, instead, to address the conditions for successful performance of various language tasks in particular contexts. Task is the primary unit of analysis rather than structures or functions of language itself. Cummins focuses on the cognitive demands and contextual supports that affect performance of language tasks in academic contexts whereas Bachman/Palmer's concern is with language tasks in general rather than specifically in academic spheres.

As noted above, the frameworks are not in any sense incompatible with each other, although they highlight different aspects of language proficiency and draw differentially on linguistic (Bachman/Palmer) as compared to psychological and developmental (Cummins) considerations. Both frameworks are also consistent in a general way with the theoretical assumptions of the CLB/CLBA. For example, Bachman and Palmer's emphasis on the notion of 'ability-task' – the inseparability under most circumstances of language ability and specific task characteristics – is highly consistent with the approach adopted in the CLB of integrating benchmark language proficiencies with specific performance and situational conditions.[1]

The Cummins framework is also consistent with this approach since its intent is to address the extent to which learners are able to cope successfully with the cognitive and linguistic demands made on them by the social and educational environment in which they are obliged to function. With respect to assessment, tasks become more difficult (and consequently require greater language proficiency for successful completion) as degree of contextualization (e.g. familiarity) decreases and as the cognitive demands of the task increase. This clearly reflects the structure of the CLB insofar as Listening/Speaking, Reading, and Writing benchmarks are closely tied to the degree of contextualization and familiarity of the tasks. Greater language proficiency is required to carry out tasks that are less familiar and less contextualized.

The relationship among components of proficiency within academic contexts can be addressed more readily within the Cummins framework as a result of the fact that the theoretical underpinnings of the framework embody explicit predictions regarding which components of proficiency are likely to cluster together and why this is so. As discussed in previous chapters, CALP-related components of language proficiency cluster together and continue to develop throughout schooling due to their strong linkage to literacy and cognitive development. Therefore, a learner's level of proficiency in the CLB Reading and Writing measures (and to a lesser extent in Listening/Speaking) might be predicted or estimated by means of measures that focus on 'core' aspects of academic language proficiency.

Conversational components of proficiency, by contrast, show different developmental trends in both L1 and L2 contexts. For example, phonology shows an early plateau in L1 contexts due to development being largely complete by about age four or five, while often in adult L2 contexts, phonology reaches an early fossilized plateau where no further progress towards native speaker norms occurs.

It is important to note that in the early stages of development (e.g. Stage I CLB Benchmarks), there is likely to be significant relationships across most components of proficiency but increasing differentiation will occur as proficiency levels increase (see Snow & Hoefnagel-Hohle, 1979). In other words, we might expect significant relationships between phonology and vocabulary knowledge at Stage I but progressively weaker relationships at Stage II and III Benchmarks.

Thus in the context of the CLBA, as we move up the Reading and Writing Benchmarks towards higher levels of proficiency, we would expect learners to be able to comprehend and use a greater proportion of relatively low-frequency (Graeco-Latin) vocabulary since this is the primary lexicon of written text. This trend might also be evident in the Listening/Speaking Benchmarks, although to a lesser extent. A hypothesis that could be investigated empirically is that learners at Stage I (Benchmarks 1–4) will rely predominantly on high frequency (Anglo-Saxon) vocabulary whereas those at Stage III will demonstrate increasing confidence in their understanding and use of low frequency vocabulary.[2] If this turns out to be the case, then vocabulary measures might represent an efficient means of indirectly estimating the language proficiency level of learners. For some purposes, this type of screening through indirect indices might be adequate, although issues of generalizability across contexts/tasks are clearly important to consider. For example, performance on a discrete-point vocabulary measure may be poorly related to an individual's ability to use that vocabulary in authentic face-to-face interactions but strongly related to ability to use that vocabulary in written essay assignments (as Laufer and Nation's (1995) research suggests).

In summary, the Cummins framework raises explicit questions about how different components of proficiency relate to each other. In particular, it permits us to ask what specific components of proficiency are most central to the construct of academic language proficiency or CALP. I argue below that lexical knowledge represents one such core component. The practical implication of this line of argument is that assessment of a core component such as lexical knowledge might permit us to estimate the broader construct in an effective (and cost-efficient) manner. Thus, under some conditions and for certain purposes, rather than administering the entire Reading and Writing CLBA (or other performance assessments), we might be able to estimate an individual's level by means of the assessment of a core component. I argue below that integrative or discrete-point testing of this core component may be just as adequate as communicative assessment for certain purposes.

Ability-Task in the Context of Communicative and Non-Communicative Assessment

As noted above, the trend in language assessment has been in the direction of communicative assessment procedures (e.g. performance assessment). Discrete-point measures that fail to reflect authentic communicative situations are very much out of favour, at least at a theoretical level. The rationale for developing a new version of the TOEFL (*TOEFL 2000*) has been based largely on the perceived need to align the test with current thinking regarding the greater appropriateness of communicative as compared to discrete-point non-communicative testing procedures (e.g. Chapelle, Grabe & Berns, 1997).

Although this trend has much to recommend it, I believe that some skepticism regarding the pendulum of fashion is also appropriate. The blanket assumption that only communicative language assessment can make claims to validity and that discrete-point tests are almost *a priori* invalid by virtue of their non-communicative nature appears to me to be highly problematic on two counts. First, 'communication' does not necessarily mean the same thing in real-life as compared to language instructional domains, to use Bachman and Palmer's (1996) terminology. As documented in Chapter 3, many investigators have argued that the task demands of highly contextualized face-to-face conversational situations are very different from those in context-reduced academic situations. To argue in favour of 'communicative language testing' in absolute terms appears to ignore these important distinctions in language use domains. In other words, the construct of 'communicative language use' is ill-defined in the absence of specification of the relevant task domains or contexts within which communication and language use will take place.

In the second place, the assumption that communicative language assessment is inherently superior to non-communicative assessment draws primarily on construct and face validity as evidence for the appropriateness of assessment procedures. For example, the Canadian Language Benchmarks (CLB), considered above, justified its format and procedures on the basis of the fact that language was used primarily for communication and thus the assessment procedure had to mirror authentic contexts of communication in non-test situations. Face validity, the extent to which the assessment procedure appears to tap the relevant construct as judged by experts and practitioners in the field, was the main evidence advanced for the validity of the approach.

However, other dimensions of validity (e.g. concurrent, predictive) are also relevant to judging the appropriateness of different assessment procedures for particular purposes. In this regard, the uncomfortable reality is that authentic/communicative measures are often no more predictive of the relevant non-test language performance than are discrete-point measures. In addition, as outlined below, authentic/communicative measures often show strong concurrent relationships with discrete-point measures (e.g. Lindholm, 1994), raising the question of whether these different procedures are in fact assessing the same construct. If they are, then the rationale for pursuing the (usually) considerably more time-consuming and expensive communicative/authentic route can be called into question.

Bachman and Cohen (1998) distance themselves from absolute endorsements of the superiority of authentic language use assessment tasks. They suggest that we need to reconceptualize authenticity as a *relative* quality – in other words, authenticity corresponds to 'the degree to which the language use we observe and sample in our research corresponds to real-life language use' (1998: 23). Following Bachman and Palmer (1996), they argue for the principle that 'if we use performance on test tasks to make inferences about individuals' language ability, then performance on these tasks must correspond, in demonstrable ways, to test takers' language use in nontest situations' (1996: 23). In other words, to be considered authentic and valid, target language use tasks should correspond in demonstrable ways to target language use domains.

This criterion is reasonable provided that 'demonstrable correspondence' is understood to include more than just superficial similarity between target language use tasks and target language use domains. I argue below, that theoretical coherence with respect to the correspondence between language use tasks and domains, together with empirical support for this correspondence, are more fundamental considerations than whether or not a particular task embodies 'real-life' authentic/communicative language. In other words, some discrete-point and integrative tests may qualify as valid and appropriate under these criteria despite the fact that they are neither 'communicative' nor 'authentic' as these terms are usually understood.

In short, in the following sections, I examine critically the assumption that only authentic/communicative task-based assessment can be considered valid or appropriate. If it can be shown that the linguistic and/or cognitive features of particular tasks (e.g. in academic contexts) vary in predictable and systematic ways with task difficulty, then assessment of these features might serve as a proxy for assessment of the entire task. For example, we know that the proportion of low-frequency words correlates strongly with the difficulty of reading tasks (e.g. Laufer & Nation, 1995); therefore a measure of vocabulary knowledge might be used as an indirect index of an individual's ability to read challenging texts. Knowledge of vocabulary is not the same as reading performance in authentic academic situations, but its correlation with reading performance is so strong that it can provide a good estimate of the individual's authentic non-test reading performance (see Read, 1997; Qian, 1998, 1999).

Empirical evidence regarding the relationship among components of proficiency and the extent to which vocabulary knowledge might be regarded as a 'core' component of a general language proficiency dimension are considered in the following sections. Of primary concern is the question of whether instruments such as the CLBA, constructed on the basis of authentic/communicative imperatives, are assessing different constructs than less communicative and less authentic forms of assessment.

The Relationship Between Authentic Performance-Based and Discrete-Point Assessment of English Language Proficiency

The CLBA has been compared to several more traditional language test batteries. Two of these comparisons are summarized below.

CLBA and IELTS (Centre for Language Training and Assessment, 1998)

The International English Language Testing System (IELTS) was developed by the British Council as a test for prospective postgraduate students. It assesses Listening, Speaking, Reading and Writing. There are two alternative assessments for reading and writing, one intended primarily for screening admission to universities (*The Academic Modules*) and the other intended for less academic purposes such as screening candidates entering training courses or employment opportunities (*The General Training Modules*). The listening and speaking sections are the same for both modules. The General Training Modules are also used by the governments of Australia and New Zealand as one criterion in the granting of residency status to prospective immigrants.

Comparison of the CLBA and General Training Modules of the IELTS on a small sample of learners (*N* = 12) showed similar rank ordering for most of the students (with two exceptions) (CLBA, 1998). The report points to the difficulty of making comparisons between the CLBA and IELTS because, although they assess a similar range of skills, their formats and purposes are very different and they have been designed for different populations.

Alderson (1993) reports on a large-scale study carried out as part of the process of developing the IELTS. At issue was whether there was a rationale for a separate test of grammar in the new test. Alderson summarizes the findings as follows:

> 'In general, an analysis of reading, grammar, and listening yielded only one common factor. The addition of writing occasionally gave rise to a second factor … The factor analyses confirm previous findings by failing to identify separate factors for reading and grammar. Whatever these tests measure appears to be common to all the tests.' (1993: 213)

In short, some form of general language proficiency appears to underlie performance on tests such as the IELTS and perhaps also the CLBA.

CLBA and TOEIC (Jones, 1998)

The Test of English for International Communication (TOEIC) is a multiple-choice norm-referenced standardized test of English proficiency focused on English in the workplace developed by a subsidiary of Educational Testing Service (ETS). It involves a 45-minute listening section (100 multiple-choice items) and a 75-minute reading section (100 multiple-choice items). Although it currently focuses only on receptive skills, Jones reports that TOEIC research reports suggest 'a definite relationship between the ability to receive language and to produce it' (p. 7). Jones reports that it was possible to establish broad equivalencies according to stages of proficiency development (Stages I–III) between the CLBA and TOEIC although direct comparison was possible only in the case of CLBA Reading.

A statistical Appendix to the Jones report provides interesting and relevant data regarding the relationship between the CLBA (Reading) and TOEIC. An overall correlation for Reading of $r = 0.867$ (*N* = 121) was found, indicating that the two measures assess very similar constructs. The TOEIC Listening Comprehension and Reading Comprehension correlate with each other at a level of $r = 0.825$ while CLBA (Reading) shows a correlation with TOEIC Listening of $r = 0.789$. The statistical report (Appendix VII in Jones, 1998) suggests that the greater correlation between CLBA Reading and TOEIC Reading in comparison to CLBA Reading and TOEIC

Listening provides further evidence that the TOEIC test discriminates between listening and reading.

This latter point is probably technically valid but what is more striking is the strength of both correlations between reading and listening. Consistent with Oller's (1979) data, in this sample of learners a general language proficiency dimension underlies much of the variance in both listening and reading. Specifically, between 62% and 68% of the variance in reading scores is explained by listening comprehension compared to 75% of shared variance between the two measures of reading comprehension.

Thus, it appears clear that the TOEIC Reading and Listening subtests are assessing a dimension of English language proficiency that is also central to CLBA assessment. A significant difference, however, is that the TOEIC is a norm-referenced measure whereas the CLBA is criterion-referenced. Thus, even though they measure the same construct, they yield different types of information. For example, as a result of its task-based design, the CLBA is likely to be much more useful for guiding instruction or for aligning the stages of proficiency with the language requirements of different employment contexts.

The close relationship, however, between a relatively traditional norm-referenced standardized test (TOEIC) and a performance measure designed according to communicative and authentic task-based criteria (CLBA) raises two issues: (1) If both assessment methods are validly tapping the same underlying construct, why should communicative/authentic measures be so strongly favoured over traditional discrete-point measures, as is the case in contemporary applied linguistics (Shohamy, 1997)? Why should the difference in face validity override the psychometric equivalence of these indices of proficiency? (2) Should we re-examine the unfashionable notion of general language proficiency in view of the extremely strong correlations between the two reading measures and the TOEIC listening measure? What other evidence is there to support such a construct?

These issues are addressed in the next section. I review a number of international studies of adult learners that are highly consistent in their results regarding the nature of language proficiency and the legitimacy of the construct of general language proficiency.

Re-Emergence of General Language Proficiency?

The pattern of intercorrelations among different standardized language tests reported by Jones (1998) and Alderson (1993) above is typical. To further illustrate, Muñoz-Sandoval *et al.* (1998) reported correlations between the English Language Proficiency (ELT) cluster of subtests on the Bilingual Verbal Abilities Test (BVAT) and a variety of school achievement and language proficiency measures. The ELT cluster (which is all oral) consists of a Picture Vocabulary subtest, an Oral Vocabulary subtest (synonyms and antonyms) and a Verbal Analogies (reasoning) subtest. At the College/University level, the ELT cluster correlated 0.74 ($N = 908$) with Reading Achievement and 0.86 ($N = 909$) with

Content Knowledge. These data illustrate the central role of vocabulary knowledge in reading and academic attainment.

One of the most convincing demonstrations of the reality of some general language proficiency factor comes from a large-scale investigation of the comparability of the TOEFL test battery and the Cambridge First Certificate in English (FCE) battery. In addition to these measures, a semi-direct test of oral performance (the Speaking Proficiency in English Assessment Kit (SPEAK)) and a writing test (Test of English Writing) were administered (Bachman, Davidson & Foulkes, 1993; Bachman, Davidson, Ryan & Choi, 1995). The SPEAK assessment involved grammar, pronunciation, fluency, and comprehensibility.

A strong general factor emerged in all analyses. Bachman *et al.* (1993) summarize the results as follows:

> These loadings suggest that all of these tests measure, to a considerable degree, a common portion of the language abilities that characterize the test takers in the sample. After this general or common ability, the next largest component appears to be associated with speaking ability. (1993: 37)

Bachman *et al.* (1995: 129) similarly comment on the construct of language proficiency that appeared to be supported in the research: '... the finding that measures as diverse as those examined in the study tap virtually the same sets of language abilities may be surprising to the test developers'.

A study by Sasaki (1996) involving 160 EFL students in Japan related performance on English (L2) language proficiency measures with L1 language aptitude and verbal and non-verbal cognitive abilities. The results indicated a strong relationship between second language proficiency and general (L1) cognitive abilities, although the constructs were not identical to each other. Sasaki also related the test performance to the verbal report protocols of her subjects as they solved problems. As summarized by Bachman and Cohen (1998: 9), these results 'suggest that a general factor of second language proficiency is related to the amount of information processing involved in correctly solving certain types of tasks. In addition, the verbal report protocols reveal that high proficiency subjects were better able to use available information to answer cloze test items correctly, spent more time planning, and used a greater variety of strategies than did low proficiency subjects.' Sasaki's data suggest that in this particular university language learning context, multiple components of second language proficiency can be distinguished but there is also support for a general factor that is strongly related to L1 cognitive abilities.

Finally, Oller has convincingly demonstrated that verbal IQ tests 'assess proficiency in the language of the tests' and non-verbal IQ tests 'mainly measure powers of reasoning accessed through the primary language of the test-takers' (1997: 467). In other words, there is a dimension of language proficiency that is strongly related to cognitive abilities and both are also involved in academic development. Vocabulary knowledge is probably the most obvious manifestation of this dimension insofar as massive amounts of research data document its strong relationship to both overall cognitive abilities and academic development.

One of the major reasons why different measures of language proficiency assessed in academic contexts tend to correlate highly with each other and with cognitive variables is that they all reflect, in varying degrees, the construct of academic language proficiency or CALP. A central component required in virtually all facets of language performance in academic contexts is lexical knowledge appropriate to the task demands of particular academic situations. The pervasiveness of lexical knowledge in all aspects of language use was expressed by Harley *et al.* (1990) in explaining why no specific measures of vocabulary knowledge were included in the test battery they administered:

> In the large-scale proficiency study described above, there were no measures specifically designed to assess lexical proficiency – not because lexical proficiency was considered unimportant, but because it was assumed to enter into performance on all the tasks assigned. (1990: 21)

As the research of Corson (1995, 1997) and Nation (1990) demonstrates, the English lexicon used in everyday conversational contexts differs dramatically both in word-frequency and word-origin from that used in literate and academic contexts. Thus, the less familiar and less contextualized tasks that assess attainment of the higher Benchmarks in measures such as the CLBA are likely to require understanding and use of more abstract and precise lexical items than is the case at lower proficiency levels. It follows that vocabulary knowledge might represent a sensitive index of the broader task-oriented dimensions of proficiency assessed by the CLBA.

In summary, the data reviewed above show clearly that despite the fact that notions of 'general language proficiency' are not particularly fashionable at the moment, this construct emerges consistently in virtually all the psychometric research on the nature of second language proficiency in academic contexts. This construct is not in any way incompatible with a notion of language performance as 'highly complex, multidimensional, and variable according to a variety of social and contextual factors' (Brindley, 1998a: 134). As noted above, context is an integral part of the construct of language proficiency and there is also considerable evidence for specific components of proficiency in addition to a general factor (e.g. Sasaki, 1996; Snow & Hoefnagel-Hohle, 1979). However, *in academic contexts*, the bulk of the variance in most batteries appears to be accounted for by a common general language proficiency factor. As noted in Chapter 3, I have argued that as proficiency increases, this construct is more accurately conceptualized as reflecting *academic language proficiency* rather than general or global language proficiency. This is particularly the case in view of the fact that most of this psychometric research has been carried out with adults or school-aged children in academic contexts.

In the final section of this chapter, I argue that knowledge of English vocabulary is a strong candidate to provide a sensitive index capable of distinguishing learners at different stages of English proficiency (e.g. CLB Benchmark Stages I, II, and III). In other words, insofar as any notion of *general language proficiency* is defensible, it is likely to be reflected most clearly and sensitively in the individual's lexical knowledge.

The Assessment of Lexical Knowledge as an Indicator of General Language Proficiency

Consider the following quotations from recent 'state-of-the-art' reviews of language testing and assessment:

> ... empirical studies have consistently shown that different types of reading tests tend to be substantially intercorrelated and test-based research has yet to verify theoretical descriptions of reading in terms of separate component skills. (Vincent, 1997: 5)

> ... in a study of the ... TOEFL conducted in the early 1970s, Pike (1979) found that, from a psychometric viewpoint, the vocabulary subtest could be regarded as a more efficient substitute for the reading comprehension one. It ranked the test-takers in essentially the same order as the reading one did, and did so more economically because the examinees did not have to spend time reading whole texts. (Read, 1997: 100)

Grabe has also argued that fluent readers need 'a massive receptive vocabulary that is rapidly, accurately, and automatically accessed' and the lack of such a vocabulary 'may be the greatest single impediment to fluent reading by ESL students' (1988: 63).

These quotations reinforce the research findings outlined earlier regarding the reality of a significant general language proficiency dimension (particularly in literacy-related contexts) and the probable contribution of lexical knowledge as enabling in many, if not all, aspects of linguistic performance (see also Anderson and Freebody, 1981; Koda, 1989; Qian, 1998, 1999).

Read (1997) suggests that there is a need to define afresh the lexical contribution to test-taker performance within the communicative paradigm. In particular, there is a need for assessment procedures that present or elicit lexical items in rich discourse contexts.

Does this perspective imply that all tests of lexical knowledge must elicit or reflect language used in authentic communicative situations if they are to have construct validity? Many applied linguists would answer affirmatively to this question. As Shohamy points out: 'Communicative language testing dominates the field' (1997: 143).

However, I believe that there are good theoretical and empirical reasons to consider a broader range of assessment procedures and contexts as potentially valid for measuring notions of general or academic language proficiency. Empirically, as noted above and in Oller's (1979) research, indices of general language proficiency (or cognitive/academic language proficiency) all seem to load on the same underlying dimension regardless of whether they are discrete-point, integrative, or communicative (such as the CLBA). In the specific sphere of vocabulary assessment, Laufer and Nation (1995) report highly significant relationships between lexical richness in a relatively authentic writing assignment and lexical richness assessed by means of the non-authentic/non-communicative Vocabulary Levels

Test (active version). Similarly, Lindholm (1994), as reported by August and Hakuta (1997: 122), 'found highly significant and positive correlations between standardized scores of Spanish reading achievement and teacher-rated reading rubric scores, as well as between the standardized reading scores and students' rating of their reading competence, for native English-speaking and native Spanish-speaking students enrolled in a bilingual immersion program.'

Oller's (1979) theoretical work provides a useful starting point for examining why 'non-communicative' discrete-point and integrative measures might be considered theoretically legitimate as indices of the constructs more directly assessed through communicative/authentic task-based measures. The essential features of Oller's approach, as summarized by McNamara are as follows:

> Oller (1979) advocated types of performance test (*pragmatic tests*) which focused not so much on replicating tasks candidates might face in the world as on tasks which demanded of candidates the same processing of language (understood in psycholinguistic terms) as is required in any real-world second language performance. Thus, tests requiring performances on relatively artificial tasks such as filling in gaps in a cloze passage or taking dictation were held to be as valid as performance tests involving more 'authentic' tasks which more obviously simulated real-world activities. (McNamara, 1996: 79–80)

Based on his notion of the *pragmatic expectancy grammar*, Oller argued that pragmatic tests must fulfil two criteria:

> First, they must cause the learner to process ... temporal sequences of elements in the language that conform to normal contextual constraints (linguistic and extralinguistic); second, they must require the learner to understand the pragmatic interrelationship of linguistic contexts and extralinguistic contexts. (1979: 33)

This description provides a coherent rationale as to how 'relatively artificial' pragmatic or integrative tasks (e.g. cloze) can be used as indices for more authentic communicative tasks. However, a similar rationale can also be constructed for legitimizing the use of non-pragmatic/non- communicative tasks (e.g. discrete-point vocabulary or reading measures) as indirect indices of communicative proficiency (both oral and written) in academic contexts.

Such tasks can be viewed as assessing the *consequences* of engaging in extensive pragmatic processing of language. If we focus on vocabulary knowledge, for example, we can justify a non-authentic task (e.g. cloze or discrete-point) by arguing that the predominant way individuals gain the vocabulary knowledge to perform well in such tasks is by engaging extensively in the processing of authentic text (usually by means of reading) that exposes them to an increasing range of the English lexicon. As noted in previous chapters, there is a very substantial amount of research supporting this position (see for example Krashen, 1993). In other words, the more language processing individuals carry out in both oral and written modes, the more rapidly and extensively their vocabulary develops. For example, the extremely strong relationship between reading ability, vocabulary growth, and the amount of reading an individual carries out has been well-established (e.g. Elley, 1991; Postlethwaite & Ross, 1992).

Thus, the fact that the multiple-choice non-communicative TOEIC test is indistinguishable from the task-based communicative/authentic CLBA in its assessment of English reading proficiency can be interpreted in the following way: the CLBA attempts to *directly* assess reading performance in an authentic/communicative manner whereas the TOEIC reading test assesses reading *indirectly* insofar as strong performance on the TOEIC reflects the consequences of engaging extensively in authentic English reading tasks. Extensive reading builds up vocabulary and grammatical knowledge as well as effective reading strategies and the TOEIC assesses the individual's knowledge of these language structures and strategies.

An additional reason why communicative/authentic and non-communicative/non-authentic assessment procedures often show relatively little difference in the way they assess academic language proficiency concerns the fact that academic tasks tend to be inherently more context-reduced than non-academic tasks. Thus, test formats that are relatively context-reduced reflect, to a considerable extent, the intrinsic nature of the academic and literacy tasks that learners are required to carry out in many school contexts. As discussed in Chapter 3, reading a book and writing a book report on it are very different from interpersonal conversation in the quantity and quality of contextual support embedded in each activity.[3]

Norton Peirce (1992) has similarly argued that a language test is a genre, no less authentic, in and of itself, than the language genres used in other social occasions:

> While test makers have generally assumed that a standardized reading test is an aberration in the 'real world', I wish to argue that it is no less authentic a social situation than an oral presentation or a visit to the doctor. In a standardized reading test, the value ascribed to texts within this genre is associated with a ritualized social occasion in which participants share a common purpose and set of expectations. (1992: 685)

In other words, to the extent that standardized reading tests mirror the context-reduced demands of schooling and many real-life reading performances (e.g. reading and completing various forms), they can be considered potentially appropriate despite the fact that they lack a task-based communicative orientation. However, such tests have been so misused and have led to such harmful consequences for ELL students in the past that they should be used with extreme caution and only when their validity has been established in relation to direct assessment of performance. This issue is addressed in more detail in Chapter 6.

Summary and Conclusion

There is considerable consensus in current applied linguistics theory regarding the need to specify relevant aspects of both traits of the individual and contexts of use in defining the construct of language proficiency. There is no universal structure of proficiency that can be defined outside of particular contexts.

Assessment of the construct of language proficiency is currently dominated by the theoretical assumptions of communicative language assessment. Among these assumptions is that language is primarily used for communication in a variety of real-life contexts and therefore tasks designed to assess proficiency should correspond in demonstrable ways to these real-life communicative contexts. Performance assessments that sample an individual's language use in authentic contexts are very much favoured over discrete-point tests that make little attempt to sample language in ways that reflect authentic communicative language use. Integrative measures occupy an intermediate position insofar as they attempt to assess the processing of authentic language but do so in a relatively non-authentic test situation.

In this chapter, I have challenged the assumption that communicative/authentic task-based performance assessment is somehow inherently superior for all purposes to less authentic discrete-point and integrative assessment procedures. The typical assumptions underlying communicative language assessment omit one central component of the construct of language proficiency: language is used not only for 'real-life' communication but also for communication and thinking in academic contexts. As documented in Chapter 3, language use in instructional domains differs dramatically from typical language use in face-to-face everyday communication. In the context of Figure 3.1, language use in Quadrant D entails very different processing demands than language use in Quadrant A. As numerous investigators have noted, language use in academic contexts tends to be more decontextualized, autonomous and abstract than language use in everyday face-to-face contexts. Bereiter and Scardamalia (1981) point out, for example, that writing an essay for a class assignment makes very different linguistic and cognitive demands on the individual than casual conversation.

In short, the nature of language use in instructional domains suggests that 'authenticity' in these contexts will be much more context-reduced than 'authenticity' in real-life everyday communicative contexts. Therefore, it can be argued that the context-reduced nature of integrative and discrete-point tests reflects, in potentially appropriate ways, the context-reduced reality of many of the tasks that individuals perform in academic contexts. Even performance or communicative assessments of reading, writing, and other academic tasks will tend to be context-reduced in comparison to performance assessments of typical face-to-face communication. Consequently, it is not surprising that we find extremely strong correlations between communicative assessments of reading and writing and discrete-point measures (e.g. Jones, 1998; Laufer & Nation, 1995). Both 'communicative' and 'non-communicative' procedures are assessing the same construct (academic language proficiency) and, because of the context-reduced nature of that construct, discrete-point and integrative tests are not necessarily inappropriate despite their contrived nature in comparison to communicative tasks. To argue otherwise requires that one explain the research showing that communicative and non-communicative measures are indistinguishable in their assessment of academic language proficiency.

The research data also show that within academic domains a general language proficiency factor consistently emerges. This is not to argue that all variance in academic assessments can be reduced to a single unitary dimension. For example, writing ability entails specific competencies that are not shared with reading ability. However, there tends to be a fairly strong correlation between these two faces of literacy, reflecting the reality of a general academic language proficiency factor (CALP).

I have argued that lexical knowledge is at the core of this general academic language proficiency factor. Therefore assessment of lexical knowledge through either communicative or non-communicative methods can provide an estimate of an individual's academic language proficiency. It is not difficult to justify theoretically the relationship between lexical knowledge and the broader construct of academic or literacy-related language proficiency. Learners who read a lot in their first or second language gain access to the low-frequency vocabulary and grammatical constructions that are found only in literate texts. It is also worth noting that most (59%) of the educators who responded to Solomon and Rhodes' survey on academic language suggested that vocabulary is a key feature of the construct and the 'language used in various content areas, such as math, social studies, science, and so on, requires mastery of specific terms and phrases unique to these areas' (1996: 5).

Clearly, lexical knowledge is displayed in many communicative spheres and each language use domain will be characterized by specific registers (e.g. street talk, baseball discussions, journalese, etc.). My intent is not in any sense to devalue these spheres of human communication and cognitive achievement. The point is that, by definition, they are not part of the instructional language use domain and therefore are less relevant to educational achievement than academic or literate registers of language.

In summary, while there are many pitfalls and threats to validity in discrete-point testing that suggest far more caution in using them than has traditionally been the case (see for example, Cummins, 1984), they should not be dismissed a priori as less valid and useful than communicative/authentic performance-based tasks. The validity and usefulness of discrete-point and integrative measures should be decided on both empirical and theoretical grounds using the criterion of 'demonstrable correspondence' as suggest by Bachman and Cohen (1998). These issues are considered further in Chapter 6 in the context of the assessment of language proficiency among school-aged students.

Notes

1. Norton and Stewart (1999) point to the complexities of developing task-based assessment while at the same time maintaining separate skill areas in the CLBA (Speaking/Listening, Reading, Writing). The mandate from the Canadian federal government called for assessment that measured ability to accomplish a variety of authentic tasks that are commonly carried out in the Canadian social and business context. At the same time, however, their mandate was to develop three separate instruments for listening/speaking, reading, and writing. As noted by Citizenship and Immigration Canada:

The CLB recognizes three skill areas, treating speaking and listening as one domain. A single global scale of proficiency description for all skills for the CLB was rejected by the ESL field in the consultation and field testing process. Separate scales reflecting competencies within skill areas were favoured for many reasons. (1996: 11)

Norton and Stewart (1999) point out that 'stakeholders soon realized, however, that many highly realistic and meaningful tasks are unsuitable for the purpose of separate-skills assessment. Authentic tasks are fluid and involve the simultaneous or rapidly alternating use of different language skills' (p. 231).

2. Obviously, there may be some adult learners who will show a different trend: for example, learners who have studied English extensively in academic contexts from authentic written texts but who have had minimal opportunity to engage in authentic conversational interactions in English may be much more proficient in academic as compared to conversational contexts.

3. This point should not be construed as an endorsement of transmission or 'banking' approaches to instruction which reduce the amount of comprehensible input that students receive and impede ELL students' academic progress. As discussed in Chapters 2 and 3, the most effective instruction for all students will tend to be cognitively challenging and context-embedded. However even at its most effective and meaningful, the language use and language demands of academic instruction are inherently more context-reduced than the language demands of everyday interaction.

Chapter 6
Dilemmas of Inclusion: Integrating English Language Learners in Standards-Based Reform

To mention the word 'assessment' to educational bureaucrats in Europe, North America, Australia and New Zealand is to risk being inundated with a dizzying array of associated jargon: *standards, performance indicators, benchmarks, outcomes-based education, quality assurance, attainment targets, minimal competency testing, accountability,* etc. These terms reflect two relatively recent trends in the educational systems of many countries: (1) the development of subject matter content and performance standards as a means of operationalizing, standardizing, and evaluating what all students should be learning; (2) the exploration of alternative approaches to evaluate attainment of curriculum standards partly as a result of dissatisfaction with traditional norm-referenced standardized tests.

The standards-based reform movement has been fuelled by parallel developments in many countries. The common context is one where educational systems are attempting to redefine themselves in light of rapidly changing economic, technological, and social conditions that are affecting countries around the world. The shift from an industrialized to a knowledge-based economy has highlighted the need for workers with higher levels of literacy and numeracy than was previously the case. Within this context, there is considerable consensus among most educational stakeholders about the need for reform to take account of changing social, economic, technological and existential realities (see Cummins & Sayers, 1995). Controversy reigns, however, in relation to the specific nature of the reforms. Educational debates since the early 1980s have been characterized by volatility and acrimony about issues such as the following:

- appropriate ways to teach literacy (e.g. whole-language versus phonics approaches);

- the perceived need to abandon what some see as fuzzy child-centred pedagogy and 'get back to basics;'
- the extent to which multicultural education is socially divisive and a cause of declining standards or, alternatively, an educational orientation that is essential to the attainment of standards (see Nieto, 1996, 1999);
- the desirability or otherwise of privatized education (e.g. through voucher systems) as a means of raising standards (and potentially reducing corporate and individual taxes).

As the current volume suggests, another common theme in educational debates in many countries concerns appropriate ways to address the growing diversity of the student population and the need to teach an increasing number of students the language of instruction.

Frequently a crisis mentality with respect to 'declining standards' has been actively encouraged by governments and business to gain public support for massive reform of the educational system. In most cases, there is little evidence to support claims of declining standards and the 'literacy crisis' (e.g. Berliner & Biddle, 1995). Regardless of whether such crises are legitimate or manufactured, in many countries a fervour for accountability has taken root as schools are increasingly being scrutinized to ensure that they are producing the 'outcomes' required to fuel economic growth and international competitiveness. Curriculum standards have been developed at both national and state levels across the United States, the United Kingdom, Canada, and elsewhere, as central governments assume more control of what is taught and frequently *how* and *when* it is taught. The degree to which schools have attained these standards is then assessed at regular intervals (usually once a year) through curriculum-based performance assessments (e.g. the Standard Assessment Tasks that accompanied the National Curriculum in the United Kingdom).

The central issue that I address in this chapter concerns the awkward reality of ELL students in the context of these standards-based educational reforms. Specifically, should the same content and performance standards be applied to ELL students as to students who are fluent in the language of instruction, or should separate standards be developed that recognize and accommodate the specific learning patterns of ELL students? Application of the same standards and assessment procedures to all students might include various exemptions and accommodations for ELL students but there is little evidence that these accommodations result in equitable assessment. If separate standards are developed for ELL students, should these be developed in all curricular areas (e.g. science, mathematics, etc.) or just in English language arts? What should such standards look like? Would they potentially reduce academic expectations for ELL students by requiring a 'lower' standard than for non-ELL students? What criteria should guide the shift from using separate ELL standards to using exclusively the 'mainstream' curriculum expectations? These issues are very much unresolved; in fact, debate on them has just begun in many educational jurisdictions.

Related to this issue is a second question. Regardless of whether separate standards are developed for ELL students, how should attainment of these standards be assessed? Currently, in the United States there exist a variety of assessment procedures ranging from a traditional norm-referenced standardized achievement test in California (the Stanford Achievement Test-9 (SAT-9)) to portfolio assessment in Vermont (Zehler *et al.*, 1994). Various kinds of performance assessment exist in other countries (e.g. Australia, the United Kingdom) but such assessments are not unproblematic. Test–retest reliability often tends to be low, and they are time-consuming and costly to administer in comparison to standardized tests.

My particular focus in this chapter concerns the implications of different assessment procedures for ELL students. I argue that, in principle, English language development standards for ELL students should be developed and implemented. This has been done in some educational jurisdictions but, as noted above, many unresolved issues remain. In particular, considerable research is required to provide an informed basis for aligning these standards with 'mainstream' language arts standards. In most jurisdictions, ELL students continue to be included in 'mainstream' standards assessment usually with a variety of accommodations. I argue that under these conditions, assessment by means of traditional standardized norm- or criterion-referenced tests provides largely meaningless and potentially harmful data. Such measures should at least be complemented by alternative assessment procedures that are sensitive to the academic growth and accomplishments of ELL students (e.g. portfolio assessment).

I also propose a procedure for curriculum-based computer-administered performance assessment that combines the advantages of standardized tests on the one hand (speed and efficiency of administration, quantitative data that can be reliably scored and interpreted in relation to norms or content criteria) and alternative performance assessments on the other (direct alignment with content standards, integration with classroom instruction, diagnostic usefulness). This procedure follows from the analysis in the previous chapter suggesting that lexical knowledge represents a core component of the construct of academic language proficiency. Language is infused across the curriculum in virtually all subject areas. Therefore, students' knowledge of the vocabulary associated with particular curriculum areas (e.g. science, social studies) can potentially be assessed as an indicator of their knowledge of the concepts taught in these curricular areas. If we take Science as an example, an extremely large item bank of words representing the concepts (e.g. photosynthesis, digestion, etc.) and processes (e.g. infer, predict, explain, etc.) covered in the curriculum for each grade level could be developed and categorized according to various criteria (e.g. difficulty/frequency level, curriculum programs in which the item appears, stage of the program or time of year that concept should be covered etc.).

The procedure could be used by individual teachers both to monitor student learning and to customize instruction to the needs of individual students. For example, students could be provided with immediate feedback and learning supports (e.g. graphic organizers) for any item they answered incorrectly. Students could then print out this information as an aid to further study of the content. Because the computer program could sample from the item bank according to pre-defined criteria selected by the teacher (e.g. time of the year, concept difficulty level, etc.), the system can be customized for each classroom rather than applying a 'one-size-fits-all' approach.

In addition to its use by individual teachers to assess student learning and identify gaps, such a system could potentially be used by school systems or broader educational jurisdictions (e.g. national or state departments of education) for summative assessment purposes. Obviously, research would be required to validate this procedure against direct performance assessment. However, based on the theoretical analysis and empirical data reviewed in this volume, I would argue that such a procedure could reliably be calibrated against direct performance assessment and would provide a useful tool for both formative and summative assessment of educational progress.

The procedure could also be developed in additional languages (e.g. Spanish) so that first language assessment for individual diagnostic or program monitoring purposes could be integrated with the system. Because the assessment system would be based directly on the curriculum, teaching to the test would not be a problem – the only way to teach effectively to the test is to teach the curriculum. Typical profiles for ELL students can be easily developed to assist in equitable and appropriate performance interpretation (e.g. according to length of residence, program (bilingual, dual language, English-only etc.)).

Trends in Performance Assessment

August and Hakuta (1997) note that the term 'performance assessment' is used in two different ways. The first usage refers to any form of assessment pertinent to performance standards. This could include discrete-point multiple-choice items such as a question requiring recall of a key fact or concept tied to a particular content standard. The second usage refers to assessment exercises requiring constructed responses or complex open-ended performances. In this sense the term is used in similar ways to the terms 'alternative assessment' and 'authentic assessment'.

Performance assessment is increasingly promoted as an alternative to multiple-choice norm-referenced standardized tests. Norm-referenced tests are designed to provide information about how students perform in relation to a norming group of other students, usually a representative sample from the same country. These tests have been criticized frequently on the grounds that they are not closely linked to the curriculum and exclude important curricular objectives (e.g. problem-solving, creative writing, etc.). Item selection criteria are based on fitting the distribution of students to the pattern defined by the bell curve rather than reflecting attainment of curriculum objectives. Furthermore, they usually provide minimal information to guide instruction and may narrow the instructional focus as a result of teachers teaching to the test.

Performance assessment, by contrast, includes a range of procedures (e.g. progress profiles, structured observations, etc.) that attempt to assess student performance in meaningful authentic contexts and in ways that reflect specific instructional goals (see Samway & McKeon, 1999, for a useful list of specific procedures). Performance assessment is generally carried out in the context where learning takes place and is designed to assess the progress that students have made towards attaining specific standards or benchmarks in particular subject areas. As in communicative assessment of language proficiency, the goal is to assess students' performance on real or authentic tasks rather than assessing only indicators of this performance.

Teachers carry out informal performance assessments to inform their instruction all the time. Most commercially available curriculum programs incorporate assessment rubrics at the end of every unit and many also encourage teachers to maintain student portfolios which can contribute to the classroom assessment process. However, as noted above, the ways in which the term 'performance assessment' is used have diverged during the past 15 years. This divergence reflects, on the one hand, the extent to which the emphasis is on accountability-oriented assessment designed to assess, in a summative way, the extent to which externally defined standards have been attained or on formative assessment designed to adjust programs to the needs of individual students.

In the context of the this latter meaning of 'performance assessment', a range of structured observational instruments has been developed to help teachers monitor their students' progress along continua of development. Two examples are the *Primary Language Record* (Barrs, 1990; Barrs *et al.*, 1988) developed by the Inner London Education Authority in the United Kingdom and the *First Steps* program developed by the Government of Western Australia (e.g. Education Department of Western Australia, 1994). These observational instruments are designed to help teachers diagnose their students' needs and plan their teaching to take account of these needs (Brindley, 1998b). The focus is generally on individual students rather than on system-wide accountability. Used in this sense, performance assessment is one branch of *authentic assessment* which O'Malley and Pierce define as 'the multiple forms of assessment that are consistent with classroom goals, curricula, and instruction' (1996: 2).

Performance assessment of school and system-wide attainment of curriculum standards in most cases falls somewhere between traditional norm-referenced standardized testing and observational records such as the Australian *First Steps* program. Unlike traditional standardized tests, the assessment is focused specifically on the attainment of explicit curriculum objectives or standards. However, in a similar way to norm-referenced standardized tests, the assessment provides comparative data that locates the performance of individual schools and students in relation to other schools and students across the country or state. The performance of students and schools is not distributed according to the bell curve (as in norm-referenced tests) but nonetheless it frequently serves the purpose of establishing 'league tables' that serve to rank schools according to performance. Thus, unlike authentic assessment procedures, performance assessment designed to monitor accountability aims to place all schools (and classrooms) on the same scale so that the attainment of standards can be gauged and comparisons can be made between schools that are successful and those that are less successful.

Accountability-oriented performance assessment also differs from authentic assessment in the extent to which students are formally tested outside of normal classroom routines. In Texas, for example, the Texas Assessment of Academic Skills (TAAS), is very much a test with high-stakes consequences for students, teachers, and administrators. A significant amount of time is spent in classrooms teaching to the test which is administered in Grades 4 through 8. Although the TAAS is articulated with Texas curriculum standards, it assesses learning in a context-reduced way as compared to the context-embedded assessment that is characteristic of authentic assessment.

By contrast, the system adopted in Ontario, Canada, assesses students (currently Grades 3, 6 and 9) in the context of a ten-day unit of work in which test items and assessment tasks are embedded. Student work is scored on a four-level scale that is linked to the provincial curriculum and standards. This system attempts to increase validity by embedding the assessment into a relatively authentic instructional situation. It also avoids at least some of the problems of curriculum narrowing as a result of teachers teaching to the test since this is precisely what teachers are supposed to do within the ten-day unit. However, there are potential costs that accompany these advantages. Unlike the TAAS, the administration of which is tightly controlled, there is considerable scope for teachers in the Ontario scheme to interpret the guidelines for assisting students leniently, thereby boosting the scores of their classroom and school.

One issue that is becoming increasingly controversial in the context of system-wide assessments is the degree to which ELL students are to be included or excluded from the assessment. If including ELL students is considered inequitable, then should separate standards be developed specifically for such students? This issue is considered in the next section.

The Awkward Reality of ELL Students

With the exception of Australia, policy-makers in English-speaking countries have generally considered the implications of state-mandated assessment schemes for ELL students only as an afterthought. This reflects the marginal status generally accorded to linguistic and cultural diversity issues in educational reform efforts in most educational jurisdictions (e.g. Nieto, 1999; Olsen *et al.*, 1994). The typical picture is that assessment regimens are initially mandated by the central authority with vague directions regarding the criteria for exemption of certain students or for accommodations of various kinds for students who might be unable to participate in the assessment without support (e.g. some categories of special education and ELL students). In subsequent years, policy-makers scramble to make the criteria more coherent but, as yet, there are few contexts where satisfactory solutions to the dilemmas of accommodations and exemptions have been implemented.

In sections below, the status of ELL students in large-scale assessment programs in the United States, Australia, and Ontario, Canada are reviewed in order to illustrate how the issues are being addressed in different jurisdictions.

The United States context

Several major reviews of the literature on the inclusion of ELL students in state-mandated assessments have been carried out in the United States (e.g. August & Hakuta, 1997; Butler & Stevens, 1997; LaCelle-Peterson & Rivera, 1994; National Clearinghouse for Bilingual Education, 1997; Zehler *et al.*, 1994). LaCelle-Peterson and Rivera note that the most common option implemented in the US for assessment of ELL students has been the testing of such students with minimal consideration of the validity of the instruments for the populations being tested. A second option has involved excluding ELL students from the accountability process by exempting them from testing for an arbitrary length of time (usually one to three years of receiving instruction primarily in English).

They point out that the first option is 'neither ethically nor educationally defensible;' it represents a negative experience for the students and generates inaccurate information about schools or systems of schools. However, the second option is also problematic insofar as it creates a type of 'systemic ignorance' about the educational progress of English language learners. With respect to these two options, they argue as follows:

> Because some ELLs may have the content knowledge and/or the cognitive ability to perform successfully on assessment tasks but are not yet able to demonstrate in English what they know, assessment procedures may be neither equitable nor yield valid results for ELLs. ... Assessing diverse groups of students – some of whom speak English as their first language, others of whom are learning it as a second or third language – with instruments written in English and normed on monolingual English-speaking students inevitably yields data of unknown validity that cannot be meaningfully aggregated. (1994: 66)

LaCelle-Peterson and Rivera suggest that any adequate assessment scheme designed to include ELL students must incorporate four characteristics: it must be

(1) *Comprehensive*: assess all that students are learning;
(2) *Flexible*: permit students to show what they know in a variety of modes;
(3) *Progress-oriented*: track student progress from year to year;
(4) *Student-sensitive*: bring into the assessment process the expertise of educators who know the needs and learning characteristics of ELL students.

They recommend that in the assessment process, students' educational program and years of schooling in English should be recorded so that meaningful disaggregations can be made to examine the performance of all students and school programs that are serving them.

Butler and Stevens (1997) distinguish two categories of accommodations for ELL students: modifications of the test and modifications of the test procedures. The former includes assessment in the native language, text changes in vocabulary, modification of linguistic complexity, addition of visual supports, use of glossaries in the native language, use of glossaries in English, linguistic modification of test directions, additional example items/tasks. Modifications of test procedures include extra assessment time, breaks during testing, administration in several sessions, oral direction in the native language, small-group administration, separate room administration, use of dictionaries, reading aloud of questions in English, answers written directly in test booklet, directions read aloud or explained.

Butler and Stevens note that the most frequently used accommodations are separate testing sessions (17 states), small-group administration or flexible scheduling (15 states), extra assessment time (14 states), and simplification of directions (11 states).[1] However, as of 1995, many states had no specific guidelines for using accommodations with ELL students. August and Hakuta (1997) note that almost no research has been conducted to determine the effectiveness of these accommodation strategies.

Butler and Stevens identify three 'potentially critical background variables' that should be taken into account in making large-scale assessments more equitable for ELL students: (1) English language proficiency, (2) prior formal schooling, and (3) length of time in the US. These three variables are likely to be highly interrelated. With respect to *English language proficiency*, they note that most performance assessments and standardized tests place a heavy language demand on the test taker. Thus, measures of English language proficiency can help determine the causes of poor test performance for ELL students. The relevance of *prior formal schooling* is evident in the fact that students with little or no formal schooling are not likely to be familiar with school culture and assessment procedures. By contrast, those with prior formal education are likely to be literate in their first language and possibly in English; they may also have been exposed to relevant academic content and have participated in large-scale assessments. *Length of residence* reflects the level of experience a student has had with the language and culture of the host country and is thus highly relevant to performance on large-scale assessments conducted in English.

Specification of these variables has implications for the kinds of information that should be gathered either from students, parents, or school staff as part of the assessment procedure. Students' profile on these variables can help determine the need for specific kinds of accommodation and for interpreting performance on the assessment procedure. Thus,

> … academic English language proficiency must be defined and levels specified along a proficiency continuum, such as beginning, intermediate, and advanced, that reflect differences in ability that have been captured through an

> evaluation procedure. With regard to prior education, it will be important to determine whether students have had previous education in the US or in their home countries, and ideally how much and of what type. Finally, in terms of time in the US, broad classifications of students, such as recent immigrants, early immigrants, and US-born learners ... need to be operationalized according to specified time parameters. (1997: 20)

Butler and Stevens conclude by stressing the need to acknowledge diversity among students who are non-native speakers of English and the importance of investigating the performance of subpopulations within the larger group on the assessments that are being used to track students' progress. Research into these issues is in its infancy but, they argue, if inclusion of English language learners in large-scale assessments is acknowledged as an important societal goal, it is crucial to pursue these directions vigorously.

The National Clearinghouse for Bilingual Education (NCBE) (1997) conference on high-stakes assessment also addressed these questions. The participants strongly recommended that ELL students should be included in assessment systems for accountability purposes with appropriate accommodations or alternative procedures (e.g. portfolios, teacher judgments as alternatives to tests) to make the assessment meaningful and useful. They argued that:

> From the outset, high-stakes assessments should be developed with ELLs in mind. They should be considered in the development of the test construct, framework, and individual items, and they should be included in sufficient numbers in the sample used to norm the instruments. (NCBE, 1997: 6)

The fact that issues related to ELL students have been very much an afterthought in most of the standards-based reforms in the United States is illustrated by the controversies that have erupted in California with respect to this issue. The state has vacillated on the issue of whether to adopt separate English Language Development standards and what they should look like. It has also adopted a statewide test (the SAT-9) that is highly traditional and is perceived by many educators as minimally reflecting the current state standards.

In 1997 the State of California passed Assembly Bill 748 which mandated the implementation of statewide English language proficiency tests for K-12 ELL students. As part of this process they commissioned the development of a set of English Language Development Standards to integrate with the 'mainstream' English Language Arts Standards that had already been developed. The standards were drawn up by a large committee under the direction of Dr Adel Nadeau of the San Diego County Office of Education (Nadeau, 1998). These standards provided a detailed 'road map' of what could be expected from beginning, intermediate and advanced ELL learners at various stages of their English language development. The standards also articulated this development with the existing English Language Arts standards. However, the California Department of Education rejected the detailed (more than 90 pages) English language development standards drawn up by Nadeau's committee and produced instead in February 1999 a nine-page streamlined document that presumably would require far less expertise and time to administer. Under pressure from educators of ELL students, the state department reversed itself again and the State Board of Education adopted in July 1999 a slightly modified version of the original standards developed by Nadeau's committee (California Department of Education, 1999a).

Merino and Rumberger articulate succinctly the rationale for development of these separate English Language Development standards:

> First ... standards developed for a native speaking population are simply not sensitive enough to capture the initial development of English language learners. Second, the process and pace of acquisition for English learners differs in significant ways from the experience of monolingual English speakers. ... The major risk in not establishing standards for English learners lies in the failure to perceive progress when it is occurring and in the failure to measure a real lack of progress. (1999: 1)

However, effective implementation of standards-based reform requires that the criterion measure used to assess attainment of the standards is closely aligned with the standards. The state of California originally implemented in 1991 an innovative performance-based assessment system, the California Learning Assessment System (CLAS). The CLAS attempted to assess higher-order thinking skills rather than the lower-order skills typically assessed in traditional standardized tests. However, according to Collins (1998), the system ran into trouble on several fronts including public skepticism with respect to its non-traditional format. In 1997, a standardized testing system (based on the SAT-9) focused on basic skills was approved by the California Assembly without much consideration regarding how the test was aligned with curriculum standards nor how it would be implemented and interpreted in relation to the large proportion (approximately 25%) of the state's school population who are classified as 'limited English proficient (LEP)' The California Statewide Testing and Reporting Program (STAR) requires all students, Grades 2–11, to take the SAT-9 in English.

The resulting controversy was predictable, particularly at a time when the impending passage of Proposition 227, designed to severely limit bilingual education, was creating major tension and acrimony among educators and policy-makers throughout the state. In 1998, the San Francisco School District and the California State Department of Education sued each other over the state's requirement that all ELL students be assessed by the state-mandated test. San Francisco refused to implement the State Department's policy of mandatory testing of all students. An Associated Press report (15 July, 1998) described the suspension of a teacher in the Fresno Unified School District because he refused to administer the state-mandated reading test to his non-English-speaking students: 'The teacher, Silvio Manno, 43, said he thought that giving the test to his second graders at Rowell Elementary School here would have been 'a humiliating insult' and ultimately harmful to them'.

Paul García points out that in the initial year of the STAR, 'results indicate LEP students scored 30 to 39 percentile ranks below all students in reading and 17 to 29 percentile ranks lower in language, depending on grade level' (1998: 29). He points out that the student population used to establish national norms for the SAT-9 represented relatively small percentages of LEP (2%), ethnic and racial minority (37%) and low SES (29%) students but in California more than 20% of the student population is classified as LEP, 61% are ethnic or racial minority students, and 25% are acutely low SES and living in poverty.

The 'crisis of accountability' in California escalated at the end of February, 2000, with the resignation from the Public School Accountability Committee of Dr Gene García, Dean of the Faculty of Education at University of California Berkeley. This committee served an advisory role to the State Board of Education on issues related to school accountability. Data from the previous year's SAT-9 testing showed that limited English proficient students were scoring at the chance level five to six times more than students who were not limited in their English proficiency. In other words, for these students the test was totally inappropriate. On the basis of these data, the Accountability Committee recommended to the State Board of Education that until a reliable, valid and fair assessment process could be put into place for ELL students, the scores of these students be excluded from the Academic Performance Index, an index developed for each school based on SAT-9 scores to reflect the quality of school performance. The State Board ignored the recommendation. García resigned from the Accountability Committee and called for a boycott of the state testing by parents and guardians of limited English speaking students.

The California experience shows how the implementation of standards-based reform can go seriously astray. The adoption of separate English Language Development (ELD) standards for ELL students is a positive development but is meaningless in the context of an assessment system that is significantly out of alignment with both the 'mainstream' Language Arts and ELD standards and makes no accommodation to the presence of large numbers of ELL students throughout the state.

Texas also has large numbers of ELL students and, as noted above, for a number of years has had a coherent, albeit controversial, assessment system. The Texas Assessment of Academic Skills (TAAS), unlike the California STAR system, is aligned with curriculum standards. In the 1990s, the state instituted mandatory testing of all ELL students because it suspected widespread abuse of existing exemption policies that permitted schools to boost scores by exempting ELL students. Grade 4 Spanish-speaking students who may have been or are in bilingual programs can take the TAAS in Spanish rather than in English but no provision is made for speakers of other languages, or Grades 5–8 students, all of whom must now take the TAAS in English regardless of length of residence or English proficiency.

Educators in Texas tend to view the TAAS in very ambivalent ways. On the one hand it is feared and resented because of the pressure from all levels of the educational hierarchy and from the general public for students to pass the test. It is also widely perceived as having negative consequential validity: unlike standards-based performance assessments which can and should drive the curriculum in a positive way to reflect the higher-order thinking and literacy skills included in most standards, the TAAS is seen as encouraging teachers to teach to the test and focus instructionally only on the basic skills that are assessed by the test. On the other hand, however, educators generally acknowledge that the TAAS has resulted in greater accountability in the educational system and this accountability extends to ELL students, although sometimes in ways that undermine the effectiveness of bilingual programs because of the pressure to exit students into English as quickly as possible.

In short, within the United States context, the issues of whether to develop separate curriculum standards for ELL students and the appropriate ways of assessing the attainment of standards among ELL (and non-ELL) students remain unresolved and subject to political controversy and confusion.

Australia

Australia is an exception to the general trend to include ELL students in mainstream standards-based assessments. Australia has developed not one, but *two*, national assessment frameworks specifically for ELL students (Brindley, 1998b; Davison, 1998; Derewianka, 1997; Moore, 1996). Some states have also developed their own ELL Standards Frameworks, based on the national ESL Scales, to accompany their general Curriculum Frameworks. Victoria, for example, published the *ESL Companion to the English CSF (Curriculum Standards Framework)* in 1996 (Board of Studies, 1996). The complex political machinations that resulted in two sets of national English Language Scales aimed at the same population of students are not of concern here (see Moore, 1996). What is more relevant is the difference in orientation and purpose of the two instruments.

The scales developed by the National Languages and Literacy Institute of Australia (NLLIA) (McKay, 1995) represent detailed descriptors of learner development within the mainstream school context with different sets of descriptors for three distinct age groups (junior primary, middle/upper, and secondary learners). According to Derewianka:

> The descriptors vary according to the maturity of the student, the student's literacy background in L1 and in English, the learner's experience of the world, and previous schooling. They attempt to avoid as far as possible, a deficit model of description of student language development. They also anticipate the various domains in which students need to develop English – personal, social, general school contexts and English for academic purposes. In addition, the descriptors suggest the various roles that the teacher might play in supporting the student's learning, thereby seeing progress as a joint responsibility, not something inherent in the individual student. (1997: 23)

By contrast, ESL Scales developed by the Curriculum and Assessment Committee (CURASS) of the Australian Education Council are much more streamlined and are designed to provide a common language for identifying and reporting progress across all key learning areas. Their primary goal is summative reporting of learner achievement; in other words, 'checking on progress at particular points in time by assigning a level on the basis of teacher-conducted observations and assessments' (Brindley, 1998b: 58). According to Brindley, the CURASS ESL scales assume uniform progress along a unidimensional scale; they do not distinguish between the use of English in social and academic contexts; they do not distinguish between primary and secondary learners, and they describe outcomes of an assumed separate ESL curriculum rather than being anchored in a mainstream context.

Despite the confusion and heated discussion that the production of two very different sets of scales generated, Derewianka suggests that a 'consensus is emerging that both sets of scales are valuable resources and can be used in complementary ways' (1997: 27). The NLLIA Bandscales demystify the typical patterns of academic and social language development of ELL students at different age ranges and provide teachers with important information to guide instruction for individual learners. However, in contrast to the CURASS ESL Scales, they are more time-consuming and cumbersome to use in any large-scale way and the latter set of scales may give an adequate 'quick-fix' indication of the student's level of English language development for some purposes. However, the usefulness of the ESL Scales to guide instruction would appear to be very limited.

Still unresolved in the Australian context is the question of how separate ELL standards should articulate with the 'mainstream' standards. Are such frameworks describing academic achievement or language proficiency? How do teachers interpret deviations from 'typical' patterns of development? Derewianka's literature review highlights these and other issues that remain problematic in the use of performance assessment scales in the Australian context. She suggests that over time both the instruments and our ability to interpret them for different purposes will continue to be refined. She summarizes the concerns that have been expressed as follows:

> Previous studies have identified a number of concerns which need to be addressed regarding the nature of the frameworks (e.g. issues of construct validity, the question of 'proficiency v. achievement'); the way in which they define the ESL learner (e.g. their ability to account for the diversity of linguistic and cultural backgrounds, the extent to which they see diversity as a positive attribute); problems with reporting to stakeholders (e.g. the information needs of different stakeholders, the use of overly technical language); and their impact on teachers (e.g. the time required to assess, record and report, the stress of change, and perceived challenges to their professionalism). (1997: 55–56)

Despite these concerns and unresolved issues, there is considerable consensus in Australia about the need for separate benchmarks for ELL students. Davison, for example, points out that national benchmarks applied to all students are not a description of 'natural' stages in literacy acquisition 'but rather a reflection of particular literacy values, beliefs, and practices in Australian society which are translated into criteria and procedures for evaluation' (1998: 5). She suggests that we need to make much more explicit 'the particular ideologies underlying the establishment of such 'norms' for literacy development and the extent to which they assume mono-lingual English-speaking background and literacy experiences, thus rendering invisible alternative starting points and pathways to English literacy' (1998: 5). Consistent with Merino and Rumberger's (1999) observation in relation to the California context (cited above), she notes that research in Australia has demonstrated that 'ESL patterns of literacy development do not conform to the English speaking norms' (1998: 6).

Ontario, Canada

A revamped curriculum was implemented in Ontario in the late 1990s and basically the same standards are in place for ELL and non-ELL students. At the secondary level there is a separate ESL curriculum for immigrant students receiving ESL support for which partial funding is provided for three years. The complexity of exemption and accommodation policies can be illustrated by examining in more detail the Ontario assessment data published by the Education Quality and Accountability Office (EQAO). In its 1997 report, EQAO specified that an exemption from assessment tasks could be granted on the basis of 'the degree of the student's facility with the English language (for example, a student in the early stages of English acquisition)' (1997: 14).

The obvious difficulty here is the considerable latitude that teachers and principals have in deciding which ELL students will participate in the assessment and what constitutes 'the early stages of English acquisition'. Some educators or school districts may decide that this criterion means only those students whose English is truly minimal should be exempted, while others may interpret it to mean that any student who is still receiving formal ELL support qualifies for exemption. Still others who may be aware of the research showing that usually at least five years are typically required for ELL students to catch up to grade norms may exempt students who have been learning English in school for several years and who are reasonably fluent in conversational aspects of the language. Some educators may consider it both unethical and invalid to subject ELL students to an assessment procedure designed for native speakers of the language on the grounds that ELL students' probable poor performance will damage their academic self-esteem. Finally, there may also be a temptation on the part of some educators to exempt a significant number of ELL students on the grounds that the scores of these students may drag down the overall school average, thereby diminishing the school's reputation in the eyes of the community. These educators, with some justification, may consider that the publication of school rankings will be interpreted as an index of school quality, regardless of any qualifications that may be included in the 'small print' with respect to nature of the student population.[2]

In short, unless the criteria for exemption and accommodations for ELL students are spelled out more precisely and monitored by the province, a range of criteria will be applied in practice. This has the potential not only to undermine the overall interpretation of assessment results from large numbers of schools (since different criteria for inclusion of and accommodations for ELL students will have been applied) but also to effectively exclude ELL students from the accountability process. Unless the data from ELL students are disaggregated in a meaningful way from the results for native speakers of English, the assessment will provide no information on the extent to which schools are succeeding in meeting the educational needs of ELL students.

The interpretation difficulties can be illustrated from examination of the Grade 3 Reading results in the 1996–97 assessment (EQAO, 1997: 11). The category of 'ESL student' was determined by asking teachers if the student was in an ESL program. This is hardly a precise process in view of the fact that an extremely wide range of provision exists for ESL students, ranging from withdrawal programs to provision by the classroom teacher within the 'mainstream' program. On the four-point scale, where Levels 3 and 4 represent satisfactory performance and Levels 1 and 2 represent less than satisfactory performance, there is a 21-point gap between the percentage of non-ESL and ESL students showing evidence of Level 2 and above (82% v. 61%). There is a 20-point gap between the percentage of non-ESL and ESL students showing evidence of Level 3 and above (52% v. 32%). While these data clearly show that students identified by their teachers as participating in ESL programs are performing more poorly than those not so designated, they tell us very little about the extent to which ELL students' needs are being adequately addressed in the schools. We also do not know what proportion of the 11% of students who were either exempted from participating or whose data were inadequate for scoring purposes came from ESL backgrounds. Finally, it is likely that some of the students not receiving ESL support but who spoke another language at home might still be in the process of catching up academically. Klesmer (1994), for example, reported a significant gap between the time periods teachers considered ELL students needed to catch up academically (two to three years for reading) as compared to the time periods indicated by formal tests (over six years for reading).

One additional potentially very useful initiative should be considered: the publication of the specific ELL standards by the Teachers of English to Speakers of Other Languages (TESOL).

The TESOL Standards

One of the most coherent ESL Standards documents to have been produced is the *ESL Standards for Pre-K-12 Students* (1997) developed by the TESOL organization which is international in its mandate. One of the strengths of this document is potentially also one of its weaknesses. It was developed independently of any national or state school system and thus is capable of reflecting research and theoretical perspectives with minimal distortion from political imperatives. However, since it is not mandated by any educational jurisdiction, there are questions regarding the extent to which it will be adopted and the uses to which it will be put.

The effort to develop the ESL Standards was motivated by a desire to ensure educational equity and opportunity for ELL students. The effort began in the early

1990s when, in the words of Deborah Short, the project director, 'it quickly became apparent to ESL educators in the United States at that time that the students we serve were not being included in the standards-setting movement that was sweeping the country' (1997: v).

The ESL Standards distinguish three broad goals for ELL learners of all ages, focusing on personal, social and academic uses of English. The three goals are:

(1)   To use English to communicate in social settings.
(2)   To use English to achieve academically in all content areas.
(3)   To use English in socially and culturally appropriate ways.

Within each of these three Goals there are three content standards that describe more specifically what students should know and be able to do as a result of instruction. In addition specific *descriptors* are designed to assist educators in identifying curriculum objectives; sample *progress indicators* list assessable, observable activities that students may perform to show progress toward meeting the designated standard; *vignettes* of classroom-based scenes demonstrate the standards in action and describe student and teacher activities that promote English language learning; and finally, *discussions* explain how the instructional activities described in the vignette encourage students to meet the standard and make explicit the reasons these practices work well with ELL students.

The need for such standards is articulated clearly in the document:

> *ESL Standards* do not and cannot stand alone. Other professional organizations and groups have developed standards that are world-class, important, developmentally appropriate, and useful, These standards mandate high levels of achievement in content learning for all learners, including ESOL (English to speakers of other languages) students. But the content standards do not provide educators the directions and strategies they need to assist ESOL learners to attain these standards because they assume student understanding of and ability to use English to engage with content. Many of the content standards do not acknowledge the central role of language in the achievement of content. Nor do they highlight the learning styles and particular instructional and assessment needs of learners who are still developing proficiency in English. (TESOL, 1997: 2)

The TESOL Standards represent a major step forward in articulating a reasonable and pragmatic interpretation of the theory underlying second language acquisition. Like the NLLIA Bandscales in Australia, the focus of the TESOL document is on formative rather than summative assessment. It focuses teachers' attention on significant aspects of their students' language development and provides guidance for furthering their linguistic and academic progress. However, it remains to be seen to what extent it will exert a significant large-scale impact on practice in light of the marginal status that ELL students, and issues related to diversity in general, occupy in the larger scheme of educational policy development.

The Dilemmas of ELL Assessment

It is clear that, at least in North America, despite the paper avalanche of K-12 Standards documents, technical reports, and pre-programmed media commentary, few administrators have any idea how to accommodate ELL students in national and state mandated assessment programs. Policy-makers have been unwilling to accept or address the reality that it typically requires at least five years for these students to catch up to grade norms in English academic proficiency. Easy solutions are provided neither by including nor excluding ELL students in the assessment process. If ELL students are included in the testing, they will reduce the overall scores of schools that have large numbers of ELL students, even with significant accommodations in the test and/or testing procedures. In view of the high-stakes nature of these large-scale assessments, this low performance by the school will inevitably be misinterpreted by parents and policy-makers as a reflection of the quality of instruction in that school.

If ELL students are exempted from participation, there is no accountability mechanism in place to encourage principals and teachers to actively support their learning in an informed way. Furthermore, if ELL students are exempted, how long should they be exempted? To exempt for the period of five years that research suggests is minimally required to catch up academically in English would entail exempting a very significant proportion of the student population in most major North American cities and risk making the whole process a farce. To set an arbitrary time period such as two years length of residence for ELL student participation does not solve the problem because we know that limited English proficiency will render the test invalid, as an index of academic performance, for at least an additional three years after this period. For example, as pointed out in previous chapters, Cummins (1981b) reported that after three years length of residence, ELL students were still about one standard deviation below grade norms (15 standard score points) in English academic proficiency. Furthermore to exempt ELL students during their first two years of learning English is to exclude them from the accountability process during their most vulnerable stage of academic development.

A number of jurisdictions (e.g. Ontario) have tried to avoid the problem by providing general guidelines for exemption and accommodation and leaving the decision essentially in the hands of educators in the schools. However, this strategy risks abuse of the process and potentially generates uninterpretable data as different criteria for exemption will be applied in different schools with potentially significant impact on the school's overall performance. This is particularly the case in a context where the legitimacy of the assessment process for ELL students is not accepted by many educators. This has been the experience in Toronto where approximately 50% of the students come from language backgrounds other than English and many teachers initially considered the imposition of external tests for these students as both invalid and ethically problematic.[3]

In short, dilemmas regarding what to do about ELL students remain unresolved in jurisdictions where state-mandated assessment has been implemented.

In the absence of coherent policies, high-stakes testing will (1) significantly disadvantage ELL students with respect to the perception of their ability and progress; (2) provide essentially meaningless data unless the results for ELL students are disaggregated in a sophisticated way that links progress to factors such as stage of English proficiency development, length of residence, program type, and socioeconomic status.

Ideally, a standards-based assessment process should integrate in a coherent way an assessment of ELL students' progress in learning English within the total accountability scheme. Both the NLLIA Bandscales in Australia and the TESOL Standards serve as excellent examples of what should be assessed in this process. They could be used as a basis for the development of more focused ELL standards in educational jurisdictions where the goal would be to integrate the ELL standards with the specific standards adopted for particular content areas in that jurisdiction. In addition, performance assessment of achievement in particular content areas (e.g. through portfolios) should be implemented for ELL students rather than tests which tend to be much less sensitive to the progress that students might have made.

The downside of this scenario is that it would require that all classroom teachers be sufficiently familiar with the process of social and academic language development among ELL students to apply procedures such as the NLLIA Bandscales or TESOL Standards. Unfortunately, most teachers have had minimal exposure to these issues in their pre-service education and policy-makers in most jurisdictions are more concerned to cut back educational funding rather than to provide the funds necessary for professional development in this area.

Thus, although there undoubtedly are important benefits to the articulation of separate standards for ELL students, they are but one step in a much longer process of adjusting educational programs and instruction to the realities of diversity in the education system. Separate standards and performance assessment of ELL achievement in content areas are by no means a panacea, particularly since the vast majority of teachers have had minimal professional development in teaching or assessing ELL students. At least, however, in the jurisdictions where these instruments are being used there is a basis for progress. Also, the dilemma about the inclusion of ELL students in standards-based assessment has brought the issue to the attention of accountability-oriented policy-makers. The grand edifice of an effective and accountable school system where clear standards are articulated and attained, which many policy-makers are anxious to construct, risks tumbling to the ground unless coherent solutions are found for when and how to integrate increasing numbers of ELL students into the accountability framework.

In the next section, I sketch the experience at one high school in New York City which shows how performance assessment for ELL students can be implemented in a creative and enlightened way. What is clear from this example is that assessment is but one component in a broader process of re-aligning school programs and language policies in schools to take account of diversity as the norm rather than as a temporary aberration. Most policy-makers are still quite some way from realizing that effective standards-based reform will become possible only when they take seriously the fact that ELL students *are* the mainstream in an increasing number of urban and rural schools.

Performance Assessment as an Integral Component of Language Policy: The International High School at Laguardia Community College, New York City

This high school was founded in 1985 and offers learners of English a four-year comprehensive program where they can satisfy state mandated subject matter requirements while they are learning English (DeFazio, 1997; DevTech Systems, 1996). The students come from over 60 countries and speak more than 50 different languages. According to DeFazio, entering students score in the lowest quartile on tests of English proficiency, yet more than 90% of them graduate within four years and move on to post-secondary education.[4] As a result of the success of the original program, the philosophy and vision have been extended to two other international high schools in different boroughs of New York City.

The philosophy underlying instruction and school organization at the International High School includes the following beliefs:

- language is key to learning and increasing proficiency in academic language emerges most naturally in experiential, language rich, interdisciplinary study;
- fluency in two languages represents a resource for the student, the school, and the society;
- students learn best from each other in heterogeneous, collaborative groupings and learning is facilitated when collaboration exists between the school and the larger community;
- assessment must support individual growth and offer a variety of opportunities for students and faculty to demonstrate what they know and what they can do.

Among the innovations of the school is an emphasis on career education throughout the curriculum to encourage students to explore career options and motivate them to continue to expand their language sophistication. In addition, the teachers select other teachers to work within the school and have developed procedures to collaborate in providing each other with support and evaluation.

Rather than being organized according to traditional subject matter, the curriculum is structured in an interdisciplinary way. The teaching staff has organized itself into six interdisciplinary teams with each team responsible for developing at least two interdisciplinary programs. Each of these programs runs for 13 weeks with the team of teachers in the program responsible for overseeing a group of approximately 75 students. An example of the kind of interdisciplinary focus is one labelled *Origins, Growth and Structure* which involves chemistry, mathematics, linguistics, and art.

Rethinking the assessment of students has been a fundamental component of the restructuring process. Portfolios and exhibitions incorporating self, peer, and instructor evaluations play a major role. DeFazio notes that:

> Students at the International High School undergo portfolio assessment where they demonstrate their academic, linguistic and social proficiencies. Traditional testing is eschewed because it is often unfair and counterproductive to linguistically diverse populations who often know much more than they may be able to articulate in English. Portfolio assessment encourages retention, higher-level cognitive skills, development of internal standards, creativity and variety in solving problems. ... Students undergo these assessments informally during the course of a semester and more formally at the end. Students also present a master portfolio as they prepare to graduate. (1997: 102)

Although English is the usual language of instruction, the school is very much a bilingual/multilingual learning environment. Students' first languages are integrated into all phases of learning and assessment. In developing their portfolios in the various interdisciplinary programs, students write in both their first language and English, according to their choice. Teachers will often ask other students or members of the wider community for assistance in translating material that has been written in a language they themselves do not know. For example, in the *American Reality* program students formally explore their native language, human development, and career education, spending at least half their school day doing academic reading and writing in their native language. The first language resources to enable students to do this 'include abundant native language materials that teachers, students, and parents purchased for the school' (DeFazio, 1997: 104)

Parents have also become significantly involved in the school. Teachers have asked students to write letters home in their native languages to describe the interdisciplinary program the student is involved with, to explain what they are learning, and to explain the portfolio/grading process. Parents are encouraged to respond to the letters in either the native language or English. When parents' letters come back in the native language, the student is requested to translate the letters for the teacher into English. According to DeFazio:

> The letter writing campaign helped instantiate several aspects of the school's language philosophy: the importance of the native language; the need for the parent/guardian and school to work together regardless of language; the development and importance of bi- and multilingualism; language respect. (1997: 103)

In other projects, students produce both native language and English language magazines and articles; their writing is read by teachers and students proficient in the native language and if no one on the school staff is proficient in the students' language 'teachers go into the community to find volunteers willing to spend time reading and commenting on the students' work' (p. 104). DeFazio notes that students often comment on how much of their native language they had forgotten.

Other projects that students carry out in the *Origins/Growth/Structures* program include writing an autobiography or a biography of another student (again in English, their L1, or both) and investigations into comparative linguistics. For example, students work with the International Phonetic Alphabet to practice the sounds in each others' languages, to write cartoon strips in phonetics, and to attempt tongue twisters and riddles in the various languages represented in the class. Their linguistics projects culminate with a community research project that focuses on some issue or question related to language in the wider community. For example, students have interviewed members of their communities about bilingual education, dialect, and language prejudice and presented their findings as the last chapter of their linguistics book. Another project involves students writing multi-lingual children's books on some aspect of language or linguistics (e.g. *How the Chinese Got Language; The Monster that Ate Polish Words*, etc.).

What is most relevant to highlight in this example is the *language planning process* (Corson, 1998a, 1998b) that educators in the International High School implemented. This planning was designed to resolve problems they identified with respect to the match between the organization of the high school and ELL students' language and academic learning needs. Students entering the high school system with limited knowledge of English were severely handicapped by the inflexibility of the original curricular and assessment requirements. They did not know enough English to gain access to and learn a challenging curriculum at the same pace as native English-speaking students; despite this they were being assessed with the same tests as native English-speaking students. Consequently, many were failing courses or receiving grades that would preclude them from going on to university or college.

The planning process involved changing the curriculum and assessment proce-dures to enable students to use their prior knowledge (much of it in their L1) to facilitate their learning and demonstrate what they had learned. Use of students' L1 was encouraged, as was a cooperative and supportive inquiry process. Language itself became a major focus of study within the program.

The performance assessment implemented in the school was a vital component in the entire restructuring process. There is no way that traditional forms of assess-ment could have evaluated the learning and project work that students undertook. There is no doubt that traditional forms of assessment would have resulted in a high failure and drop-out rate because most students entering the school with minimal English would not have been capable of passing the tests at each grade level. This is illustrated in the fact that in New York City as a whole the drop-out rate among limited English proficient students is close to 30% compared to only 3.9% at the International High School (DevTech Systems, 1996).

There are two major implications of this program for the general issues discussed in this chapter: first, attempts to resolve the assessment and account-ability dilemmas discussed above that focus only on assessment are likely to experience minimal success; equitable assessment, whether performance-based or traditional, is meaningful only in the context of equitable and appropriate instruction, as illustrated in the program at the International High School. Thus, standards-based reform should place ELL students at the forefront of consideration rather than as a footnote; this implies focusing on how school programs can be adjusted to permit ELL students to demonstrate what they know (e.g. through their L1), apply this prior knowledge to their new learning, and experience affirmation of their identities in their interactions with educators. These directions are consistent with the theoretical framework outlined in Chapter 2 and have clearly been implemented in highly creative and effective ways at the International High School. Implementation of these initiatives at the International High School was possible only because alternative high schools are permitted the flexibility to develop their own design, including approaches to student assessment and accountability.

A second implication is that authentic performance assessment might be introduced as a complement to more traditional forms of standards assessment. Let us take Texas as an example. The problems of discrimination against ELL students, teaching to the test, and an instructional focus on lower-level basic skills associated with the TAAS have been noted above. These problems might be addressed to some extent if more extensive project-based work and associated portfolio assessment were introduced into the school program. As DeFazio (1997) notes, informal portfolio assessment could be carried out during the course of the year with a more formal assessment at the end. To integrate this process into the TAAS, the formal evaluation of students' portfolios could be combined with performance on the TAAS so that reliance on a formal test is reduced. An evaluation team at each school comprising the classroom teacher, school principal, and possibly school district representative could carry out the evaluation according to explicit guidelines provided by the state. A sample of portfolio evaluations could be audited by the state each year to ensure compliance with the state guidelines.

This system would have several clear advantages over the current situation. First, the proportion of overall evaluation contributed to by the portfolio and TAAS score could vary according to the student's length of residence and stage of English academic development. Thus, the portfolio assessment might contribute 100% of the evaluation for a beginning ELL student in Grade 5 but only 25% for advanced ELL students and fluent English-speaking students. Second, as noted by DeFazio, mandatory project-based work and portfolio assessment tends to drive positive instructional practices and encourage concept retention, 'higher-level cognitive skills, development of internal standards, creativity and variety in solving problems' (1997: 102). This would simultaneously reduce the focus on lower-level basic skills and the tendency to teach to the test.

An additional advantage of this type of system is that equitable and appropriate assessment practices become integrated into the overall functioning of the school. By contrast, the current TAAS procedure is imposed from outside, constricts the curriculum and takes time away from instruction. In this way the costs associated with training teachers to implement performance assessment can be viewed as costs for professional development and improved instruction.

In the final section of this chapter, I outline an additional direction that might be pursued to implement a system of curriculum-based assessment that is equitable, efficient and cost-effective while at the same time having positive consequential validity.

Lexical Knowledge as a Performance Indicator

Language permeates all facets of the curriculum and thus measures of performance in any content area are also likely to be measures of language (Oller, 1997). To illustrate this point, August and Hakuta quote the description of *mathematical communication*, one of seven mathematical performance areas for elementary school children, from the New Standards (1995) document which outlines performance standards in English Language Arts, Mathematics, Science, and Applied Learning. Students are required to:

> 'use appropriate mathematical terms, vocabulary, and language based on prior conceptual work; show ideas in a variety of ways including words, numbers, symbols, pictures, charts, graphs, tables, diagrams, and models; explain clearly and logically solutions to problems, and support solutions with evidence, in both oral and written form; consider purpose and audience when communicating; and comprehend mathematics from reading assignments and from other sources.' (cited in August & Hakuta, 1997: 120–121)

They note that 'quite clearly, this assessment of mathematical skills is also an assessment of language proficiency' (1997: 121). In a similar way, concepts in other areas of the curriculum are also linguistic concepts. The concepts of *democracy* in Social Studies and *photosynthesis* in Science are expressed through language, and linguistic communication in both oral and written modes is the primary means through which we come to understand these concepts. As noted in the previous chapter, comprehension is not an all-or-nothing phenomenon; it operates on a continuum that reflects increasing depth of understanding. Comprehension of the concept and lexical knowledge are two sides of the same coin and both can range from simple recognition of the concept/word to an ability to explain and define it, and use or apply it appropriately in a variety of contexts.

I suggest here a rationale for developing a system to assess the curriculum-based lexical knowledge that students have gained as a result of their instruction and engagement with literacy. This system would be a form of computer-adaptive assessment that could provide both a general assessment of lexical knowledge linked to language arts curricula and a more specific assessment aligned to the content of particular subject areas. The assumptions underlying the system are as follows:

- Lexical knowledge is a core component of academic language proficiency and consequently assessment of lexical knowledge can serve as an indicator of academic language proficiency.
- In the context of schooling, the lexical content of the curriculum progresses

from relatively high frequency words in the lower grades to increasing proportions of less frequent words at higher grades. By the same token, students' knowledge of the English lexicon grows in predictable ways. Students assimilate more and more low frequency words (predominantly from Greek and Latin sources) as they progress through the grades.

- Language is infused in all areas of the curriculum and is the medium through which instruction and assessment are carried out. While academic language proficiency is implicated to a greater extent in some areas of the curriculum than in others (e.g. Language Arts as compared to Mathematics), it represents an important dimension even in relatively 'non-verbal' areas.

- Assessment of the extent to which students have gained mastery of the general academic lexicon (as represented by the total vocabulary in school curriculum materials for each grade level) and the specific vocabulary of particular subject areas (as represented by the total vocabulary in curriculum materials for content areas such as Science, Social Studies, Mathematics) can serve as an indicator of the extent to which the content of those areas has been mastered. Its validity as an indicator will vary within and between subject areas; for example, it is likely to be a better indicator of reading ability than writing ability and of mathematical communication than mathematical calculation. These validity coefficients can easily be established by means of concurrent validation with full performance assessments of these curricular areas.

- Computer-adaptive assessment of students' academic lexical knowledge can be customized for particular purposes and groups of students. For example, it can be used as a classroom tool by individual teachers to monitor student mastery of material covered during instruction, to diagnose gaps in student knowledge, and to provide immediate feedback and instructional support for students. This can, in principle, be done in either L1 or L2 for ELL students, at least in the more common languages in a particular context. The system can also be used for quick summative assessment of programs after it has been validated against performance assessments in the relevant areas.

The way the system might work can be illustrated as follows: take a Grade 4 science unit on *sounds*, extract the concepts and vocabulary that are taught in this unit, and then construct a set of vocabulary assessment items using the same procedure as Laufer and Nation (1995, 1999) used in their research (the active version of the Vocabulary Levels Test). Consider the following items:

(1) Sound is made of <u>vib___</u> moving through matter such as air.
(2) When sound <u>wa___</u> travel through the air, your outer ear catches them.
(3) You should never stick objects in your ear because they could damage your <u>eard___</u>.
(4) The shell-shaped part of the inner ear is called the <u>co___</u>.

These items would be presented on the computer and the student would complete the word that has been partially omitted. When used as curriculum support, students could be given immediate feedback by the system, indicating the correct answer, an explanation of the concept and possibly graphics or illustrations from the curriculum program.

Bilingual versions of this procedure can be developed (e.g. Spanish–English) such that students could take the assessment/practice in their L1 (e.g. if they had recently immigrated or were in a bilingual program) or receive L1 support for an assessment/practice administered in English. In addition, the system could present the items aurally to younger students or those with lower literacy levels in English. Another variation would be to adopt the procedure of the *Bilingual Verbal Abilities Tests* (Muñoz *et al.*, 1998) and present items initially in English but re-test failed items in the L1 in order to get a better assessment of the student's overall (L2 + L1) verbal conceptual knowledge.

The system could sample from the universe of items for particular grade levels and content areas according to a variety of criteria depending on the purpose of the assessment. If the assessment were part of an accountability-oriented summative assessment process for Grade 4 Science, the system might select 60 items representing equally the different areas specified in Grade 4 science standards and including a range of items within each area from relatively easy to relatively difficult. Word frequency values might serve as a starting point for assessing difficulty even within particular technical content areas.

There is no problem in principle in having the same system used for accountability-oriented summative assessment as for formative assessment and instructional support because the system would choose different sets of items from the universe for each administration or practice session within the parameters set by teachers or test administrators. Furthermore, as in most forms of authentic performance assessment, it is fine for teachers to 'teach to the test' because the 'test' reflects the totality of the curriculum.

Such a system would be relatively straightforward to update to keep aligned with curriculum changes and, as it was used, norms could be generated for native speakers and for ELL students according to level of English proficiency (as assessed through a system such as the TESOL Standards), length of residence, L1 literacy level/previous schooling, and grade. In other words, performance of ELL students could be interpreted in much more valid and precise ways than the present simple score on a test that may or may not align with curriculum standards.

One potential objection to the system is that vocabulary items of the kind outlined above do not assess real depth of vocabulary knowledge. A student may know the word 'vibrations' in item (1) above but have very limited understanding of the concept beyond the fact that it has something to do with hearing (see for example, Schmitt, 1999). This is an issue in any test situation and obviously is one of the arguments for authentic performance assessment which can reflect the depth of students' understanding in a variety of ways. However, the downside is that this form of authentic assessment is difficult and expensive to carry out on a large scale and also difficult to quantify on a reliable basis.

The issue of the extent to which curriculum-based vocabulary assessment of the kind being proposed reflects depth of vocabulary in addition to range is at one level an empirical question. To what extent are vocabulary size and depth related to each other? Also, if the curriculum-based vocabulary size procedure correlates highly with authentic performance assessments, then this would constitute evidence for validity despite the fact that range rather than depth of vocabulary is being assessed. There is empirical evidence available on some of these issues. For example, Qian's (1998) study with Korean and Chinese adult learners showed equivalent and extremely high (0.78-0.82, $N = 74$) correlations between reading comprehension (based on a TOEFL test) and measures of both vocabulary size (Nation's Vocabulary Levels Test) and vocabulary depth (a modified version of Read's (1993, 1995) depth of vocabulary knowledge procedure). Vocabulary depth and vocabulary size showed a correlation of 0.82 with each other and 0.63 and 0.69 respectively with a test of morphological knowledge. The correlations between vocabulary size and depth are similar to those reported by Read (1995). Thus, the evidence suggests that vocabulary size represents a reliable indicator of vocabulary depth (at least as measured by Read's test).

However, it is also possible in principle to accommodate an assessment of vocabulary depth within the system in a variety of ways. For example, for a sample of the items that students get correct, they could be asked a series of more challenging questions reflecting greater depth of understanding. Or they could be asked to write a one-paragraph explanation of how sound is caused by vibrations. In this second instance, the response would be evaluated either by the teacher (in a formative assessment context) or by an outside team of evaluators (in an accountability-oriented assessment context).

The essential point I want to make is that such a system potentially incorporates considerable flexibility to address the concerns of both construct and consequential validity. It can be customized for a variety of contexts and purposes to take advantage of the positive features of both authentic performance assessment and standardized tests without most of the limitations of either. The items are drawn directly from the curriculum and assess students' mastery of that curriculum content. It also provides immediate feedback and diagnostic information of direct usefulness to learning and instruction. At the same time, the achievement levels of particular students, classrooms, and schools can be quantified and interpreted for accountability purposes. This accountability is attained in ways that do not discriminate against ELL students who can (to the extent feasible) take the procedure in both their L1 and English and whose performance can easily be disaggregated from that of non-ELL students. Furthermore, the performance of ELL students can be interpreted in light of their length of residence, previous schooling, and general academic proficiency in English.

Conclusion

In analyzing the dilemmas of including ELL students in statewide large-scale assessments we are faced once again with questions such as: What exactly are we assessing when we test ELL students' achievement in language arts or science or mathematics? How does 'language proficiency' relate to 'academic achievement?' Are they very much the same construct as some would argue (e.g. Oller, 1997), or are they different?

I have suggested that because the curriculum is infused with language and academic language proficiency is implicated across curricular areas, standards-based assessment procedures that ignore the reality of ELL students are undermining their own validity and credibility. There are no easy or cheap solutions to the problem of ensuring valid assessment of ELL students and including them in the accountability process. The positive aspect of this is that school systems and policy-makers are finally required to address the broader issues of providing equitable instruction and assessment for culturally and linguistically diverse students who now constitute the mainstream population in many North American cities.

The appropriate directions to pursue entail developing separate ELL standards (e.g. for English Language Development) or adapting existing standards frameworks (e.g. NLLIA Bandscales or TESOL Standards) for both English Language Development and specific curricular areas. Despite the problems of cost, reliability, and large-scale feasibility, authentic task-based performance assessment is warranted in educational contexts where summative standardized assessment of language proficiency or academic development will result in inappropriate inferences regarding ELL students' progress or learning potential. As noted above in relation to the TAAS in Texas, summative assessments of this type can also constrict the curriculum in ways that are highly problematic from a pedagogical perspective. By contrast, various forms of performance and portfolio assessment provide a much more accurate picture of ELL students' progress and academic potential and are more likely to promote effective instructional practices (e.g. DeFazio, 1997; O'Malley & Pierce, 1996). In some contexts, a combination of traditional and authentic performance-based assessment might be feasible where more weight would be given to the performance assessment among ELL students who are still in the process of learning English and catching up academically.

Finally, I proposed the development of a computer-adaptive curriculum-based assessment and instructional support system that attempts to combine the advantages of both performance assessment and more traditional forms of assessment. The bottom line, however, is that whatever assessment system is adopted, it will be truly equitable and effective for ELL students only to the extent that the instructional program is equitable and effective. Unfortunately, issues of program effectiveness for ELL students are also mired in controversy, particularly in the United States context. I address some of the theoretical issues underlying the controversies surrounding bilingualism and bilingual education in the following chapters.

Notes

1. August and Hakuta (1997) report slightly different figures based on several studies and surveys. According to their review, 55% of states allow modifications in the administration of at least one of their assessments to accommodate ELL students. The most common modifications are extra time (20 states), small-group administration (18 states), flexible scheduling (16 states), simplification of directions (14 states), use of dictionaries (13 states) and reading of questions aloud in English (12 states). They note that only five states require ELL students to take state-wide assessments required of other students and in three of these ELL students may be exempted under certain conditions. Thirty-six states exempt ELL students from such assessments, although 22 of those states require these students to take the assessments after a given period of time (usually one to three years).

2. In the Ontario system there are disincentives for exempting ELL students, not least of which is the fact that if a school totally exempts a student, he or she must be physically removed from the class during the full ten days of the test. A spare classroom or other location must be found for students who are exempted. In addition, a teacher is required to supervise these students, at a point when all teacher resources are required to assist with those students needing accommodations (but not exemptions). What does happen are partial exemptions: the ELL child participates in the test activities, but some of the sections are not sent in (personal communication, October 1999, Burns Wattie, ESL Consultant, Toronto District School Board). In addition, the Ontario data appear to suggest that factors associated with socioeconomic level and parental education are more significant than ESL background alone in determining test performance, although analyses that disaggregate the relevant factors have not been published. It is not clear to what extent this pattern is affected by the nature of the performance assessment (which attempts to assess learning that all students have had opportunities to participate in) or by the accommodations provided for ELL students whose need for assistance might be more obvious than that of English-speaking low socioeconomic students.

3. Burns Wattie (personal communication, October 1999) points out that the way in which the tests are administered over the ten-day teaching and testing period will make a significant difference. When 'the testing is achieved in a very respectful way' it is unlikely to exert negative effects on students' self-esteem even when they are in the relatively early stages of learning English.

4. DevTech Systems (1996) report somewhat different graduation statistics based on 1993 New York City Board of Education data. They report that 54% of International High School students graduated in four years compared to 34% of all Limited English proficient students and 44% of all students in New York City.

Part 3
From Bilingual Education to Transformative Pedagogy

Introduction

Bilingual education programs are being increasingly implemented in countries throughout the world and a considerable volume of research exists on the outcomes of these programs under different conditions. Yet bilingual education continues to be politically controversial in some countries (e.g. the United States) and its underlying theoretical basis is still not well understood either by policy-makers or the general public. The following four chapters address aspects of the politics, theory, and practice of bilingual programs in the international arena. My goal is to give a sense of how coercive relations of power operating in the wider society affect what transpires between educators and students in the classroom. I also want to illustrate how academic discourse regarding bilingual education in the United States has become embroiled in the pattern of societal power relations.

There is an Alice-in-Wonderland quality to much of the debate in the United States. For example, opponents of bilingual education have attempted to constrict the framework of discourse to the issue of 'transitional bilingual education' versus 'structured English immersion' (e.g. Rossell & Baker, 1996). This strategy may be intended to obscure the fact that:

- most academic advocates of bilingual education have argued strongly *against* quick-exit transitional programs as very much inferior to programs that attempt to develop bilingualism and biliteracy;
- most academic opponents of bilingual education have argued strongly *for* two-way bilingual immersion programs which involve far greater amounts of L1 instruction than the transitional programs they oppose.

Not surprisingly, the issues remain confused in the minds of many policy-makers. However, there is increasing consensus among applied linguists that the central issue is not whether a program is labelled 'bilingual education' or 'English-only' but whether it is *enrichment-oriented* as compared to *remedial-oriented* (see Fishman,

1976; Hornberger, 1991). At a more 'macro' level, the extent to which the program views students' languages as *resources* to be developed as compared to *problems* to be resolved also appears to distinguish effective from ineffective programs. Although the term 'enrichment bilingual education' was introduced by Fishman (1976), it has recently been reconceptualized by Cloud, Genesee, and Hamayan (2000) in the context of the outcomes of three specific program types. These are outlined below and then placed in the context of Richard Ruiz' (1984) discussion of language as resource, language as right, and language as problem. The concepts of *Enrichment Education* and *language as resource*, together with the empowerment framework presented in Chapter 2, frame the discussion of bilingual education in Chapters 7 through 10.

Extending Enrichment Bilingual Education: Revisiting Typologies and Redirecting Policy

Cloud *et al.* (2000) cluster three types of programs under the heading of what they label *Enriched Education* (EE).

Second language immersion programs

These serve language majority students and use a language other than English to teach at least 50% of the curriculum during the elementary or secondary grades. Canadian French immersion programs fall into this category.

Developmental bilingual education programs

These serve language minority students and use the minority language for close to 50% of instruction during the elementary grades (and occasionally into high school) to develop academic proficiency in students' first language. Bilingual programs for minority francophones in Canada represent a strong form of developmental bilingual education with instruction primarily through French from kindergarten through Grade 12 (K-12). Similarly, Maori-medium programs in New Zealand use Maori for most of the instruction throughout elementary school and into secondary school. In the United States, most developmental programs involve Spanish and English as languages of instruction with the proportion of Spanish falling to between 25 and 50% of instruction by the end of elementary school.

It is important to note that the line between developmental and transitional bilingual programs is not always clear. Sometimes the term 'late-exit transitional' is used for developmental programs (e.g. Ramírez, 1992). Also, not all early-exit programs are remedial in orientation. Educators in some of these programs attempt to communicate a strong affirmative message to students regarding the value of their first language and a genuine attempt is made to promote biliteracy within the constraints of the program. However, this pattern is probably the exception rather than the rule in programs labelled 'transitional bilingual education' in the United States.

Two-way immersion or 'dual language' programs

These represent a combination of immersion and developmental bilingual programs. They serve both language minority and language majority students in the same classrooms with approximately half the students coming from each group. There are two major models of two-way programs: 90/10 and 50/50 programs, representing the proportion of time devoted to the minority and majority languages in the early grades of the program. The 90/10 model aims to promote the minority language as much as possible in the early grades on the assumption that this is the language that requires the most support since it is generally of lower status in the wider community than English. The 50/50 model is based on the belief that both languages need to be acquired from the beginning of schooling and the best way to do this is to split the instructional time between the two. The available research data suggest that both of these programs can work well. Although these programs are primarily associated with the United States, variants have been implemented in other contexts also. For example, a number of the *Gaelscoileanna* (all-Irish schools) in Ireland involve native speakers of Irish and English (Cummins, 1978) and the bilingual programs in Edmonton, Alberta, also involve native speakers of both languages (e.g. Ukrainian–English; German–English, etc.) as well as second language learners (Lupul, 1985).

Enrichment programs generally fall into the *language-as-resource* or *language-as-right* orientation in Richard Ruiz' language planning framework.

Ruiz' framework for language planning

In distinguishing between language-as-problem, language-as-right, and language-as-resource, Ruiz (1984) notes that the *language-as-problem* orientation focuses on the resolution of societal problems associated with language learning or linguistic diversity. Provision of transitional bilingual education programs in the United States illustrates this orientation. The goal is to solve 'problems' associated with the fact that children enter school not speaking the usual language of instruction in school.

The *language-as-right* orientation is illustrated in the language rights enacted in many European countries during the past 20 years (see Skutnabb-Kangas, 2000). Another prominent example is the language rights that Canadian official language minorities (English in Quebec and French in the rest of Canada) have to education conducted through their mother tongue. Ruiz notes that these two orientations have been the predominant ones in the international literature: 'While problem-solving has been the main activity of language planners from early on …, rights-affirmation has gained in importance with the renewed emphasis on the protection of minority groups' (1984: 17). He suggests that while problem- and rights-orientations are valid and important they are inadequate alone as a basis for language planning in linguistically diverse societies because hostility and divisiveness are often inherent in these orientations. He argues that greater emphasis should be given to a *language-as-resource* orientation in which linguistic diversity is seen as a societal resource that should be nurtured for the benefit of all groups within the society. An implication is that majority groups should be encouraged to acquire minority languages and opportunities for trilingualism should be provided for all students in schools that promote a minority language in addition to the dominant language.

The chapters that follow focus on some of the ways in which theory, politics, and research intersect in debates regarding the medium of instruction in schools. Chapter 7 examines the status of two hypotheses I proposed during the 1970s: the threshold and interdependence hypotheses. These hypotheses have been influential, controversial, and widely misinterpreted both by advocates and opponents of bilingual education. I try to clarify the hypotheses and their educational implications and review recent research data that speak to their validity (e.g. the Ramírez (1992) study).

Chapter 8 turns to the controversies surrounding research in the United States context. I critique the paradigms of research that have been widely implemented, arguing that the role of theory in research implementation and interpretation has been neglected. Both opponents and many advocates of bilingual education have assumed that only experimental or quasi-experimental treatment versus control group studies are relevant to policy issues regarding program effectiveness. I argue that this perspective is extremely narrow and a much wider array of research studies are directly relevant to policy when viewed through a theoretical lens. In this chapter, I also review different interpretations of the large-scale Thomas and Collier (1997) study as well as outcomes from dual language (two-way bilingual immersion) programs to illustrate the types of conclusions that can be drawn from different orientations to research, theory and policy.

Chapter 9 examines how rational communication regarding the education of bilingual students might be re-established in contexts where the issues have become highly politicized. I illustrate the politicized nature of the debate with reference to the account provided by Lourdes Diaz Soto (1996) of the ugly controversy surrounding bilingual education in 'Steeltown', Pennsylvania. This sad story of racism in action demonstrates how everybody loses in a context of coercive relations of power. I also draw on Marcia Moraes' (1996) use of Bakhtin's theoretical framework to suggest ways in which dialogue might be re-established between opponents and advocates of bilingual education on the basis of a rational interpretation of the available research evidence.

Chapter 10 returns to the perspective outlined in Chapter 2 that the micro-interactions between educators and students are the central determinants of both knowledge generation (learning) and identity formation. The theoretical issues regarding the nature of language proficiency and bilingual development discussed in Chapters 3–9 amount to very little unless their implications are built into classroom instruction. This final chapter charts directions towards a transformative pedagogy designed to create contexts of empowerment for ELL students.

An assumption of this chapter is that many of the issues that are currently being debated both within bilingual programs (e.g. whether L1 or L2 should be used as the initial language of reading instruction, how much instructional time should be spent in L1 and L2) and between advocates and opponents of bilingual education are 'surface structure' issues. These issues are much less significant than the issue of the extent to which the instruction is genuinely transformative of student experience and challenges the operation of coercive relations of power in school and society.

Chapter 7
The Threshold and Interdependence Hypotheses Revisited

Not all regions in Scotland had schools, even well into the nineteenth century. And where schools existed, students and educators alike faced another dilemma: largely for political reasons, English was the preferred medium of instruction, despite obvious problems in communication. Worse, many schools ignored Gaelic entirely, both because it was politically expedient and because there were no Gaelic texts to use. Fortunately, by the early nineteenth century, attitudes had softened somewhat; the Scots had not risen against the English recently, and *educators discovered that Gaelic students learned to read English more easily if they had a basic grounding in Gaelic grammar and literature*. The fluency of MacDougall's written Gaelic indicates that he was one of the lucky ones, taught in both Gaelic and English.

(From Elizabeth Thompson's Introduction to Robert MacDougall's *The Emigrant's Guide to North America*, published originally in 1841 and republished in English translation, 1998, pp. x–xi; emphasis added)

The interdependence hypothesis was proposed to address exactly the same type of observation that Elizabeth Thompson refers to in the quotation above with reference to the early 1800s in Scotland: academic language proficiency transfers across languages such that students who have developed literacy in their L1 will tend to make stronger progress in acquiring literacy in L2. For much of the 20th century, however, educators held to a very different set of assumptions. They considered bilingualism to be a source of academic retardation and cognitive confusion and actively sought to rid bilingual students of the encumbrance of their mother tongue (see Hakuta, 1986). Currently, this perspective is expressed in the strong opposition to bilingual education for minority language students in the United States and elsewhere, as illustrated by the passage of Proposition 227 in California in June 1998.

The major assumption regarding language learning that props up arguments against bilingual education is the *maximum exposure* or *time-on-task* hypothesis. Rosalie Pedalino Porter has expressed this perspective as follows:

> The evidence of direct correlation between early, intensive second-language learning and high level of competence in the second language is inescapable, as is the on-task principle – that is, the more time spent learning a language, the better you do in it, all other factors being equal. (1990: 119)

According to Porter, the major problem with transitional bilingual education is that the time spent through the medium of L1 does not contribute to the learning of English. She suggests that the success of French immersion programs for majority language students in Canada augurs well for the implementation of English immersion for minority language students in the United States. She has more recently described bilingual education as 'terribly wrongheaded' and 'a failure' (Porter, 1998). Clearly, the time-on-task hypothesis predicts diametrically opposite outcomes of bilingual programs than the interdependence hypothesis; specifically, if time-on-task or maximum exposure to English is the determining factor in English academic achievement then all forms of bilingual education will dilute instructional time devoted to English and will result in significant adverse effects. By contrast, the interdependence hypothesis predicts no adverse effects on English from well-implemented bilingual programs as a result of transfer of academic knowledge and skills across languages.

The threshold and interdependence hypotheses were proposed more than 20 years ago as an attempt to account for research data showing that:

- Many bilingual students experience academic failure and low levels of literacy in both their languages when they are submersed in an L2-only instructional environment; however, bilingual students who continue to develop both languages in the school context appear to experience positive cognitive and academic outcomes.
- Contrary to what the time-on-task notion would predict, instruction through a minority language does not appear to exert any adverse consequences on students' academic development in the majority language. This holds true for students from both minority and majority language backgrounds in various kinds of bilingual programs.

During the past 20 years, both hypotheses have exerted significant influence on educational policy and practice. Most opponents of bilingual education in the United States, and even some advocates, would claim that the influence of these hypotheses has been negative and prejudicial to the educational success of bilingual children (e.g. Edelsky, 1990; Rossell & Baker, 1996). Both hypotheses have been the focus of considerable empirical research, with overwhelming evidence in support of the interdependence hypothesis and also some research support for the threshold hypothesis.

I believe that the interdependence hypothesis is of crucial importance in understanding the nature of bilingual students' academic development and in planning appropriate educational programs for students from both minority and majority language backgrounds. The threshold hypothesis, by contrast, is less relevant to policy and practice. I noted in Chapter 2 that the hypothesis remains speculative and is not essential to the policy-making process. What *is* relevant is the well-supported finding that the continued development of bilingual children's two languages during schooling is associated with positive educational and linguistic consequences. This 'additive bilingualism enrichment principle' (Cummins, 1996) highlights the fact that bilingualism is not just a societal resource, it is also an individual resource that potentially can enhance aspects of bilingual children's academic, cognitive and linguistic functioning.

The threshold hypothesis went further than this, however. It speculated about the conditions under which language as an intervening variable might affect cognitive and linguistic growth. Specifically, it was hypothesized that continued academic development of both languages conferred cognitive/linguistic benefits whereas less well-developed academic proficiency in both languages limited children's ability to benefit cognitively and academically from interaction with their environment through those languages (e.g. in school). Simply put, students whose academic proficiency in the language of instruction is relatively weak will tend to fall further and further behind unless the instruction they receive enables them to comprehend the input (both written and oral) and participate academically in class. A student whose academic proficiency in the language of instruction is more strongly developed is less vulnerable to inappropriate instruction (e.g. English submersion programs). In other words, educational treatment interacts with students' academic language proficiency to produce positive or negative educational and cognitive outcomes.

The threshold hypothesis was initially vague in many respects; for example, with respect to the lower threshold necessary to avoid adverse developmental consequences, the extent to which students need to attain strong proficiency in both L1 and L2 as opposed to just the predominant language of their environment and school instruction was never specified, for the simple reason that these conditions will vary so extensively. In some cases, academic and conceptual input is provided in both languages whereas in others this input is predominantly in the L2. In the former case, the hypothesis would argue that a certain degree of academic proficiency in both languages is required whereas in the latter, attaining sufficient proficiency in just the L2 (the language of school instruction) might suffice.

The hypothesis also left vague what aspects of proficiency were being referred to and, as noted in Chapter 4, initially used the highly problematic term 'semilingualism' to refer to relatively limited academic knowledge of both languages. As Martin-Jones and Romaine (1986) pointed out, notions of 'native-speaker competence' were also problematic in the absence of specification of what aspects of proficiency were being referred to.

My concern in this chapter is to clarify the empirical and theoretical status of both the threshold and interdependence hypotheses and also their respective relevance to the education of bilingual students. Why bother focusing on the threshold hypothesis when I have said that it is not directly relevant to policy and practice? Simply because both advocates and opponents of bilingual education have frequently misinterpreted this hypothesis and its implications. The major misinterpretation derives from conflating the threshold and interdependence hypotheses. For example, some educators in countries as diverse as the United States and New Zealand have invoked the 'threshold hypothesis' as justification for delaying the introduction of English literacy instruction for a considerable period. They assume that the minority language must be built up to a 'threshold level' before literacy in the majority language should be introduced; they also assume that transfer of knowledge and academic skills across languages will happen automatically. As noted in Chapter 1, I see these extrapolations of the threshold and interdependence hypotheses as problematic and unsupported by the research evidence.

One source of the confusion is the conflation of the two hypotheses. Rebecca Freeman, for example, expresses a common (mis)understanding of what the threshold hypothesis is saying: 'Cummins ... argues that a certain 'threshold' level of proficiency in the native language (e.g. Spanish) is necessary for Spanish-speaking students' development of high levels of proficiency in English' (Freeman, 1998: 12–13). Although she does not link this interpretation to recommendations regarding the organization of L1 and L2 instruction, many policy-makers and practitioners who are strongly supportive of bilingual education have conflated the hypotheses as a way of legitimating the strong promotion of literacy in students' L1 and avoiding premature exit from bilingual programs. These educational goals are certainly legitimate but this particular interpretation of the threshold and interdependence hypotheses is inaccurate. Conflating the two hypotheses has resulted in considerable confusion regarding their theoretical claims and also their practical implications for bilingual programs. This is particularly the case regarding the appropriate time to introduce reading instruction in the majority language within a bilingual program. *Neither hypothesis says anything about the appropriate language to begin reading instruction within a bilingual program nor about when reading instruction in the majority language should be introduced.*

Opponents of bilingual education have also inappropriately conflated the two hypotheses. Christine Rossell, for example, expressed herself more colourfully than Freeman when she was quoted in *Education Week* as saying:

> The advantage of native-tongue instruction is that it's easier to read and write in a language you understand. ... So why do they not get bigger effects? Because of this cockamamie theory that the academics have constructed that you have to reach a high level of proficiency in your native tongue before you can be transitioned to English. (Viadero, 1999: 12)

A second source of confusion regarding the interpretation of the threshold hypothesis is that the term currently is being used in academic research to refer to two related but distinct phenomena. On the one hand, there is the use that I and others have employed to refer to the operation of language proficiency as an intervening variable in explaining the different educational and cognitive outcomes associated with bilingualism. The other use is in the context of second language reading research and the hypothesis has also been labelled the 'short-circuit' hypothesis (Bernhardt & Kamil, 1995; Bossers, 1991; Clarke, 1979, 1980). Hulstijn characterizes this 'threshold hypothesis' succinctly as follows: 'L1 reading performance can only begin to correlate substantially with L2 reading after knowledge of L2 has attained a threshold' (1991: 9). Much of this research has originated from the question posed by Alderson in 1984: 'Is second language reading a language problem or a reading problem?' Bernhardt and Kamil express the linguistic threshold or short-circuit hypothesis as follows:

> In order to read in a second language, a level of second language linguistic ability must first be achieved. ... Firm first language reading skills could not help readers compensate when reading in a second language. A lack of second language linguistic knowledge ultimately 'short-circuited' the first language reading knowledge. In other words, a given amount of second language grammatical/linguistic knowledge was necessary in order to get first language reading knowledge to engage. (1995: 17)

As Hulstijn points out, 'these two distinct threshold notions do not rule out each other; they are evidently compatible with each other' (1991: 10). In discussing this research, I will revert to the original term – short-circuit hypothesis – simply to avoid confusion with the use of the term 'threshold' in my own work. It is evident from Bernhardt and Kamil's description that the short-circuit hypothesis is more related to the interdependence hypotheses than to the (Cummins) threshold hypothesis. In fact, it can be read as an argument regarding the conditions under which interdependence (L1/L2 transfer) will occur. Thus, there is again the potential confusion that results from conflating the two hypotheses.

In the first two sections, I summarize some of the recent research that addresses the threshold and interdependence hypotheses and then I address three issues: (1) the relationship between the interdependence hypothesis and the enhancement of cognitive and linguistic processes associated with additive forms of bilingualism; (2) the educational implications of the interdependence and threshold hypotheses and (3) the relationship of these hypotheses to the 'short-circuit' hypothesis. My goal is to clarify both the theoretical status of the hypotheses and their implications for policy and practice.

Empirical Research on the Threshold Hypothesis

As I noted briefly in Chapter 2, there is considerable empirical research supporting the positive consequences of continued development of academic skills in two or more languages. When bilingualism and biliteracy develop under these additive conditions, students experience demonstrable metalinguistic, academic, and possibly cognitive advantages. Claims regarding 'cognitive' advantages are somewhat tentative for several reasons; first, if 'cognitive' is taken to refer to 'non-verbal abilities' then the evidence supporting positive effects is weak and inconsistent. If, however, 'cognitive' is seen as including 'verbal cognitive abilities' (e.g. vocabulary/concept knowledge, metalinguistic knowledge, deductive verbal reasoning), then there is strong evidence that 'cognitive' abilities are also enhanced by the development of biliteracy skills. These data have been reviewed extensively (e.g. Baker, 1996; Cummins, 1984, 1996; Hakuta, 1986) and only the research that pertains directly to the threshold hypothesis will be outlined here.

Levels of bilingualism and metalinguistic awareness

The findings of a series of Australian studies (Ricciardelli, 1992, 1993) are consistent with the threshold hypothesis and illustrate the types of advantage that bilingual information processing might confer on the developing child. Ricciardelli conducted two studies to investigate the influence of bilingualism on children's cognitive abilities and creativity. The first involved 57 Italian–English bilingual and 55 English monolingual children who were aged five or six at the time of the study. This study found that children who were proficient in both Italian and English performed significantly better than children who were proficient in English only (the high English monolingual group) and those bilinguals who were proficient in English but less proficient in Italian, on several measures reflecting creative thinking (the Torrance Fluency and Imagination measures), metalinguistic awareness (Word Order Correction), and verbal and non-verbal abilities.

The second study was conducted in Rome with 35 Italian–English bilingual and 35 Italian monolingual five- and six-year-old children. Again, those children who were proficiently bilingual in Italian and English performed significantly better than the other groups on the Torrance Fluency and Imagination measures as well as on Word Order Correction and Word Reading. Ricciardelli concludes that these data are consistent with the threshold hypothesis:

> Furthermore, [both studies] are consistent with Cummins' Threshold Hypothesis … in that an overall superiority on the examined cognitive measures was found only for those children who had attained a high degree of bilingualism. (1993: 346)

Another series of seven studies, carried out between 1978 and 1987 in a totally different socio-cultural context (Orissa, India), shows a consistent pattern of results. Mohanty (1994) studied large numbers of monolingual and bilingual Kond tribal children who had varying degrees of contact with the dominant language of Orissa, namely Oriya. The monolingual children came from areas where the original Kui language of the Konds had given way to Oriya monolingualism as a result of contact with speakers of the dominant language. In other areas, a relatively stable form of Kui–Oriya bilingualism exists where Kui is used predominantly in children's homes but contact with Oriya through peers and others in the neighbourhood results in most children having a considerable degree of bilingualism by the time they start school, which is conducted through the medium of Oriya. Despite the differences in language use, the Konds are relatively homogenous with respect to Kond identity, socioeconomic, and cultural characteristics. The context thus provides a unique opportunity to study the impact of bilingualism in relative isolation from the social, political and economic factors which frequently confound comparisons between monolingual and bilingual groups.

Mohanty's studies show a clear positive relationship between bilingualism and cognitive performance including measures of metalinguistic ability. He suggests that bilinguals' awareness of language and their cognitive strategies are enhanced as a result of the challenging communicative environment in which their bilingual abilities have developed. He interprets the findings as supporting both the threshold and interdependence hypotheses.

Bialystok (1987a, 1987b, 1988) has also carried out a series of studies that suggest a positive influence of bilingualism on children's metalinguistic awareness. The advantages are more evident for bilinguals who are more fully fluent in their two languages. She suggests that 'the level of bilingualism is decisive in determining the effect it will have on development' (1988: 567). Bialystok (1991) has interpreted the research data as indicating that bilingual children have enhanced ability in the analysis and control components of linguistic processing. She argues that processing systems developed to serve two linguistic systems are necessarily different from the same processing systems that operate in the service of only one.

Similar enhancement of bilinguals' ability to focus on the form of linguistic input is reported by Galambos and Hakuta (1988) with low-income Spanish–English bilinguals in the United States. They suggest that the degree of enhancement of metalinguistic awareness is related to the degree to which the child's two languages are developed, a position which is obviously consistent with the threshold hypothesis.

The threshold hypothesis is also supported by research carried out in the Basque country. Lasagabaster (1998) set out to investigate the extent to which the threshold hypothesis could be applied to a trilingual school situation (Basque, Spanish, English). Participants were 126 Grade 5 and 126 Grade 8 students. The Grade 5 students were in their second year of studying English and the Grade 8 students were in their third year. Students' academic knowledge of Basque, Spanish, and English was assessed together with a non-verbal ability test (Raven's Progressive Matrices) as a control measure and a test of metalinguistic abilities as dependent variable. Groups were formed based on median splits carried out on the three language measures (Basque, Spanish, English) and comparisons made between those 'highly competent' (i.e. above the median) in three languages, those highly competent in two languages, those highly competent in one language, and those below the median in all three languages.

Lasagabaster reported that performance on the metalinguistic ability test was directly related to the levels of bilingualism/trilingualism in the order outlined above. Those above the median in three languages performed significantly better than all other groups with those below the median in all three languages demonstrating less well-developed metalinguistic abilities than the other three groups. Although in the predicted direction, differences were not significant between those above the median in two languages as compared to those above the median in just one, possibly, as Lasagabaster suggests, because those who had become highly proficient in three languages would have been the ones who might have made the differences between the other two groups significant. The differences between the groups could not be attributed to non-verbal ability or socioeconomic or sociocultural status. Lasagabaster concludes that 'these findings confirm the threshold hypothesis' (1998: 131).

Enhancement of third language learning

Two studies carried out in Canada suggest that development of bilingual students' L1 academic proficiency can positively influence the learning of additional languages. Both studies were conducted in a large Metropolitan Toronto school board that offers French as a second language for 20 minutes a day from Grades 1 through 4 followed by the option of a French–English bilingual program (50% English, 50% French) from Grades 5 through 8. Students also have the option of participating in a heritage language program involving the teaching of languages other than English or French from Kindergarten through Grade 8.

The first study (Bild & Swain, 1989) reported that Grade 8 students from heritage language backgrounds who were enrolled in the French–English bilingual program performed better than an English-background group in the same program on a variety of grammatical measures of French but not on measures of lexical knowledge. A significant positive correlation between the number of years in heritage language classes and indices of French proficiency was also noted in this study.

The second study (Swain & Lapkin, 1991; Swain, Rowen & Hart, 1991) involved more than 300 Grade 8 students in the same bilingual program. Swain *et al.* compared four groups of students on various measures of French proficiency: (1) those who had no knowledge of a heritage language (HL); (2) those with some knowledge but no literacy skills in the HL; (3) those with HL literacy skills but who mentioned no active use of HL literacy; and finally, (4) those who understood and used the HL in the written mode. The first group had parents with higher educational and occupational status than the other three groups who did not differ in this regard.

Highly significant differences in favour of those students with HL literacy skills (groups 3 and 4) were found on both written and oral measures of French. These differences are particularly noteworthy in view of the fact that these students came from considerably lower socio-economic backgrounds than students who spoke English as their first language. There was also a trend for students from Romance language backgrounds to perform better in oral aspects of French but the effect of this variable was much less than the effect of literacy in the heritage language. The authors conclude that there is transfer of knowledge and learning processes across languages and development of L1 literacy entails concrete benefits for students' acquisition of subsequent languages.

These two studies taken together suggest that trilingualism is a feasible educational goal and that the development of literacy in the minority language spoken in the home facilitates the learning of a third language in school.

Bilingualism and mathematical reasoning

Several studies have reported findings consistent with the threshold hypothesis in the area of mathematics reasoning (Clarkson, 1992; Clarkson & Galbraith, 1992; Dawe, 1983; Li, Nuttall & Zhao, 1999). Dawe's study was designed to provide a direct test of the threshold hypothesis. It involved a sample of 53 Punjabi, 50 Mirpuri, and 50 Italian bilinguals together with 167 English monolingual children. All the children were between 11 and 14 years old, had been born in Britain, and were considered by their teachers to be fluent in English. The measuring instruments included a test of deductive reasoning in mathematics in English, tests of English reading comprehension and logical connectives in English, both designed to tap cognitive competence in the language rather than just surface fluency, and a test of L1 listening comprehension, again designed to tap deeper levels of academic or logical competence in the language. Finally, all students were administered a measure of non-verbal reasoning ability. The English logical connectives measure assessed knowledge of words and phrases which serve to link propositions in reasoned argument (e.g. 'if ... then', 'either ... or' etc.) and was included because of the relevance of this kind of linguistic knowledge for deductive reasoning in mathematics.

The threshold hypothesis was strongly supported for the Mirpuri sample (all boys) and partially supported for the Punjabi and Italian samples. Dawe summarizes the data for the Mirpuri sample as follows:

> The overall picture which emerges is that high scores on the test of deductive reasoning for Mirpuri boys are associated with high L1 and L2 competence and a specific knowledge of logical connectives in English. Low scores are associated with low L1 and L2 competence, poorer knowledge of logical connectives and a tendency to switch languages more frequently in mathematics lessons at school. (1983: 339)

For the Punjabi group the trends were in the predicted direction. Those strong in both languages performed best followed by those with one language dominant and those weak in both languages. However, the differences did not attain significance. For the Italian group there was strong support for the lower threshold (those weak in both languages did more poorly) and weak support for the upper threshold insofar as the trends were in the predicted direction but did not attain significance. However, Dawe notes that a far greater proportion of the high achieving Italian students were literate in Italian, a trend which is consistent with the threshold hypothesis.

Although it did not directly set out to investigate the threshold hypothesis, a study carried out by Li, Nuttall & Zhao (1999) reports results that are consistent with its tenets. They reported that Chinese-American students who had developed

Chinese writing skills (i.e. were literate in Chinese) performed significantly better on the mathematics subtest of the Scholastic Aptitude Test (used for university entrance) than equivalent Chinese-American students who had not developed literacy in Chinese. They suggest that the training in spatial and geometrical relationships entailed in learning written Chinese may have contributed to the mathematical differences observed.

My point in reviewing these data is not to argue for the threshold hypothesis. In its specifics it is largely irrelevant to the theoretical framework presented in this volume and elsewhere (e.g. Cummins, 1986, 1996). What is highly relevant for policy is that the continued development of academic proficiency in bilinguals' two languages is associated with enhanced metalinguistic, academic, and cognitive functioning. However, the data summarized above and considerably more research summarized elsewhere (e.g. Baker, 1996; Cummins, 1984) demonstrate that the threshold hypothesis is not an unreasonable idea.[1] My view has not changed from that which I expressed in 1991:

> The threshold hypothesis, on the other hand, while it has had valuable heuristic impact, goes beyond what can be empirically validated at this point, given our limited ability to specify and operationalize the nature of language proficiency. The empirical evidence continues to mount that bilingualism is associated with enhanced metalinguistic functioning (and possibly with advantages in other aspects of cognitive performance), but whether or not there are specific 'thresholds' associated with these metalinguistic and cognitive outcomes is unclear. The issue may be of only academic interest since the practical implication of the data is the same: schools should attempt to encourage minority students to develop their L1 abilities to as great an extent as possible both to stimulate transfer to L2 and to reap the significant personal and more subtle educational benefits of additive bilingualism. (1991a: 86)

Empirical Research on the Interdependence Hypothesis

Some of the research evidence for the interdependence or common underlying proficiency (CUP) hypothesis has been reviewed in Chapter 2, including Fitzgerald's review which concluded that 'considerable evidence emerged to support the CUP model' (1995: 181). Some examples will suffice to demonstrate the overwhelming trend of research evidence in support of the interdependence hypothesis. There are two major sources of evidence: first from research on the relationships between academic proficiency in L1 and L2, and second, from research on bilingual education that demonstrates transfer of academic knowledge and skills across languages.

Relationships between L1 and L2 academic proficiency

Umbel and Oller (1995) reported strong positive relationships between receptive vocabulary in Spanish (L1) and English (L2) in a sample of 102 English-Spanish first, third and sixth graders in Miami, Florida. Spanish vocabulary knowledge accounted for almost 27% of the variance in English vocabulary knowledge. They conclude that:

Spanish receptive vocabulary development was the strongest predictor of English receptive vocabulary scores. This finding is consistent with Cummins' (1979, 1984) interdependence hypothesis, which postulates that a strong foundation in one language facilitates second language development. (1995: 73)

An evaluation study of five schools attempting to implement the Theoretical Framework for the Education of Language Minority Students developed by the California State Department of Education (1985) showed consistently higher correlations between English and Spanish reading skills (range $r = 0.60$ to 0.74) than between English reading and oral language skills (range $r = 0.36$ to 0.59) (California State Department of Education, 1985). Oral language skills were assessed by a detailed rating scale completed by teachers. In these analyses scores were broken down by months in the program (1–12 months through 73–84 months). It was found that the relation between L1 and L2 reading became stronger as English oral communicative skills grew stronger ($r = 0.71$, $N = 190$ for students in the highest category of English oral skills). This is not surprising in view of the fact that some basic knowledge of the second language is necessary before we would expect transfer of L1 reading skills and knowledge to make a difference in L2 reading.[2]

González (1986, 1989) similarly demonstrated a considerably stronger relationship between English and Spanish reading skills than between English reading skills and English oral communicative skills in a study involving Spanish-speaking immigrant students in the United States. Two groups of Grade 6 students attending a bilingual program were compared on English and Spanish measures: 34 students who were born and schooled for at least two years in Mexico prior to immigrating to the United States and 38 students who were born in Mexico but immigrated to the United States before beginning school. Both groups were of low socioeconomic status. It was found that the Mexican-schooled group performed significantly better on both Spanish and English reading tasks (assessed by means of the CTBS Español and Stanford Reading Test respectively) than the group schooled entirely in the United States. The US-schooled group outperformed the Mexican-schooled group on an English oral language measure (the Bilingual Syntax Measure (BSM) II) and on ratings of English communicative proficiency. Both groups showed a high level of competence in conversational aspects of Spanish proficiency. In the total sample, Spanish and English reading comprehension scores showed a correlation of 0.55 (p <0.01) with each other whereas the respective correlations between reading in English and Spanish and oral language measures in each language (BSM II) was 0.33 for English and 0.22 for Spanish. Ratings of communicative competence in each language did not correlate significantly with reading measures in either language. González concluded that the academic foundation developed by the Mexican-schooled students transferred to the acquisition of English academic skills, giving these students an advantage over their US-schooled peers. This academic advantage in English was evident despite the fact that both groups attended the same bilingual program and the US-schooled children were more conversationally fluent in English.

It is interesting to note that ratings of communicative competence were also strongly related across languages in González' study, suggesting that personality attributes of the child underlie their communicative behaviour in each language. Similar findings are reported by Cummins *et al.* (1984) for Japanese–English bilingual students (Grades 2–6) and by Verhoeven (1991b) for Turkish–Dutch six-year-old bilingual children. Measures of interactional style (Cummins *et al.*) and pragmatic competence (Verhoeven) derived from spontaneous speech in face-to-face oral interaction situations were even more strongly related across languages than was the case for cognitive/academic measures.[3]

A large number of other studies demonstrating significant cross-lingual relationships for cognitive/academic aspects of L1 and L2 proficiency are reviewed in Cummins (1991c). These studies demonstrate interdependence for writing abilities in addition to reading (e.g. Canale, Frenette & Bélanger, 1987; Cumming, 1987, 1989).They involve languages that are linguistically distant from each other (e.g. Japanese–English, Chinese–English, Hebrew–English, Turkish–Dutch, etc.) as well as languages that are relatively close to each other linguistically (e.g. English–French, English–Spanish). As noted also by Genesee (1979), the cross-lingual correlations for dissimilar languages tend to be less, albeit still significant, than for languages that are similar. This suggests that in the case of linguistically distant languages, interdependence across languages derives primarily from cognitive and personality attributes of the individual; in the case of linguistically more congruent languages, the relationship derives from both underlying attributes and linguistic factors (e.g. cognate relationships between L1 and L2). The conclusion reached on the basis of the Cummins (1991c) review highlights the importance of both input in the L2 and the attributes that the learner brings to the task of acquiring L2 (e.g. L1 literacy) in explaining the development of L2 conversational and academic proficiencies:

> The data reviewed in this paper suggest that both attributes of the individual learner and aspects of the input received by the learner contribute in important ways to the development of different aspects of L2 proficiency. The importance of quantity of input is clearly indicated by the consistently strong relationships observed between length of residence (LOR) and L2 acquisition. However, LOR was not equally related to all aspects of proficiency. For example, in the Cummins *et al.* (1984) study, acquisition of L2 conversational syntax was considerably more dependent on LOR than either L2 academic proficiency or interactional style. Cognitive and personality attributes of the individual contributed as much to the explanation of variance in these dimensions as did LOR. These learner attributes, however, were unrelated to individual differences in L2 conversational syntax. In general, moderately strong cross-lingual relationships are observed for attribute-based aspects of L1 and L2 proficiency as a result of the fact that underlying attributes of the individual manifest themselves in the individual's performance in both languages. (Cummins, 1991c: 84)

The consistency of the research evidence with the interdependence hypothesis can be seen from several studies reported in a recent volume edited by Durgunoğlu and Verhoeven (1998). For example, in a study involving children in a Hebrew–English bilingual program in Toronto, Geva and Wade-Wooley report that 'positive and significant correlations among parallel L1 and L2 reading and spelling measures provide evidence for common underlying cognitive and linguistic mechanisms' (1998: 105). Their findings, together with other data which they review involving Hebrew–English, Persian–English, and French–English bilinguals, supports the existence of 'a central linguistic-cognitive processing executive which controls the development of literacy skills' (p. 104) but they also show that some aspects of reading acquisition are orthography-specific and thus the development of reading and spelling skills in Engish and Hebrew is not isomorphic.

Verhoeven and Aarts (1998) examined the relationship between school literacy and functional literacy in both L1 and L2 of 188 Turkish-speaking students in their first year of Dutch secondary school. The average length of residence of the students in Turkey was about 10 years. In addition, a sample of 140 Dutch-L1 and 276 Turkish-L1 students in Turkey participated in the study. The functional literacy instrument consisted of authentic text from a letter, a page of a TV guide, the front page of a newspaper, an application form, and a map, items commonly found in both Turkey and the Netherlands. According to Verhoeven and Aarts, LISREL analysis showed two important trends:

> In both languages, school literacy skills influence functional literacy skills. Furthermore, the literacy level in Turkish has an effect on literacy level in Dutch. The interdependency of literacy skills in the L1 and L2 as well as the possibilities for transfer of L1 skills to the L2, are valid not only with respect to school literacy, but also with respect to functional literacy skills. (1998: 130)

In a study of 46 first graders in two bilingual education classes in the United States, Durgunoğlu (1998) reported that Spanish phonological awareness by itself explained 47% of the variance in English phonological awareness. Furthermore, Spanish phonological awareness and letter identification accounted for 84% of the variance in English spelling performance. In the letter identification test, children were given credit for letters correctly identified in either Spanish or English. English and Spanish word recognition were significantly correlated ($r = 0.51$). Identical correlations were observed between English word recognition and English spelling as between English word recognition and Spanish spelling ($r = 0.55$). These data are very similar to the findings of Cummins (1991b) with kindergarten and Grade 1 English–Portuguese bilingual children in Toronto. Durgunoglu concludes by noting that there are many different rationales for providing good bilingual education, but 'the rationale of L1 helping L2 literacy development is the one supported by these data' (1998: 144).

Finally, Wagner's (1998) longitudinal study of Arabic-L1 and Berber-L1 students' acquisition of French (introduced in Grade 3) demonstrated a strong relationship between Arabic and French literacy development (assessed at Grade 5) despite the fact that the two languages are unrelated in terms of orthography, lexicon, and syntax. He concludes: 'The finding that Arabic skills were strongly predictive of French-literacy acquisition further suggests that second-literacy acquisition is substantially dependent on first literacy acquisition' (1998: 179).

Evidence for interdependence from bilingual education

As noted in Chapter 2, the results of virtually all evaluations of bilingual and second language immersion programs are consistent with predictions derived from the interdependence hypothesis insofar as instruction through a minority language appears to result in no adverse consequences for students' academic development in the majority language (see for example, Baker & Prys Jones, 1998; Cummins & Corson, 1997). In other words, transfer across languages of conceptual knowledge and academic skills (such as learning and reading strategies) compensates for the reduced instructional time through the majority language. Three studies illustrate the process, one from Africa (Williams, 1996), one from Europe (Verhoeven, 1991a), and one from the United States (Ramírez, 1992).

Williams examined the impact of language of instruction on reading ability in L1 and L2 in Malawi and Zambia. In Malawi, Chichewa is the language of instruction for Years 1–4 of primary school with English taught as a subject. In Zambia, English is the medium of instruction with one of seven local languages taught as a subject. Williams administered an English reading test and a local language reading test (Chichewa in Malawi and the almost identical Nyanja in Zambia) to Year 5 learners in six schools in each country. He reported no significant difference in English reading ability between students in each country, despite the huge difference in amount of English instruction, but large differences in favour of Malawi in local language reading ability. He concludes that these results 'are consistent with research on minority groups suggesting that instruction in L1 reading leads to improved results in L1 with no retardation in L2 reading' (1996: 183).

Similar conclusions come from longitudinal research with Turkish–Dutch bilingual students in the Netherlands (Verhoeven, 1991a). The study involved 138 Turkish working class children in The Netherlands who had been in the country for at least two years during which time they attended nursery school. Some of the children were taught to read first in Dutch in Grade 1 after which they were given some hours per week of Turkish (L1) literacy classes in Grade 2. Other children experienced a transitional approach in which initial reading instruction was in Turkish with instruction in Dutch reading introduced two months later in the context of simultaneous instruction in L1 and L2 literacy. Using LISREL structural equation analysis, Verhoeven found evidence of bidirectional relations of causality between L1 and L2. Among students in the transitional program where students were taught to read initially in Turkish, there was evidence of positive transfer from Turkish to Dutch in both decoding and reading comprehension. In the program that taught reading initially through Dutch with later (Grade 2) Turkish literacy instruction, the direction of causality was from Dutch (L2) to Turkish (L1). This pattern of findings suggests that in an additive educational context where there is opportunity and motivation to develop literacy skills in both languages, interdependence will operate both from L1 to L2 and from L2 to L1. Verhoeven concludes:

> With respect to linguistic measures, it was found that a strong emphasis on instruction in L1 does lead to better literacy results in L1 with no retardation of literacy results in L2. On the contrary, there was a tendency of L2 literacy results in the transitional classes being better than in the regular submersion classes. Moreover, it was found that the transitional approach tended to develop a more positive orientation toward literacy in both L1 and L2. ... Finally, there was positive evidence for ... the interdependence hypothesis. From the study on biliteracy development it was found that literacy skills being developed in one language strongly predict corresponding skills in another language acquired later in time. (1991a: 72)

The Ramírez (1992) study was funded by the US Department of Education and involved 2352 Latino elementary schoolchildren in nine school districts, 51 schools and 554 classrooms. It compared the academic progress of children in three program types: (1) English immersion, involving almost exclusive use of English throughout elementary school, (2) early-exit bilingual in which Spanish was used for about one-third of the time in kindergarten and first grade with a rapid phase-out thereafter, and (3) late-exit bilingual that used primarily Spanish instruction in kindergarten, with English used for about one-third of the time in Grades 1 and 2, half the time in Grade 3, and about 60% of the time thereafter. One of the three late-exit programs in the study (Site G) was an exception to this pattern in that students were abruptly transitioned into primarily English instruction at the end of Grade 2 and English was used almost exclusively in Grades 5 and 6. In other words, this 'late-exit' program is similar in its implementation to early-exit. Students were followed through to the point where each program model assumes they would be ready for mainstreaming into the regular program; in the case of the early-exit and immersion students this was Grade 3 while late-exit students were followed to the end of Grade 6.

It was possible to compare directly the progress of children in the English immersion and early-exit bilingual programs but only indirect comparisons were possible between these programs and the late-exit program because these latter programs were offered in different districts and schools from the former. The comparison of immersion and early-exit programs showed that by the end of Grade 3 students were performing at comparable levels in English language and reading skills as well as in mathematics. Slightly more of the early-exit bilingual students were reclassified as fully English proficient by the end of Grade 3 than was the case for immersion program students (72% v. 67%). Students in each of these program types progressed academically at about the same rate as students in the general population but the gap between their performance and that of the general population remained large. In other words, they tended not to fall further behind academically between first and third grade but neither did they bridge the gap in any significant way.

While these results do not demonstrate the superiority of early-exit bilingual over English immersion, they clearly do refute the argument that there is a direct relation between the amount of time spent through English instruction and academic development in English. If the 'time-on-task' notion were valid, the early-exit bilingual students should have performed at a considerably lower level than the English immersion students, which they did not.

The 'time-on-task' notion suffers even further indignity from the late-exit bilingual program results. In contrast to students in the immersion and early-exit programs, the late-exit students in the two sites that continued to strongly emphasize primary language instruction throughout elementary school (at close to 40% of instructional time) were catching up academically to students in the general population. This is despite the fact that these students received considerably less instruction in English than students in early-exit and immersion programs and proportionately more of their families came from the lowest income levels than was the case for students in the other two programs. It was also found that parental involvement (e.g. help with homework) was greater in the late-exit sites, presumably because teachers were fluent in Spanish and students were bringing work home in Spanish in addition to English.

Differences were observed among the three late-exit sites with respect to mathematics, English language (i.e. skills such as punctuation, capitalization etc.) and English reading; specifically, according to the report:

> As in mathematics and English language, it seems that those students in Site E, who received the strongest opportunity to develop their primary language skills, realized a growth in their English reading skills that was greater than that of the norming population used in this study. If sustained, in time these students would be expected to catch up and approximate the average achievement level of this norming population. (Ramírez, 1992: 37–38)

By contrast, students in Site G who were abruptly transitioned into almost all-English instruction in the early grades (in a similar fashion to early-exit students) seemed to lose ground in relation to the general population between Grades 3 and 6 in mathematics, English language and reading. The report concludes that:

> Students who were provided with a substantial and consistent primary language development program learned mathematics, English language, and English reading skills as fast or faster than the norming population used in this study. As their growth in these academic skills is atypical of disadvantaged youth, it provides support for the efficacy of primary language development in facilitating the acquisition of English language skills. (1992: 38–39)

An additional conclusion highlighted by Ramírez (1992) was that learning English language skills by ELL students requires six or more years of special instructional support, a finding clearly consistent with the results of studies other studies that have addressed this issue (e.g. Collier, 1987; Cummins, 1981b; Hakuta *et al.*, 2000; Klesmer, 1994).

These findings are entirely consistent with the results of other bilingual programs and show clearly that, as predicted by the interdependence hypothesis, there is no direct relationship between the instructional time spent through the medium of a majority language and academic achievement in that language. On the contrary, there appears to be an inverse relation between exposure to English instruction and English achievement for Latino students in this study.

Beykont (1994) has carried out insightful additional analyses of the Ramírez data from Site E which involved Puerto Rican students in New York City. The sample of two cohorts for whom data were available from Grades 3 through 6 consisted of 139 students (74 girls and 65 boys), the majority of whom were born in the United States. The progression of Spanish and English reading scores from Grades 3 through 6 was related to a variety of predictor variables (preschool attendance, parental attitudes towards bilingual education, classroom organization (grouping patterns)).

Beykont reported the following findings:

- Students made significant progress between Grades 3 and 6 in both English and Spanish reading. Spanish reading scores remained higher than English reading throughout this period but students approached grade norms rapidly in both languages.
- Academic progress in English reading was faster for those students whose initial (Grade 3) Spanish reading scores were high and slower for those with low initial Spanish reading scores. A strong relationship was also observed between English and Spanish reading at the Grade 3 level.
- Students whose parents held favourable attitudes towards bilingual education made faster progress in both English and Spanish reading between Grades 3 and 6 than those whose parents held unfavourable or ambivalent attitudes.
- Students tended to show higher English and Spanish academic performance in classrooms that relied on smaller groups rather than on larger or whole class grouping.

Beykont concludes that:

In fact, children's consistently rapid progress in both English and Spanish reading through the sixth grade is remarkable, considering that the academic performance of native speakers typically levels off starting in the fourth grade, when children are expected to move beyond 'learning to read' and start 'reading to learn' difficult content matter. ... Of those Puerto Rican children who stayed in the program, about 50% of Cohort 1 read at or above the sixth grade level in both English *and* Spanish; an additional 21.4% read at or above grade level in Spanish only and the rest read one or two years below grade level in English and Spanish. In Cohort 2, which was followed for three years [to the end of Grade 5], about 37% read at or above fifth-grade level in English *and* Spanish; an additional 31% read at or above fifth-grade level in Spanish only by the end of the study. ... These results clearly indicate that early assessment of

English skills conceals the long-term benefits of extensive Spanish instruction for biliteracy development. (1994: 140)

In summary, both the correlational research and the outcomes of bilingual programs are overwhelmingly consistent with predictions derived from the interdependence hypothesis. Wagner has expressed clearly the major educational implication of these data in commenting on the strong relationship he observed between Arabic and French literacy development:

> This particular result seems to suggest that increasing a child's competence in a first literacy … may be a good way to promote second-literacy acquisition. Because first- versus second-language literacy training is a critical policy issue in many multilingual and multiliterate societies, this outcome may be useful in helping to think about which languages will be most effective for teaching reading, whether for children or in adult literacy programs. (1998: 181)

Interdependence and Additive Bilingual Enrichment

As noted above, the cross-lingual interdependence of academic language proficiency reflects both the cognitive attributes of the individual (broadly defined) and, in the case of related languages, linguistic similarities between L1 and L2. The cognitive attributes of the individual essentially refer to what the individual has learned up to this point, both with respect to conceptual knowledge (knowing that) and skills (knowing how). Thus the linguistic and literacy-related knowledge and skills that an individual has learned in his or her L1 will be brought to bear on the learning of academic knowledge and skills in L2. This would include, as Bernhardt notes, literacy variables such as 'operational knowledge that refers to knowing how to approach text, why one approaches it, and what to do with it when a text is approached' (1991: 35). Also clearly relevant is the background knowledge, or knowledge of the world, which permits learners to derive meaning from text in both L1 and L2. We can talk of the influence of these factors loosely in terms of 'transfer', although in reality they form the underlying cognitive apparatus that is used to interpret textual meaning rather than being 'transferred' directly across languages.

Linguistic knowledge, on the other hand, does transfer across languages in a more direct way than underlying operational or conceptual knowledge. Letter recognition among languages that share a Roman orthography is one example. Clearly, cognate relationships across languages also provide opportunities for transfer of linguistic knowledge.

As Verhoeven's (1991a) research demonstrates, cross-lingual influence can operate in both directions, from L1 to L2 and from L2 to L1, depending on the degree of motivation and opportunity generated by the particular acquisition contexts. For example, in an L2 submersion context where there is no L1 literacy instruction either in school or home, transfer of L2 literacy knowledge and strategies to L1 literacy is less likely than in an additive context where literacy development in both languages is encouraged.

The way context influences transfer across languages is illustrated by the findings of Cashion and Eagan (1990) in a Canadian French immersion program. In these programs, initial literacy instruction is usually totally through the medium of French (L2). Cashion and Eagan report that as students spontaneously acquired English reading and writing skills prior to formal instruction in English reading, they transferred this knowledge from English (L1) to French (L2). This process of transfer from the stronger (English) to the weaker language (French) was much more evident than transfer of literacy-related skills from French to English despite the fact that literacy instruction in school was only through French.

In additive contexts where literacy in both languages is being developed, it is easy to see how the two-way transfer that frequently occurs (i.e. interdependence) can evolve into greater metalinguistic awareness among bilingual students. In this sense, the interdependence and additive bilingual enrichment hypotheses are related. In a frequently quoted passage, Vygotsky (1962) expressed the linkage between L1–L2 interdependence and the potential for enhancement of L1 metalinguistic awareness:

> Success in learning a foreign language is contingent on a certain degree of maturity in the native language. The child can transfer to the new language the system of meanings he already possesses in his own. The reverse is also true – a foreign language facilitates mastering the higher forms of the native language. The child learns to see his native language as one particular system among many, to view phenomena under more general categories, and this leads to awareness of his linguistic operations. Goethe said with truth that 'he who knows no foreign language does not truly know his own'. (1962: 110)

In short, although the interdependence and threshold hypotheses are addressed to separate issues, the cognitive and linguistic enhancement associated with additive bilingualism will operate through the same central processing system that underlies the interdependence of L1 and L2 proficiencies. As noted above, I have used the term *common underlying proficiency* to refer to the interdependence of concepts, skills and linguistic knowledge that makes transfer possible. In reference to the interdependence of L1–L2 academic proficiencies, this common underlying proficiency is probably better conceived in a more dynamic way in terms of a *central processing system* comprising (1) attributes of the individual such as cognitive and linguistic abilities (e.g. memory, auditory discrimination, abstract reasoning, etc.) and (2) specific conceptual and linguistic knowledge derived from experience and learning (e.g. vocabulary knowledge). The positive relationship between L1 and L2 can thus be seen as deriving from three potential sources: (1) the application of the same cognitive and linguistic abilities and skills to literacy development in both languages; (2) transfer of general concepts and knowledge of the world across languages in the sense that the individual's prior knowledge (in L1) represents the foundation or schemata upon which L2 acquisition is built; and (3) to the extent that the languages are related, transfer of specific linguistic features and skills across languages.

Educational Implications of the Interdependence and Threshold Hypotheses

The research data reviewed above show clearly that within a bilingual program, instructional time can be focused on developing students' literacy skills in their primary language without adverse effects on the development of their literacy skills in English. Furthermore, the relationship between first and second language literacy skills suggests that effective development of primary language literacy skills can provide a conceptual foundation for long-term growth in English literacy skills. These data unequivocally refute the time-on-task hypothesis.

It is important, however, to highlight what the research data are *not* saying in addition to what they are saying. Neither the research data sketched above nor the interdependence or threshold hypotheses say anything about:

- whether L1 or L2 should be the *initial language* of reading instruction within a bilingual program;
- the *amount of time* that should be spent through each language in the early grades, except that there should be sufficient emphasis on academic development in *both* languages during the elementary school years to provide students with the opportunity to develop academic knowledge and skills in each language;
- *when to introduce* English reading and language arts within a bilingual program;
- whether there is any *specifiable or threshold level of 'oral English'* that students should have acquired before formal English reading instruction is introduced.

On all of these issues, no definitive statements can be made since a variety of models appear to work well under different conditions. For example, Noonan, Colleaux and Yackulic (1997) showed that the order of introduction of reading instruction in a Canadian French–English bilingual program (intended for English-L1 students) made no difference either to English or French reading achievement.

My own interpretation of the data is that these issues represent 'surface structure' issues that are much less central than 'deep structure' issues. These deep structure issues include the extent to which the school is making a serious attempt to promote students' L1 literacy (and awareness of language generally), and the extent to which the teacher–student interactions in the school are affirming of students' academic and cultural identities and strive to establish genuine partnerships with culturally diverse parents. In other words, what distinguishes effective from ineffective programs is the extent to which the program challenges the historical pattern of coercive relations of power. The promotion of biliteracy is one important component of this process.

With respect to the role of students' L1, the research is very clear that for groups that appear to be at risk of school failure promotion of strong L1 literacy makes a powerful contribution to students' academic success. In most bilingual programs for Spanish-speaking students, it will also make much more sense to introduce reading in L1 rather than in L2 for three reasons: (1) Spanish is the language students know best; (2) it is generally considered much easier to acquire decoding skills in Spanish than in English because of the greater regularity of sound–symbol relationships; and (3) introduction of reading in Spanish affirms students' identity as a result of communicating to students and parents the importance of the family language and culture.

However, the same arguments may not apply as clearly to groups such as Chinese or Japanese students because of the much more complex literacy systems in those languages which take even native speakers in monolingual contexts many years to acquire. Also, the potential advantages of introducing reading in L1 to Spanish-speakers should not blind us to the fact that other models that have introduced reading in L2 before L1 or in both language in quick succession have also been successful (e.g. El Paso Independent School District, 1987). The central factor appears to be the extent to which the school is making a serious attempt to promote students' L1 literacy rather than the specific linguistic order in which reading is introduced. Similarly, the exact amount of instructional time spent through each language is less important than the commitment of the program to develop strong biliteracy and bilingualism among students.

The 'collaborative empowerment' framework elaborated in Chapter 2 is much more relevant to explaining the conditions under which various kinds of educational provision will result in positive academic outcomes than the threshold or interdependence hypotheses in isolation. Furthermore, speculation regarding 'thresholds' of proficiency is just that: speculation. The more directly relevant research finding is that continued development of both languages (additive bilingualism) is associated with subtle positive academic and linguistic outcomes. However, this additive bilingualism enrichment principle says nothing directly about which program models are likely to result in additive bilingualism, apart from the fact that the program should encourage L1 literacy development.

As noted above, both advocates and opponents of bilingual education have sometimes conflated the threshold and interdependence hypotheses and drawn inappropriate conclusions as a result. Rossell and Baker, for example, conflate them under the label 'the facilitation theory' arguing that together the two hypotheses predict that 'transitional bilingual education' will result in positive academic outcomes, provided students stay in the program for at least seven years and reach a certain threshold in the native language (1996: 27). On the basis of this interpretation, they dismiss as contrary to the 'facilitation theory' the findings of Hébert *et al.* (1976) showing that the amount of French (L1) instruction in programs for minority francophones in Canada was unrelated to achievement in English. In other words, those receiving 80% of their instruction in French (L1) were performing as well in English as those in programs that provided 80% of the instruction through English. It is clear that Hébert *et al.*'s findings are exactly what the interdependence hypothesis would predict but this is certainly not apparent from Rossell and Baker's highly distorted account.

Some advocates of bilingual programs have also interpreted the threshold and interdependence hypotheses as implying that instruction for bilingual students should be virtually all through the medium of L1 with English reading instruction delayed for as long as possible. In the United States this might mean Grade 3 when students are frequently transitioned to all-English programs. Another example is in New Zealand where some Maori-medium programs (*kura kaupapa Maori*) delay formal English instruction until students are at the secondary school level. The rationale is the minority language (Maori) needs maximum reinforcement and transfer of academic skills to English will happen 'automatically' without formal instruction. Although there may be instances where this does happen, in my view, this assumption is seriously flawed. 'Automatic' transfer of academic skills across languages will not happen unless students are given opportunities to read and write extensively in English in addition to the minority language. In addition, *there is a significant role for formal explicit instruction in order to teach specific aspects of academic registers in both languages.* The potential benefits of developing literacy in both languages are much more likely to be realized if instruction gives the process a helping hand by promoting students' awareness of language and how it works (e.g. focusing on similarities and differences between the two languages). If one of the two languages is ignored instructionally with the expectation that it will 'take care of itself', students may experience significant gaps in their knowledge of and access to academic registers in that language, particularly in areas related to writing.

In short, while the delay of formal English literacy instruction might be appropriate under some circumstances (e.g. in the context of a well-designed 90:10 two-way bilingual immersion program), neither the threshold nor interdependence hypotheses, individually or together, provides support for any specific configuration of L1/L2 instruction within bilingual education. The interdependence hypothesis posits that transfer of academic skills and knowledge will occur across languages under appropriate conditions of student motivation and exposure to both languages. It does *not* argue that initial instruction in the early grades should be totally through the minority language. Nor does it suggest that a 90:10 model of dual language or two-way bilingual immersion program is intrinsically better than a 50:50 program model. In situations where bilingual students may have varying levels of proficiency in their L1 and English on entry to the program, it may be more effective to promote literacy in both L1 and English simultaneously or in close succession, rather than delaying the introduction of English reading instruction. The goal here would be to work for transfer across languages from an early stage by encouraging Grades 1 and 2 students to read literature in both languages and write in both languages (e.g. produce and publish bilingual books).

In this regard, the almost sacrosanct principle of keeping the two languages instructionally separate within a bilingual or second language immersion program needs to be qualified. When the two languages are kept rigidly separate, students are given much less opportunity and encouragement to engage in the 'incipient contrastive linguistics' that Lambert and Tucker (1972) reported French immersion students often spontaneously engaged in. This kind of enriching metalinguistic activity is much more likely to occur and exert positive effects if it is actively promoted by instruction. Within the context of Vygotsky's theory, the greater metalinguistic awareness that bilingualism seems to promote can be seen as an opportunity for teachers to intervene within the zone of proximal development. When teachers draw students' attention to similarities and contrasts between their two languages and provide them with opportunities to carry out creative projects on language and its social consequences, students will be enabled to transform their spontaneous use and experience of two languages into a more conscious and 'scientific' awareness of their linguistic operations. In other words, despite the generally accepted principle of keeping the two languages within a bilingual program instructionally separate, there is also an important role for focusing on the two languages together in order to enhance students' awareness of language and the relationships between language and power.

The Short-Circuit/Linguistic Threshold Hypothesis

The basic idea of the short-circuit hypothesis is similar to the (Cummins) threshold hypothesis, namely, that low L2 proficiency restricts a reader's ability to understand and interact with an L2 text. Clarke (1979, 1980) referred to this as a *linguistic ceiling* while Carrell (1988, 1991) suggested that a threshold level of L2 language proficiency must be attained before L1 reading strategies and background knowledge can transfer to L2 reading performance.

Although the idea seems intuitively reasonable and is consistent with the empirical data, there is a serious conceptual problem with this whole line of research. The problem derives from failure to adequately address how 'L2 proficiency' is conceptualized (which was also a problem with early versions of the Cummins threshold hypothesis). The research data related to the short-circuit hypothesis is reviewed first and then the problematic aspects of the research are discussed.

The short-circuit hypothesis is consistent with the California State Department of Education's (1985) case studies project, reviewed above, showing that the relationship between Spanish and English reading achievement increased significantly as oral proficiency in English increased. It is also consistent with Hakuta and Diaz' (1985) finding with Spanish-speaking elementary school students that correlations between English and Spanish academic skills increased over time. Between kindergarten and Grade 3 the correlation between English and Spanish went from 0 to 0.68.

Research designed specifically to investigate the short-circuit hypothesis is generally supportive of the involvement of both L1 reading and L2 linguistic knowledge as significant contributors to L2 reading performance. When the research question is posed in terms of which is the stronger predictor of L2 reading performance, L2 linguistic knowledge usually emerges as a stronger predictor than L1 reading proficiency (Bernhardt & Kamil, 1995; Bossers, 1991; Lee & Schallert, 1997). Bossers provides a clear overview of the findings up to 1991:

> In summary, the findings above provide the following picture. Firstly, although both variables contribute significantly to L2 reading, L2 knowledge is a more

powerful predictor than L1 reading. … Secondly, differences between the least skilled L2 readers are predicted only by differences in L2 knowledge. … Thirdly, L1 reading comes into play as a significant predictor variable only at a relatively high level of L2 reading. … The picture indicates, in other words, that knowledge of the target language plays a dominant role initially, and that L1 reading becomes a prominent factor at a more advanced level. This is exactly what a threshold or language ceiling hypothesis would predict concerning the relation between L1 reading, L2 reading, and L2 knowledge: direct transfer of L1 reading skills occurs only when a certain amount of L2 knowledge has been acquired. (1991: 56–57)

Bernhardt and Kamil (1995) working with 187 students learning Spanish in the US Air Force Academy found a correlation of 0.53 between Spanish and English reading measures. Students came from three levels of Spanish proficiency according to amount of instructional time in Spanish (beginners, intermediate who had taken up to five semesters of Spanish, and advanced with up to seven semesters of Spanish). Bernhardt and Kamil note that English (L1) reading accounted for 28% of the variance in Spanish reading when entered first into the regression equation. However, when entered after Spanish language/instructional level the amount of unique variance accounted for by English reading was reduced to 10% with language/instructional level accounting for 38%. They conclude that linguistic level in the target language is a more powerful predictor.

Lee and Schallert (1997) also investigated the short-circuit/linguistic threshold hypothesis with 809 14–17-year-old Korean students learning English as a foreign language. Their measure of English (L2) language proficiency was comprised of vocabulary and grammatical judgment items administered through a written test. They reported that 56% of the variance in L2 reading could be accounted for by L2 proficiency and only 30% by L1 reading, suggesting that this difference 'supports the contention that L2 reading ability owes more to L2 proficiency than to L1 reading' (1997: 732). They also found significantly higher correlations between L1 and L2 reading at higher levels of L2 language proficiency than at lower levels which they interpret as providing support for a threshold level of language proficiency below which L1 reading will exert less impact on L2 reading than at higher levels of L2 proficiency.

Critique: What is meant by 'language proficiency?'

The Bernhardt and Kamil (1995), Bossers (1991), and Lee and Schallert (1997) studies illustrate the problematic nature of the either–or question posed by Alderson (1984) regarding the extent to which L2 reading performance is a language problem or a reading problem. This question fails to define the construct of 'language proficiency'. Thus, we return once again to the familiar issue of how do we conceptualize the nature of language proficiency.

In all three studies, the way 'language proficiency' was operationally defined reflects academic rather than conversational aspects of proficiency. As such, it is not at all surprising that measures of academic proficiency in L2 relate strongly to measures of reading proficiency in L2 – these measures are essentially assessing the same construct.

In Bernhardt and Kamil's study, L2 proficiency was operationally defined as the level of proficiency attained in L2 academic courses, a variable that presumably reflects academic L2 proficiency. Bossers (1991) assessed vocabulary and grammar knowledge from a widely used Dutch-as-a-second-language test battery. Lee and Schallert opted for measures of vocabulary and knowledge of grammatical structures on the grounds that these measures were typically included in batteries designed to assess 'language proficiency' in previous studies. Almost apologetically, they note that 'in this article, we refer to L2 proficiency as knowledge of vocabulary and grammatical structures while acknowledging the limitations that such an operationalization of the construct imposes' (1997: 717). The fact that these were written measures which required students to read the L2 clearly indicates that the construct of 'language proficiency' in this study (and in Bossers, 1991) overlaps considerably with the construct of 'reading proficiency'. Thus, in the Lee and Schallert study, the strong correlation of 0.75 between 'L2 proficiency' and 'L2 reading' simply reflects the fact that they are both indices of L2 academic language proficiency. The same is true for Bossers' finding that L2 knowledge was a considerably stronger predictor of L2 reading than was L1 reading, although both variables contributed uniquely to the explanation of variance.

One can go further and suggest that the relationships among the *three* variables investigated by Lee and Schallert reflect the construct of academic language proficiency. The cross-lingual correlations between English (L2) proficiency and Korean (L1) reading, and English reading and Korean reading were 0.47 and 0.55 respectively, both significant at $p < 0.0001$. These cross-lingual relationships are remarkably high in view of the linguistic differences between Korean and English and the large number of participants in the study. From the theoretical perspective developed in previous chapters, they strongly support the construct of academic language proficiency and the interdependence of academic skills and knowledge across languages.

My goal here is not to dispute the validity of the data in the Bernhardt/Kamil, Bossers, or Lee/Schallert studies. These sets of data strongly support the interdependence hypothesis. Furthermore, the discontinuity in the L1/L2 reading correlations between low and high levels of L2 proficiency in the Bossers and Lee/Schallert study adds to the evidence that there may be an identifiable threshold of L2 proficiency that must be attained before L1 reading strategies can positively influence L2 reading performance. In this regard, the pattern of findings is similar to those observed by the California State Department of Education (1985) and Hakuta and Diaz (1985).

My point is rather that Alderson's question regarding the extent to which reading in L2 is a reading or a language problem cannot be addressed meaningfully in the absence of a coherent definition and operationalization of 'language proficiency'. It is essentially trivial to discover that L2 proficiency is a better predictor of

L2 reading than is L1 reading when the measures of 'L2 proficiency' and 'L2 reading' are indices of the same underlying construct. When conversational measures of 'L2 proficiency' have been assessed, as in González' (1989) study and to some extent in the California State Department (1985) study, L1 reading emerged as a much stronger predictor of L2 reading than did L2 conversational proficiency.

In summary, studies that have investigated the 'short-circuit' version of the 'threshold hypothesis' have consistently supported the interdependence of L1 and L2 academic proficiencies. Some of these studies also provide evidence that relationships between L1 and L2 reading are stronger among relatively advanced L2 learners as compared to beginning L2 learners (e.g. Bossers, 1991; Lee and Schallert, 1997). Finally, it should be emphasized that these studies are addressed to different phenomena than the (Cummins) threshold hypothesis which focuses on the consequences of bilingualism for cognitive, linguistic, and academic growth.

Conclusion

The interdependence hypothesis has been consistently supported in empirical research across a wide range of sociolinguistic contexts. As discussed in the next chapter, this hypothesis entails significant implications for policy in the area of bilingual education. It helps to explain why instruction through a minority language in a well-implemented bilingual program results in no adverse effects on academic development in the majority language.

The research data also provide considerable support for the positive consequences of additive bilingualism for children's metalinguistic development, learning of additional languages, and more general verbal cognitive operations. For these positive effects to exert a long-term impact, it appears that both languages must be given the opportunity to continue to develop into the school years. There is also some evidence that there may be threshold levels of bilingual proficiency that act as intervening variables in mediating the consequences of bilingualism on cognitive and linguistic growth. However, the positing of linguistic thresholds is still speculative and is not in any sense necessary for the overall theoretical framework outlined in Chapter 2. Contrary to the views of both advocates and opponents of bilingual education, the threshold hypothesis, by itself, carries few policy implications. It is certainly *not* the case that instruction in the majority language should be delayed until a certain 'threshold' level of L1 literacy has been attained.

By contrast, the finding that positive educational and metalinguistic consequences are associated with additive bilingualism does have important policy and instructional implications. For policy, this finding reinforces the legitimacy of strongly promoting bilingualism and biliteracy in school. Instructionally, the appropriate implication is that there should be an explicit focus on augmenting bilingual students' awareness of language in general and the roles that it plays in their lives and in societal power relations. If we focus only on one of the bilingual's two languages, or keep them rigidly separate, then we miss a very significant opportunity to enhance bilingual students' linguistic and academic development.

In the next chapter, I examine the controversy and confusion regarding which research approaches are appropriate and legitimate to inform policy in bilingual education. I argue that the confusion derives largely from the failure to consider adequately the role of *theory* in policy formation.

Notes

1. Jean Lyon (1996), based on a study of childhood bilingualism in Wales, has proposed an expanded version of the threshold model to describe the stages that young bilingual children go through in their acquisition of two languages in the home and into the school years. She distinguishes four stages: *early language* involving words/phrases in one (or two) languages; *potential bilingualism* involving simple sentences in one language plus words/phrases in the second; *developing bilingualism* involving age appropriate level in one language plus simple sentences in the second; and *proficient bilingualism* involving age appropriate levels in both languages.

2. Gándara (1999) discusses further analyses of the California Case Studies data conducted by Samaniego and Eubank (in press). The Case Studies schools made extensive use of the primary language in the first three grades with increasing use of English thereafter until students were fully mainstreamed in English by the sixth grade. Samaniego and Eubank found that the timing and extent of transfer of reading skills across languages was influenced by the community context. In one of the five schools (Rockwood School) which was located in an area of high transiency near the Mexican border, relatively little growth in English reading was found during the elementary years despite the fact that scores in Spanish reading and math were high. This contrasted with the findings from Eastman Avenue School in urban Los Angeles where superior English reading performance was demonstrated in comparison to district norms and students taught in an alternative program. As reported by Gándara, the researchers concluded that

   > … while the study showed clear transfer of skills from the primary language to English in subjects such as math, English reading scores were more dependent upon the community context [reflected in the] stability of the community, opportunities for exposure to English, and the economic pressure to acquire English language skills. As in other studies, high levels of Spanish reading proficiency continued to be a good predictor of English language reading – but in some sites this was likely to take longer to demonstrate. (1999: 11)

   The implication is that in schools such as Rockwood where exposure to and motivation to learn English are relatively low, there should be a greater emphasis on English in the early grades (together with strong L1 literacy development) if the goal is to have students at grade level in English academic skills by Grade 6. Alternatively, expectations regarding the amount of time required for students to catch up in English academic skills could be revised upward to a higher grade level.

   These data are consistent with the interdependence hypothesis which specifies exposure and motivational conditions required for transfer to take place (see Chapter 2). They also reinforce the point made in Chapter 1 that dogmatic assumptions should not be made regarding the optimal amounts of L1 and L2 instruction in the early grades. Decisions on these issues should be made with reference to the community context and the realities of educational organization and politics in particular situations (e.g. timing of state-mandated assessments in English). In all situations, literacy in the first language should be promoted strongly for optimal development in both languages to take place; however, the appropriate timing and intensity of literacy instruction in English may be determined by contextual factors.

3. One frequent misinterpretation of the interdependence hypothesis is that it applies to academic (CALP) but not conversational (BICS) aspects of language proficiency (e.g.

Devlin, 1997; Verhoeven, 1994). In fact, Cummins *et al.* (1984) reported stronger cross-lingual relationships for an 'interactional style' (BICS) factor than for a CALP factor in a study of Japanese-L1 students in Toronto. The cross-lingual relationships for some aspects of conversational proficiency have been interpreted as reflecting underlying personality attributes of the individual (e.g. sociability) in the same way that the cross-lingual relationships for CALP reflect cognitive attributes of the individual. It is certainly not true to claim, as the authors cited above do, that the existence of cross-lingual relations for aspects of conversational skills is contrary to any claims that I have made. I have tended to emphasize cross-lingual aspects of L1/L2 CALP rather than L1/L2 BICS for the simple reason that the former (by definition) have more relevance to schooling and academic development than do the latter.

Chapter 8

Research, Theory and Policy in Bilingual Education: Evaluating the Credibility of Empirical Data

As noted in Chapter 2, few educational issues in North America have become as volatile or as ideologically loaded as the debate on the merits or otherwise of bilingual education. Research has played a prominent role in this debate. Unfortunately, the research evidence has been interpreted in very different ways by advocates and opponents of bilingual education.

In this chapter, I review how the research on bilingual education has been interpreted by academics and also raise ethical issues about the way in which research evidence has been infused into the public discourse on bilingual education. Unlike courtroom lawyers who advocate for their clients regardless of the merits of the case, academics have an ethical responsibility to analyze the research evidence as objectively as possible and to recommend policy options that are consistent with the evidence. Academics also bear a responsibility to address, and attempt to reconcile, internal contradictions in their stated positions and interpretations of the research.

The academic debate on bilingual education in the United States contrasts markedly with the treatment of the issue in the media. Media articles on bilingual education have tended to be overwhelmingly negative in their assessment of the merits of bilingual programs (McQuillan & Tse, 1996). By contrast, the academic debate lines up virtually all North American applied linguists who have carried out research on language learning as advocates of bilingual programs against only a handful of academic commentators who oppose bilingual education. These opponents tend to come from academic backgrounds other than applied linguistics. The most prominent of these are Rosalie Pedalino Porter, Keith Baker, Christine Rossell, and Charles Glenn. Others such as Nathan Glazer and Herbert Walberg have made occasional forays into the debate to express their skepticism about bilingual education.

First, in order to provide a context for the debate on research methods, I sketch some interpretations of the research that I believe would be endorsed by a large majority of applied linguists. These five points essentially summarize the positions that have been discussed in previous chapters. Then I examine three major reviews of the literature on bilingual education in the United States, two carried out by advocates of bilingual programs (August & Hakuta, 1997; Greene, 1997, 1998) and one by opponents (Rossell & Baker, 1996). I critique the orientation to research adopted in each of these reviews, arguing that the role of theory in interpreting the implications of research for policy has been neglected and misunderstood. Next, I examine three case studies of bilingual programs from New Zealand, Belgium, and the United States, to illustrate what can be inferred from studies that might be regarded as 'methodologically unacceptable' in more conventional reviews. Finally, the credibility of the large-scale ongoing study by Wayne Thomas and Virginia Collier (1997) is assessed in light of a vehement critique from Christine Rossell (1998).

Common Ground Within Applied Linguistics

Obviously social and educational policy decisions depend on sociopolitical considerations as much as, or more, than on information derived from educational research. Nevertheless, policy-makers usually need to rationalize their decisions in terms of what is in the best interests of children and the society at large. The following points appear to me to be relatively non-controversial among applied linguists who have examined the research upon which they are based, although they might be expressed differently according to the theoretical orientation of individual researchers.

(1) Bilingual programs for students from minority and majority language backgrounds have been implemented successfully in countries around the world

As documented in many sources (e.g. Baker & Prys Jones, 1998; Cenoz & Genesee, 1998; Cummins & Corson, 1997; Dutcher, 1995; Skutnabb-Kangas, 1995), students educated for part of the day through a minority language do not suffer adverse consequences in the development of academic skills in the majority language. If there were adverse consequences associated with bilingual instruction, there would hardly be more than 300,000 English-background students in various forms of French–English bilingual programs in Canada. Similarly, in the Basque country of Spain during the past decade, there has been a dramatic increase in the number of students being enrolled in bilingual (Model B) and Basque immersion/maintenance (Model D) programs, as compared to Model A programs which are conducted in Spanish with Basque taught only as a second language.

(2) Bilingual education, by itself, is not a panacea for students' underachievement

Underachievement derives from many sources and simply providing some first language (L1) instruction will not, by itself, transform students' educational experience. Bilingual instruction *can* make a significant contribution, but the predominant model of bilingual education implemented in the United States (quick-exit transitional programs) is inferior to programs that aim to develop bilingualism and biliteracy, such as developmental (late-exit) and two-way bilingual immersion (dual-language). Dual-language programs also serve English-background students in the same classes as minority language students with each group acting as linguistic models for the other.

(3) The development of literacy in two languages entails linguistic and perhaps cognitive advantages for bilingual students

As noted in Chapters 2 and 7, there are close to 150 research studies carried out since the early 1960s that report significant advantages for bilingual students on a variety of metalinguistic and cognitive tasks.

(4) Significant positive relationships exist between the development of academic skills in L1 and L2

These cross-lingual relationships reflect the transfer of academic and conceptual knowledge across languages as well as the fact that the same cognitive and linguistic processing system operates on the acquisition and use of both languages.

(5) Conversational and academic registers of language proficiency are distinct and follow different developmental patterns

As noted in previous chapters, this distinction has major educational implications for pedagogy and assessment of ELL students.

Research Orthodoxies in the United States

Despite the relative consensus that exists among applied linguists regarding the five points sketched above, interpretation of the voluminous research on bilingual education within the United States has been highly controversial among both academics and policy-makers for more than 25 years. Clearly the political sensitivity of the issue has contributed to confusion about what the research is actually saying. A more fundamental cause of this confusion, however, is the extremely limited way in which most educational researchers have examined the research, and in particular the quantitative research on this issue. The dominant assumption has been that we can draw policy-relevant conclusions regarding the effectiveness of bilingual education only from 'methodologically acceptable studies'. Typically, these studies are program evaluations that involve treatment and control groups compared in such a way that outcome differences can be attributed to the treatment rather than to extraneous factors.

I argue that this approach represents an appropriate, but extremely limited, orientation to research in bilingual education. It is limited on two counts:

- It has proven virtually impossible to apply rigorous controls or random assignment to treatment groups in comparisons between programs due to the myriad human, administrative, and political influences that impact the implementation of programs over time.[1]
- Underlying this approach is the assumption that there is a direct connection between research and policy: researchers will discover which program alternatives work best and policy-makers will develop funding and implementation policies based on these findings. While this straightforward linkage between research and policy may work well in some spheres (e.g. opinion surveys), it seldom yields clearcut results in an area as multifaceted as educational research where the treatment variable of interest (e.g. proportion of L1 instruction) is intertwined and interacting with hundreds of other variables that will affect program outcomes.

As I document below, it is not surprising that this dominant research paradigm has yielded such paltry pickings for policy. The only thing that academic opponents and many advocates of bilingual education seem to agree on with respect to the policy-related research is that it is of almost universally poor quality (August & Hakuta, 1997; Greene, 1997, 1998; Rossell & Baker, 1996).

I argue in this chapter that 'poor quality' is in the eye of the beholder. Viewed through the lens of 'methodologically acceptable studies', it is possible to find fault with virtually all of the research studies, including many of those that survived the 'rigorous criteria' established by Greene (1997, 1998) and Rossell and Baker (1996). However, there is an enormous amount of relevant and interpretable research, both internationally and within the United States, that speaks directly to the bilingual education policy issues. I suggest that the policy issues have remained confused and contested at least partly because the bulk of the relevant research has been virtually ignored, both by advocates and opponents of bilingual education. The relevance of this research is not apparent within the dominant paradigm because the studies do not conform to the criteria of acceptability within this paradigm. However, when we examine this voluminous research from the perspective of an alternative paradigm, its relevance is immediately apparent.

The alternative paradigm claims that the relevance of research for policy is mediated through theory. In complex educational and other human organizational contexts, data or 'facts' become relevant for policy purposes only in the context of a coherent theory. It is the *theory* rather than the individual research findings that permits the generation of predictions about program outcomes under different conditions. Research findings themselves cannot be directly applied across contexts. For example, the fact that students in a Spanish–English bilingual program in New York City performed extremely well academically in relation to grade norms (as demonstrated in a methodologically sophisticated study carried out by Beykont, 1994) tells us very little, by itself, about whether a similar program might be effective with Mexican-American students in San Diego. Yet when certain patterns are replicated across a wide range of situations, the accumulation of consistent findings suggests that some stable underlying principle is at work. This principle can then be stated as a theoretical proposition or hypothesis from which predictions can be derived and tested.

In contrast to research findings, within a 'scientific' or positivistic paradigm, theories are almost by definition applicable across contexts. The validity of any theoretical principle is assessed precisely by how well it can account for the research findings in a variety of contexts. If a theory cannot account for a particular set of research findings, then it is an inadequate or incomplete theory. Thus, while no individual research finding can 'prove' a theory or confirm a hypothesis, any research finding can disconfirm or refute a theory or hypothesis. Thus, the criterion of validity for any hypothesis is extremely stringent: it must be consistent with *all* of the research data or at least be able to account for inconsistencies (e.g. poor implementation of a program). The examination of the consistency between the hypothesis and the data in a wide variety of sociolinguistic conditions constitutes a form of randomization that only extremely robust theoretical constructs can survive (Pogrow, 1999).[2]

I label the former paradigm the 'Research–Policy' paradigm and the latter the 'Research–Theory–Policy' paradigm. In order to show the strengths and limitations of each, I examine how they have been employed in the bilingual education debate and the policy-relevant findings that each yields. I conclude that the former paradigm yields largely trivial information for policy purposes and perpetuates misconceptions regarding bilingual education that have persisted for almost 30 years. By contrast, the latter paradigm yields considerable information that has direct relevance to policy and addresses many of the most contentious issues in the bilingual education debate.

The Research–Policy Paradigm: Debunking the Mythology of 'Methodologically Acceptable Studies'

Both advocates and opponents of bilingual education have largely concurred on the conditions under which research in general and evaluation studies in particular can be considered 'methodologically acceptable'. For example, Greene (1997, 1998), whose interpretation of research is favourable to bilingual education, and Rossell and Baker (1996) whose conclusions are highly unfavourable to bilingual education, agreed on the appropriateness of the following criteria for designation of studies as 'methodologically acceptable:'

(1) Studies had to compare students in bilingual programs to a control group of similar students.
(2) The design had to ensure that initial differences between treatment and control groups were controlled statistically or through random assignment.
(3) Results were to be based on standardized test scores in English.

(4)   Differences between the scores of treatment and control groups were to be determined by means of appropriate statistical tests.

The approaches diverged on several additional points. Greene, for example, focused only on studies that had been carried out in the United States and which measured the effects of bilingual education after at least one year of the treatment whereas Rossell and Baker (1996) included international research data in their review. Rossell and Baker also categorized programs according to pre-defined labels (structured immersion, transitional bilingual education, submersion, English as a second-language (ESL)) whereas Greene adopted a more straightforward categorization of bilingual education as a program in which all students are taught using at least some of their native language. An additional difference was that Greene (like Willig, 1985) used meta-analysis to take into account effect sizes in individual studies whereas Rossell and Baker (like Baker and de Kanter, 1983) used what is now considered a very crude technique of simply counting studies that were favourable or unfavourable to different treatments.

Using their respective criteria of 'methodologically acceptable' studies, Rossell and Baker rejected 228 studies and accepted 72 while Greene could find only 11 studies whose design permitted conclusions to be drawn.

August and Hakuta (1997) and their colleagues reviewed both the basic and policy-oriented research on schooling for language-minority children. Their review is comprehensive, balanced, and useful for researchers and policy-makers alike. It also offers very appropriate suggestions for improving the quality of program evaluations. However, it suffers from the same problematic orientation to research and policy as do the reviews by Greene (1997, 1998) and Rossell and Baker (1996). In interpreting both the basic research and program evaluations relevant to language learning and bilingual education, the authors pay only lip-service to the role of theory in mediating the relevance of research for policy (Fitzgerald & Cummins, 1999). As a result, their conclusions are considerably weaker than they might have been and also considerably less useful for policy purposes.

I critique these three literature reviews below. My focus is directed towards identifying the limitations of the research paradigm these authors have adopted rather than attempting a comprehensive analysis of their literature reviews and conclusions.

Greene's meta-analysis

Greene (1997, 1998) reported that participation in a bilingual program over a period of two years made a difference of about 1/5 of a standard deviation in achievement. Thus, if a student in an English-only program performed at the 26th percentile at the end of those two years, the bilingual student would be at the 34th percentile. The problematic nature of this type of meta-analysis can be seen from examining some of the 11 studies included. One of the large-scale 'methodologically acceptable' studies included in the analysis (and in Rossell and Baker's review) was the American Institutes of Research (AIR) study (Danoff, Coles, McLaughlin &

Reynolds, 1978). This study aggregated a variety of programs labelled 'bilingual education' and compared them to non-bilingual programs, ignoring the fact that many bilingual programs are bilingual in name only or involve minimal amounts of L1 instruction by a non-trained paraprofessional (see, for example, Gándara, 1999). In addition, as pointed out by August and Hakuta (1997) there was no clear demarcation between treatment and control groups:

> Nearly three-quarters of the experimental group had been in bilingual programs for two or more years, and the study measured their gains in the last few months. Additionally, about two-thirds of the children in the control group had previously been in a bilingual program; these children did not represent a control group in the usual sense of the term. Thus the AIR study did not compare bilingual education with no bilingual education. (1997: 140)

Krashen (1999a) has also pointed out that Greene's analysis included several 'methodologically acceptable' studies in which 'bilingual education' was either not described in any detail or involved minimal use of the L1 (e.g. use of bilingual paraprofessionals)

In short, Greene's meta-analysis makes no attempt to test the theoretical propositions underlying bilingual education or alternative English-only programs. The apparent rigor involved in reducing the extensive corpus of bilingual education data to 11 'methodologically acceptable' studies seems destined to end up in *rigor mortis* for this approach as the credibility of even these 11 studies is whittled away. However, this is not because most of the research is inadequate; the inadequacy is rather in the lens through which we are examining the research.

August and Hakuta's (1997) National Research Council Report

This report was intended to provide researchers and policy-makers with a 'state-of-the-art' review of what basic and applied research could tell us about improving schooling for language-minority students. One might have expected to find clear and coherent answers to volatile policy-relevant questions such as:

- How long does it take English language learners (ELL) to catch up academically to their native English-speaking peers?
- Should reading instruction be provided initially through bilingual students' first language?
- What outcomes can be expected from different kinds of bilingual programs?
- How important is time-on-task, understood as the amount of instructional time spent through the target language, on second language academic development?' etc.

Although most of these questions are addressed to some extent in the report, the answers are at best tentative and not particularly helpful for policy-purposes. This lack of incisiveness can be attributed to the focus on research in isolation from theory. Crucial theoretical issues such as the nature of language proficiency and its relationship to academic development are barely considered in the report. Similarly, the report fails to address the validity of the competing hypotheses that have been advanced to support either English-only programs (the 'time-on-task' or maximum exposure to English hypothesis (e.g. Porter, 1990)) or certain forms of bilingual program (the 'linguistic interdependence' hypothesis (see Chapter 7)).

Consequently, the first question listed above is barely considered in the report despite the fact that this has been a central issue to emerge in the context of Proposition 227 in California and the many policy debates leading up to this initiative.

Answers are given to some of the other questions; for example, the report states that 'the degree of children's native-language proficiency is a strong predictor of their English-language development' (p. 28). However, the authors fail to address what this finding means for policy. As I illustrate below, when this finding is integrated with theory in the form of the linguistic interdependence hypothesis, it provides an empirically testable basis for interpreting the outcomes of bilingual education programs in widely different sociolinguistic and sociopolitical contexts.

Similarly, the authors' treatment of the question of learning to read through a second language correctly identifies the major pattern of research findings but then lets the issue drop as though the findings were contradictory and few policy implications could be drawn:

> With respect to reading instruction in a second language, there is remarkably little directly relevant research. Clearly, one of the major intellectual stimuli to bilingual education programs has been the belief that initial reading instruction in a language not yet mastered orally to some reasonable level is too great a cognitive challenge for most learners. The evidence that better academic outcomes characterize immigrant children who have had 2 to 3 years of initial schooling (and presumably literacy instruction) in their native countries (Collier & Thomas, 1989; Skutnabb-Kangas, 1979) is consistent with the claim that children should first learn to read in a language they already speak. However, it is clear that many children first learn to read in a second language without serious negative consequences. (1997: 59–60)

By contrast, I would argue that there is a significant amount of directly relevant research. Reviews of this research from 25 years ago were able to conclude that the language of initial literacy instruction is not, in itself, a significant determinant of academic outcomes (Cummins, 1979a; Engle, 1975; Wagner, 1998), although it may play a role as part of a much broader constellation of variables related to power relations and identity negotiation (Cummins, 1996).

Finally, overwhelming amounts of data on bilingual education programs internationally should have permitted the authors to state definitively that the major theoretical argument underlying the push for all-English programs is without merit. The *time-on-task* (maximum exposure) hypothesis predicts that any form of bilingual education that reduces the amount of instructional time through the medium of English will result in academic difficulties in English. As a theoretical proposition, this hypothesis is refuted by the outcomes of countless bilingual programs evaluated in countries around the globe which demonstrate that students suffer no adverse effects in their mastery of the majority language (English in North America) as a result of spending significant instructional time through the minority language (see Corson, 1993, 1998b; Cummins, 1996).

The policy implication is not that bilingual programs are necessarily 'effective', or will necessarily succeed better than alternative programs. Outcomes of any program will depend on a variety of implementation factors; rather the data and associated theory show clearly that linguistic minority and linguistic majority students in well-implemented bilingual programs (of various types) will suffer no adverse consequences as a result of spending instructional time through both languages.

This type of clear policy-relevant conclusion is not forthcoming from the report, not because relevant data are lacking, but because the data are viewed through a very fuzzy lens. The authors' conclusion seems designed to provide policy-makers on both sides of the bilingual education issue with what they want to hear:

> The beneficial effects of native-language instruction are clearly evident in programs that have been labelled 'bilingual education', but they also appear in some programs that are labelled 'immersion' (Gersten & Woodward, 1995). There also appear to be benefits of programs that are labelled 'structured immersion' (Baker & de Kanter, 1981; Rossell & Ross, 1986). (1997: 147)

Theory is required to bring the data into focus. As I illustrate below, definitive answers could have been provided to many of the most contentious policy-related questions in the area of bilingual education had the authors articulated the major theoretical positions in the literature on bilingual education and examined the consistency of these positions with the available data.

Rossell and Baker (1996)

The outcomes of Rossell and Baker's review of the literature on the educational effectiveness of bilingual education are clearly stated in the Abstract:

> The research evidence indicates that, on standardized achievement tests, transitional bilingual education (TBE) is *better* than regular classroom instruction in only 22% of the methodologically acceptable studies when the outcome is reading, 7% of the studies when the outcome is language, and 9% of the studies when the outcome is math. TBE is never better than structured immersion, a special program for limited English proficient children where the children are in a self-contained classroom composed solely of English learners, but the instruction is in English at a pace they can understand. (1996: 1)

Furthermore, the comparisons of reading scores between TBE and structured immersion showed that structured immersion was superior in 83% of cases and no differences were observed in 17%.

These conclusions, published in a reputable refereed journal, and apparently based on rigorous methodological criteria, would cause any policy-maker to question the merits of transitional bilingual education.

Cracks appear very quickly, however, in the facade of objective rationality that this review of the literature projects. One problem is immediately obvious: When we look more closely at the research studies that supposedly demonstrated the superiority of 'structured immersion' over 'transitional bilingual education' in reading it turns out that *90% of these studies are interpreted by their authors as supporting the effectiveness of bilingual and even trilingual education.*

Seven of the ten studies that Rossell and Baker claim support structured immersion over TBE in reading were studies of French immersion programs in Canada. Typically, in these programs English-speaking students are 'immersed' in French (their second language (L2)) in kindergarten and Grade 1 and English (L1) language arts are introduced in Grade 2. The proportion of English instruction increases to about 50% by Grades 4 or 5. The closest equivalent to the program in the United States is dual language immersion which, as documented below, has repeatedly demonstrated its effectiveness for both majority and minority language students (e.g. Christian *et al.*, 1997; Dolson & Lindholm, 1995; Thomas & Collier, 1997). Note that, as in the US dual language programs, Canadian French immersion programs are bilingual programs, taught by bilingual teachers, and their goal is the development of bilingualism and biliteracy.

Even at the level of face validity, it seems incongruous that Rossell and Baker use the success of the Canadian French–English bilingual programs to argue for monolingual immersion programs taught largely by monolingual teachers with the goal of developing monolingualism. This is particularly the case since two of the seven programs they cite as evidence for monolingual structured immersion were actually *trilingual* programs involving instruction in French, English, and Hebrew (Genesee & Lambert, 1983; Genesee, Lambert & Tucker, 1977).

In addition to these seven French immersion program evaluations, one of the ten studies (Malherbe, 1946) was an extremely large-scale study of Afrikaans–English bilingual education in South Africa involving 19,000 students. The other two were carried out in the United States (Gersten, 1985; Peña-Hughes & Solis, 1980).

The Peña-Hughes and Solis program (labelled 'structured immersion' by Rossell and Baker) involved an hour of Spanish language arts per day and was viewed as a form of bilingual education by the director of the program (Willig, 1981/82). I would see the genuine promotion of L1 literacy in this program as indicating a much more adequate model of bilingual education than the quick-exit transitional bilingual program to which it was being compared. Gersten's study involved an extremely small number of Asian-origin students (12 immersion students in the first cohort and nine bilingual program students, and 16 and seven in the second cohort) and hardly constitutes an adequate sample upon which to base national policy.

Malherbe's study concluded that students instructed bilingually did at least as well in each language as students instructed monolingually despite much less time through each language. He argues strongly for the *benefits* of bilingual education (however, see Krashen, 1999c, for a critique of the design of this study).

In short, Rossell and Baker's conclusions are immediately suspect as a result of the fact that they use the documented success of bilingual and trilingual programs to argue against bilingual education. There are many other problems with their literature review which bring the entire enterprise of basing policy decisions primarily on 'methodologically acceptable' treatment-control group studies into question. Some of the problems are briefly outlined below (see also Cummins, 1999; Dicker, 1996; Escamilla, 1996; Krashen, 1996).

The criteria for deciding which studies are 'methodologically acceptable' are unclear and are applied in an arbitrary manner

Krashen (1999c), for example, points out significant design problems with Malherbe's study and, as noted above, the AIR study confounds the experimental and control treatments since both groups experienced some (unknown) forms of bilingual education.

The labels assigned to different programs are arbitrary and applied in an inconsistent manner

For example, Rossell and Baker claim to compare French immersion (structured immersion) programs in Canada with 'transitional bilingual education'. There are no transitional bilingual education programs in Canada. The programs which Rossell and Baker label 'transitional bilingual education' were termed 'partial immersion programs' by Swain and Lapkin (1982) and involve at least half the time through the minority language from kindergarten through Grade 6 with the intent of developing a high level of bilingualism and biliteracy.

A complete disregard for consistency is also evident in the way the El Paso Independent School District (1987) program was labelled. In 1992, Baker termed it a 'Spanish-English dual immersion' program (in a critique of Porter's (1990) work), but by 1996 it had become a 'submersion' program (Rossell and Baker, 1996 – Appendix C, p. 72) and it finally found peace as a 'structured English immersion' program (Baker, 1998). This program involved a 'native language cognitive development' component of 90 minutes a day at Grade 1, gradually reducing to 60 minutes a day by Grade 3 and 30 minutes a day by Grade 4 (Gersten & Woodward, 1995; Krashen, 1996).

Limiting the framework of discourse to exclude bilingual programs designed to promote bilingualism and biliteracy

An additional example of arbitrary labelling is their treatment of Legaretta's (1979) kindergarten study. Originally labelled a 'structured immersion' program by Baker and de Kanter (1983), this study demonstrated the superiority of a 50% Spanish, 50% English kindergarten program over both English-only and other bilingual program options with respect to students' learning of English. Rossell and Baker (1996) list this study as showing 'no difference' between TBE and submersion (English-only) treatments. Yet the program option that was significantly better than all others was neither TBE nor submersion! The consistently positive outcomes of this kind of 'Enriched Education' program (Beykont, 1994; Cloud, Genesee & Hamayan, 2000) are nowhere represented in Rossell and Baker's review. By limiting the framework of discourse to 'transitional bilingual education' versus varieties of

English-only programs, they have excluded the type of dual-language program option endorsed by virtually all applied linguists and also by some commentators who have been highly critical of bilingual education (Glenn & LaLyre, 1991; Porter, 1990; see Chapter 9). There appears, in fact, to be an emerging consensus among advocates and opponents of 'bilingual education' that dual language and other programs that aspire to bilingualism and biliteracy are effective in developing English academic skills among both linguistic minority and majority students.

Rossell and Baker's reporting of French immersion data is blatantly inaccurate

In response to critiques from Kathy Escamilla (1996) and Susan Dicker (1996) regarding the fact that French immersion programs are fully bilingual in both goals and implementation, Rossell (1996) pointed out:

> In the first two years, the program is one of total immersion, and evaluations conducted at that point are considered to be evaluations of 'structured immersion'. It is really not important that, in later years, the program becomes bilingual if the evaluation is being conducted while it is still and always has been a structured immersion program. (1996: 383)

The significance of this point is that the major empirical basis of Rossell and Baker's entire argument for structured English immersion rests, according to their own admission, on the performance in French of English-background students *in the first two years* of Canadian French immersion programs. They interpret this research as follows:

> Both the middle class and working class English-speaking students who were immersed in French in kindergarten and Grade 1 were almost the equal of native French-speaking students until the curriculum became bilingual in Grade 2, at which point their French ability declined and continued to decline as English was increased. (1996: 22)

Rossell and Baker seem oblivious to the fact that at the end of Grade 1 French immersion students are still at very early stages in their acquisition of French. Despite good progress in learning French (particularly receptive skills) during the initial two years of the program, they are still far from native-like in virtually all aspects of proficiency – speaking, listening, reading, and writing. Most Grade 1 and 2 French immersion students are still incapable of carrying on even an elementary conversation in French without major errors and insertions of English. Similarly, it is bizarre to claim, as Rossell and Baker do without even a citation to back it up, that the French proficiency of Grade 6 immersion students is more poorly developed than that of Grade 1 students, and to attribute this to the fact that L1 instruction has been incorporated in the program.

The research data show exactly the *opposite* pattern to that claimed by Rossell and Baker. Lambert and Tucker (1972), for example, report highly significant differences between Grade 1 immersion and native French-speaking students on a variety of vocabulary, grammatical and expressive skills in French, despite the fact that no differences were found in some of the sub-skills of reading such as word discrimination. By the end of Grade 4, however, (after three years of English (L1) language arts instruction), the immersion students had caught up with the French controls in vocabulary knowledge and listening comprehension, although major differences still remained in speaking ability. Similarly, in the United States, the one large-scale 'methodologically acceptable' study that investigated this issue (Ramírez, 1992) found that early-grade students in 'structured immersion' were very far from grade norms in English even after *four* years of English-only immersion.

In summary, to claim that two years of immersion in French in kindergarten and Grade 1 results in almost native-like proficiency in French in a context where there is virtually no French exposure in the environment or in school outside the classroom flies in the face of a massive amount of research data. This can be verified by anyone who cares to step into any of the thousands of Grade 1 French immersion classrooms across Canada.

In conclusion, Rossell and Baker's literature review is characterized by inaccurate and arbitrary labelling of programs, inconsistent application of criteria for 'methodological acceptability', and highly inaccurate interpretation of the results of early French immersion programs. Ironically, the data they review (both methodologically 'acceptable' and 'unacceptable') does have considerable relevance for policy purposes, if the interpretive paradigm is changed.

The Research–Theory–Policy Paradigm: Progressive Refinement of Theory to Explain and Predict Phenomena

In most scientific disciplines, knowledge is generated not by evaluating the effects of particular treatments under strictly controlled conditions but by observing phenomena, forming hypotheses to account for the observed phenomena, testing these hypotheses against additional data, and gradually refining the hypotheses into more comprehensive theories that have broader explanatory and predictive power.[3] Take just one example: meteorology or climatology – the understanding and prediction of weather patterns. What scientists do to generate knowledge in this discipline (and many others) is to observe phenomena (e.g. the conditions under which hurricanes appear) and build up theoretical models that attempt to predict these phenomena. With further observations they test and refine their predictive models. There is no control group, for obvious reasons, yet theory-based predictions are constantly being tested and refined.

In a similar way, I would suggest that a much wider body of research data is both theoretically and policy relevant than typical reviews in the area of bilingual education have suggested. For example, case studies of particular programs or evaluations that assess student progress in relation to grade norms are potentially theoretically relevant. They become relevant for theory and policy when their outcomes are assessed in relation to the predictions derived from particular hypotheses or theoretical frameworks. The process is as follows:

(1) Establish that the phenomenon is genuine and not an artifact of measurement or observational procedures (e.g. data collection errors).

(2) Once the phenomenon has been established as genuine, ask what theoretical constructs can potentially account for the data.

(3) The third stage involves examining hypotheses in relation to additional data (e.g. designing research to test the hypotheses explicitly). As noted above, it takes only one contrary finding to refute a theoretical proposition or cause it to be modified.

(4) The final stage involves continual refinement of hypotheses and increasing integration into broader theoretical frameworks capable of more comprehensive explanations and accurate predictions.

There is nothing new in any of this. It reflects, for example, the process whereby we came to understand the movement of the planets and countless other scientific phenomena. Why then has this process not been applied in the recent policy-oriented literature reviews relating to bilingual education? Had this process been applied, a much clearer picture of the research findings and their implications would have emerged. The three literature reviews outlined above would have been able to communicate to policy-makers and the general public the following answers to at least some of their central questions:

(1) In response to the relatively unsophisticated question, *'Does bilingual education work?'*, the research shows clearly that successful bilingual education programs have been implemented in countries around the world for both linguistic minority and majority students and exactly the same patterns are observed in well-implemented programs: students do not lose out in their development of academic skills in the majority language despite spending a considerable amount of instructional time through the minority language (see, for example, Williams, 1996). This pattern is demonstrated in the vast majority of the 300 studies listed by Rossell and Baker (1996) as well as in the broader reviews of literature undertaken by August and Hakuta (1997) and Dutcher (1995). These data are consistent with predictions derived from the interdependence hypothesis which suggests that this theoretical construct can be used as a predictive tool by policy-makers.

(2) In response to the question, *'Does bilingual education work better than English-only instructional programs?'* no definitive answers can be given until the term 'bilingual education' is defined more precisely. The trend in much of data is that programs that aspire to develop bilingualism and biliteracy (Enriched Education programs) show much better outcomes than English-only or quick-exit transitional bilingual programs that do not aspire to develop bilingualism and biliteracy. Specific hypotheses (e.g. regarding the positive effects of bilingualism on cognitive and linguistic functioning) and more comprehensive theoretical frameworks (e.g. Ovando & Collier, 1998; Cummins, 1996; Lucas, Henze & Donato, 1990) have been advanced that are consistent with this trend for Enriched Education programs to show highly

positive outcomes. However, considerably more research is required to refine these frameworks to take account of the multiple interactions that occur among variables that contribute to bilingual students' academic success.

(3)   In response to the question, '*Will students suffer academically if they are introduced to reading in their second language?*' the research indicates that the language of initial introduction of reading is not, in itself, a determinant of academic outcomes. The linguistic mismatch hypothesis therefore has no credibility as a theoretical principle, as was evident in the 1970s (Engle, 1975; Cummins, 1979; Noonan *et al.*, 1997). In the context of US bilingual education, there are many persuasive arguments for introducing reading to Spanish-speaking students in their L1; but the benefits of this strategy have more to do with factors associated with the affirmation of students' identity (see Chapter 2) and the relatively regular pattern of sound–symbol relationships in Spanish as compared to English than with any axiomatic principle that children should always be introduced to literacy in their first language.

(4)   In response to the question, '*Will greater amounts of English instruction (time-on-task) result in greater English achievement?*' the answer is simply, no. The research data overwhelmingly fails to show any positive relationship between the amount of English instruction in a program and student outcomes.

In arguing for the theoretical and policy relevance of research findings that report student outcomes in relation to grade norms without direct control group comparisons, I am not suggesting that individual studies in isolation provide any definitive information. Rather the findings of individual evaluations or research studies represent phenomena that require explanation. Specific conditions in any particular context may have contributed to program outcomes such that similar findings are not observed in contexts where these conditions are absent. What we can state is that a particular set of findings is consistent or inconsistent with hypothesis X. However, before much credibility can be placed in the general relevance of hypothesis X, it is necessary to assess its consistency with a much broader set of findings in contexts where a variety of other unique conditions may be present. If the predictions that derive from hypothesis X are confirmed across these diverse contexts, then the credibility of hypothesis X increases significantly despite the fact that control group comparisons may not have been carried out.

Let us take a hypothetical example. Suppose that dual language or two-way bilingual immersion programs (which usually have between 50% and 90% minority language instruction in the early grades) were to show consistently the pattern that most of those that have been evaluated to this date apparently do show: by the end of elementary school, students from majority language backgrounds develop high levels of biliteracy skills at no cost to their English (L1) academic development; students from minority language backgrounds by Grade 6 show above average L1 literacy development and come close to grade norms in English (L2) academic skills. Let us suppose, hypothetically, that we have 100 such programs demonstrating this pattern from around the United States and the few programs that do not demonstrate this pattern can be shown to have been poorly implemented or not to have followed the prescribed model in some important respects.

Do these 100 programs demonstrating a consistent pattern of achievement in relation to grade norms tell us anything that is policy relevant? Rossell and Baker would say no – these studies are not 'methodologically acceptable' because control groups were not used and results are reported only in relation to grade norms.

I have argued, by contrast, that such a pattern is directly relevant to policy because it permits us to test certain theoretical predictions against the research data. Thus, the hypothetical pattern described for both minority and majority students is clearly inconsistent with the 'time-on-task' hypothesis because students instructed through the minority language for significant parts of the school day suffered no adverse effects in English language academic development. These data would also refute the linguistic mismatch hypothesis since majority language students whose initial literacy instruction was through Spanish experienced no long-term difficulty in either English or Spanish literacy skills. This pattern of data, however, would be consistent with the interdependence hypothesis which predicts that instruction through a minority language will result in no adverse consequences for academic development in the majority language.

In conclusion, the alternative Research–Theory–Policy paradigm conforms more closely to typical scientific procedures than the virtual elimination of theoretical considerations in the Research–Policy paradigm that has dominated the recent bilingual education policy debate. Not surprisingly, it also yields information for policy that is much more interpretable and useful. Experimental and quasi-experimental research is an appropriate approach to inquiry but by itself is limited in its ability to answer the major policy-related questions in the education of linguistic minority students, as the inadequacies of the three literature reviews analyzed above illustrate.

In the next section, I summarize three case studies of bilingual and trilingual programs that have been implemented in widely different sociolinguistic and geographical contexts. All conform to the general definition of Enriched Education insofar as they all aim to develop biliteracy skills and also to affirm students' cultural and linguistic identities. The goal of reviewing these studies is to illustrate what can be learned from detailed descriptions of how programs are implemented and the outcomes they produce despite the fact that the evaluations may not conform to the 'methodologically acceptable' orthodoxy of treatment/control group comparisons. Again, I would emphasize that none of these studies stands alone as evidence of the effectiveness of bilingual education. Their credibility derives from the fact that their outcomes are consistent with predictions derived from theoretical propositions (e.g. the interdependence hypothesis) and together they demonstrate the robustness of the pattern of findings across a wide range of sociolinguistic and sociopolitical contexts. I first sketch the general pattern of findings and then examine their consistency with the theoretical framework presented in Chapter 2 that highlights the centrality of the ways in which identities are negotiated in the school context.

Case Studies of Bilingual and Trilingual Programs

In describing each of the three programs, I first provide a summary of the main features in tabular form and then draw out some of the commonalities that characterize all three programs. In each case, I draw primarily on book-length documentation relating to the school so there is ample scope for those interested to pursue further information. All three programs were 'mature' at the time the reports were written, ranging from 10–25 years of operation. The information is accurate as of the time of the publications cited; however, schools evolve and personnel change so it is quite likely that the portraits presented here do not fully represent these schools as they are now. The point, however, is that they illustrate what educators, students, and communities *can* achieve when the ideology that permeates the school challenges the constricting and devaluing ideology that subordinated groups have typically endured in the wider society.

Richmond Road School

Location:	New Zealand (Auckland)
Languages:	Cook Islands, English, Maori, Samoan
Students:	Cook Islands L1, English L1, Maori L1, Samoan L1
L1/L2%:	Model A: 100 % English
	Model B: 50 % Maori, 50 % English
	Model C: 50 % Samoan, 50 % English
	Model D: 50 % Cook Islands, 50 % English
Goals:	To affirm and incorporate the languages and cultures of the students within the school.
Results:	By the end of elementary school, students' reading attainment improved dramatically compared to their performance in the first few years of schooling. Most children (26/35) in the cohort analyzed longitudinally were performing at or above grade expectations compared to only 3/35 who were at or above grade norms on entry to school. This contrasts with the pattern in large scale studies which showed similar students in New Zealand far below grade level with the gap increasing as students progressed through the grades (Elley, 1992).
Comments:	The classes are organized in vertical family groupings rather than according to chronological age. Peer tutoring and cooperative learning are central to the instructional approach. Students stay in the same program from 5 to 13 years old and parents are given the choice of which model to enter. Thus, children from English-speaking backgrounds also entered the bilingual (Maori) program (Cazden, 1989; May 1994).

Oyster Bilingual School

Location:	USA (Washington, DC)
Languages:	Spanish, English

Students: For 1998/99, 59% Hispanic (primarily Salvadorean), 24% White, 14% African-American and 3% Asian; 31% are Language Majority and 69% Language Minority; 28% limited English proficient and 46% Free/Reduced Lunch (low-income background) (Oyster Bilingual School, 1999).

L1/L2 %: Approximately 50% Spanish, 50% English; students read in both languages each day. Each class is taught by two teachers, one responsible for English-medium instruction and one for Spanish-medium instruction. This organization is achieved through larger class sizes and by assigning ancillary or resource teacher allocations to classroom instruction.[4]

Goals: The development of students who are biliterate and bicultural.

Results: Grade 3 Reading, Mathematics, Language and Science scores were more than one median grade equivalent above norms (percentiles 74–81); Grade 6 grade equivalents were more than 3.5 years above norms (percentiles 85–96) (1991 data). The school was ranked in the top 8% of Washington DC schools in reading and mathematics on the SAT-9 test (1997/1998 data).

Comments: Started in 1971, the school has evolved a social identities project (Freeman, 1998) that communicates strongly to students the value of linguistic and cultural diversity. In the words of one of the teachers: 'It's much more than language'.

The Foyer Model of Trilingual/Bicultural Education

Location: Belgium (Brussels)

Languages: Dutch, French, and one of the following: Arabic, Italian, Spanish, Turkish.

Students: Students from the following backgrounds: Italian (2 schools), Spanish (2 schools), Turkish (1 school) and Moroccan (1 school)

L1/L2%: Nursery school (ages 3–5): 50% L1 (L1 grouping), 50% Dutch (integrated in multi-ethnic groups);
Primary school (ages 6–12):
Year 1:   60% L1 (reading, writing, mathematics)
         30% Dutch-medium (L1 grouping)
         10% Dutch-medium (multi-ethnic groups)
Year 2:   50% L1 (language, culture)
         20% Dutch-medium (L1 grouping)
         30% Dutch-medium (multi-ethnic groups)
Year 3+: 10% L1
         90% Dutch-medium + French lessons (multi-ethnic groups)

Goals:
1. To prepare all children and teachers to live together in a complex, multicultural society;
2. To enable migrant children to acquire fluency and literacy in three languages by the end of elementary schooling;

3. To increase migrant children's opportunities for integration in both the host country and in their countries of origin;

4. To increase family involvement in the school and society in general.

Results: Project students develop better L1 knowledge than those in monolingual Dutch schools, although their L1 knowledge is less than that of students in their countries of origin. Students also develop a level of Dutch sufficient to enable them to keep up with subsequent classes at secondary school, although there are still differences between them and Dutch-L1 Belgian students.

Comments: Started in 1981 by Foyer (a non-state organization concerned with the well-being of immigrant communities in Brussels), the project assumed as axiomatic that children should be taught in part by teachers of the same origin as themselves in order to support their sense of identity (Byram & Leman, 1990; Reid & Reich, 1992). According to the evaluation report on Dutch proficiency 'children in the experimental group succeed in catching up on most of their arrears in proficiency in the course of primary school'. (Jaspaert, 1989: 47)

The Collaborative Creation of Power in Three School Programs

Some commonalities are immediately obvious. All three schools articulate the value for individual students and their families of developing strong L1 proficiency in both oral and written modes. In doing so, they are challenging the still pervasive devaluation and sometimes 'linguicidal' orientation towards the mother tongues of subordinated groups in the wider society (Skutnabb-Kangas, 2000) The goals of these schools reflect both *language as right* and *language as resource* orientations (Ruiz, 1984).

The following quotations from evaluation reports and other documentation illustrate other aspects of the deep structure of collaborative empowerment and willingness to challenge coercive relations of power that characterizes these schools.

Richmond Road

From Courtney Cazden's (1989) report come these quotes from teachers in Richmond Road that illustrate the ways in which identities are negotiated between teachers and students and among teachers from different backgrounds:

> We, as teachers, share our various ethnic backgrounds with each other. This helps to enrich us as a group working together. And not only that – the children also share their backgrounds with each other and with the teachers. The whole basis of the subject content matter of the school is who we are in *this* school. (1989: 148)

I'm learning from the kids – their cultures, and not only that, their languages as well. (1989: 148)

It's taken a long time, but for me – like many people before – I think of Richmond Road now as my *turangawaiwai* [a place to stand]. It's the place, and what it represents to me, in my mind and my heart. I left Fiji with a chip on my shoulder, and I had nothing to do with Fijian people for ten years. It's only by being involved with the philosophy here: we're constantly telling people not to be sucked up in the system that says you have to speak English and be like an English person before you can succeed. And I realized that here *I* was, telling them to do these things, and *I* wasn't even doing them myself. I had never spoken to *my* children in Fijian. This was a big discovery to me. I felt good about myself before, but as a *New Zealand* person. Whereas now, because of the experiences that I had here, I feel totally different. (1989: 149)

When I was a child, my mother never came near the school, because she felt she didn't have a place in it. Here people come and feel they're *helping*, and I think that's what's important – that everybody's got something they can *do* for the school. If parents and children feel that school is a special place for them, then the child benefits from this liaison. When you, as a teacher, have the support of the parents who feel good about the place, then there's nothing that can't be done for that child. That's special about Richmond Road. And, of course, it's happening for *each* ethnic group. (1989: 158–159)

When teachers who belong to groups with differential status in the wider society share as equals within the school, this constitutes a challenge to the pattern of coercive macro-interactions in the society. Similarly, when teachers *learn* from their culturally diverse students, a shift in the pattern of power relations has occurred. When the school creates a climate of two-way partnership with parents from varied backgrounds and values the language and cultural resources they can bring to school, collaborative empowerment is taking place.

Oyster Bilingual School

Rebecca Freeman (1998) provides detailed discourse analyses that illustrate how the micro-interactions between educators and students in Oyster bilingual school 'refuse' the discourse of subordination that characterizes the wider society and most conventional school contexts. She points out that the discourse practices in the school 'reflect an ideological assumption that linguistic and cultural diversity is a resource to be developed by all students, and not a problem that minority students must overcome in order to participate and achieve at school' (p. 233). Specifically, educators have *choices* in the way they organize discourse practices and these choices entail significant consequences for both language minority and majority students. The school *requires* all students to become bilingual and biliterate in Spanish and English, and 'to expect, tolerate, and respect diverse ways of interacting' (1998: 27).

> Oyster's bilingual program has two complementary agendas that together challenge the unequal distribution of rights in mainstream US schools and society. First, the dual-language program is organized so that language minority and language majority students have the opportunity to develop the ability to speak two languages and to achieve academically through two languages. Second, the social identities project is organized so that language minority students gain experience seeing themselves as having the right to participate equally in the academic discourse, and the language majority students gain experience respecting that right. (1998: 231)

In other words, the school 'aims to promote social change on the local level by socializing children differently from the way children are socialized in mainstream US educational discourse' (1998: 27).

> Rather than pressuring language minority students to assimilate to the positively evaluated majority social identity (white middle-class native English-speaking) in order to participate and achieve at school, the Oyster educational discourse is organized to positively evaluate linguistic and cultural diversity. ... this socializing discourse makes possible the emergence of a wide range of positively evaluated social identities, and offers more choices to both language minority and language majority students than are traditionally available in mainstream US schools and society. The Oyster educators argue that students' socialization through this educational discourse is the reason that [limited English proficient], language minority, and language majority students are all participating and achieving more or less equally. (1998: 27)

The Oyster Bilingual School Local School Plan for the school year 1999–2000 provides more information about the outstanding achievement levels of the students and insight into the conditions that nurture this achievement. It notes that Oyster has moved from being ranked 25th out of 119 Washington DC elementary schools in the results of standardized tests in 1982 (top 21%) to being ranked 9th out of 111 elementary schools in the results of the SAT-9 reading and mathematics assessment in 1998 (top 8%). On the Spanish achievement test (APRENDA) 51% of Oyster students scored at the proficient or advanced levels in reading and 77% scored at the proficient or advanced levels in mathematics (Oyster Bilingual School, 1999).

The Local School Plan also notes that:

> The hallmark of Oyster's dual-language immersion program is that it nurtures students' valuing of themselves and their valuing of others. That cherishing of human growth comes in significant measure from the way that the dual language immersion program is delivered at Oyster. From Pre-Kindergarten, students learn in an atmosphere where language and culture are integrated. ... the equal valuation of two languages communicates to the children that cultures and the people who are products of those cultures are also to be equally valued. (1999: 3)

There is an obvious congruence between these accounts of why and how the Oyster Bilingual School succeeds so well and the *empowerment/negotiating identities framework* presented in Chapter 2.

The Foyer Model

A number of themes run through the various evaluation reports of the Foyer project. One is the necessity for schools to focus directly on issues of *identity* if they are to prepare students to thrive in a complex multilingual multicultural social context. In Brussels (and Belgium as a whole), French is the more prestigious language but Dutch is the majority language. Because of the similarity of languages, Spanish and Italian children often acquire French on the street and are frequently more fluent in French than their Dutch-speaking peers. These students speak their L1 in the home and frequently visit their countries of origin during the summer. So three languages permeate many aspects of their lives and constitute significant components of their *Belgian* identity.

At one level the school simply reflects and positively valorizes this multilingual and multicultural reality. However, the apparent logic and 'obviousness' of this approach masks its uniqueness and the challenge it constitutes to the educational status quo. Unlike more traditional schools that ignore and (implicitly or explicitly) devalue students' home language and culture, Foyer communicates to students (and their parents) the fact that their languages and cultures are *resources* that provide them with expanded options or *choices* with respect to both identity and future life choices (e.g. employment possibilities, place or residence etc.).

Also clear from the Foyer case study is the fact that trilingualism can be developed at no cost to students' achievement in the dominant language of society and school (Dutch). Although the evaluation comparisons involve small numbers, it is clear that teachers, researchers, and parents consider the program to be highly successful with most students coming close to Dutch (L1) norms by the end of elementary school.

In short, the organizational structures of the project together with the ways in which educators have defined their roles or identities result in a pattern of micro-interactions that expand the identity options and academic opportunities available to language minority students. The *language as resource* orientation that permeates the ethos of the Foyer schools challenges and refutes the *language as problem/minorities as inferior* orientation that characterizes more typical educational contexts.

In the next section, we turn to a very different form of research from the case studies considered above. Wayne Thomas and Virginia Collier have been conducting an extremely large-scale study of the outcomes of different kinds of programs over the past decade. Their data support the efficacy of dual language or two-way bilingual immersion programs together with developmental (late-exit) programs as compared to traditional withdrawal ESL programs. Not surprisingly, their study has been controversial.

The Thomas/Collier Study

The study entitled *School Effectiveness for Language Minority Students* carried out by Wayne Thomas and Virginia Collier (1997) is undoubtedly one of the largest investigations of educational effectiveness ever conducted. It involved analysis of more than 700,000 student records compiled from five large school systems during the years 1982–1996. Student progress was examined both cross-sectionally and longitudinally. The core analyses were carried out on 42,317 students who had attended the participating schools for four years or more. More than 150 home languages are represented in the sample with Spanish the largest language group comprising 63% overall.

Thomas and Collier investigated two central questions: (1) How long does it take ELL students to reach the 50th Normal Curve Equivalent (NCE), taking account of age on arrival in the US and type of program attended? (2) What is the influence of school program and instructional variables on the long-term academic achievement of ELL students? With respect to the first question, Thomas and Collier report that:

> It takes typical bilingually schooled students who are achieving on grade level in L1, from 4–7 years to make it to the 50th NCE (normal curve equivalent) in L2. It takes typical 'advantaged' immigrants with 2–5 years of on-grade-level home country schooling in L1 from 5–7 years to reach the 50th NCE in L2, when schooled all in L2 in the US. It takes the typical young immigrant schooled all in L2 in the US 7–10 years or more to reach the 50th NCE, and the majority of these students do not ever make it to the 50th NCE, unless they receive support for L1 academic and cognitive development at home. (1997: 36)

They report that the amount of formal schooling in L1 that students have received is the strongest predictor of how rapidly they will catch up academically in L2. This factor is a stronger predictor than socioeconomic status or the extent to which parents may or may not speak English.

Thomas and Collier interpret this pattern of findings in terms of Collier's (1995) *Prism Model*. This model has four major components that 'drive' language acquisition for school: sociocultural, linguistic, academic, and cognitive processes. Within the prism are the social and cultural processes that impact on the child's experience in home, school, community, and the broader society. These sociocultural processes incorporate the influences that I have discussed in terms of both macro-interactions and micro-interactions in Chapter 2. In a similar way to the discussion of *negotiating identities* in Chapter 2, Thomas and Collier note that sociopolitical and affective factors will strongly influence the student's response to the new language, 'affecting the process positively only when the student is in a socioculturally supportive environment' (1997: 42).

The boundaries of the prism are formed by L1 + L2 language development, L1 + L2 cognitive development, and L1 + L2 academic development. Thomas and Collier note the interdependence of all four components: 'If one is developed to the neglect of another, this may be detrimental to a student's overall growth and future success'

(1997: 44). Thus, programs that focus only on language development in English tend to ignore both cognitive development and sociocultural processes and provide support for overall academic development either minimally or not on grade level.

With respect to the second question, Thomas and Collier report major differences in long-term academic outcomes (in English) across programs. They point out that their results are aggregated from a series of four to eight year longitudinal studies from well-implemented, mature programs in five school districts. Students whose achievement is represented in the following table are those who began schooling in the US in kindergarten with no proficiency in English and whose background is low socioeconomic status as measured by eligibility for free or reduced lunch. However, a similar pattern was found for other cohorts from different socioeconomic levels. The pattern of mean NCE findings for students at the Grade 11 level is presented below. The proportion of the samples (at the elementary school level) in each of these program types is represented in parentheses.

Two-way developmental bilingual education programs (two-way bilingual immersion):	NCE	61	(3%)
One-way developmental bilingual education (late-exit) with content-based ESL support:	NCE	52	(7%)
Transitional bilingual education with content ESL:	NCE	40	(9%)
Transitional bilingual education together with ESL, both taught traditionally:	NCE	35	(17%)
ESL taught through academic content:	NCE	34	(13%)
ESL pullout, taught traditionally:	NCE	24	(51%)

Thomas and Collier interpret the differences in programs in terms of the fact that the developmental bilingual programs 'address all of the Prism model dimensions, rather than only one or two as in the other program types' (1997: 54).

Critique of the Thomas/Collier Study

The Thomas and Collier study has been critiqued by Christine Rossell (1998) on several grounds. She characterizes them as arguing that treatment and control groups are unnecessary and claims that this represents an 'unscientific' position; she further criticizes them for the lack of detailed statistical and sampling information in their report; and finally, she argues that their results do not conform to the outcomes of small-scale two-way bilingual immersion programs and are thus not credible.

Rossell's first point has been addressed earlier in this chapter. As noted above, her literature review (with Keith Baker) is characterized by inaccurate and arbitrary labelling of programs, inconsistent application of criteria for 'methodological acceptability', and highly inaccurate interpretation of the results of early French immersion programs. It is hardly a model of 'scientific' inquiry and the

Thomas/Collier study does not suffer in comparison to what Rossell characterizes as 'scientific'.[5]

Rossell's second point reflects the fact that methodological details in the Thomas/Collier report are sketchy. A detailed report providing the kind of information lacking in the Thomas/Collier (1997) overview is in preparation and will address many of the concerns raised regarding the sketchiness of the data reported to date (personal communication, Virginia Collier and Wayne Thomas, January 2000). However, even if Thomas and Collier provide extremely detailed information on sample selection and analysis, it is unlikely to satisfy anti-bilingual critics because they selected programs, in consultation with school district educators, that were mature, well-implemented, and illustrative of particular pedagogical approaches (e.g. content-based ESL, traditional pedagogy, etc.). Thus, anyone inclined for political reasons to disbelieve the outcomes would likely claim that there is significant danger of selection bias that might have affected the program comparisons.[6]

By contrast, however, it could be argued that Thomas and Collier have provided educators and policy-makers with exactly the kind of information they need to implement appropriate programs. They have shown the kinds of educational outcomes that are possible when certain sociocultural, linguistic (L1/L2), cognitive and academic components are included in the program design and implemented in a consistent and sustained way. Their *Prism Model* is coherent theoretically and useful for program planning. It highlights in a concise way most of the considerations that have formed the basis of the framework articulated in the present volume and in Cummins (1996) (e.g. the relationship between macro- and micro-interactions (power relationships) and the development of academic language proficiency in L1 and L2).

The credibility of the Thomas/Collier results is clearly related to their consistency with other data. If Rossell's (1998) claim were valid that the outcomes of individual two-way bilingual immersion programs are much more modest than the trends reported by Thomas and Collier, then this inconsistency would require explanation. Comparisons can be made with the trends emerging in two-way and one-way bilingual (developmental) programs and with the performance of ELL students who receive only traditional ESL support.

Consistency of Thomas/Collier Data with Dual Language Program Evaluations

Relatively few two-way programs have students who have reached the 11th grade but some trends are evident. The Oyster two-way program reviewed earlier in this chapter does not disaggregate the results for English L1 and Spanish L1 students but the Grade 6 results reported in Freeman (1998) show students performing more than three grade levels above expectations. These results have been consistent over time (Oyster Bilingual School, 1999). About 73% of the students are either Hispanic or African American, both groups that have tended to underachieve in monolingual English-only programs and thus the outstanding performance of the Oyster students cannot be attributed only to middle-class white Euro-American students. These results are thus consistent with the Thomas/Collier trends.

The River Glen school in San Jose has disaggregated data for English L1 and Spanish L1 students. Dolson and Lindholm (1995) present longitudinal evaluation data from this program. The program involved 90% Spanish instruction in Grades K and 1, 80% in Grades 2 and 3, and 50% in Grades 4 through 5. Thirty percent of instruction in middle school (Grades 6 through 8) was through Spanish. Almost two-thirds of the school population are low-income, based on participation in the Free School Lunch program, and 72% are of Latino/Latina origin. Performance of the Latino/Latina students in Grades K though 5 was compared to a Spanish-speaking comparison group in a high quality late-exit transitional program, and a sample of middle-class English speaking Grades 1–4 students served as a comparison group for the English L1 students.

With respect to conversational skills development, a large majority (more than 90%) of the Grades 3–5 Spanish-speaking students were rated as fluent in English in spite of the limited quantity of English instruction in the school day. Almost 80% of the English-speaking students were rated as fluent in Spanish by Grade 5. All students made much better than average progress in content areas such as science, math, and social studies taught in Spanish. Spanish reading and language scores for both groups were also extremely high (greater than 95th percentile at Grade 5). Dolson and Lindholm summarize the results in English reading as follows:

> In English reading achievement by third grade, English speaking students scored average to above average. By fifth grade, 85% of the English speakers were scoring above the 50th percentile, and over 50% of the students above the 75th percentile. The English speaking students' performance was also slightly higher than English speaking counterparts in the regular English-only instructional program. Among the Spanish speakers, performance in English reading increased steadily across the grade levels. However, their reading achievement in English did not approach average until seventh grade … Comparisons of the Spanish speaking two-way bilingual immersion students with Spanish speaking students in a high quality transitional bilingual education program in the district indicated that the bilingual immersion students scored higher in every area: Spanish reading, language, and mathematics, and English reading and mathematics. (1995: 91–92)

The fact that the River Glen Spanish L1 students outperformed similar students in a high quality transitional bilingual program and were close to grade norms in English academic achievement by Grade 7 is consistent with the trends reported by Thomas and Collier. They note, for example, that minority language students in the enrichment two-way and one-way developmental programs reach the 50th percentile sometime between the fourth and seventh grade. Recall also that the late-exit (one-way developmental) students in the Ramírez (1992) study were projected to reach grade expectations by Grade 7.

Another two-way bilingual program that has reported detailed longitudinal data is the *Amigos* Spanish–English program in the Robert F. Kennedy School in Cambridge, Massachusetts (Cazabon, Nicoladis & Lambert, 1998; Nicoladis, Taylor, Lambert & Cazabon, 1998; Office of Educational Equity, 1990; Pérez-Sélles, 2000. See also the *Portraits of Success* web site (http://www.lab.brown.edu/public/NABE/portraits.taf) for a detailed description of the program). This program is implemented from kindergarten through Grade 8 and approximately half the time is spent through each language. All subject areas (i.e. language arts, mathematics, science, and social studies) are taught in each language by a native-speaker of that language.

The research design included comparison from Grades 4 through 8 with both Spanish-speaking and English-speaking control groups using results from a sequence of several years in each comparison. The English controls were native-English-speaking students enrolled in the regular all-English program that is housed in the same school as the Amigos program. The Spanish controls were native-Spanish-speaking students enrolled in the transitional bilingual stream in the Cambridge Public Schools. At later grade levels, most of these students would have been relatively recent arrivals from Spanish-speaking countries whose previous schooling was through Spanish. Non-verbal ability, assessed by means of Raven's Coloured Progressive Matrices, was controlled in all of the comparisons. A large majority of the Spanish-L1 and English-L1 students in the Amigos program come from low-income backgrounds, reflected in the fact that in the years covered by the evaluation approximately 75% qualified for the free or reduced lunch program.

On the California Achievement Test which was used to assess English reading, the English Amigos performed above the English control group at all grade levels between Grade 4 and 8, with differences statistically significant in four out of five comparisons. The Spanish-L1 Amigos also performed above the English control group in four out of five comparisons but the differences were not statistically significant. The Spanish Amigos were performing very close to grade level in English reading at Grades 6 and 8 but below grade level at Grade 7.[7] Significant differences in English reading were observed between English and Spanish Amigos (in favour of English Amigos) at Grades 4, 5, and 6 but not at Grades 7 and 8.

The Spanish Amigos performed significantly better than English Amigos in Spanish reading at the Grades 4 and 5 level but not in subsequent grades (on the Spanish Achievement in Bilingual Education (SABE) test). It is worth noting that the Spanish Amigos' grade equivalents in Spanish reading are lower at all grade levels than their grade equivalents in English, possibly reflecting a somewhat greater emphasis on English than on Spanish in this 50:50 program.

More recent data from the 1999 Massachusetts Comprehensive Assessment System (MCAS), the state-mandated Grades 4 and 8 test (conducted in English), showed the Amigos program to be performing extremely well (Pérez-Sélles, 2000). At Grade 4, Amigos ranked fourth in the Cambridge School District (out of 15 schools) in the combined Average Scaled scores for Math, Language Arts, and Science and Technology. The district average combined MCAS score was 693, the state average was 706 while Amigos scored at 711. The top-ranked school in the district had a combined MCAS score of 724. These results are all the more remarkable considering the fact that Amigos has far greater numbers of students classified as limited English proficient, qualifying for free or reduced lunch, and with a home language other than English compared to the three higher ranked schools or the district average. The comparative data are presented below:[8]

School	Combined MCAS	% LEP	Reduced Lunch	Home Language
Cambridgeport	724	<1%	23%	14%
Graham Parks	715	20%	33%	37%
King Open	713	5%	21%	16%
Amigos	711	61%	55%	64%
District Average	693	16%	45%	44%

In short, although there is some fluctuation in scores from grade to grade, the equivalent performance in English reading of the Spanish Amigos to the English-speaking controls from Grades 4–8, together with the fact that the Grade 8 scores of the Spanish Amigos are very close to grade level, supports both the efficacy of this form of two-way bilingual immersion program and the outcomes reported by Thomas and Collier (1997).

One other set of scores from a two-way bilingual immersion program can be reported. The Korean–English Dual Language program at Cahuenga Elementary School in Los Angeles has compiled the achievement test scores up to Grade 5 (1997–98) for both Korean L1 and English L1 students in the program over several years. The school is located near Korean Town in the heart of Los Angeles and about 90% of the students in the school qualify for free lunch. Despite the fact that over 90% of the Korean L1 students in the program were classified as non- or limited-English speaking on entry, their Grade 4 English reading scores were at the 61st Normal Curve Equivalent (NCE), compared to NCEs of 67.7 for English-L1 students in the dual language program and 53.9 for Korean background students in the Los Angeles Unified School District as a whole (all of the data reported for this program are based on personal communication from Shelley Kwock, Coordinator, Asian Pacific and Other Languages Office of the Los Angeles Unified School District).

On the statewide assessment using the Stanford 9 Test (SAT-9) administered in the 1997/98 school year, Grade 4 Korean L1 students in the dual language program scored at the 85th percentile ($N = 23$) in Reading compared to the 88th percentile ($N = 3$) for the English L1 students in the program and the 65th percentile for students of all backgrounds in the Cahuenga school as a whole ($N = 63$). On the Language and Math subtests of the SAT-9, the Grade 4 Korean L1 students in the dual language program scored at the 98th and 97th percentile respectively. The Grade 5 Korean L1 students ($N = 20$) in the dual language program performed at the 62nd,

69th, and 76th percentiles respectively on the SAT-9 Reading, Language, and Math subtests administered in 1998.

The UCLA Korean Reading Test was administered to the students, again with impressive results for the Korean L1 students in the program. The 1995/96 Grade 2 students scored a mean of 51.7 on this test compared to 56.1 for Korean students in Seoul, Korea who were receiving instruction exclusively in Korean. The English L1 students in the program scored 27.2 and Korean L1 students in the district who were not enrolled in the dual language program scored 25.9. Other comparisons showed Grade 4 Korean L1 students in the district scoring 90.1% correct on this measure in 1996/97 compared to 59.6% correct for Korean students in the district who were not enrolled in the program.

In short, the English reading data for language minority students in this Korean dual language program clearly surpass the average performance levels reported by Thomas and Collier for dual language programs, adding credence to their claims regarding the comparative effectiveness of this bilingual model.

To conclude, these examples from well-implemented two-way bilingual programs suggest that low socioeconomic status language minority students can attain grade norms by the middle school stage (Grade 7) in these programs. For Latino/Latina students, performance in these programs is much better than has traditionally been reported in either all-English or quick-exit transitional bilingual programs. Furthermore, the Ramírez (1992) late-exit program data and the additional analyses by Beykont (1994) suggest that the same trends are evident in well-implemented one-way developmental programs. The comparatively lower performance of students in both quick-exit transitional bilingual education and English-only ESL programs, reported by Thomas and Collier (1997) conforms to well-established trends for Spanish-L1 Latino/Latina students born in the US to drop out more frequently than English-L1 students and show significantly lower levels of educational performance.[9]

Thus, I find the Thomas and Collier study highly credible because of its consistency with the trends emerging from well-implemented individual two-way and one-way developmental bilingual programs. These trends are also consistent with predictions derived from the theoretical frameworks elaborated in their own work and in the present volume.

In the next chapter, I discuss the sociopolitical nature of the debate on bilingual education in the United States and the steps required to shift from a pattern of coercive relations of power to dialogue aimed at establishing collaborative relations of power.

Notes

1. Wayne Thomas (personal communication, January 2000) points out that another limitation to this approach is that it:

    severely limits the 'scientific' research questions that might be investigated. Specifically, the research questions one can ask are limited to ones of the form: 'What differences among groups remain at post-test time when initial differences among groups have been controlled?' Other potentially informative research questions (e.g.

'What trends in achievement gains are evident over the past 5–10 years among groups of interest, irrespective of initial achievement levels?') are thereby eliminated or inappropriately dismissed as 'unscientific' by the over-emphasis on the pre-post control-group design in its experimental (randomized) or quasi-experimental (unrandomized) forms. Thus, longer-term, time-series questions and questions where *achievement change or achievement trends*, not final achievement levels, are the variable of interest are perfectly legitimate and scientific.

2. I do not want to suggest here that a 'scientific' or positivistic paradigm is non-problematic or in any way superior to other paradigmatic approaches to research or theory construction (see Carr and Kemmis (1986) for discussion). It simply happens to be the major paradigm within which the debate on the effectiveness of bilingual education has been conducted. The point I wish to make is that even within the framework of this paradigm, it is highly inappropriate to restrict the evidence only to quasi-experimental research.

3. This is true for both positivistic and non-positivistic orientations to scientific research. For example, ethnographic research into social realities employs these processes to generate theory in much the same way as quantitative research on physical phenomena, as in the example of meteorology.

4. Fern (1995) provides the following account (based on interviews with Paquita Holland, school principal in 1993) of how Oyster Bilingual School achieves its two teachers per class organization:

> Holland estimates that the additional staff costs about 20% more than with traditional staffing patterns; however, she maintains that this added cost is recuperated by saving the school system approximately $100,000 that is allocated to Oyster each year for substitute teachers. If a teacher is absent at Oyster, her teamed teacher is able to teach the class alone. Holland points to the team model as one of the school's ongoing challenges; it does have its disadvantages, it seems. Teachers do not always have the option of choosing their teaching partners, and sometimes generational, philosophical, and personality conflicts develop. (1995: 501)

5. In response to Rossell's (1998) characterization of the Thomas and Collier (1997) position, Wayne Thomas (personal communication, January 2000) notes that:

> Actually, we said that true control groups are unavailable (each program group is a treatment group) and that the portion of the test norm group with the same pre-test scores as the program (treatment) groups can serve as a suitable 'no treatment' comparison group in the necessary absence of true 'no treatment' control groups. Rossell mangled this into 'treatment and control groups are unnecessary'. She further muddied the water by confusing the concepts of comparison groups and 'no treatment' control groups by using them interchangeably, by asserting incorrectly that one cannot construct a comparison group from the subset of the norm group with the same pretest scores. … [This is] possibly true in a short-term study but not in a long-term study, and ours is a long-term study.

Thomas (personal communication, January, 2000) also points out that the fact that Rossell and Baker (1996) in their literature review 'used the outmoded and primitive vote counting technique, instead of cumulative probabilities or effect sizes is prima-facie evidence of un-scientific analysis'.

6. Thomas (personal communication, January, 2000) notes in relation to the issue of selection bias:

> If what is meant is that we could have selected 'bad' ESL pullout programs with low scores, thus underestimating this program's true effect, and selected only 'good' two-way programs with high scores, thus over-estimating this program's true effect, we stated that we selected programs based on criteria of 'full and faithful' implementation *long before we knew what their scores were like over time*. Also, we now know that the

highest scores seen for ESL Pullout are very low (18th percentile is the all-time maximum from any district) and that scores for two-way programs vary above and below the program mean, but are always at or above those for the best English-only programs.

7. Unfortunately Cazabon *et al.* (1998) do not specify what kind of score they are reporting in their Tables. Based on Rossell's (1998) discussion of Grades 1–3 Amigos data, I am assuming that the figures in the Cazabon *et al.* reports are in fact grade equivalents. Also, since the figures reported by Cazabon *et al.* (1998) represent mean scores adjusted for group differences in non-verbal ability, they should be treated with caution since the unadjusted scores are not provided. My assumption also is that the Amigos students in the Grades 4 through 8 comparisons have been in the program continuously at least over this period; in other words, the Grade 8 students have been in the program for at least five years and are not recent arrivals.

8. These data were compiled by Marla Pérez-Sélles, Assistant Director of Bilingual Education, Cambridge Public Schools. The Grade 8 MCAS data (1999) showed the Amigos students performing better than the non-Amigos students in Robert F. Kennedy school in all curricular areas. Also, 'when compared with district and state scores, a higher rate of Amigos 8th graders, 63% of whom are Hispanic, passed the 1999 MCAS Language Arts test' (Pérez-Sélles, 2000: 1). However, according to Pérez-Sélles (personal communication, March, 2000), the 8th grade scores were less impressive than the 4th grade scores for two reasons: (1) After Grade 4, a considerable number of newly arrived Spanish-speaking students enter the Amigos program and these students are still catching up in their acquisition of academic English at the time of the Grade 8 testing; (2) At the Grade 5 level students across the district are selected for an accelerated (gifted) program and this results in attrition of some of the most academically advanced students from the Amigos program in Grades 6 through 8.

9. Virginia Collier (personal communication, January, 2000) points out:

> Another point we often make when referring to Baker's and Rossell's summaries of the research is that they generally are referring to short-term studies of 1–3 years, when student achievement is similar across program types initially. But when we follow students long term (at least four years or more), we find increasingly significant differences in student achievement, with students in the enrichment bilingual programs outperforming those who received remedial models of bilingual and/or ESL programs. Thus we feel that the short-term studies don't give policy makers the information they need to make decisions; whereas the long-term studies provide significant policy-making information.

Chapter 9

Challenging the Discourse of Disempowerment Through Collaborative Dialogue

In the debate on bilingual education in the United States, discourses of educational equity collide with discourses that are xenophobic and racist. In between are discourses that are not overtly xenophobic but rather portray themselves as concerned with 'rationality', effectiveness, and cost. As noted in the previous chapter, interpretation of research evidence about the effectiveness of bilingual education in promoting ELL students' academic achievement occupies a central role in this debate. I suggested in Chapter 8 that the research findings permit some clear conclusions to be drawn when they are viewed through the lens of theory.

A recurrent source of frustration for bilingual educators is the difficulty of communicating the research findings to those who actively oppose or just remain skeptical of bilingual education. As suggested above, one group of opponents is primarily concerned with the sociopolitical aspects of bilingual education and the perceived infiltration of 'divisive' multicultural perspectives into public policy. For these commentators, the research is secondary. It is important only as a backup and/or rationalization for more deeply rooted sociopolitical objections to bilingual education.

There is also a communication problem to another group of opponents who are not overtly racist or xenophobic but have been 'disinformed' regarding what the research says. Typically, in the absence of any real understanding of the research, these opponents revert to the common sense view that ELL children should be immersed in English as the self-evidently best way to learn the language.

Two recent volumes by Marcia Moraes (1996) and Lourdes Diaz Soto (1996) each address, in very different ways, the barriers to communication regarding bilingual education. Moraes' treatment of the issue is primarily theoretical, an attempt to establish the foundations of a critical-dialogic pedagogy within bilingual education based on the theoretical contributions of Bakhtin and his colleagues in the 1920s and 1930s Soviet Union. Soto's volume, by contrast, details the struggle of a Puerto Rican community in 'Steel Town' Pennsylvania to preserve a nationally recognized bilingual education program, with 20-years of success to its credit, in the face of opposition from the school superintendent, school board and majority community. I review each of these volumes focusing on the barriers to communication and dialogue that inhibit the implementation of rational and equitable educational policies.

Soto: Language, Culture and Power

The ugly reality of racism jumps off the pages of Soto's volume, making it gripping but also painful reading. The legitimation for the school board's eventual decision to eliminate the bilingual program, despite strong and sustained opposition from the bilingual community, was grounded by attitudes in the broader community that encouraged the following kinds of discourse:

> Listeners heard about the 'Blue E' on the local radio station. The 'Blue E' referred to a proposed city ordinance encouraging local merchants to post a 'Blue E' on their doorways to signify their support for the English-only ordinance. The ordinance provided store owners with the ability to price goods based upon the English language proficiency of their prospective buyer. For example, if the store clerk detected an accent or felt that the buyer's English was not up to par, they were expected to pay an additional 10% to 20% on their purchase since this signified additional paperwork and expense for the merchant.

> Supporters of this ordinance called the radio talk show, expressing views such as: 'Send all the spics back to their country'; 'This is America … for whites only'; 'Our city was better off without all this trash'; 'English is the language my grandparents had to learn'; 'One state should be set aside for these people … but not Pennsylvania'. (Soto, 1996: 65)

The re-emergence of this racism was no doubt stimulated by the growth of bilingual communities in Steel Town (and elsewhere) and by the fact that the community decided to stop 'swallowing hard' and remain silent in the face of discrimination as they historically had done; instead, they mobilized to demand their educational rights and became both audible and visible. In the eyes of the dominant majority, they no longer knew their place.

Soto details some extraordinary scenes that demonstrate the community's commitment to education and the high aspirations parents held for their children. She quotes newspaper accounts of a crucial public hearing on 28 January, 1993 in which more than 100 people approached the table of board members 'who became noticeably frightened when a congregation knelt and prayed on behalf of the bilingual children in Steel Town' (1996: 77):

> The pastor of the Church on Steel Town's Southside took the microphone off its stand and approached board members, speaking softly, 'Bendito, please listen to the parents', he said. 'I've seen too many kids suffer and too many kids don't make it. Let's give the kids a chance.' Facing the audience, the pastor motioned Latino members to come to the front and began to pray as board members found themselves looking up at a solid wall of standing people. 'Bless this administration. Let us love.' The two security guards tensed. (1996: 78)

The vice-president of the board was reported to say later that he appreciated the blessing but that he had seen the light before the hearing: 'I've heard them all before', he said (p. 78).

In Soto's account, the 'bad guys' win: despite the unprecedented mobilization of the Puerto Rican community and a positive report on the bilingual program from a district-wide committee, the bilingual program is eliminated in favor of an English immersion program, a new school is commissioned in a white middle-class district rather than in the much more overcrowded South Side where the Puerto Rican community live, South Side students are bussed out of their neighborhood because of overcrowding and the refusal of the school board to construct additional facilities, the school superintendent gets generous salary increases and accolades from the board, an outspoken Puerto Rican advocate for the bilingual program loses his job in a community college, pastors and priests from various religious groups who supported the community are transferred to other locations, a complaint from the community to the Office of Civil Rights remains in limbo, and the Puerto Rican community emerges from the struggle with emotions ranging from frustration and anger to despondency and resignation.

In her chronicle of these events, Soto makes no pretense to be an outside neutral observer. She participates with the community as an advocate for the bilingual program and equal educational opportunities. Her own voice is strong and articulate as she asks questions such as:

> Is the American Dream for monolinguals only? What will it take to have children's voices heard? …
> To the high school principal who shared how blatant and acceptable racism has become by stating, 'This is America!' I will say that many of us will resist being a part of such an oppressive America. Our schoolchildren are taught about a different America, an America that promises democracy, freedom, and equal educational opportunities. Where is our democratic America? (1996: 94–96)

Unfortunately, as the histories of the United States, Canada and many other countries show, democracy (understood as the rule of the majority) provides only very limited safeguards for subordinated minorities. The brutal physical and sexual abuse suffered by generations of Canadian First Nations children in residential schools run by religious orders under the 'supervision' of government illustrates just how much protection of rights subordinated minorities can expect when the democratic majority considers them to be inherently inferior. As Soto's account illustrates, coercive relations of power persist under the rhetorical veneer of democracy, respect for human rights, and equality of opportunity. What has changed during the past 30 years in many (but by no means all) countries is the perceived need to rationalize and legitimate the hegemony of dominant groups in terms of these latter constructs. Within a democracy, the continued dominance of dominant groups requires the consent of the majority of those who vote. Only a relatively small proportion of members of a society will readily admit (to others or to themselves) that they are racist or bigoted; the majority see themselves, and their nation, as fair, reasonable, and committed to freedom and human rights (within 'reason'). The fact that large doses of historical amnesia are required to preserve and reinforce this individual and collective social identity is not at all problematic for dominant groups. Discourse can readily be mobilized through institutions such as the media and schools (largely controlled by dominant groups) to legitimate coercive relations of power as being reasonable, fair, and in the best interests of both the subordinated minority and the society as a whole. It is desirable, albeit not essential, that members of the subordinated minority also accept this legitimation; it makes for a smoother democratic process.

It is in this light that we can understand the school district superintendent's argument in favor of the new proposal he recommended to the school board:

> Its main premise is early English acquisition, which would ensure success equipping students with the ability to communicate in the language of this country – English! The fact is that English immersion programs are legal and have been implemented successfully all over the United States for many years ... As superintendent, please know that my single motivation for changing the current bilingual education program is my deep and sincere belief that the earlier children master the English language, the better their chances for success. (newspaper column, 27 January, 1993; quoted in Soto, 1996: 76–77)

There is no reason to suspect the superintendent of hypocrisy; he no doubt had (and probably still has) a 'deep and sincere belief' that English immersion is in bilingual children's best interests. Those who hold power also usually hold 'deep and sincere beliefs' that they act in the best interests of the society as a whole and that they have more insight than subordinated communities into what is in the best interests of these communities. Apartheid in South Africa was rationalized in these terms.

The questions left hanging at the end of Soto's volume are 'How can racist educational structures and provision be changed?' 'How can coercive relations of power in schools be transformed into collaborative relations of power?' 'How can marginalized children and communities make their voices heard by those who occupy the centers of power?'

Not surprisingly, she provides no definitive answers to these questions. She invokes the President's Commission on Foreign Language and International Studies (1980) to point out that the society as a whole can benefit from the linguistic and cultural resources of ethnic minority groups. Paulo Freire's (1970, 1985) approach to transformative educational change through grassroots organization and action is also suggested as an appropriate direction for communities. However, the reader is left with the distinct impression of a community at least temporarily spent and dispirited. Community organization and action was tried but to no avail. Those who held power used it to reinforce the barriers between the center and the margins. Largely unresolved in Soto's volume is the issue of why dominant groups should do otherwise and how can marginalized communities generate the power to persuade or force them to abandon coercive models of power relations in favor of more collaborative models.

Interestingly, this is the central issue that Brazilian educator Marcia Moraes attempts to address in her treatment of bilingual education in the United States.

Moraes: A Dialogue with the Bakhtin Circle

Moraes uses the work of the Bakhtin Circle (e.g. Bakhtin, 1986) to argue both for a dialogic-critical pedagogy within bilingual education programs and for an approach to educational and societal change that goes beyond the Freirean model of the oppressed struggling for liberation from the oppressor. She suggests that whereas the Freirean social movement towards awareness and struggle is from the margins to the center, a Bakhtinian movement would be from the margins but also from the center. We need a pedagogy of the oppressor as much as a pedagogy of the oppressed, she asserts. Dominant/oppressive groups have been educated 'toward a tacit understanding that they are superior. Therefore the oppressed can be best empowered if we also turn our attention to the oppressor' (1996: 115). Moraes elaborates on this point as follows:

> We need to create conditions for oppressors to critically analyze their own situation; to critically analyze the levels in which they are also oppressed because they live under various forms of social control and are discursively positioned in contradictory ways that blind them to their own situatedness in relations of power and privilege. Then students from the oppressive groups will be able to understand the oppression of the oppressed, since they are also part of the oppressed group that is ideologically controlled. (1996: 115)

> ... if we do not reinforce the relevance of a dialogic interaction between the oppressed and oppressor, it will be more difficult for the oppressed to overcome social constraints and, therefore, to be empowered. From this perspective, the awareness of the oppressed is fundamental, but the awareness of the oppressor is crucial in the sense that the oppressor can understand that he or she must collaborate for a better society, for his or her own emancipation as part of the social arena ... Then we can take a truly liberatory step toward emancipation and social freedom and a step toward democracy because the oppressive groups will be able to understand that oppression toward the other becomes their own imprisonment. (1996: 112)

How does the work of a group of Soviet intellectuals in the 1920s and 1930s, who were more directly focused on the nature of language and communication than on social change, lead us to these conclusions? Bakhtinian constructs such as *dialogue* and *heteroglossia* are analyzed as follows by Moraes to make the connection between the nature of language and social interaction, on the one hand, and social transformation on the other:

> According to Bakhtinian theory, *an individual does not exist outside of dialogue* – a dialogue in which the consciousness of the speaker encounters the consciousness of another speaker; a dialogue that reveals conflicts; a dialogue that embodies history and culture; … In the Bakhtinian sense of dialogue … the existence of the self and the other is a simultaneous existence; a dialogical existence. The Bakhtinian notion of language embraces the idea that the other cannot be silenced or excluded … language never exists outside historical forces and … the dialogic essence of language implies that a unique group can never dominate all other languages completely. (1996: 94–95)

The notion of *heteroglossia* refers to the multiple ideologically infused discourses that intersect in all utterances and forms of language use. Thus, 'language must be understood as a site of political struggle in which meanings collide and have to be negotiated' (p. 95). Moraes quotes Quantz and O'Connor (1988: 99) to the effect that the heteroglossic essence of social life can be better understood through the concept of *multivoicedness*:

> Multivoicedness seems to be the term that best captures the idea that any particular, concrete, historical dialogue is best described in tems of the multiple voices participating … The concept of dialogue as a multivoiced social activity explains how the ideas of the powerful gain and maintain legitimacy as well as how the disempowered can attempt to legitimate their ideas and beliefs to others. (Moraes, 1996: 100–101)

The foundations of a dialogic-critical pedagogy are rooted in the fact that 'both oppressed and oppressor must understand that our dialogic existence is something that cannot be denied' (p. 112). Thus, we must construct a pedagogy that initiates and maintains a living dialogue between oppressed and oppressors whereby both groups can understand the social constraints that inhibit progress toward an emancipatory democracy and become more aware of the different forms of oppression each group experiences.

Moraes asks the obvious question 'How can we make the oppressor aware that society cannot function fairly while people just think in egocentric and binaristic terms of domination and subordination?' (p. 113) She replies to this question as follows:

> The fact is the oppressor must also understand and be aware of social inequalities … [We have to construct] a dialogic-critical pedagogy in which students who occupy the position of oppressors understand that the oppositional relationship between oppressor and oppressed is not a relationship that will guarantee social freedom or social hope. It is important that the oppressor

recognizes that both social freedom and social hope can be reached through dialogic interaction. (1996: 113)

While these sentiments are difficult to contest, we are still left with the same question that faced us on the final pages of Soto's volume. Why should dominant groups give up or share their (coercive) power? How can subordinated/oppressed groups convince their oppressors that it is also in their best interests to move towards more collaborative models of social progress? I know of no opponent of bilingual or multicultural education who is likely to be convinced by the argument that 'our dialogic existence is something that cannot be denied' (Moraes, 1996: 112). In response to the argument that 'the oppressor must understand and be aware of social inequalities' (p. 113), those positioned as oppressors are likely to respond that they are very much aware of social inequities and that's why they are adamant that bilingual children must learn English as early and as quickly as possible.

It is tempting to dismiss the Bakhtinian-inspired perspective of reciprocal two-way dialogue between oppressed/oppressors advanced by Moraes as naive and impractical. It is much more straightforward to work from a Freirean perspective where the oppressed identify their oppression and its source in coercive power structures and take steps to transform their world through language and concrete action. The open racism and unwillingness to engage in any form of serious dialogue that the Puerto Rican community encountered in Soto's account reinforces the view that rights will only be achieved by means of active community-based struggle against oppression.

It is possible to speculate on further measures that the community might have taken to assert their children's right to a culturally sensitive and equitable education. In addition to pursuing the Civil Rights complaint, they might have considered the action taken by a Finnish community in Sweden who withdrew their children from school for an eight-week period in protest against the school's termination of a successful Finnish–Swedish bilingual program (Skutnabb-Kangas, 1988). The community demands were eventually met by the school who found it difficult to defend its arbitrary decision in the face of national attention and community mobilization in support of the strike. The accounts of this strike demonstrate how coercive power relationships break down when the subordinated group refuses to play their (essential) part in being the recipients of this form of power.

However, I believe it would be highly unfortunate to dismiss Moraes' Bakhtinian perspective as impractical. On the contrary, I believe her work embodies important insights into the nature of progressive social change and how it can be promoted. Moraes is quite explicit in fully supporting the struggle of oppressed groups against the forces that oppress them. In addition to challenging coercive power structures directly, however, she appears to be suggesting that marginalized communities can also engage in other strategies aimed at promoting an identity change among dominant groups through engaging them in dialogue. Her discussion of this process remains largely at a theoretical level and thus, without elaboration, is not particularly helpful to communities whose struggles for educational rights and attempts at dialogue are rebuffed. In what follows I attempt to elaborate in a concrete way what a 'Bakhtinian-inspired' two-way dialogical process involving dominant and subordinated communities might look like, and how pressure and persuasion can be exerted on dominant groups to engage in this type of collaborative dialogue.

Towards Collaborative Dialogue in the Bilingual Education Debate

I see four components to the process of collaborative dialogue when we take it from the theoretical to the practical level:

(1) Recognition that dominant groups are no more homogenous than subordinated groups and to dismiss all of those who enjoy privileged status in our society as 'oppressors' amounts to essentialization that will curtail rather than promote the dialogic process; there is a need to identify and reach out to those within dominant groups who are prepared to engage in meaningful dialogue.
(2) Identification of shared goals and common vested interests that transcend more superficial *Us versus Them* divisions between dominant and subordinated communities.
(3) Demystification of research findings related to the issues under dispute (e.g. bilingual education) and exposure of contradictions and inconsistencies inherent both in academic attempts to distort these research findings and in the media discourse related to diversity.
(4) Promotion of programs that explicitly challenge *Us versus Them* divisions and demonstrate in a concrete way the advantages for all in establishing collaborative relations of power.

Each of these components can be illustrated briefly.

Identification of the possibilities for dialogue

If we consider the fact that approximately 70% of those who voted in California's Proposition 187 plebiscite in 1994 were in favour of severe restrictions on the use of languages other than English, and 61% supported Proposition 227 in 1998, we might well be apprehensive about the impact of further 'democratic' action on minority rights in general and bilingual education in particular. Both these propositions expressed the fear of diversity, the fear of the *Other*, the fear of strangers – xenophobia. They are about power, both social and economic, who has it and who intends to keep it. They can also legitimately be described as racist insofar as they were intended to deny educational and linguistic rights to subordinated groups and to intimidate those who advocate for human rights. These realities must be recognized if we are to fight this type of initiative.

However, we should also recognize that a large proportion of those who supported these two propositions do not see themselves as racist and are not in any sense overtly or actively racist. They would see themselves as supportive of 'the common good' despite the fact that they have bought into (or been indoctrinated into) the discourse of xenophobia. If we dismiss all those who support anti-immigrant initiatives as 'racist' or 'oppressors' then the possibilities of change through democratic action are remote indeed. If we are to challenge the discourse of xenophobia and work toward a saner and more tolerant society we must communicate and engage in dialogue with many of those who currently see diversity as a threat. In fact, we must join forces with them to articulate a vision of our society where there is cooperation rather than competition across cultural boundaries and where cultural and linguistic differences enrich rather than fragment the whole.

Recognition of common goals and shared vested interests

Among the common goals in which all members of society have a vested interest are the following:

Promote Academic Achievement for All

At a time when both corporations and nations acknowledge that intellectual resources are paramount to their future progress, it should not be difficult to agree on the desirability of maximizing the academic and intellectual potential of all students. Every dropout carries a huge price tag for the society: these students' potential to contribute to the economic and social well-being of their society is not realized, there are increased costs for social services ranging from welfare to incarceration, and tax revenues that they might have generated are lost. Subordinated group students are massively over-represented among statistics of school failure in many countries and thus any means of reversing school failure among these students will pay dividends to the society in both short and long term. Initiatives such as bilingual and multicultural education should thus be examined not only through an ideological lens but as dispassionately as possible for their potential to reverse underachievement and realize the intellectual and academic resources of the nation.

Develop Society's Cultural and Linguistic Resources

At a time of dramatically increased global interdependence (e.g. economic and ecological interdependence, the need for cooperation in conflict avoidance and resolution, etc.), the cultural and linguistic resources of any nation assume particular significance. Ability to work together to solve problems across cultural, linguistic, racial, and national boundaries is not only part of the 'job description' coming down from Corporate America, it is essential for social cohesion both in domestic and international arenas. As Robert Hughes succinctly put it: 'In the world that is coming, if you can't navigate difference, you've had it' (1993: 100). From this perspective, it makes no economic or other form of sense for a society to squander its cultural and linguistic resources when, for a minimal investment, they could be so easily developed.

Demystification of research findings

The suspicion that bilingual education is some form of 'Hispanic Plot' to destabilize the nation is fuelled by the apparent counter-intuitive nature of its rationale. This rationale suggests that English proficiency will be better developed if children are taught in Spanish (or some other language) rather than in English. It makes more sense to many skeptics to argue that success in learning English is more likely to be assured if instructional time through English is maximized. As noted in previous chapters, this maximum exposure hypothesis is totally at variance with *all* the research findings from bilingual programs around the world that involve either minority or majority language students. Despite the empirical support for bilingual programs and the fact that some form of bilingual education is implemented in almost every country around the world, there has been a sustained attempt since the early 1980s to discredit both the rationale and empirical foundation of bilingual programs (e.g. Rossell & Baker, 1996).

As noted in the previous chapter, it is not difficult to expose the superficial logic and sociopolitical functions of the attempt to undermine the empirical basis of bilingual education. For example, Rossell and Baker argue for a monolingual program, taught by monolingual teachers, aimed at promoting monolingualism, on the basis of the success of a fully bilingual program (Canadian French immersion), taught by bilingual teachers, whose goal is bilingualism.

In addition, Keith Baker appears to have little problem drawing diametrically opposite conclusions from the same research study at different points in time. Consider the following two interpretations of the El Paso Independent School District research. The El Paso program was labelled 'bilingual immersion' by the district and involved 90 minutes a day of L1 instruction at Grade 1, gradually reducing to 60 minutes a day by Grade 3 and 30 minutes a day by Grade 4 (Gersten & Woodward, 1995; Krashen, 1996). The first quotation comes from a critical review of Porter's book *Forked Tongue* (Baker, 1992) while the second is from a more recent article in the journal *Phi Delta Kappan* (Baker, 1998). The first quotation argues for more intensive forms of bilingual education on the basis of the El Paso data while the second highlights how the El Paso data document the harm that bilingual education does to children's academic development:

> She [Porter] summarizes a report from El Paso (1987) as finding that an all-English immersion program was superior to bilingual education programs. The El Paso report has no such finding. What Porter describes as an all-English immersion program in El Paso is, in fact, a Spanish–English dual immersion program. The El Paso study supports the claims of bilingual education advocates that most bilingual education programs do not use enough of the native language. It does not support Porter's claims that they should use less.

> … Like El Paso, San Diego has an extensive two-language program. Like El Paso, there is evidence that the extensive bilingual education program worked better than the typical bilingual education program. … Like El Paso, the results of the San Diego study argue for more bilingual education programs, not fewer as Porter maintains. (1992: 6)

> El Paso created an SEI (structured English immersion) program in which Spanish instruction was reduced to 30 minutes a day. The district followed

students from this program and from the state-mandated bilingual education program for 12 years. The SEI students scored significantly higher on all tests for 11 straight years. In the 12th year, the SEI students still scored higher, but their advantage was no longer statistically significant, suggesting that, after a decade or so, the harm that bilingual education programs do to learning English is more or less wiped out by continued exposure to English outside the classroom. (1998: 201)

It is clearly an extreme example of *doublethink* (Orwell, 1983/1949)[1] to be able to describe in 1992 a program as 'a Spanish–English dual immersion program' whose positive results support the 'claims of bilingual education advocates that most bilingual education programs do not use enough of the native language' and six years later to describe exactly the same program as a 'structured English immersion' program whose positive results illustrate 'the harm that bilingual education programs do to learning English'. Furthermore, Baker's reporting of the El Paso results in his 1998 article is at variance with Gersten and Woodward's (1995) data. They report that there were no differences between the programs by Grade 7 whereas Baker, citing Gersten and Woodward, claims that the 'structured immersion' program was 'significantly higher on all tests for 11 straight years' (p. 201). Baker (1998) also implies that the El Paso program involved only 30 minutes a day of L1 instruction when, in fact, between 90 and 60 minutes a day of L1 instruction designed to develop Spanish literacy was employed between Grades 1 and 3.

This type of patently contradictory anti-bilingual discourse becomes interpretable when seen as the discourse of the courtroom lawyer whose goal is to present the most persuasive case for her/his client with little regard for the truth. In these courtroom situations, lawyers frequently attempt to obscure the facts so that 'reasonable doubt' is created in the jury. In a climate of xenophobia, all that is needed to confirm the paranoia in relation to 'Hispanic activists' is to create soundbites to the effect that: 'In reading, 83% of the studies showed TBE (transitional bilingual education) to be worse than structured immersion' (Rossell & Baker, 1996: 21). As illustrated in Soto's volume, these soundbites then get recycled through the media and into the discourse of policy-makers providing 'scientific proof' for what was obvious anyway to reasonable observers: namely, bilingual education doesn't work and simply constitutes at best a make-work program for Hispanics and at worst a plot to undermine American values. Even among policy-makers and members of the public who try to look at both sides of the issue, the soundbite's regime of truth highlights the 'fact' that the experts disagree. Thus, decision-makers must invoke other criteria, such as 'common sense' or 'American values' as a basis for action.

Promotion of programs that challenge 'Us versus Them' discourse

The 'Achilles heel' of bilingual education opponents is the success of dual language or two-way bilingual immersion programs considered in previous chapters. According to the 'maximum exposure/time-on-task' argument, these programs should be a disaster for language minority students since they involve much less English instruction than the vast majority of transitional bilingual education or all-English (structured immersion) programs. In fact, as noted above, minority language students in these programs consistently attain or come very close to grade norms in English academic skills by Grade 6 or 7. It is ironic that these two-way programs have been explicitly endorsed by two of the most prominent *opponents* of bilingual education: Rosalie Pedalino Porter and Charles Glenn. The possibility of transforming *Us versus Them* discourse scenarios into *Win–Win* scenarios is clear from an examination of their published statements on these programs.

According to Porter (1990), a two-way or dual immersion program is:

- 'particularly appealing because it not only enhances the prestige of the minority language but also offers a rich opportunity for expanding genuine bilingualism to the majority population' (p. 154);

Such programs promise:

- 'mutual learning, enrichment, and respect' (p. 154). They
- 'are also considered to be the best possible vehicles for integration of language minority students, since these students are grouped with English-speakers for natural and equal exchange of skills' (p. 154).

Furthermore, two-way programs are:

- 'the best opportunity for families that are seriously committed to genuine bilingualism for their children' (p. 154) and these programs
- 'do not cost any more than the average single-language classes to maintain' (p. 156).

There is clearly a *doublethink* process here involving the simultaneous endorsement of (1) English-only immersion programs as the most promising option for bilingual students' academic success because they provide maximum English exposure (time-on-task); and (2) two-way bilingual immersion programs that typically entail *less* English-medium and more L1 instruction than any other bilingual education option. Nevertheless, the identification of points of agreement provides a starting point for collaborative dialogue on the basis of the fact that advocates and opponents of bilingual education both endorse exactly the same form of program option (two-way bilingual) as far superior to the usual form of bilingual education (quick-exit transitional bilingual).

Charles Glenn, a well-respected Massachusetts academic and administrator, has also been critical of bilingual programs that segregate bilingual students from the mainstream but, like Porter, has been one of the strongest and most consistent advocates of two-way bilingual immersion as *the best* program alternative for all students. His own five children have attended a two-way bilingual program:

> More than any other model of education for linguistic minority pupils, two-way bilingual programs meet the diverse expectations that we set for our schools. Properly designed and implemented, they offer a language-rich environment with high expectations for every child, in a climate of cross-cultural

respect. Linguistic minority pupils are stimulated in their use of English, while being encouraged to value and employ their home language as well. (Glenn, 1990: 5).

The best setting for educating linguistic minority pupils – and one of the best for educating *any* pupils – is a school in which two languages are used without apology and where becoming proficient in both is considered a significant intellectual and cultural achievement. (Glenn & LaLyre, 1991: 43)

In summary, the four stages outlined above clearly show the possibilities for collaborative dialogue in the bilingual education debate. Two-way bilingual programs have expanded rapidly in the United States during the past five years (to a current level of close to 300). They clearly chart positive directions for educational enrichment for *all* students. To focus on these programs, and their endorsement by supposed opponents of bilingual education, is probably the most effective strategy for transforming the discourse from a pattern of coercive relations of power to one of collaborative relations of power.[2]

Conclusion

Soto's account of the community struggle for effective bilingual programs in Steel Town shows the ugly face of racism and xenophobia that peers through the transparent veneer of 'deep and sincere beliefs that the earlier children master the English language, the better their chances for success'. Addressing the same issues from the perspective of semiotic theory, Moraes concludes that dialogic interaction between oppressed and oppressor is crucial to the possibility of social change. She combines Freirean and Bakhtinian analyses in arguing for a critical dialogic pedagogy that would equip students (and communities) with the tools both to struggle directly against oppression and to work for dialogue with the oppressor.

In exploring the implications of these volumes for the current debate over bilingual education in the United States, I have attempted to elaborate some of the forms that a collaborative dialogue might take. However disdainful some academics might be of the media's soundbite discourse through which coercive power relations are perpetuated, the reality is that this is the primary discursive arena for the political process. A major implication of Moraes' theoretical analysis is that it is irresponsible to abandon this arena to the forces of racism and xenophobia. In the absence of dialogue, the 'democratic' voice of the dominant majority, infused with pre-recorded soundbite formulas, will ensure that the coercive status quo will remain intact.

Dialogue, by contrast, has at least the potential to identify common concerns and priorities shared by various sectors of the society, expose the superficial logic and sociopolitical manipulation underlying opposition to programs such as bilingual education, and finally work towards concrete social and educational changes that overturn xenophobic '*Us versus Them*' perspectives and implement programs that are self-evidently for the 'common good'. Collaborative dialogue of this type has the potential to cause soundbites to implode because their apparent logic can be sustained only in the absence of dialogue. However, for this process to begin, the 'real' world that Soto describes must be engaged by the 'theoretical' world that Moraes explores in more concrete ways than just subjecting the real world to further theoretical analyses.

Undoubtedly the most effective way to challenge the discursive perpetuation of coercive relations of power it to demonstrate the positive outcomes of programs that implement a transformative pedagogy, as sketched in Figure 2.2. The final chapter attempts to analyze how transformative pedagogies can give rise to micro-interactions between educators and students that challenge coercive relations of power operating in both the discourse and educational structures of the broader social context.

Notes

1. The term *doublethink* was coined by George Orwell in his futuristic novel *Nineteen EightyFour* (1983/1949) to refer to the simultaneous belief in two contradictory ideas. Orwell describes the process of *doublethink* as follows:

   Doublethink means the power of holding two contradictory beliefs in one's mind simultaneously, and accepting both of them. The Party intellectual knows in which direction his memories must be altered; he therefore knows that he is playing tricks with reality; but by the exercise of *doublethink* he also satisfies himself that reality is not violated. The process has to be conscious, or it would not be carried out with sufficient precision, but it also has to be unconscious, or it would bring with it a feeling of falsity and hence of guilt. (1983: 865)

2. Guadalupe Valdés (1997) has sounded an important cautionary note in relation to dual language immersion programs. She suggests that, as currently constituted, they may benefit dominant group students more than subordinate group students and may also fail to address adequately the relationships between language and power in both school and society. This reinforces aspects of the theoretical framework presented in Chapter 2 to the effect that any program, whether it be dual language immersion or some form of English-only program, will be successful for subordinated language minority students only to the extent that it effectively challenges coercive relations of power in the wider society.

   While I agree with Valdés' point that dual language immersion programs are no panacea for students' underachievement, I would argue that they currently present an important opportunity to transcend the *Us versus Them* divisions of the bilingual debate and re-focus the issues on enriched versus remedial education. Also, it is important to remember that by virtue of incorporating the minority language as an equal instructional partner with English throughout elementary school, dual language programs *do* challenge central components of the coercive power structure. However, to be truly effective structural changes in patterns of parental involvement, pedagogy, and assessment must also be incorporated. An excellent example of a dual language program that explicitly sets out to challenge coercive power structures by means of a transformative pedagogy is *La Escuela Fratney* in Milwaukee (Ahlgren, 1993; Peterson, 1994; see Chapter 10).

Chapter 10
Transformative Pedagogy: Who Needs It?

As noted in Chapter 2, transformative pedagogy is realized in interactions between educators and students that attempt to foster collaborative relations of power.[1] Empowerment, understood as the collaborative creation of power, results from classroom interactions that enable students to relate curriculum content to their individual and collective experience and to analyze broader social issues relevant to their lives. This process affirms and extends students' identities and at the same time develops the linguistic and intellectual tools necessary for collaborative critical inquiry. It is important to note that affirmation of identity is a critical process that brings alternative perspectives into the open and encourages students to reflect on and evaluate their own experiences and beliefs.

The theoretical framework attributes the historical patterns of underachievement among marginalized groups to the devaluation of identity that has typically been played out in the interactions between educators and students (e.g. punishment for speaking L1). This devaluation of linguistic, cultural and academic identity reflected the pattern of coercive relations of power that characterized intergroup relations in the broader society. Under these conditions, students quickly became convinced that academic effort was futile and many resisted further devaluation of their identities by mentally withdrawing from participation in the life of the school.

To turn this scenario around and reverse the pattern of academic failure inevitably requires that educators, students, and communities challenge the historical pattern of subordination that has characterized relations in the broader society. When educators encourage culturally diverse students to develop the language and culture they bring from home and build on their prior experiences, they, together with their students, challenge the perception in the broader society that these attributes are inferior or worthless. When educators and culturally diverse parents become genuine partners in children's education, this partnership repudiates the myth that culturally diverse parents are apathetic and don't care about their children's education. When classroom instruction encourages students to inquire critically into social issues that affect their lives (e.g. racism, environmental deterio-ration, omissions of marginalized groups from official histories, etc.), students' intelligence is activated in ways that potentially challenge the societal status quo.

This chapter elaborates on the scope of transformative pedagogy and raises the issue of whether there is any empirical research or 'hard data' that would support the claims that (1) negotiation of identity is a central explanatory construct in under-standing the academic achievement of culturally and linguistically diverse students, and (2) transformative pedagogy is a key element in implementing effec-tive instruction and reversing the historical process of underachievement.

My rationale for raising this issue is the fact that educational debates on school effectiveness for culturally and linguistically diverse students have been enacted in parallel discourses that have rarely been brought together. On the one hand, there is the research-driven mainstream discourse that focuses on 'effective schools' and has spawned a plethora of school restructuring activities across the United States (for reviews see August & Hakuta, 1997; Olsen *et al.*, 1994; Stedman, 1987). This tradition typically relates different instructional and organizational practices to performance on standardized tests in order to identify the most effective interven-tions or structural configurations. On the other hand, there is an increasing body of theoretical analysis and ethnographic research deriving from the perspectives of multicultural education and critical pedagogy that highlights a very different set of practices and interventions as potentially 'effective' for culturally and linguistically diverse students (e.g. Banks & Banks, 1993; Frederickson, 1995; Giroux, 1999; Igoa, 1995; Ladson-Billings, 1995; May, 1999; McCaleb, 1994; McLaren & Muñoz, 1999; Nieto, 1996, 1999; Skutnabb-Kangas, 1995; Wink, 2000).

With a few notable exceptions, these discourses have largely ignored each other. My impression from interactions with members of both 'camps' is that the mainstream effectiveness researchers consider the more critically-oriented scholars to be ideologically-driven and hence 'unscientific'. Because critically-oriented researchers rarely employ 'outcome measures' such as test scores, their case study and ethnographic research is considered 'soft' and therefore fails to make it into large-scale meta-analyses of school effectiveness.

By contrast, critical educators tend to be disdainful of what they see as an obses-sion with test scores and the extremely narrow concept of 'achievement' that characterizes the 'effectiveness' research. They ignore the 'effectiveness' research because they reject its premises and the educational status quo upon which it is based. Giroux expresses the perspective of many critical educators when he argues that schools play a vital role in developing students' political and moral conscious-ness, and furthermore this critical conception of education 'is also grounded in a notion of educational leadership that does not begin with the question of raising test scores or educating students to be experts, but with a moral and political vision of what it means to educate to govern, lead a humane life, and address the social welfare of those less fortunate than themselves' (1999: 59).

Laurie Olsen and her colleagues at *California Tomorrow*, a social research and advocacy organization based in Oakland, have attempted to bring these two perspectives into dialogue with each other. Their study of 73 California schools in the process of restructuring revealed a silence about issues of culture and identity and 'heavy barriers to bringing diversity and equity issues into the school's plans to better serve their students' (Olsen *et al.*, 1994: 31). In spite of genuine commitment, the agenda for the reform process was largely determined by the concerns of dominant group educators and the voices of culturally diverse educators and parents were rarely heard around the table. Not surprisingly, these observations were not well received by many of those involved in the California restructuring effort and hopes for genuine dialogue have faded even more in recent years with overtly coercive policies such as the Proposition 227 'final solution' to the problems of bilingual students' underachievement.

The emphasis in the framework presented in Chapter 2 on the relationships between classroom interactions and societal power relations clearly reflects a 'critical' rather than 'effectiveness' orientation to these issues. However, the reality for virtually all public schools in North America (and elsewhere) is that they are now required to meet curriculum standards that are enforced by means of performance standards and often backed up with standardized tests, such as the SAT-9 in California. The ill-conceived, confused, and contradictory nature of many of these accountability initiatives has been discussed in Chapter 6. For the forseeable future, however, this is the context within which the education of culturally and linguistically diverse students must operate. 'Effectiveness' as defined by standardized tests is already determining the reward structure within school systems for students, teachers, principals, and administrators (e.g. in Texas).

I argue in this chapter that a critical perspective must address this reality in at least two ways. It must continue to highlight the discriminatory structure of the accountability apparatus and its internal contradictions (see Chapter 6) so that educators can collectively explore ways to resist the potentially negative effects of cultural and linguistic bias against ELL students and also the narrowing of the curriculum brought about by teaching to the test. But critical perspectives must also move from rhetoric and theoretical analysis to a more detailed focus on the specific forms of pedagogy that will develop the 'basic skills' assessed by most tests while at the same time expanding students' personal, intellectual, and academic horizons in transformative ways.

I believe that these goals are compatible with each other. In fact, I argue in this chapter that transformative pedagogy constitutes the most effective means of developing basic skills, and much beyond. My perspective here is similar to that of Lisa Delpit (1995) who argues for a rigorous approach to developing literacy skills among African American students as an essential component of a transformative pedagogy:

> We must take the responsibility to *teach*, to provide for students who do not already possess them, the additional codes of power. ... They must be encouraged to understand the value of the code they already possess as well as to understand the power realities in this country. Otherwise they will be unable to work to change these realities. (1995: 40) (emphasis original)

Sonia Nieto (1999) has also emphasized that multicultural education will ultimately be judged by how well it succeeds in teaching basic subject matter content in addition to critical thinking skills and social awareness. If it fails to reorient itself to its primary focus on student learning, and working to increase equity in access to learning opportunities, then it risks being dismissed as simply an ineffectual 'feel-good' melange of 'ethnic additives or cultural celebrations' (1999: xvi). By contrast, she argues that 'when it is conceptualized as broad-based school reform, multicultural education can have a decisive impact on how and to what extent students learn' (1999: 163).

Is it possible to find the evidence for these perspectives in the more narrowly conceived school effectiveness research? Do we really need to adopt a transformative pedagogical orientation in order to reverse underachievement, or can we simply implement the technical strategies that research suggests are effective? I argue below that evidence for the 'effectiveness' of a transformative pedagogical orientation in developing basic literacy and content knowledge is clearly discernable in the literature on school and classroom effectiveness. Furthermore, the failure of the mainstream educational reform movement to acknowledge the sociopolitical roots of student failure is a major factor in the limited impact that this research has exerted to date on the process of reversing educational inequality.

I start with two vignettes that illustrate the consequences of locating the 'problem' of ELL student underachievement in the students themselves rather than in the sociopolitical conditions under which their schooling operates. My intent here is to highlight the centrality of educator role definitions and their relationship to educational structures that frequently discriminate against culturally and linguistically diverse students. On the basis of this analysis, I address the nature of transformative pedagogy which essentially requires that educators be prepared to challenge systemic manifestations of coercive power relations as they impact policy decision and educator–student interactions in schools. Next, I describe the major differences between three orientations to pedagogy – traditional, progressive, and transformative – as a means of placing current educational controversies in context. Then I examine the consistency of the mainstream research on school effectiveness with the claims of transformative pedagogy and highlight several orientations that are likely to succeed in affirming student identities and promoting knowledge generation among culturally and linguistically diverse students. Finally, I outline a fairly simple scheme for integrating the perspectives of school and classroom effectiveness research with the principles of transformative pedagogy.

Where Does the 'Problem' Reside? Within ELL Students or in Coercive Educational Structures?

'In recent years, increasing numbers of ESL students have come into my [science] classes. This year, one of my classes contains almost as many non-English speaking students as there are English speaking ones. Most of the

ESL students have very limited English skills, and as a result are not involved in class discussions and cannot complete assignments or pass tests.

I respect these students as I recognize that often they have a superior prior education in their own language. They are well-mannered, hard-working and respectful of others. I enjoy having a multiracial society in my classroom, because I like these students for themselves and their high motivational level. However, I am troubled by my incompetence in adequately helping many individual students of that society. Because of language difficulties, they often cannot understand me, nor can they read the text or board notes. Each of these students needs my personal attention, and I do not have that extra time to give.

As well, I have to evaluate their ability to understand science. They cannot show me their comprehension. I have to give them a failing mark! I question the educational decisions made to assimilate ESL students into academic subject classes before they have minimal skills in English.' (extracted from 'A teacher's daily struggle in multi-racial classroom', B. Dudley Brett, Letter of the Week, *Toronto Star*, 1994, 2 April, p. B3)

B. Dudley Brett's letter expresses well the dilemmas experienced by committed and caring educators faced with rapidly increasing numbers of ELL students in their schools and classrooms. As in other countries, immigration to Canada has increased substantially during the past 15 years, with the result that many schools in large urban centres have large numbers of ELL students whose knowledge of the language of instruction varies widely. Many teachers, particularly at the secondary level, are confused and often frustrated at the new challenges they are facing. They feel prepared and competent to teach science, mathematics, or regular English courses but totally unprepared to teach these courses to students who are still in the process of acquiring the language of instruction. Many, like B. Dudley Brett, would like to see more intensive and prolonged instruction in English as a second language so that students would be fluent in English by the time they enter 'mainstream' classes.

Brett's letter also illustrates well, however, the consequences of viewing the education of ELL students only as a technical instructional problem rather than as a sociopolitical issue related to power relations in the broader society. Although he acknowledges his own 'incompetence' to help ELL students, Brett fails to problematize the system that gave rise to, and perpetuates, his incompetence. Instead, he sees the 'problem' as residing almost exclusively with ELL students themselves (through no fault of their own) and his 'solution' is to keep students out of the 'mainstream' until they can cope with the instructional demands of the regular curriculum. It is instructive to analyze the scenario described by Brett in terms of the framework of micro- and macro-interactions outlined in Chapter 2.

It is clear that despite his frustration, Brett is positively oriented towards his students and probably attempts to communicate this respect to them in his classroom interactions. However, this positive orientation may amount to very little in comparison to the message communicated to them as a result of their failure to pass his science course. They fail not because they do not know the content nor make the effort to learn, but because they are unable to demonstrate their learning in English.

Brett clearly defines his role as a committed and caring teacher, but nowhere in his letter is there a sense of the need to address his own acknowledged 'incompetence'. It is the ELL student who requires 'fixing' through more intensive and extensive ESL instruction rather than Brett's own teaching abilities or strategies. Brett does not problematize his own identity as a competent science teacher despite the fact that he is unable to teach science to almost half of the students in his science class. He also shows no awareness of the time periods typically required for ELL students to catch up academically (over five years) despite the fact that this research was carried out in Toronto (Cummins, 1981a; Klesmer, 1994) and widely publicized among ESL teachers for more than 15 years. Had he, or the administrators in his school, been aware of these data they might have reflected more on the need for *all* teachers, rather than just the ESL teacher, to provide English language learning support.

Also unquestioned is the educational structure encompassing curriculum, assessment, pre-service education, in-service education, criteria for advancement to leadership positions in the school district etc. that has largely ignored issues related to diversity and second language learning. In Ontario, as in most other jurisdictions, these issues, if considered at all, remain as footnotes to more general policies designed to address the needs of the 'generic' or typical student who is still imagined as white, middle-class, and monolingual (despite massive evidence to the contrary). Thus, Brett questions why ELL students are admitted to his science class before they have minimal English, rather than questioning the structure of a school system and a policy framework that excludes ELL students from any meaningful participation in the instructional process.

This exclusion is particularly evident at the secondary level as evidenced by Watt and Roessingh's (1994) data. They report that, over a number of years, almost 75% of the ESL student population in one Alberta high school failed to complete graduation requirements. For students who had minimal English skills on entry to high school (Grade 9), the drop out rate was a staggering 95.5%. These figures are influenced by the fact that Alberta in the 1990s imposed a ceiling of age 19 for enrolment in high school, but they nonetheless suggest a disregard for considerations of social justice in government policies as well as massive wastage of educational and economic potential.

Many of the adjustments that might begin to address the blatant inequities of access would cost nothing to implement. For example, faculties of education could ensure that *all* new teachers who graduate have had at least some preparation with respect to making academic content comprehensible to ELL students. Similarly, school systems could institute as a criterion of advancement to principal and vice-principal positions, some demonstrated expertise or success in working with ELL students. If such expertise is not a criterion of advancement, why should we expect any leadership in our schools in relation to issues of diversity and academic language learning? Had B. Dudley Brett been in a school where the 'problem' of ELL students was at least being discussed under the leadership of a knowledgeable principal, ESL teachers and content teachers might have been able to collaboratively design strategies to facilitate ELL students' comprehension and participation in the 'regular' classroom. These strategies might have ranged from the simple use of graphic organizers to cooperative planning of lessons between ESL and content teachers so that the same content is being reinforced in both settings.

None of this appears to have happened in the school setting described by Brett. This lack of collaborative action to address the learning needs of ELL students is not surprising. Issues related to diversity and educational equity for ELL students remain marginal in the priorities of the wider society. Lurking behind the veneer of vacuous multicultural rhetoric in many Canadian (and other) school systems is the reality of coercive relations of power. The good intentions and commitment of B. Dudley Brett and his equally committed colleagues are not enough by themselves to provide an equitable and effective education for linguistically and culturally diverse students. Change requires that educators become aware of, and be willing to challenge, the power relations operating in the wider society and in the school as a reflection of that society. When they fail to problematize their own identities and the structure within which they operate, educators inadvertently reinforce the operation of coercive relations of power.

Consider another vignette from the same school system:

> Ms. Sampson (not real name), an ESL teacher in a large multiethnic Toronto high school, was concerned that Phan Nguyen (not real name), a Vietnamese-origin student in one of her classes, was experiencing speech and possibly auditory discrimination difficulties that were impeding his learning of English and, as a consequence, other academic subjects. This student's difficulties were much greater than those of other students from the same background. She contacted the Student Services department of the school system to explore the possibility of arranging a Speech and Hearing assessment for the student. She was referred to one of the speech/language pathologists in the department who listened sympathetically to the description of the student's difficulties but who declined to become involved on the grounds that she had 'no expertise in assessing ESL students'. When pressed as to whether the department's policy excluded ESL students, the speech/language pathologist replied that 'We have no instruments that would be valid for such students'. When further pressed as to why intervention to assist the student's obvious articulation problems could not be undertaken, the speech/language pathologist reiterated that 'There are just too many variables involved' to make intervention feasible. In the absence of any specialized assistance from the Student Services department, the ESL teacher whose Philology training in Europe had included development of expertise in the phonetic alphabet, used this strategy with some success to help Phan acquire strategies to deal with his articulation difficulties in English.

The speech/language pathologist here has defined her role as helping monolingual English-speaking students overcome any speech difficulties they might experience. These are the students she has been trained to help, there are instruments that can validly be applied to diagnosing the nature of their difficulties, and they fit into the special education system of which she is a part. By contrast, with ELL students 'there are just too many variables'.

Clearly, this professional educator is intent on defending rather than challenging the special education system that operates in the school district. The system is coercive insofar as power is exercised throughout the system to the detriment of marginalized groups. In this instance, a student obviously in need of articulation assistance receives no help simply because he is in the process of learning English.

The power relations operating in special education systems have been documented repeatedly (e.g. Cummins, 1984; Harry, 1992; Smith, 1999). For example, in the early 1970s, Jane Mercer (1973) showed that there were between three and four times as many African American and Latino/Latina students in classes for the educable mentally retarded as would be expected based on their proportion in the school population. In Texas, Ortiz and Yates (1983) similarly found a threefold over-representation of Latino/Latina students in the 'learning disability' category. More recent documentation indicates that the problem persists (e.g. Jitendra & Rohena-Diaz, 1996; McNamara, 1998; Oller, 1997). Johnson and Supik (1999), for example, reported that the number of limited English proficient students assigned to special education classes in Texas rose by 11.7% between the 1996–97 and 1998–99 school years.

If equity is to be injected into such a system, it is clear that individual special educators must challenge the way the system operates and the assumptions underlying their own professional training. In the vignette outlined above, despite the fact that she was sympathetic to the student's plight, the speech/language pathologist was effectively reinforcing a system of coercive relations of power.

I argue in the sections below that effective instruction and/or 'delivery' of services requires that educators pursue a transformative pedagogy that problematizes both their own role definitions and the educational structures within which they operate as a first step toward challenging the operation of coercive relations of power in the school and wider society.

Transformative Pedagogy, Identity Negotiation, and Power Relations

The framework elaborated in Chapter 2 (Figures 2.1 and 2.2) defined *transformative/intercultural* pedagogy as interactions between educators and students that attempt to foster collaborative relations of power in the classroom. This orientation to pedagogy challenges the operation of coercive relations of power in the school and wider society. It focuses not just on the student as *learner* with the implied assumption that the teaching/learning process is neutral with respect to social realities and intergroup power relations. Rather, it recognizes that the process of identity negotiation is fundamental to educational success for all students, and furthermore that this process is directly determined by the micro-interactions between individual educators and students. Micro-interactions are a function of the way educators have defined their roles in relation to culturally and linguistically diverse students, together with the educational structures that frame the 'delivery' of education. These, in turn, are strongly influenced by the macro-interactions or power relations between groups in the wider society.

The starting point for elaborating this framework with a focus on classroom implementation is the argument that any set of classroom interactions can and should be examined from at least two inter-related perspectives: (1) the effectiveness of the instruction in fostering learning, or what I prefer to label *knowledge generation*; (2) the impact of the instruction on the way students view themselves, or expressed differently, the identity messages and options for future identity choices that educators reflect back to the students with whom they interact. Implied in the framework is a reciprocal relationship between these two perspectives. The ways in which identities are negotiated will affect the long-term outcomes of the teaching/learning process and, by the same token, the effectiveness of instruction in enabling students to generate knowledge will affect the academic and personal identities that students develop. As discussed in Cummins (1996), both processes can be conceived within a sociocultural framework using Vygotsky's (1962) metaphor of the *zone of proximal development* (ZPD):

> Expressed simply, the ZPD is the interpersonal space where minds meet and new understandings can arise through collaborative interaction and inquiry. Newman, Griffin and Cole (1989) label this interpersonal space *the construction zone*. In the present volume, the dual process of reciprocal negotiation of identity and collaborative generation of knowledge take place within this 'construction zone' and are seen as being intimately related to each other. Teacher–student collaboration in the construction of knowledge will operate effectively only in contexts where students' identities are being affirmed. Essentially, this conception extends the ZPD beyond the cognitive sphere into the realms of affective development and power relationships. It also makes clear that the *construction zone* can also be a *constriction zone* where student identities and learning are constricted rather than extended. (Cummins, 1996: 26)

As noted above, the centrality of identity negotiation, and its roots in societal power relations, has been virtually ignored in most of the mainstream literature on educational effectiveness and educational restructuring despite the fact that it has been a significant theme in the writings of academics and educators focused on equity and multicultural education (e.g. Darder, 1991; Fordham, 1990; Hayes, Bahruth & Kessler, 1991; Igoa, 1995; Nieto, 1996, 1999; Walsh, 1996). The focus of much of the educational effectiveness research related to language education has been on 'technical' issues related to instruction and achievement. Prominent among these are the following:

- The relative merits of a phonics approach to initial reading as compared to whole language approaches.
- The extent to which formal teaching of grammar and 'language skills' is effective in developing students' writing abilities.
- The status of 'child-centred' approaches to instruction as compared to 'direct instructional' methods.
- The role of explicit teaching of learning strategies in promoting academic achievement.
- The role of corrective feedback in helping second language learners acquire fluency and literacy in the target language.
- The benefits of different forms of student assessment in helping students learn.
- The extent to which students' L1 should be used in ESL or foreign language instruction; etc.

These issues are important but they are far from the whole story in designing effective instructional contexts. The exclusive focus on these and related issues assumes that the process of implementing effective instruction is a technical rather than a sociopolitical issue. By contrast, the present framework, following that of Freire (1970) and many other critical educators, assumes that instruction is never neutral with respect to societal power relations. Thus, research relating to technical instructional issues must be viewed through the lens of transformative pedagogy in order to bring implications for culturally and linguistically diverse students into focus.

The next section describes transformative pedagogy in relation to two other major pedagogical orientations: traditional and progressive pedagogy.

Instructional Landscapes: Traditional, Progressive and Transformative Pedagogies

The public discourse on education has largely ignored the claims and successes of transformative pedagogy. In many countries, recent educational debates have been framed as conflicts between 'conservative' and 'progressive' (or 'liberal') educators that revolve around the merits or otherwise of 'direct' versus 'child-centred' instruction and phonics versus whole language approaches to reading. Traditional versus constructivist approaches to the teaching of mathematics and science also enter the fray from time to time. Transformative pedagogies that many theorists and educators argue are essential for educational equity are not even on the map of public concerns at this point in time. Traditional and progressive pedagogies will be described briefly in order to contrast their assumptions with those of transformative pedagogy (see also Miller, 1996, for discussion of these orientations).

Traditional Pedagogy

The basic premise of the traditional model is that the teacher's task is to impart knowledge or skills to students. This implies that the teacher initiates and controls the interaction, constantly orienting it towards the achievement of instructional objectives. The instructional content in this type of program derives primarily from the internal structure of the language or subject matter; consequently, it frequently involves a predominant focus on surface features of language or literacy and emphasizes correct recall of content taught. Content is frequently transmitted by means of highly structured drills and workbook exercises, although in many cases the drills are disguised in order to make them more attractive and motivating to students.

Within this instructional orientation, language is decomposed into its component parts (e.g. phonics, vocabulary, grammatical rules) which are then transmitted in isolation from each other; learning is assumed to progress in a hierarchical manner starting with simple elements and progressing to more complex forms. Thus, explicit phonics instruction is a prerequisite for reading development; grammar, vocabulary, and spelling must be taught before students can start writing; and knowledge is viewed as static or inert, to be internalized and reproduced by students when required.

The social assumptions of traditional pedagogy are straightforward. Curriculum should present the 'cultural literacy' of the society – in Hirsch's (1987) terms 'what every American needs to know'. However, by virtue of what it omits, this type of curriculum also operates to restrict access to alternative perspectives on historical and contemporary events (Macedo, 1993, 1994; Peterson, 1994). The curriculum is sanitized with respect to issues of historical and current power relations, and students are expected to emerge from schooling as 'good citizens' who will comply with the expectations of the societal power structure. By sanitizing the curriculum, traditional pedagogy attempts to make coercive power structures invisible, thereby reinforcing their discriminatory effect.

Despite the concern among many policy-makers and the general public that traditional models of pedagogy have been abandoned in favour of 'liberal' child-centred models, the evidence overwhelmingly shows that traditional or transmission models persist (e.g. Goodlad, 1984). This trend was very evident in both bilingual and structured immersion programs studied by Ramírez and his colleagues:

> Of major concern is that in over half of the interactions that teachers have with students, students do not produce any language as they are only listening or responding with non-verbal gestures or actions. … Of equal concern is that when students do respond, typically they provide only simple information recall statements. Rather than being provided with the opportunity to generate original statements, students are asked to provide simple discrete close-ended or patterned (i.e. expected) responses. This pattern of teacher/student interaction not only limits a student's opportunity to create and manipulate language freely, but also limits the student's ability to engage in more complex learning (i.e., higher order thinking skills). In sum … teachers in all three programs offer a passive language learning environment, limiting student opportunities to produce language and develop more complex language and thinking skills. (Ramírez, Yuen, Ramey & Pasta, 1991: 8)

Similarly, Sirotnik, in discussing the implications of Goodlad's study, points to the fact that the typical American classroom contains 'a lot of teacher talk and a lot of student listening … almost invariably closed and factual questions … and predominantly total class instructional configurations around traditional activities – all in a virtually affectless environment. It is but a short inferential leap to suggest that we are implicitly teaching dependence upon authority, linear thinking, social apathy, passive involvement, and hands-off learning' (1983: 29).

With respect to the education of culturally and linguistically diverse students, the major problems with this form of 'banking' education are:

- It devalues the identities of marginalized group students by providing no opportunity for students to express and share their experience with peers and teachers; students are silenced or rendered 'voiceless' in the classroom (Giroux, 1991; Walsh, 1991). Their prior knowledge is untapped and there are few if any opportunities to reflect critically on social issues of direct relevance to their lives. Students are being prepared to accept the societal status quo and their own inferior status therein.
- It contravenes central principles of language and literacy acquisition that highlight the importance of ample opportunities for meaningful communicative interaction in both oral and written modes.

Progressive Pedagogy

Kalantzis and Cope (1999) note that the roots of progressivism go back to the pioneering work of John Dewey and Maria Montessori. They describe the central features of progressivism as follows:

> Its founding principles were that students should be active learners; that they should learn by doing; that education should be through practical experience rather than having to absorb facts; that the process of learning was more important than the content; that learning had to be meaningful rather than formal; and that the most effective learning was relevant to the individual rather than institutionally imposed. (1999: 255)

With respect to language and literacy instruction, 'whole-language' represents the most prominent approach that draws on a progressivist philosophy. Whereas traditional approaches decompose language – break it up into its component parts for easier transmission – progressive or whole-language approaches insist that language can be learned only when it is kept 'whole' and used for meaningful communication either in oral or written modes. Knowledge within traditional curriculum is viewed as fixed and inert whereas in progressive pedagogy it is seen as catalytic in the sense that new information acts as a catalyst for further inquiry. Learning in traditional pedagogy is largely memorization whereas in progressive pedagogy learning is constructed collaboratively through interaction with peers and teachers.

Within a progressive pedagogical approach, the teacher's encouragement for students to use both written and oral language actively allows students' experience to be expressed and shared within the classroom context. This expression and sharing of experience makes possible the affirmation of students' identity. By contrast, 'banking' approaches usually employ textbooks that reflect only the values and priorities of the dominant group, thereby effectively suppressing the experience of culturally diverse students.

Progressive approaches highlight the role of collaborative inquiry and the construction of meaning as central to students' academic growth. The classroom is seen as a community of learning where knowledge is generated by teachers and students together.

There is considerable research evidence supporting the general principles underlying a whole-language, inquiry-based progressivist pedagogy (see, for example, Freeman & Freeman, 1994, 1998; Krashen, 1999b; McQuillan, 1998). This can be seen most obviously in the area of reading where, despite public and policy perceptions to the contrary, the whole-language emphasis on immersion in a literacy-rich environment, together with active promotion of student writing, is strongly supported by the research (e.g. Allington & Woodside-Jiron, 1999). As documented below, this research identifies extensive reading as the major causal variable underlying the development of reading comprehension. Extensive reading (and writing) are also central components of a transformative pedagogy.

Reading research – a quick reality check

Elley and Mangubhai (1983) demonstrated that fourth and fifth grade students in Fiji exposed to a 'book flood' program during their 30 minute daily English (L2) class in which they simply read books either alone or with the guidance of their teacher, performed significantly better after two years than students taught through more traditional methods. Elley (1991) similarly documented the superiority of book-based English language teaching programs among primary school students in a variety of other contexts.

The importance of time spent reading has also been documented in large-scale international studies of first language reading development. Postlethwaite and Ross (1992) in a large-scale international evaluation of reading achievement in 32 systems of education showed that the amount of time students reported they spent in voluntary reading activities was amongst the strongest predictors (#2) of a school's overall reading performance. The first ranked indicator was the school's perception of the degree of parent cooperation, which is probably an indicator of socioeconomic status. The significance of reading frequency in promoting reading development is also evident from the high rankings of variables such as *Amount of reading materials in the school* (#8), *Having a classroom library* (#11), and *Frequency of borrowing books from a library* (#12). With respect to teaching methods, a focus on *Comprehension instruction* was ranked #9 and *Emphasis on literature* was ranked #17, both considerably higher than whether or not the school engaged in explicit *Phonics teaching* (#41).

Consistent with these results, Fielding and Pearson's (1994: 62) review of research in this area highlights four components of a reading program that contribute to the development of reading comprehension:

- large amounts of time for actual text reading;
- teacher-directed instruction in comprehension strategies;
- opportunities for peer and collaborative learning; and
- occasions for students to talk to a teacher and one another about their responses to reading.

The centrality of extensive reading to students' performance in both L1 and L2 is also documented by Day and Bamford (1996), Krashen (1993, 1999b) and McQuillan (1998). Unfortunately, most policy-makers and media commentators do not identify this emphasis on immersion in literacy as the defining feature of whole-language or progressive approaches to reading. Instead, they understand whole-language as an approach to reading that advocates the elimination of any type of direct instruction, particularly the explicit teaching of phonics in reading. Certainly the stridency with which some whole-language advocates have argued against any type of 'skills instruction' or formal assessment has contributed to the backlash against whole-language and the public perception that it is an 'anti-phonics' program.[2]

The perception that whole-language eschews all forms of direct instruction has resulted in critiques from the political 'left' as well as from the political 'right'. Several critics of whole-language approaches (e.g. Delpit, 1988; Kalantzis & Cope, 1993, 1999) have argued convincingly that some children require more explicit forms of instruction and corrective feedback than is the case in many whole-language classrooms. Specifically, there is a need for explicit instruction in how to use language powerfully to achieve social goals. This would entail developing competence in the conventions of different genres (e.g. report writing, formal letters etc.) and an awareness of how language is used in a wide variety of social contexts. In Lisa Delpit's words, teachers must learn not only how to 'help students to establish their own voices, but to coach those voices to produce notes that will be heard clearly in the larger society' (1988: 296). Maria de la Luz Reyes (1992) has also criticized the 'one size fits all' assumptions of some whole-language classrooms, arguing that there is a need to affirm more explicitly culturally diverse students' cultural knowledge and to promote multicultural awareness.

These criticisms of whole-language instructional approaches can easily be accommodated by reiterating that a focus on immersion of children in literacy is not at all incompatible with an explicit focus on teaching learning strategies and developing students' awareness of language, ranging from phonemic awareness in the early grades to the intersections of power and language in later grades. The transformative pedagogy framework elaborated later in this chapter incorporates these emphases.[3]

While the instructional assumptions underlying progressive pedagogy are generally appropriate and supported by research, the social assumptions underlying progressive pedagogy are seldom articulated. With some exceptions, contemporary whole-language theorists have tended to focus on instructional rather than social realities. Their focus is on the child, either as an individual or within the classroom learning community. An unfortunate consequence of this, as Reyes (1992) has pointed out, is that without explicit attention to the social realities of diversity, many whole-language classrooms will be just as monocultural and blind to students' cultural realities as are more traditional classrooms. Similarly, issues of power and status are rarely the focus of instruction within whole-language classrooms. Any focus on multiculturalism is frequently limited to 'celebrating diversity' – promotion of tolerance and acceptance that is aimed at increasing students' self-esteem but does little to challenge inequities of power and status distribution in the society.

In short, contemporary progressive approaches to pedagogy usually focus narrowly on the teaching–learning relationship and fail to articulate a coherent vision of the broader social implications of instruction. Tolerance and acceptance of cultural difference are often implied but critical reflection on students' own experience, and critique of social realities are not.

Transformative Pedagogy

The instructional assumptions of transformative pedagogy are similar to those of progressive pedagogy. However, they diverge with respect to social assumptions. Transformative pedagogy uses collaborative critical inquiry to enable students to analyze and understand the social realities of their own lives and of their communities. Students discuss, and frequently act on ways in which these realities might be transformed through various forms of social action. Instruction aims to go beyond the sanitized curriculum that is still the norm in most schools. It strives to develop a critical literacy which Ira Shor has defined as follows:

> Habits of thought, reading, writing, and speaking which go beneath surface meaning, first impressions, dominant myths, official pronouncements, traditional clichés, received wisdom, and mere opinions, to understand the deep meaning, root causes, social context, ideology, and personal consequences of any action, event, object, process, organization, experience, text, subject matter, policy, mass media, or discourse. (1992: 129)

In short, critical literacy reflects the analytic abilities involved in cutting through the surface veneer of persuasive arguments to the realities underneath and analyzing the methods and purposes of particular forms of persuasion. Critical literacy in this sense is similar to James Banks' concept of transformative academic knowledge which he defines as 'the facts, concepts, paradigms, themes, and explanations that challenge mainstream academic knowledge and expand and substantially revise established canons, paradigms, theories, explanations and research methods' (1996: 9). Transformative scholars, according to Banks, 'assume that knowledge is not neutral but is influenced by human interests, that all knowledge reflects the power and social relationships within society, and that an important purpose of knowledge construction is to help people improve society' (1996: 16). Although his primary focus is on academic scholars, Banks' description applies equally well to the pursuit of critical literacy by school-age students under the guidance of a teacher oriented to transformative pedagogy (see, for example, Jasso & Jasso, 1995; Students for Cultural and Linguistic Democracy, 1996; Terrazas, 1995).

Fifth grade teacher Bob Peterson, one of the editors of a volume devoted to analyzing and describing transformative pedagogy entitled *Rethinking Our Classrooms*, illustrates the difference between traditional, progressive, and transformative pedagogy by contrasting the likely response of a teacher from each of these orientations to a student who brings in a flyer about a canned food drive that is being organized during the December holiday season:

> The traditional teacher affirms the student's interest – 'That's nice and I'm glad you care about other people' – but doesn't view the food drive as a potential classroom activity. The progressive teacher sees the food drive as an opportunity to build on students' seemingly innate sympathy for the down-trodden, and after a class discussion, has children bring in cans of food. They count them, categorize them and write about how they feel. The critical teacher does the same as the progressive teacher – but more. The teacher also uses the food drive as the basis for a discussion about poverty and hunger. How much poverty and hunger is there in our neighbourhood? Our country? Our world? Why is there poverty and hunger? What is the role of the government in making sure people have enough to eat? Why isn't it doing more? What can we do in addition to giving some food? (1994: 30)

In short, transformative pedagogy shares a common instructional orientation with progressive pedagogy (with some qualifications) but incorporates an explicit focus on social realities that relate to students' experience. It also is informed by a coherent vision of the kind of society it hopes students will promote – one founded on principles of social justice – and classroom instruction is oriented to building students' awareness of democratic ideals and giving them the academic and critical literacy tools they will need for full participation.

The editors of *Rethinking Our Classrooms* (Bigelow, Christiansen, Karp, Miner & Peterson, 1994) articulate eight interlocking components that are reflected in curriculum and classrooms oriented toward collaborative critical inquiry. These components of transformative pedagogy are:

- *Grounded in the lives of our students*. All good teaching begins with a respect for children, their innate curiosity, and their capacity to learn. Regardless of what subject is being taught, ultimately the class has to be about students' lives as well as about a particular subject. Students should probe the ways their lives connect to the broader society and are often limited by that society.
- *Critical*. Students must learn to pose essential critical questions: Who makes decisions and who is left out? Who benefits and who suffers? Why is a given practice fair or unfair? What are its origins? What alternatives can we imagine? What is required to create change? Through this type of inquiry, students learn to think about advertising, cartoons, literature, legislative deci-

sions, military interventions, job structures, newspapers, movies, agricultural practices, or school life.

- *Multicultural, antiracist, pro-justice.* A social justice curriculum must strive to include the lives of all those in our society, especially those who have been marginalized or excluded historically. A rigorous multiculturalism should engage students in a critical analysis of the roots of inequality in curriculum materials, school structure, and the larger society.

- *Participatory, experiential.* Whether through projects, role-playing, simulations, mock trials, or experiments, students need to be mentally and physically active. Students also must be stimulated to develop their capacity for democratic participation through questioning, challenging, decision making, and collaborative problem-solving.

- *Hopeful, joyful, kind, visionary.* The ways we organize classroom life should seek to make children feel significant and cared about – by the teacher and by each other. Unless students feel emotionally and physically safe, they won't share real thoughts and feelings.

- *Activist.* A critical curriculum should reflect the diversity of people from all cultures who acted to make a difference, many of whom did so at great sacrifice. We want students to come to see themselves as truth-tellers and change-makers, capable of acting in pursuit of social justice.

- *Academically rigorous.* Far from devaluing the vital academic skills young people need, a critical and activist curriculum speaks directly to the deeply rooted alienation that currently discourages millions of students from acquiring those skills. Critical teaching aims to inspire levels of academic performance far greater than those motivated or measured by grades or test scores. When students write for real audiences, read books and articles about issues that really matter, and discuss big ideas with compassion and intensity, 'academics' starts to breathe.

- *Culturally sensitive.* These days, the demographic reality of schooling makes it likely that white teachers will enter classrooms filled with children of colour. Teachers must be prepared to learn from their students and to call on parents, culturally diverse colleagues, and community resources for insights into the students and communities they seek to serve.

Peterson also describes how critical thinking can be integrated with diverse subject matter. Mathematics can be integrated with social studies, for example, by having students:

> tally numbers of instances certain people, viewpoints, or groups are presented in a text or in mass media. One year my students compared the times famous women and famous men were mentioned in the fifth grade history text. One reaction by a number of boys was that men were mentioned far more frequently because women must not have done much throughout history. To help facilitate the discussion, I provided background resources for the students, including biographies of famous women. This not only helped students better

understand the nature of 'omission', but also generated interest in reading biographies of women. In another activity I had students tally the number of men and women by occupation as depicted in magazine and/or TV advertisements. By comparing their findings to the population as a whole, various forms of bias were uncovered. (1994: 36–37)

These examples illustrate the potentially unlimited scope of collaborative critical inquiry and how it can be integrated with basic numeracy and literacy skills (see also Powell & Frankenstein, 1997). The different cultural perspectives represented in the classroom become important resources for insight into the social issues that surround the classroom. Students' identity options and their views of their own potential are expanded as they engage in discussion, reading, and writing about issues that relate directly to their lives and the power relations that exist both in their own society and globally. Many other illustrations of critical teaching can be found in Frederickson (1995), Shor (1992) and Wink (2000). Theoretical discussions of these issues can be found in Giroux (1993, 1999), Nieto (1996, 1999) and McLaren (1994).

How does transformative pedagogy relate to the more general research on educational effectiveness for culturally and linguistically diverse students? As noted above, the term 'transformative pedagogy' is not exactly a household word in the mainstream of educational policy discussions. For example, there is no mention of the term in August and Hakuta's (1997) comprehensive review of the literature on school and classroom effectiveness for language-minority students. To what extent are the eight components of transformative pedagogy highlighted in *Rethinking Our Classrooms* (outlined above) simply a pious ideologically motivated wish-list or do they have any basis in more 'objective' research and theory? Certainly most of the components mesh very well with the focus elaborated in this volume on the centrality of identity negotiation in the classroom and its roots in societal power relations. Thus, another way of posing the question is to ask if the academic underachievement of culturally and linguistically diverse students can be reversed simply by making the basic teaching/learning process more efficient without any focus on issues of identity negotiation or the creation of contexts of empowerment for culturally and linguistically diverse students?

In the sections below I review the research on school and classroom effectiveness to assess the extent to which the outcomes of this research are consistent with the central role ascribed to identity negotiation in the present framework and to transformative pedagogy as an essential orientation in reversing the underachievement of culturally and linguistically diverse students.

I argue on the basis of this examination of the research that identity negotiation and knowledge generation represent essentially two sides of the same transformative pedagogy coin. To be truly effective in reversing patterns of school failure, classroom interactions must engage the totality of students' language and cognitive abilities in the learning process and also create contexts of empowerment where student identities are being affirmed as they participate academically.

Transformative Pedagogy and the Research on School Effectiveness

A good place to start in addressing the consistency of a transformative pedagogy orientation with the research evidence on school effectiveness is August and Hakuta's (1997) comprehensive review of this research. They identified 13 attributes of effective schools and classrooms in the 33 studies they reviewed. These attributes are outlined below:

(1) *A supportive school-wide climate.* This refers to the beliefs, assumptions, and expectations that teachers, students, and parents bring to the learning environment; in the terminology of Figure 2.1, the collective 'role definitions' or mindsets that educators adopt in relation to bilingual students and their communities. Included are factors such as the 'value placed on the linguistic and cultural background of English language learners, high expectations for their academic achievement, and their integral involvement in the overall school operation' (August & Hakuta, 1997: 172). Also highlighted is the celebration of diversity and encouragement for bilingual students to enhance their native-language skills.

(2) *School leadership.* The principal of the school is seen as a key player in ELL students' academic achievement in most of the studies reviewed. She or he makes the achievement of ELL students a priority, monitors curricular and instructional improvement, recruits and keeps talented and dedicated staff, involves the entire staff in improvement efforts, and maintains a good social and physical environment.

(3) *A customized learning environment.* Successful programs adapt to the realities of their particular circumstances; for example, by providing special programs to meet the needs of recently arrived immigrant students.

(4) *Articulation and coordination within and between schools.* Unlike the situations described in the two vignettes at the beginning of this chapter, successful schools implement collaboration between all educators who are addressing the needs of ELL students. A central aspect of the positive outcomes reported by the Success for All program, for example, is the fact that *all* of the school personnel work together to ensure the success of every child (Slavin, Madden, Dolan & Wasik, 1996; Slavin & Fashola, 1998). Other successful schools have devoted considerable energies to making explicit connections between students' prior learning and experiences in Spanish and their learning of English as they prepare for transition to English-only classes.

(5) *Some use of native language and culture in the instruction of language-minority students.* August and Hakuta (1997: 176) note that the 'advantages of native-language use are a prominent theme' in the research on effective schools and classrooms for ELL students. They cite Lucas and Katz' conclusion from exemplary sheltered English programs (in California known as 'Special Alternative Instructional Programs') that these classrooms were 'multilingual environments' in which 'native language use emerged as a persistent and key

instructional strategy realized in very site-specific ways' (Lucas & Katz, 1994: 545).

(6) *A balanced curriculum that incorporates both basic and higher-order skills.* A characteristic of successful classrooms in the studies reviewed is that teachers combine basic and higher-order skills. According to August and Hakuta (1997), this balance is characteristic of the Success for All program which explicitly teaches letter sounds, sound blending, word recognition skills, writing skills and metacognitive strategies for reading comprehension; however, it also makes extensive use of student-directed activities such as cooperative learning, peer tutoring, and partner reading. In the early grades the program engages students in story telling and retelling while in later elementary grades the emphasis is on the development of thinking skills, fluency, pleasure reading, and the use of increasingly complex material.[4]

(7) *Explicit skills instruction.* Explicit teaching emerges as an important factor for basic skills instruction and for teaching well-structured skill and knowledge domains.

(8) *Opportunities for student-directed activities.* Teachers in effective classrooms for ELL students supplement explicit skills instruction with considerable opportunities to produce oral and written English and to exchange ideas in intellectual conversations and collaborative inquiry.

(9) *Use of instructional strategies that enhance understanding.* The explicit teaching of learning and metacognitive strategies to ELL students has proven effective across a significant number of studies (for reviews see Chamot, Barnhardt, El-Dinary & Robbins, 1999; Echevarria & Graves, 1998). In a similar way to the Cognitive Academic Language Learning Approach (CALLA) (Chamot & O'Malley, 1994), Success for All encourages students to develop metacognitive skills to enable them to think about and plan for a task, monitor their completion of the task and evaluate the outcomes.

(10) *Opportunities for practice.* August and Hakuta's description of this attribute of effective instruction is far from the passive notion of 'practice' that is entailed in filling out worksheets or teacher-imposed assignments. Rather what emerges from the research is the importance of providing ELL students with opportunities to interact with fluent English-speaking peers and the kind of extended dialogue that occurs in *instructional conversations* (e.g. Patthey-Chavez & Goldenberg, 1995; Saunders & Goldenberg, 1999). Students who are encouraged to use language to elaborate and develop ideas in writing and discussion perform better academically than those who do not engage in these forms of extended language use.

(11) *Systematic student assessment.* The monitoring of student progress on a regular basis is associated with higher achievement. The Success for All program, for example, assesses students every 8 weeks to determine who needs tutoring and to identify students who might need some other form of assistance.

(12) *Staff development.* August and Hakuta note that staff development for all teachers in the school, not just language specialists, was a significant compo-

nent of many of the effective schools. All teachers were expected to know how to teach ELL students effectively and were given the support to do so.

(13) *Home and parent involvement.* A number of studies highlight the fact that an ongoing community/school process is an important contributor to the success of a school in working with bilingual students. In effective schools, teachers have a strong commitment to home–school communication and parents are involved in formal parent support activities (e.g. García, 1991). Lucas, Henze, and Donato (1990) point out that one of the ways in which the school demonstrates its commitment to parental involvement is by hiring staff who can speak the parents' languages. Moll, Amanti, Neff and González (1992) have highlighted how educators can work with parents to discover the *funds of knowledge* that exist in the community and integrate their instruction in a culturally responsive way with this knowledge base. Success for All schools have an extremely comprehensive family support program for each grade level in both Spanish and English. According to Calderón and Carreón (1999) 'a family support team helps families feel respected and welcomed in the school and to become active supporters of their children's education. ... parents learn strategies to use in reading with their own children in their primary language or in facilitating literacy by enjoying stories with their children' (1999: 182). Two other outstanding examples of school community collaboration in promoting literacy development are documented by Ada (1988a) and McCaleb (1994).

Clearly there is overlap among several of the categories extracted from the research by August and Hakuta and the labels by themselves do not always convey the essence of the effective practice. An example is 'opportunities for practice' (# 10) where the description highlights extended oral and written language use focused on meaning, together with higher-order thinking, rather than the more passive teacher-directed activity which the term 'practice' often connotes. Calderón, Hertz-Lazarowitz and Slavin's (1998) study is cited as illustrating the positive effects of providing opportunities for practice. They describe their Bilingual Cooperative Integrated Reading and Composition (BCIRC) program (which is one component of the Success for All program in bilingual contexts) as engaging 'students in frequent cognitively complex interactions around the solution of real problems' (p. 163) and giving students daily opportunities to use language to find meanings and solve problems. These types of activities emerged as particularly important for students in transitional bilingual programs at the critical point of transition from their home language to English. Thus, 'practice' here has clearly more affinity to 'progressive' orientations to pedagogy than to 'traditional' orientations.

It seems to me that the 13 attributes of effective schools for ELL students outlined by August and Hakuta can be expressed in terms of three overlapping dimensions. Some of the categories apply to more than one of these dimensions:

- Coherent school organization and leadership (#1, 2, 3, 4, 11, 12).
- Affirmation of student and community identity (#1, 3, 5, 13).

- Balance between, on the one hand extensive meaning-focused oral and written language input and use designed to promote problem-solving and higher-order thinking, and, on the other, explicit formal instruction designed to develop linguistic and metacognitive awareness (#6, 7, 8, 9, 10).

Several of the instructional features included in the third dimension above could also be seen as affirming students' identities insofar as they prioritize student voice by encouraging oral and written language use in higher-order thinking and problem-solving.

These three dimensions can readily be identified in some of the studies and related theoretical frameworks that were part of the August and Hakuta review as well as some that were not. For example, the Lucas *et al.* (1990) study of effective high schools for Latino/Latina students strongly emphasized the affirmation of student and community identity in at least five of the eight dimensions they identified. These were:

- Value is placed on the students' languages and cultures.
- High academic expectations are communicated to language-minority students.
- School leaders make the education of language-minority students a priority.
- Parents of language-minority students are encouraged to become involved in their children's education.
- School staff members share a strong commitment to empower language-minority students through education.

Collier and Thomas (1999), as noted in Chapter 8, highlight the success of two-way and one-way developmental bilingual programs which, by definition, set out to affirm students' linguistic and cultural identities. The pedagogical characteristics of successful programs are expressed as follows:

> In these enrichment programs, students receive the mainstream curriculum through both their primary language and English, with challenging academic work that is cognitively on grade level. Teachers use cooperative learning, thematic interdisciplinary units, and hands-on materials and make ample use of video and microcomputers. Materials and books present a cross-cultural perspective, and lessons activate students' prior knowledge for bridging to new knowledge. Enrichment bilingual classes for older students include problem-posing, knowledge gathering, reflective thinking, and collaborative decision-making. (1999: 1, 6)

In this brief description we see again the integration of identity negotiation and knowledge generation as core components of effective instruction for culturally and linguistically diverse students. Affirmation of identity is communicated through the reinforcement of students' L1, the cross-cultural perspective of the classroom materials and resources, and the activation of students' prior knowledge which communicates to students that what they are bringing into the classroom is important and relevant to their learning. The high expectations communicated through cognitively challenging work such as problem-posing and active knowledge gathering also serve to reinforce students' academic self-concept. These components of quality instruction are very similar to those emphasized by other investigators (e.g. Brisk, 1998).

Thomas and Collier (1997) explicitly highlight *sociocultural support* as a central component of their *Prism Model*. While acknowledging that it is difficult to measure, they note that sociocultural support emerged as a consistent theme in interviews with school staff regarding the conditions under which ELL students tended to experience academic success. As is clear from the following quotation, the notion of sociocultural support is similar to what I am calling *identity affirmation*:

> Language minority students in these (socioculturally supportive) schools are respected and valued for the rich life experiences in other cultural contexts that they bring to the classroom. Their bicultural experience is considered a knowledge base for teachers to build on. The school is a safe, secure environment for learning. Native-English speakers treat language minority students with respect, and there is less discrimination, prejudice, and open hostility. Often sociocultural support includes an additive, enrichment bilingual context for schooling, where students' L1 is affirmed, respected, valued, and used for cognitive and academic development. Sometimes native-English speakers choose to join the bilingual classes, and both groups work together at all times in an integrated schooling context. (1997: 51)[5]

In short, the mainstream research literature on school and classroom effectiveness for ELL students provides ample support for the centrality of identity negotiation as a determinant of student outcomes. School success is created in educator–student interactions that simultaneously affirm student identities and provide a balance of explicit instruction focused on academic language, content, and strategies together with extensive opportunities for students to engage with literacy and collaborative critical inquiry.

The importance of identity negotiation and the role of the teacher in affirming student identities also emerges in a significant number of qualitative studies. Cristina Igoa (1995), for example, provides a moving and powerful account of how her immigrant students, many from war-torn countries, gradually developed the confidence and spiritual strength to express them*selves* and their inner worlds. The teacher's role in this process is crucial: 'As they revealed their inner worlds, together we set the nest and created the environment for the true selves to emerge' (1995: 190).

Sonia Nieto similarly notes 'the inescapable truth that has emerged in this book is that teachers' attitudes and behaviors *can* make an astonishing difference in student learning' (1999: 167). She clearly identifies the sociopolitical as well as the interpersonal aspects of this process:

> In the end, if teachers believe that students cannot achieve at high levels, that their backgrounds are riddled with deficiencies, and that multicultural educa-

tion is a frill that cannot help them to learn, the result will be school reform strategies that have little hope for success. On the other hand, if teachers begin by challenging social inequities that inevitably place some students at a disadvantage over others; if they struggle against institutional policies and practices that are unjust; if they begin with the strengths and talents of students and their families; if they undergo a process of personal transformation based on their own identities and experiences; and finally, if they engage with colleagues in a collaborative and imaginative encounter to transform their own practices and their schools to achieve equal and high-quality education for all students, then the outcome is certain to be a more positive one than is currently the case. (1999: 175–176)

What Nieto articulates so well is precisely the dimension of the change process that the notion of *transformative pedagogy* attempts to capture and which is completely missing from the rather soulless notion of 'school and classroom effectiveness'. This dimension of transformative pedagogy corresponds to what I have termed *educator role definitions* in Figure 2.1. The ways in which educators define their roles represent a central two-way conduit between inter-group power relations in the wider society, on the one hand, and educator–student micro-interactions in the classroom, on the other. These interactions are never neutral with respect to societal power relations; rather, they serve always to promote either collaborative relations of power or coercive relations of power. The problem with focusing only on 'instructional effectiveness' is the implication that school improvement is a technical process that is sociopolitically neutral. When the emphasis is placed only on the technical aspects of instruction, human relationships and their sociopolitical roots fade into the background. By contrast, the emphasis in the present analysis is that identity negotiation and knowledge generation (learning) are equally important facets of educational effectiveness.

This perspective also implies, however, that multicultural education and transformative pedagogy must root themselves as much in the learning process as in the sociopolitical dimensions of learning. As Nieto points out, multicultural education and critical pedagogy have often not been taken seriously because they are viewed simply as ideological orientations that have little intrinsic relationship to student learning. The connections to student learning must be made explicit. In the next section, I attempt to do this. I examine three frameworks which, in varying degrees, articulate conditions for ELL student learning that incorporate both 'effectiveness' and 'transformative' perspectives.

Instructional Frameworks for Knowledge Generation and Identity Negotiation

The first of these frameworks is the Cognitive Academic Language Learning Approach (CALLA) which was originally developed in the 1980s and has been extensively implemented and researched (Chamot & O'Malley, 1994). Although this framework does not incorporate an explicitly transformative orientation, it is compatible with such an orientation. It also illustrates the kind of coherent instructional framework that becomes more powerful in its impact when harnessed to transformative goals.

The Cognitive Academic Language Learning Approach (CALLA)

The CALLA was developed by Chamot and O'Malley (1994) as a means of accelerating academic achievement for ELL students. The framework emphasizes the role of students' prior knowledge, the importance of collaborative learning, and the development of metacognitive awareness and self-reflection. Three components are the focus of instruction: high priority curriculum content, academic language development, and learning strategies.

The CALLA instructional design is task-based and has five phases: *preparation, presentation, practice, evaluation,* and *expansion.* In each of these phases the three components of content, language, and learning strategies are combined. The *preparation* phase involves teachers finding out what prior knowledge students have about the content topic to be taught as well as relevant information about their language proficiency and learning strategies. As noted above, activating the prior knowledge that culturally and linguistically diverse students bring to the classroom acknowledges and validates the 'funds of knowledge' (Moll *et al.,* 1992) that these students and their communities possess. This process of identity affirmation is probably at least as important as the impact of prior knowledge on facilitating the acquisition of new knowledge (see Dochy, Segers & Buehl, 1999, for a review of this research).

In the *presentation* phase teachers focus on making new information and skills accessible and comprehensible to students using techniques such as demonstrations, modelling, and visual support.

The *practice* phase involves students using the new information and skills in activities requiring collaboration, inquiry, problem-solving, and hands-on experiences.

The fourth phase, *evaluation,* entails students self-evaluating their understanding and proficiency with the content, language, and learning strategies they have been practising. O'Malley (1996: 3) has clearly expressed the importance of self-assessment in affirming students' sense of academic efficacy: 'Self-assessment is the key to student empowerment because it gives students an opportunity to reflect on their own progress toward instructional objectives, to determine the learning strategies that are effective for them, and to develop plans for their future learning'.

In the final phase, *expansion,* students engage in activities that apply what they have learned to their own lives including their families and communities and aspects of their cultural and linguistic backgrounds.

Different components of the CALLA framework are supported by extensive cognitive science research and the overall approach has been implemented successfully in ESL and foreign language instructional settings. Chamot and her colleagues have recently developed an extremely useful resource book for the teaching of learning strategies (Chamot *et al.,* 1999).

CALLA has been implemented primarily at upper elementary and higher grade levels but it overlaps with aspects of the Success for All program, implemented primarily in the early grades, in its emphasis on learning strategies, metacognition, and integration between content and academic language development (Slavin *et al.*, 1996; Slavin & Fashola, 1998).

The New London Group's Pedagogy of Multiliteracies

The New London Group (1996) is the self-appellation of a group of Australian, North American, and European academics who met originally in New London, in the US state of New Hampshire, to articulate an orientation to literacy education that took account of the rapidly increasing cultural and linguistic diversity of students in western education systems and the multiple manifestations of literacy reflected in these diverse communities and in new forms of technology. According to the New London Group, if literacy pedagogy is to be effective, it must take account of and build on the various forms of vernacular literacy that are manifested in ethnocultural communities (e.g. Hardman, 1998; Lotherington *et al.* 1998; Martin-Jones & Bhatt, 1998; Vásquez, *et al.* 1994) as well as expand the traditional definitions of literacy beyond the text-based reading and writing of western schooling.

The New London Group proposes the notion of *Design* as a central construct for schooling whereby learners become familiar with available designs (e.g. of grammars, of genres of discourse, of visual representation (e.g. film, photography, etc.) and other forms of media); they then work to construct meaning and knowledge in the context of these designs. Students also work to *redesign* these semiotic systems in the sense of creating transformed designs to express new meanings. Traditional teaching of language and culture aims to transmit standard forms and conventions of the language and official versions of culture and national identity with an emphasis on stability and regularity. According to Kalantzis and Cope (1999), the Design notion starts with a very different set of assumptions:

> The starting point is language variation – the different accents, registers and dialects that serve different ends in different social contexts and for different social groups. And the key issue of language use is agency and subjectivity – the way in which every act of language draws on disparate language resources and remakes the world into a form that it has never quite taken before. ... In this sense, language is both an already Designed resource and the ground of Designs for social futures. (1999: 271)

In a similar way, with respect to culture, the focus is on change and transformation rather than on stability and regularity: 'the breadth, complexity and richness of the available meaning-making resources are such that representation is never simply a matter of reproduction' (1999: 271).

The creation and critical analysis of Designs for meaning involves four sets of pedagogical processes. Although all four are crucial for the learning process, they do not have to be implemented in any particular fixed sequence or as neatly separate bits:

(1) *Situated practice* involves immersion in meaningful practice and experience within a community of learners using Available Designs.
(2) *Overt instruction* requires explicit instruction on the part of the teacher to demystify skills and content and scaffold learner progress; its goal is systematic, analytic, and conscious understanding.
(3) *Critical framing* entails a focus on the historical, cultural, sociopolitical, and ideological roots of systems of knowledge and social practice; students step back from the meanings they are studying and view them critically in relation to their social and cultural context.
(4) *Transformed practice* aims to put transformed meanings and knowledge gained from previous practice, instruction, and critical reflection to work in other contexts or cultural sites.

This framework represents a useful integration of the concerns of the three pedagogical orientations discussed earlier in this chapter – traditional, progressive, and transformative. Progressive educational concerns for immersion in meaningful practice in a community of learners are incorporated in the first dimension (situated practice). The relevance of direct instruction by the teacher, which has been the focus of traditional pedagogy, is accommodated in the dimension of overt instruction. Finally, transformative pedagogy's concerns with critical literacy and social action are addressed in the dimensions of critical framing and transformed practice. Warschauer (1999: 166) reports that the New London Group framework could be applied productively to interpreting 'the best of what occurred' in the classes using new technologies for literacy promotion which he studied.

Kalantzis and Cope point out that cultural and linguistic diversity are central to all four of the pedagogical orientations:

> The inevitability of heterogeneous lifeworlds is highlighted by Situated Practice. The discussion of patterns of meaning that work in different social and cultural contexts sees a kind of contrastive linguistics replace the grammar of standard language forms (Overt Instruction). One can then analyze why these patterns of meaning work and in whose interests (Critical Framing). And finally, the learner can make or change their own world, even in the smallest of meaning-interventions (Transformed Practice). (1999: 272)

The New London framework represents a significant advance in thinking about how the research on school effectiveness (which emphasizes both situated practice and overt instruction) can be combined with a transformative orientation which exposes mainstream linguistic and cultural practices to critical scrutiny. Hornberger and Skilton-Sylvester (2000) have also used this framework together with Hornberger's (1989) continua of biliteracy to make visible the ways in which mainstream school practices and assumptions surrounding literacy and bilingualism have acted to disempower students from marginalized communities. They focus on the power relations embedded in the contexts of biliteracy, the development of biliteracy, the content of biliteracy and the media of biliteracy and argue that traditionally devalued aspects of language and literacy (e.g. vernacular varieties) must be re-evaluated by educators so that student voice and agency can find expression and make a difference in schools and the wider society. From this perspective, many of the unquestioned assumptions regarding literacy that underlie the educational effectiveness research constitute part of the invisible screen that obscures the operation of power relations in the school context.

The final framework to be considered attempts to integrate the concerns of traditional, progressive, and transformative pedagogies in a similar way to that of the New London Group. It was formulated specifically to illustrate how knowledge generation and identity negotiation could be combined within a transformative orientation. It attempts to reflect the core knowledge base relevant to academic language learning among ELL students in a way that lends itself to reflection, dialogue, and critical application by teachers.

Academic Language Development and Identity Negotiation Through a Pedagogical Focus on Meaning, Language and Use

The framework outlined in Figure 10.1 provides a general guide to the implementation of pedagogy that will effectively promote second language learners' linguistic and cognitive development as well as encourage the growth of critical literacy skills. It assumes that for optimal progress to occur, cognitive challenge and intrinsic motivation must be infused into the interactions between teachers and students.

Focus on meaning

The starting point is to acknowledge that effective instruction in a second language must focus initially on meaning or messages. Virtually all applied linguists agree that access to sufficient comprehensible input in the target language is a necessary condition for language acquisition; most applied linguists, however, also assign a role to (1) a focus on formal features of the target language, (2) development of effective learning strategies, and (3) actual use of the target language. These components are incorporated in the Focus on Language and Focus on Use components of the framework.

The Focus on Meaning component argues that the interpretation of the construct of *comprehensible input* must go beyond just literal comprehension. Depth of understanding of concepts and vocabulary as well as critical literacy are intrinsic to the notion of comprehensible input when we are talking about the development of academic language proficiency. This implies a process whereby students relate textual and instructional meanings to their own experience and prior knowledge (i.e. activate their cognitive schemata), critically analyze the information in the text (e.g. evaluate the validity of various arguments or propositions), and use the results of their discussions and analyses in some concrete, intrinsically motivating activity

FIGURE 10.1 Framework for academic language learning

A. FOCUS ON MEANING
   Making Input Comprehensible
   Developing Critical Literacy

B. FOCUS ON LANGUAGE
   Awareness of Language Forms and Uses
   Critical Analysis of Language Forms and Uses

C. FOCUS ON USE
   Using Language to:
      Generate New Knowledge
      Create Literature and Art
      Act on Social Realities

---

or project (e.g. making a video or writing a poem or essay on a particular topic). In short, for learning of academic content, the notion of *comprehensible input* must move beyond literal, surface-level comprehension to a deeper level of cognitive and linguistic processing.

The following scheme incorporates aspects of the *experience–text relationship* (ETR) approach (Au, 1979) as well as Ada's (1988a, 1988b) *creative reading* approach as a way of elaborating on what a focus on meaning entails. The scheme attempts to show how interpersonal spaces can be created between teachers and students that encourage students to share and amplify their experience within a collaborative process of critical inquiry. The process is also consistent with the emphases in recent work on instructional conversations (e.g. Saunders *et al.*, 1999; Saunders & Goldenberg, 1999 – see Note 3). Each of the five phases below progressively opens up possibilities for the articulation and amplification of student voice. The 'texts' that are the focus of the interaction can derive from any curricular area or from newspapers, popular songs, or current events. The process is equally applicable to students at any grade level and the phases can be intertwined rather than follow a strict sequence.

Much conventional reading instruction has focused only on the *literal phase* or on comprehensible input in a very narrow sense. The *experiential, personal, critical* and *creative phases* are essential if we are to speak of knowledge generation or transformative pedagogy rather than just transmission of information.

Experiential Phase

There is extensive research showing the relationship of prior knowledge to reading comprehension (e.g. Carrell, 1988; Dochy, Segers & Buehl, 1999). Activating students' prior knowledge serves several important functions in promoting reading comprehension. First, it makes the learning process more efficient since we learn by integrating new input into our existing cognitive structures or schemata. Our prior experience provides the foundation for interpreting new information.

Finding out what students know about a particular topic (e.g. through brain-storming) allows the teacher to supply relevant concepts or vocabulary that some or all students may be lacking but which will be important for understanding the upcoming text or lesson.

In addition to making the learning process more efficient, activating students' prior knowledge also:

- permits teachers to get to know their students better as individuals with unique personal histories and cultural experiences;
- creates a context in the classroom where students' cultural knowledge is expressed, shared and validated, thereby motivating students to participate more actively in the learning process.

In short, activating students' prior knowledge affirms students' identities while simultaneously increasing the effectiveness of the teaching/learning relationship.

Literal Phase

In this phase the focus of interaction is on the information contained in the text. Typical questions at this level might be: Where, when, how, did it happen? Who did it? Why? These are the type of questions for which answers can be found in the text itself. Ada points out that these are the usual reading comprehension questions and that 'a discussion that stays at this level suggests that reading is a passive, receptive, and in a sense, domesticating process' (1988a: 104). When the process is arrested at this level, the focus remains on internalization of inert information and/or the practice of 'reading skills' in an experiential and motivational vacuum. Instruction remains at a safe distance from any challenge to the societal power structure. A danger of using standardized tests or narrow performance assessments as outcome measures is that they may encourage instruction that stays at this literal level. It promotes 'comprehensible input' only in a very superficial way.

Personal Phase

After the basic information in the text has been discussed, students are encouraged to relate it to their own experiences and feelings. Questions that might be asked by the teacher at this phase are: Have you ever seen (felt, experienced) something like this? Have you ever wanted something similar? How did what you read make you feel? Did you like it? Did it make you happy? Frighten you? What about your family? Ada (1988a) points out that this process helps develop children's self-esteem by showing that their experiences and feelings are valued by the teacher and classmates. It also helps children understand that 'true learning occurs only when the information received is analyzed in the light of one's own experiences and emotions' (p. 104). This phase deepens students' comprehension of the text or issues by grounding the knowledge in the personal and collective narratives that make up students' histories.

Critical Phase

After children have compared and contrasted what is presented in the text with their personal experiences, they are ready to engage in a more abstract process of critically analyzing the issues or problems that are raised in the text. This process involves drawing inferences and exploring what generalizations can be made. Appropriate questions might be: Is it valid? Always? When? Does it benefit everyone alike? Are there any alternatives to this situation? Would people of different cultures (classes, genders) have acted differently? How? Why? When students pursue guided research and critical reflection, they are clearly engaged in a process of knowledge generation; however, they are equally engaged in a process of self-definition; as they gain the power to think through issues that affect their lives, they simultaneously gain the power to resist external definitions of who they are and to deconstruct the sociopolitical purposes of such external definitions.

Creative Phase

This is a stage of translating the results of the previous phases into concrete action. The dialogue is oriented towards discovering what changes individuals can make to improve their lives or resolve the problem that has been presented. Let us suppose that students have been researching problems relating to environmental pollution. After relating the issues to their own experience, critically analyzing causes and possible solutions, they might decide to write letters to elected officials, highlight the issue in their class/school newsletter in order to sensitize other students, write and circulate a petition in the neighbourhood, write and perform a play that analyzes the issue, etc. Once again, this phase can be seen as extending the pursuit of meaning insofar as when we act to transform aspects of our social realities we gain a deeper understanding of those realities.

Focus on language

The Focus on Language component in Figure 10.1 attempts to put controversial issues such as the appropriate time and ways to teach L2 grammar under the 'umbrella' of *Language Awareness*. The development of language awareness would include not just a focus on formal aspects of the language but also the development of *critical language awareness* which encompasses exploring the relationships between language and power. Students, for example, might carry out research on the status of different varieties of language (e.g. colloquial language versus formal 'standard' language) and explore critically why one form is considered by many educators and the general public to be 'better' than the other. They might also research issues such as code-switching and the functions it plays within their own lives and their bilingual communities. Or they might analyze letters to the editor on bilingual education and inquire why certain kinds of letters tend to get published while others do not.

In short, a focus on formal features of the target language should be integrated with critical inquiry into issues of language and power. Also, to be effective, a focus on language must be linked to extensive input in the target language (e.g. through reading) and extensive opportunities for written and oral use of the language.

A number of scholars and educators have focused on the importance of developing language awareness not only as a means of demystifying language and how it works but also as a way of reinforcing students' sense of identity. Lisa Delpit (1998), for example, talks about encouraging African American speakers of Ebonics to become 'language detectives' investigating similarities and differences between their own vernacular and other forms of English such as that found in school texts. For example, groups of students can work together to create bilingual dictionaries of their own language forms and Standard English. A significant goal is to reinforce students' understanding that their language is legitimate and powerful in its context of use but that other forms of English are necessary in different contexts of use. She also illustrates how an affirmation of identity can be associated with a focus on language by referring to the practice of a teacher who has her middle school students listen to rap songs in order to develop a rule base for their creation:

> The students would teach her their newly constructed 'rules for writing rap', and she would in turn use this knowledge as a base to begin a discussion of the rules Shakespeare used to construct his plays, or the rules poets used to develop their sonnets. (1995: 67)

John Baugh (1999) discusses a series of 'Lyric Shuffle' games which he devised to help African American students bridge the gap between their oral language and the more formal language of literacy. Students bring in popular music that they listen to outside of school (excluding music with a 'parental advisory' designation); they either transcribe the lyrics or the teacher provides a copy of the lyrics to them. Students listen to the song and then engage in a variety of games that reinforce vocabulary and other aspects of language awareness. According to Baugh, 'every Lyric Shuffle game has a basic format that requires student game players to rearrange the words from the song to form new sentences, new poems or lyrics, or an original short story' (1999: 35). Tasks can be adjusted to fit the needs of individual students and the complexity of the games can be increased to present new challenges and advance students' literacy. In addition to activities that focus on basic literacy knowledge such as sentence formation and phonic regularities, the substance of the lyrics can be discussed and more complex linguistic topics like ambiguity, puns, homonymy, and synonymy can be introduced to students 'without direct reference to the acquisition of dominant literary or linguistic norms' (1999: 36).

This latter point highlights the importance of introducing literacy to students in a way that reinforces rather then undermines their identities. Baugh notes the crucial importance of both literacy and access to standard English for African American students. However, he also points out:

> But I am equally aware that many young minority students value their vernacular dialects, including languages other than English. And many come to equate the acquisition of literacy with two negative characteristics: an abandonment of their native linguistic identity and an abhorrence of any behavior that could be considered 'acting white' (Fordham and Ogbu, 1985). (1999: 34)

Baugh's discussion illustrates how a Focus on Language for culturally and linguistically diverse students will be particularly effective when it simultaneously affirms students' identities as well as increases their critical awareness of language and its intersection with power relationships.[6]

Focus on use

The Focus on Use component is based on the notion that L2 acquisition will remain abstract and classroom-bound unless students have the opportunity to express themselves – their identities and their intelligence – through that language. There is convincing evidence that target language use contributes to acquisition of that language (Swain, 1997) but the focus here is on the importance of language use for overall literacy development and identity affirmation.

In order to motivate language use there should ideally be an authentic audience that encourages two-way communication in both oral and written modes. The three examples of language use presented in Figure 10.1 (*generate new knowledge, create literature and art, act on social realities*) are intended to illustrate important components of critical literacy. Language must be used to amplify students' intellectual, aesthetic, and social identities if it is to contribute to student empowerment, understood as the collaborative creation of power. Unless active and authentic language use for these purposes is promoted in the classroom, students' grasp of academic (and conversational) English is likely to remain shallow and passive.

Clearly, a major aspect of the *Focus on Use* involves writing across curricular areas. Observations by the staff of the Oyster Bilingual School highlight the importance of writing for academic achievement in general but also more specifically for performance on the SAT-9 standardized test:

> Further analysis of test scores on a class-by-class basis indicated that the teachers who were most successful in raising test scores provided a very strong writing program for their students. Schoolwide priorities this year include reading 25 books a year and writing two books, one in English, one in Spanish. We will hold, for the first time, a Young Authors' Night where students will have the opportunity to read their books to parents and to other students. ... a schoolwide Writing Process is being implemented across all classes and grades. Teachers are required to implement the Writing Process to enable students to write two books. (Oyster Bilingual School, 1999: 4)

Here again, we see the positive effects of integrating students' sense of self with active language use and engagement with literacy. A student who sees herself as a Young Author, capable of writing creatively in *two* languages, will read more extensively and write more enthusiastically than one who is confined to a passive role within the classroom. The Oyster example also suggests how a transformative orientation that focuses on meaning, language, and use, can result in superior performance on standardized tests of basic skills. Thus, educators do not have to choose between an 'effectiveness' orientation (teach to the test) and a transformative orientation. Implemented appropriately, a transformative orientation incorporates everything that students need to perform well on tests, and as an additional benefit, it aspires to truly educate children. Krashen (1993, 1999b) has also reviewed research that demonstrates that students who spend more time reading extensively as opposed to experiencing direct instruction in 'reading skills' performed significantly better on standardized tests.

Another example of a language use activity that clearly promotes identity exploration together with literacy skills development is the writing of critical autobiographies in which culturally and linguistically diverse students write about experiences and events in their lives (Benesch, 1993; Brisk, 1998). Brisk points out that in writing the autobiographies students should examine and discuss their lives from a variety of perspectives: linguistic, cultural, political, economic, sociological, and psychological, and try to understand why things are the way they are. In the course of class discussion exploring various themes, teachers can ask questions to students to probe deeper into issues. Parents can also be interviewed for relevant information and resources (e.g. photographs).

A variation of the critical autobiography is to have pairs of students collaborate to write each others' biography. In some cases, a more fluent English-speaker will collaborate with a less fluent student to construct and write the biography of the less fluent student. Publication of the biographies in paper or electronic (e.g. class web page) format can also be pursued for sharing with a wider audience (e.g. parents, other students, etc.).

Recently arrived ELL students can be encouraged to write in their L1. Edwards documents how this process simultaneously develops writing expertise and affirms students' identities:

> While it is clearly very difficult for language learners to write in English in the early stages, there is no reason why they cannot draft, revise and edit in their first language. This approach allows them to develop their skills while joining in the same activity as their peers. It can also enhance their status in the class. Instead of emphasizing what they cannot do, the focus shifts to their achievements. This is precisely what happened with Julia, a ten-year-old girl who had recently arrived from Russia. Classmates – and teacher – were fascinated by the appearance of the Cyrillic script on the page and very impressed by her beautiful handwriting. A Russian-speaking member of staff provided a translation so that she was able to share her story with the class. (1998: 67)

Another set of examples of language use in the context of transformative pedagogy comes from the computer-mediated sister class projects documented by Brown (1999), Cummins and Sayers (1995) and Brown, Figueroa, Sayers and Cummins (1998). Brown, for example, describes a project dubbed 'New Places' by the participating classes in which students who had moved described their experiences. Students who hadn't moved interviewed peers at their school about how they were received in their new schools and communities. Students from a dozen countries were involved in this project, including those who had moved from rural China to Beijing, African Americans who had moved from the south to the north within the United States, and immigrant students who had moved from many countries to the United States. Students investigated what motivates migration and how people from different cultural, racial, and linguistic backgrounds were received by their new communities. Brown concludes:

> One of the outcomes of this project was that together the students analyzed the linguistic, cultural, and institutional barriers at their schools and drew up guidelines for teachers and students about how to make their schools better places for newcomers. The idea that collaborative problem solving might make the world a better place motivates much online learning. (1999: 312)

Once again, it is clear how the power of a project such as this derives from its dual and complementary focus on knowledge generation and identity negotiation.

Conclusion

A framework such as that outlined in Figure 10.1 can be used by educators almost as a simple checklist to think about their own instruction and the extent to which culturally and linguistically diverse students are being given opportunities for both knowledge generation and identity affirmation. Each of the Focus areas can be viewed through these two lens and, as they look back on a week with their students, educators should be able to identify the activities that fell into each category (Meaning, Language, and Use) and the ways in which these activities contributed to students' identity formation and learning of academic content. A transformative orientation is built into each of the three Focus areas by means of the specification of *critical literacy, critical language awareness* and *acting on social realities* as core components of a focus on meaning, language, and use respectively.

In answer to the question posed in the title of this chapter (Transformative Pedagogy: Who Needs It?), I have argued that transformative pedagogy represents a crucial component of any educational reform process that is serious about reversing patterns of underachievement among marginalized groups. As emphasized by Nieto (1996, 1999) and Kalantzis and Cope (1999), it is 'mainstream' schooling that requires transformation if all students are to succeed academically within its structures.

A transformative orientation does not entail sacrificing a concern with basic skills. On the contrary, although it uses a different lexicon, the research on school effectiveness identifies many aspects of transformative pedagogy as strongly related to student achievement measured by conventional tests. It is also clear that the instructional approaches emphasized within a transformative orientation engage students in extensive reading, critical discussion, and writing, all of which have been shown to be significant determinants of reading comprehension.

Where transformative pedagogy goes beyond the notion of 'effective instruction' is in its understanding that sustained effectiveness requires that students engage actively with the instructional process and this will happen among subordinated group students only in contexts where their identities are being affirmed. Creation of contexts of empowerment in the classroom, by definition, entails a challenge to coercive power structures operating in the educational system and wider society. Transformative educators acknowledge that educational structures are rooted in a sociopolitical context that traditionally has disempowered subordinated group students and they orchestrate interactions with their students that challenge these forms of disempowerment. In short, their conception of what education is all about and why they are in the classroom is fundamentally different than that of most policy-makers who see education primarily in terms of the efficient delivery of a service. The struggle between these very different conceptions of education will ultimately determine the extent to which schools continue to reproduce social inequalities or alternatively, effectively challenge the roots of inequality.

Notes

1. I use the term *transformative pedagogy* rather than *critical pedagogy* because it more clearly communicates that an active focus on social change is its central goal. Transformative pedagogy aims to create patterns of teacher–student interaction that effectively challenge and transform the ways in which schools have traditionally reproduced social and economic inequalities.

2. The tone of the traditional versus progressive pedagogy debates can be seen from the conflict that erupted in Texas in early November 1999 over the issue of how much 'decodable text' should be in reading textbooks from kindergarten through Grade 3. Decodable text is text that is structured so as to be easily sounded out by students who have been taught using a phonics approach to reading. In 1998, the Texas State Board of Education ruled that 'most' words in early reading texts should be 'decodable'. The Texas Education Agency interpreted this ruling as indicating that 51% of the words should conform to this criterion and publishers developed their reading programs based on this ruling. When members of the State Board discovered in September 1999 that 'most' had been defined as 51%, several influential members were outraged and called for an average of at least 80% decodable words in reading texts from kindergarten through Grade 3. Publishers complained that making these changes at this stage would cost them millions of dollars but the power of the Texas market was such that most of them did make the changes. The following excerpts from the *Dallas Morning News* (4 November, 1999) illustrate the fierceness of the traditional versus progressive pedagogy debate as manifested in the contemporary reading wars:

   > Their battles over what is taught in classrooms are well-known. Human evolution. Sex education. Creeping federal programs. Flawed textbooks. Those have all been rallying cries for such social conservative groups as the Christian Coalition and the Eagle Forum. Now they have embraced another cause with equal fervour – the use of phonics to teach young children to read. Christian radio stations across Texas and the nation are among the individuals and organizations who call frequently for a return to phonics – teaching students letters and their sounds to develop reading skills …

   > Critics contend the conservatives' agenda is driven by a desire to have a more rigid learning structure in schools, one that avoids critical thinking by students. 'They have a paranoia about teaching children to think critically', said Samantha Smoot of the Texas Freedom Network, a political watchdog group created to counter the influence of religious conservatives. 'The more simple and standardized they can make learning, the safer they feel'. …

   > Texas Eagle Forum founder Phyllis Schlafly … blames illiteracy in schools on the lack of phonics instruction. 'My answer [to illiteracy] is, scrap the failed method called

whole language and instead teach children how to read by the proven phonics method so they will be able to realize the American dream', she wrote in a column in August. But, she cautioned, 'The schools aren't going to do that because their teachers are brainwashed into believing that phonics is a 'far right' religious and educational conspiracy.' (Stutz, 1999: 1A, 17A)

See Dressman (1999) and Allington and Woodside-Jiron (1999) for insightful analyses of the relationship between the research data and the Texas and California reading policy initiatives. Coles (1998), Krashen (1999b, 1999d), McQuillan (1998), and Neumann (1999) also make for fascinating reading in this respect. It is clear, for example, from Allington and Woodside-Jiron's analysis that many of the prescriptions regarding phonics instruction that have been implemented in Texas and California policies have absolutely no basis in research.

3. The importance of relating ELL students' prior knowledge to the text they are reading and providing extensive opportunities for small group discussion and writing about personal reactions to the text emerges from research conducted at the Center for Research on Education, Diversity & Excellence (CREDE) in Santa Cruz, California. Saunders, O'Brien, Lennon and McLean (1999), for example, found four strategies to be effective in raising achievement levels in a multi-year Spanish-to-English language arts transition curriculum. Students were in Grades 2–5 of a transitional bilingual program whose goal is to promote first and second language acquisition and academic achievement. The four strategies are:
   - Building students' background knowledge.
   - Drawing on students' personal experiences.
   - Promoting extended discourse through writing and discussion.
   - Assisting students in re-reading pivotal portions of the text.

   A related study carried out by Saunders and Goldenberg (1999) among 116 fourth and fifth graders found that for ELL students the most effective of four treatments they evaluated was the combination of literature logs and instructional conversations. Students at the fourth grade level were still receiving Spanish language arts instruction in addition to English language arts instruction. A literature log might involve prompts to students to write about a personal experience related to the story, elaborate on something that has happened in the story (e.g. assume the role of a character), or analyze or interpret some aspect of the story or theme. This process is integrated with small group discussions or *instructional conversations* in which the teacher and students meet in small groups to discuss the story, log entries, related personal experiences, and the theme(s) for the unit. These instructional conversations 'allow students to hear, appreciate, and build on each others' experiences, knowledge, and understandings' (Saunders & Goldenberg, 1999: 28). It is clear that this process combines identity affirmation with knowledge generation.

4. The research evidence supporting the efficacy of the Success for All program has been hotly debated (e.g. Pogrow, 1999). The program also arouses strong emotions among teachers. Many that I have spoken to dislike the 'deskilling' of their professional expertise entailed in the prescribed scripts they are required to deliver to students in some components of the program. For inexperienced and insecure teachers such scripts may serve a useful transitional function and they do provide a measure of consistency of implementation across school contexts. However, they are rooted in a transmission or 'banking' model of pedagogy and they introduce a rigidity into the program that appears likely to constrict rather than enhance the interaction and relationship between teachers and students.

5. This description links in well with the *socioacademic framework* developed by De Villar and Faltis (1991, 1994) which emphasizes the centrality of *communication, integration* and *cooperation* in creating appropriate learning contexts for ELL students. These dimensions each involve both cognitive and interpersonal aspects and draw primarily on sociocultural

theory (Vygotsky's work), prejudice reduction research (Allport's (1954) contact theory), and research on cooperative learning (e.g. Johnson & Johnson, 1981).

6. Norah McWilliam (1998) has written a wonderful book highlighting the possibilities for developing language awareness in multilingual classrooms. The book is entitled *What's in a Word? Vocabulary Development in Multilingual Classrooms*. It highlights the cultural, linguistic, and academic enrichment that derives from a focus on language in the classroom where students' linguistic and cultural knowledge become resources for creative linguistic exploration.

References

Ada, A.F. (1988a) The Pajaro Valley experience: Working with Spanish-speaking parents to develop children's reading and writing skills in the home through the use of children's literature. In T. Skutnabb-Kangas and J. Cummins (eds) *Minority Education: From Shame to Struggle* (pp. 223–238). Clevedon: Multilingual Matters.

Ada, A.F. (1988b) Creative reading: A relevant methodology for language minority children. In L.M. Malave (ed.) *NABE '87. Theory, Research and Application: Selected Papers* (pp. 97–112). Buffalo: State University of New York.

Ahlgren, P. (1993, Fall) La Escuela Fratney: Reflections on a bilingual, anti-bias, multicultural elementary school. *Teaching Tolerance*, 26–31.

Aitchison, J. (1994) *Words in the Mind. An Introduction to the Mental Lexicon (2nd edn)*. Oxford: Blackwell.

Alderson, J.C. (1984) Reading in a foreign language: A reading problem or a language problem? In J.C. Alderson and A.H. Urquhart (eds) *Reading in a Foreign Language* (pp. 122–135). London: Longman.

Alderson, J.C. (1993) The relationship between grammar and reading in an English for Academic Purposes test battery. In D. Douglas and C. Chapelle (eds) *A New Decade of Language Testing Research* (pp. 203–219). Alexandria, VA: TESOL.

Allington, R.L. and Woodside-Jiron, H. (1999) The politics of literacy teaching: How 'research' shaped educational policy. *Educational Researcher* 28 (8), 4–13.

Allport, G.W. (1954) *The Nature of Prejudice*. New York: Doubleday Anchor.

Anderson, R.C. and Freebody, P. (1981) Vocabulary knowledge. In J. Guthrie (ed.) *Comprehension and Teaching: Research Reviews* (pp. 77–117). Newark, DE: International Reading Association.

Appel, R. and Muysken, P. (1987) *Language Contact and Bilingualism*. London: Edward Arnold.

Arnaqaq, N., Pitsiulak, P. and Tompkins, J. (1999, April) Geese flying in a northern sky. Paper presented at the American Education Research Association Conference, Montreal.

Au, K.H. (1979) Using the experience–text–relationship method with minority children. *Reading Teacher* 32 (6), 677–679.

Au, K.H. and Jordan, C. (1981) Teaching reading to Hawaiian children: Finding a culturally appropriate solution. In H. Trueba, G.P. Guthrie and K.H. Au (eds) *Culture and the Bilingual Classroom: Studies in Classroom Ethnography*. Rowley, MA: Newbury House.

August, D. and Hakuta, K. (eds) (1997) *Improving Schooling for Language-Minority Children: A Research Agenda*. National Research Council, Institute of Medicine, National Academy Press.

Bachman, L.F. (1990a) *Fundamental Considerations in Language Testing*. Oxford: Oxford University Press.

Bachman, L.F. (1990b) Constructing measures and measuring constructs. In B. Harley, P. Allen, J. Cummins and M. Swain (eds) *The Development of Second Language Proficiency* (pp. 26–38). Cambridge: Cambridge University Press.

Bachman, L.F. (1998) Appendix: Language testing–SLA interfaces. In L.F. Bachman and A.D. Cohen (eds) *Interfaces Between Second Language Acquisition and Language Testing Research.* Cambridge: Cambridge University Press.

Bachman, L.F. and Cohen, A.D. (1998) Language testing–SLA interfaces: An update. In L.F. Bachman and A.D. Cohen (eds) *Interfaces Between Second Language Acquisition and Language Testing Research* (pp. 1–31). Cambridge: Cambridge University Press.

Bachman, L.F., Davidson, F. and Foulkes, J. (1993) A comparison of the abilities measured by the Cambridge and Educational Testing Service EFL test batteries. In D. Douglas and C. Chapelle (eds) *A New Decade of Language Testing Research* (pp. 24–45). Alexandria, VA: TESOL.

Bachman, L.F., Davidson, F., Ryan, K. and Choi, I.-C. (1995) *An Investigation into the Comparability of Two Tests of English as a Foreign Language. The Cambridge-TOEFL Comparability Study.* Cambridge: Cambridge University Press.

Bachman, L.F and Palmer, A.S (1982) The construct validation of some components of communicative proficiency. *TESOL Quarterly* 16, 449–465.

Bachman, L.F. and Palmer, A.S. (1996) *Language Testing in Practice.* Oxford: Oxford University Press.

Baker, C. (1996) *Foundations of Bilingual Education and Bilingualism.* Clevedon: Multilingual Matters.

Baker, C. and Prys Jones, S. (1998) *Encyclopedia of Bilingualism and Bilingual Education.* Clevedon: Multilingual Matters.

Baker, K. (1992) Review of *Forked Tongue. Bilingual Basics* (Winter/Spring), 6–7.

Baker, K. (1998) Structured English immersion: Breakthrough in teaching limited-English-proficient students. *Phi Delta Kappan* (November), 199–204.

Baker, K.A. and de Kanter, A.A. (1981) *Effectiveness of Bilingual Education: A Review of the Literature.* Washington: US Department of Education.

Baker, K.A. and de Kanter, A.A. (1983) *Effectiveness of Bilingual Education: A Review of the Literature.* Washington, DC: Office of Planning and Budget, US Department of Education.

Bakhtin, M.M. (1986) *Speech Genres and Other Late Essays.* Austin, TX: University of Texas Press.

Banks, J.A. (1996) The canon debate, knowledge construction, and multicultural education. In J.A. Banks (ed.) *Multicultural Education, Transformative Knowledge and Action: Historical and Contemporary Perspectives* (pp. 3–29). New York: Teachers College Press.

Banks, J.A. and Banks, C.A.M. (eds) (1993) *Multicultural Education, Issues and perspectives.* Needham Heights, MA: Allyn and Bacon.

Baril, A. and Mori, G.A. (1991) Educational attainment of linguistic groups in Canada. *Canadian Social Trends* (Spring), 17–18.

Barrs, M. (1990) *Words Not Numbers: Assessment in English.* Exeter: Short Run Press.

Barrs, M., Ellis, S., Hester, H. and Thomas, A. (1988) *The Primary Language Record.* London: Centre for Language in Primary Education.

Baugh, J. (1999) *Out of the Mouths of Slaves: African American Language and Educational Malpractice.* Austin: University of Texas Press.

Benesch, S. (1993) Reading and writing in critical autobiographies. In J.G. Carson and I. Leki (eds) *Reading in the Composition Classroom.* Boston: Heinle and Heinle.

Bereiter, C. and Scardamalia, M. (1981) From conversation to composition: The role of instruction in a developmental process. In R. Glaser (ed.) *Advances in Instructional Psychology. Vol. 2.* Hillsdale, NJ: Erlbaum.

Berko Gleason, J. (1993) *The Development of Language (3rd edn).* New York: Macmillan.

Berliner, D.C. and Biddle, B.J. (1995) *The Manufactured Crisis: Myths, Fraud, and the Attack on America's Public Schools.* Reading, MA: Perseus Books.

Bernhardt, E.B. (1991) A psycholinguistic perspective on second language literacy. In J.H. Hulstijn and J.F. Matter (eds) *Reading in Two Languages* (pp. 31–44). Amsterdam: AILA.

Bernhardt, E.B. and Kamil, M.L. (1995) Interpreting relationships between L1 and L2 reading: Consolidating the linguistic threshold and linguistic interdependence hypotheses. *Applied Linguistics* 16 (1), 15–34.

Bethell, T. (1979, February) Against bilingual education. *Harper's Magazine.*

Beykont, Z.F. (1994) Academic progress of a nondominant group: A longitudinal study of Puerto Ricans in New York City's late-exit bilingual programs. Doctoral dissertation presented to the Graduate School of Education, Harvard University.

Bialystok, E. (1987a) Influences of bilingualism on metalinguistic development. *Second Language Research* 3 (2), 112–125.

Bialystok, E. (1987b) Words as things: Development of word concept by bilingual children. *Studies in Second Language Learning* 9, 133–140.

Bialystok, E. (1988) Levels of bilingualism and levels of linguistic awareness. *Developmental Psychology* 24, 560–567.

Bialystok, E. (1991) Metalinguistic dimensions of bilingual language proficiency. In E. Bialystok (ed.) *Language Processing in Bilingual Children* (pp. 113–140). Cambridge: Cambridge University Press.

Biber, D. (1986) Spoken and written textual dimensions in English: Resolving the contradictory findings. *Language* 62, 384–414.

Bigelow, B., Christensen, L., Karp, S., Milner, B. and Peterson, B. (1994) *Rethinking our Classrooms: Teaching for Equity and Justice.* Milwaukee, WI: Rethinking Schools Ltd.

Bild, E.R. and Swain, M. (1989) Minority language students in a French immersion programme: Their French proficiency. *Journal of Multilingual and Multicultural Development* 10 (3), 255–274.

Board of Studies (1996) *ESL Companion to the English CSF.* Melbourne: Board of Studies (Victoria).

Bossers, B. (1991) On thresholds, ceilings and short-circuits: The relation between L1 reading, L2 reading and L2 knowledge. In J.H. Hulstijn and J.F. Matter (eds) *Reading in Two Languages* (pp. 45–60). Amsterdam: AILA.

Bostwick, R.M. (1999) A study of an elementary English language immersion school in Japan. Doctoral dissertation, Temple University, Philadelphia.

Bracey, G.W. (1999, November 2) Poverty issues get short shrift in today's education debate. *USA Today*, p. 19A.

Brathwaite, K.S. and James, C.E. (1996) *Educating African Canadians.* Toronto: James Lorimer and Company.

Brindley, G. (1998a) Describing language development? Rating scales and SLA. In L.F. Bachman and A.D. Cohen (eds) *Interfaces Between Second Language Acquisition and Language Testing Research* (pp. 112–140). Cambridge: Cambridge University Press.

Brindley, G. (1998b) Outcomes-based assessment and reporting in language learning programmes: A review of the issues. *Language Testing* 15 (1), 45–85.

Brisk, M.E. (1998) *Bilingual Education: From Compensatory to Quality Schooling.* Mahwah, NJ: Lawrence Erlbaum Associates.

Brown, K. (1999) Global learning networks: Heartbeats on the Internet. In J.V. Tinajero and R.A. DeVillar (eds) *The Power of Two Languages 2000* (pp. 309–319). New York: McGraw-Hill School Division.

Brown, K., Cummins, J., Figueroa, E. and Sayers, D. (1998) Global learning networks: Gaining perspective on our lives with distance. In E. Lee, D. Menkart and M. Okazawa-Rey (eds) *Beyond Heroes and Holidays: A Practical Guide to K-12 Anti-Racist, Multicultural Education and Staff Development* (pp. 334–354). Washington, DC: Network of Educators on the Americas.

Bruner, J.S. (1962) Introduction. In L.S. Vygotsky *Thought and Language* (pp. v–x). Cambridge, MA: MIT Press.

Bruner, J. S. (1975) Language as an instrument of thought. In A. Davies (ed.) *Problems of Language and Learning*. London: Heinemann.

Bullock Report (1975) *A Language for Life: Report of the Committee of Inquiry Appointed by the Secretary of State for Education and Science under the Chairmanship of Sir Alan Bullock*. London: HMSO.

Bunyi, G. (1997) Language in education in Kenyan schools. In J. Cummins and D. Corson (eds) *Bilingual Education. Vol. 5. Encyclopedia of Language and Education* (pp. 33–44). Dordrecht, The Netherlands: Kluwer Academic Publishers.

Butler, F.A. and Stevens, R. (1997) *Accommodation Strategies for English Language Learners on Large-Scale Assessments: Student Characteristics and Other Considerations* (CSE Technical Report No. 448). National Center for Research on Evaluation, Standards, and Student Testing (CRESST), University of California.

Byram, M. and Leman, J. (1990) *Bicultural and Trilingual Education*. Clevedon: Multilingual Matters.

Calderón, M. and Carreón, A. (1999) In search of a new border pedagogy: Sociocultural conflicts facing bilingual teachers and students along the US–Mexico border. In C.J. Ovando and P. McLaren (eds) *The Politics of Multiculturalism and Bilingual Education: Students and Teachers Caught in the Cross Fire* (pp. 167–187). Boston: McGraw Hill.

Calderón, M., Hertz-Lazarowitz, R. and Slavin, R. (1998) Effects of bilingual cooperative integrated reading and composition on students making the transition from Spanish to English reading. *The Elementary School Journal* 99 (2), 160–164.

California Department of Education (1999a) *English Language Development Standards*. Sacramento, CA: Standards, Curriculum, and Assessment Division, California Department of Education.

California Department of Education (1999b) *California Two-Way Bilingual Immersion Programs Directory*. Sacramento, CA: California Department of Education.

California State Department of Education (1985) *Case Studies in Bilingual Education: First Year Report*. (Federal Grant #G008303723) Sacramento, CA: California Department of Education.

Campos, J. and Keatinge, R. (1988) The Carpinteria language minority student experience: From theory, to practice, to success. In T. Skutnabb-Kangas and J. Cummins (eds) *Minority Education: From Shame to Struggle* (pp. 299–308). Clevedon: Multilingual Matters.

Canale, M. (1983a) On some dimensions of language proficiency. In J.W. Oller (ed.) *Issues in Language Testing Research* (pp. 333–342). Rowley, MA: Newbury House.

Canale, M. (1983b) From communicative competence to communicative language pedagogy. In J. Richards and R. Schmidt (eds) *Language and Communication* (pp. 2–25). New York: Longman.

Canale, M., Frenette, N. and Bélanger, M. (1987) Evaluation of minority students writing in first and second languages. In J. Fine (ed.) *Second Language Discourse: A Textbook of Current Research*. Norwood, NJ: Ablex.

Canale, M. and Swain, M. (1980) Theoretical bases of communicative approaches to second language teaching and testing. *Applied Linguistics* 1, 1–47.

Candelaria-Greene, J. (1996) A paradigm for bilingual special education in the USA: Lessons from Kenya. *Bilingual Research Journal* 20 (3/4), 545–564.

Carr, W. and Kemmis, S. (1986) *Becoming Critical: Education, Knowledge and Action Research*. London: The Falmer Press.

Carrell, P.L. (1988) SLA and classroom instruction: Reading. *Annual Review of Applied Linguistics* 9, 223–242.

Carrell, P.L. (1991) Second language reading: Reading ability or language proficiency? *Applied Linguistics* 12, 159–179.

Cashion, M. and Eagan, R. (1990) Spontaneous reading and writing in English by students in total French immersion: Summary of final report. *English Quarterly* 22 (1–2), 30–44.

Cazabon, M.T., Nicoladis, E. and Lambert, W.E. (1998) *Becoming Bilingual in the Amigos Two-Way Immersion Program*. Washington, DC: CREDE/CAL.

Cazden, C.B. (1989) Richmond Road: A multilingual/multicultural primary school in Auckland, New Zealand. *Language and Education* 3, 143–166.

Cenoz, J. and Genesee, F. (eds) (1998) *Beyond Bilingualism: Multilingualism and Multilingual Education*. Clevedon: Multilingual Matters.

Centre for Language Training and Assessment (1998) *A Comparison Study of the International English Language Testing System (IELTS) and the Canadian Language Benchmarks Assessment (CLBA)*. Mississauga, ON: Centre for Language Training and Assessment.

Chamot, A.U., Barnhardt, S., El-Dinary, P.B. and Robbins, J. (1999) *The Learning Strategies Handbook*. White Plains, NY: Longman.

Chamot, A.U. and O'Malley, M. (1994) *The CALLA Handbook: Implementing the Cognitive Academic Language Learning Approach*. Reading, MA: Addison-Wesley.

Chapelle, C., Grabe, W. and Berns, M. (1997) *Communicative Language Proficiency: Definitions and Implications for TOEFL 2000* (TOEFL Monograph Series No. 10). Princeton, NJ: Educational Testing Service.

Chapelle, C.A. (1998) Construct definition and validity inquiry in SLA research. In L.F. Bachman and A.D. Cohen (eds) *Interfaces Between Second Language Acquisition and Language Testing Research* (pp. 32–70). Cambridge: Cambridge University Press.

Chomsky, N. (1959) Review of B.F. Skinner: 'Verbal Behavior'. *Language* 35, 26–57.

Chomsky, N. (1965) *Aspects of the Theory of Syntax*. Cambridge, MA: MIT Press.

Chomsky, N. (1987) *On Power and Ideology: The Managua Lectures*. Boston: South End Press.

Christian, D., Montone, C.L., Lindholm, K.J. and Carranza, I. (1997) *Profiles in Two-Way Immersion Education*. Washington, DC: Center for Applied Linguistics and Delta Systems.

Citizenship and Immigration Canada (1996) *Canadian Language Benchmarks. Working Document*. Ottawa: Ministry of Supply and Services Canada.

Clapham, C. (1997) Introduction. In C. Clapham and D. Corson (eds) *Language Testing and Assessment. Vol. 7. Encyclopedia of Language and Education* (pp. xiii–xix). Dordrecht: Kluwer Academic Publishers.

Clarke, M.A. (1979) Reading in Spanish and English: Evidence from adult ESL students. *Language Learning* 29, 121–150.

Clarke, M.A. (1980) The short-circuit hypothesis of ESL reading – or when language competence interferes with reading performance. *The Modern Language Journal* 64, 203–209.

Clarkson, P.C. (1992) Language and mathematics: A comparison of bilingual and monolingual students of mathematics. *Educational Studies of Mathematics* 23, 417–429.

Clarkson, P.C. and Galbraith, P. (1992) Bilingualism and mathematics learning: Another perspective. *Journal for Research in Mathematics Education* 23 (1), 34–44.

Cline, T. and Frederickson, N. (eds) (1996) *Curriculum Related Assessment, Cummins and Bilingual Children*. Clevedon: Multilingual Matters.

Cloud, N., Genesee, F. and Hamayan, E. (2000) *Dual Language Instruction: A Handbook for Enriched Education*. Boston, MA: Heinle and Heinle.

Coles, G. (1998) *Reading Lessons: The Debate over Literacy*. New York: Hill and Wang.

Collier, V.P. (1987) Age and rate of acquisition of second language for academic purposes. *TESOL Quarterly* 21, 617–641.

Collier, V.P. (1995) *Promoting Academic Success for ESL Students*. Elizabeth, NJ: New Jersey Teachers of English to Speakers of Other Languages-Bilingual Educators.

Collier, V.P. and Thomas, W.P. (1989) How quickly can immigrants become proficient in school English? *Journal of Educational Issues of Language Minority Students* 5, 26–38.

Collier, V.P. and Thomas, W.P. (1999) Making US schools effective for English language learners, Part 2. *TESOL Matters* 9 (5), 1,6.

Collins, T. (1998) *California English Language Proficiency Assessment Project*. San Diego County Office of Education.

Cook, V. (1992) Evidence for multicompetence. *Language Learning* 42 (4), 557–591.

Corson, D. (1993) *Language, Minority Education and Gender: Linking Social Justice and Power.* Clevedon: Multilingual Matters.

Corson, D. (1995) *Using English Words.* New York: Kluwer.

Corson, D. (1997) The learning and use of academic English words. *Language Learning* 47 (4), 671–718.

Corson, D. (1998a) *Language Policy in Schools.* Mawah, NJ: Lawrence Erlbaum Associates.

Corson, D. (1998b) *Changing Education for Diversity.* Buckingham: Open University Press.

Crawford, J. (1992a) *Language Loyalties: A Source Book on the Official English Controversy.* Chicago: University of Chicago Press.

Crawford, J. (1992b) *Hold Your Tongue: Bilingualsm and the Politics of 'English Only'.* New York: Addison Wesley.

Crawford, J. (1998). The bilingual education story: Why can't the news media get it right? Presentation to the National Association of Hispanic Journalists, Miami, June 26, 1998. Available at: http://ourworld.compuserve.com/homepages/jwcrawford.

Cumming, A. (1987) Writing expertise and second language proficiency in ESL writing performance. Doctoral dissertation, University of Toronto.

Cumming, A. (1989) Writing expertise and second-language proficiency. *Language Learning* 39 (1), 81–141.

Cumming, A. (1995) Changing definitions of language proficiency: Functions of language assessment in educational programs for recent immigrant learners of English in Canada. *Journal of the Canadian Association of Applied Linguistics* 17, 35–48.

Cumming, A. (1997) The testing of writing in a second language. In C. Clapham and D. Corson (eds) *Language Testing and Assessment. Vol. 7. Encyclopedia of Language and Education* (pp. 51–64). Dordrecht: Kluwer Academic Publishers.

Cummins, J. (1976) The influence of bilingualism on cognitive growth: A synthesis of research findings and explanatory hypotheses. *Working Papers on Bilingualism* 9, 1–43.

Cummins, J. (1977) Delaying native language reading instruction in immersion programs: A cautionary note. *Canadian Modern Language Review* 34, 46–49.

Cummins, J. (1978) Immersion programs: The Irish experience. *International Review of Education* 24, 273–82.

Cummins, J. (1979a) Linguistic interdependence and the educational development of bilingual children. *Review of Educational Research* 49, 222–251.

Cummins, J. (1979b) Cognitive/academic language proficiency, linguistic interdependence, the optimum age question and some other matters. *Working Papers on Bilingualism* 19, 121–29.

Cummins, J. (1980) Psychological assessment of immigrant children: Logic or intuition? *Journal of Multilingual and Multicultural Development* 1, 97–111.

Cummins, J. (1981a) The role of primary language development in promoting educational success for language minority students. In California State Department of Education (ed.) *Schooling and Language Minority Students: A Theoretical Framework.* (pp. 3–49). Los Angeles: Evaluation, Dissemination and Assessment Center California State University.

Cummins, J. (1981b) Age on arrival and immigrant second language learning in Canada: A reassessment. *Applied Linguistics* 1, 132–149.

Cummins, J. (1983) Language proficiency and academic achievement. In J.W. Oller Jr. (ed.) *Issues in Language Testing Research* (pp. 108–129). Rowley, MA: Newbury House.

Cummins, J. (1984) *Bilingualism and Special Education: Issues in Assessment and Pedagogy.* Clevedon: Multilingual Matters.

Cummins, J. (1986) Empowering minority students: A framework for intervention. *Harvard Education Review* 15, 18–36.

Cummins, J. (1989) The sanitized curriculum: Educational disempowerment in a nation at risk. In D.M. Johnson and D.H. Roen (eds) *Richness in Writing: Empowering ESL Students.* New York: Longman.

Cummins, J. (1991a) Conversational and academic language proficiency in bilingual contexts. In J.H. Hulstijn and J.F. Matter (eds) *Reading in Two Languages* (pp. 75–89). Amsterdam: AILA.

Cummins, J. (1991b) The development of bilingual proficiency from home to school: A longitudinal study of Portuguese-speaking children. *Journal of Education* 173, 85–98.

Cummins, J. (1991c) Interdependence of first- and second-language proficiency in bilingual children. In E. Bialystok (ed.) *Language Processing in Bilingual Children* (pp. 70–89). Cambridge: Cambridge University Press.

Cummins, J. (1996) *Negotiating Identities: Education for Empowerment in a Diverse Society.* Los Angeles: California Association for Bilingual Education.

Cummins, J. (1997) Minority status and schooling in Canada. *Anthropology and Education Quarterly* 28 (3), 411–430.

Cummins, J. (1999) Beyond adversarial discourse: Searching for common ground in the education of bilingual students. In C. Ovando and P. McLaren (eds) *The Politics of Multiculturalism and Bilingual Education: Students and Teachers Caught in the Cross Fire* (pp. 126–147). Boston: McGraw Hill.

Cummins, J. and Corson, D. (eds) (1997) *Bilingual Education. Vol. 5. Encyclopedia of Language and Education.* Dordrecht, The Netherlands: Kluwer Academic Publishers.

Cummins, J. and Sayers, D. (1995) *Brave New Schools: Challenging Cultural Illiteracy Through Global Learning Networks.* New York: St. Martin's Press.

Cummins, J. and Swain, M. (1983) Analysis-by-rhetoric: Reading the text or the reader's own projections? A reply to Edelsky *et al. Applied Linguistics* 4 (1), 23–41.

Cummins, J., Swain, M., Nakajima, K., Handscombe, J., Green, D. and Tran, C. (1984) Linguistic interdependence among Japanese and Vietnamese immigrant students. In C. Rivera (ed.) *Communicate Competence Approaches to Language Proficiency Assessment: Research and Application* (pp. 60–81). Clevedon: Multilingual Matters.

Danoff, M.V., Coles, G.J., McLaughlin, D.H. and Reynolds, D.J. (1978) *Evaluation of the Impact of ESEA Title VII Spanish/English Bilingual Education Program.* Palo Alto, CA: American Institutes for Research.

Darder, A. (1991) *Culture and Power in the Classroom: A Critical Foundation for Bicultural Education.* New York: Bergin and Garvey.

Davies, A. (ed) (1975) *Problems of Language and Learning.* London: Heinemann.

Davies, A., Grove, E. and Wilkes, M. (1997) Sub-project 1: Review of literature on acquiring literacy in a second language. In P. McKay, A. Davies, B. Devlin, J. Clayton, R. Oliver and S. Zammit (eds) *The Bilingual Interface Project Report: The Relationship Between First Language Development and Second Language Acquisition as Students Begin Learning English in the Context of Schooling* (pp. 17–74). Canberra: Department of Employment, Education, Training and Youth Affairs, Commonwealth of Australia.

Davison (1998) Aiming even higher: More effective accountability and intervention in ESL learning and teaching. *Australian Language Matters* 6 (4), 5–7.

Dawe, L. (1983) Bilingualism and mathematical reasoning in English as a second language. *Educational Studies in Mathematics* 14, 325–353.

Day, R.R. and Bamford, J. (1996) *Extensive Reading in the Second Language Classroom.* Cambridge: Cambridge University Press.

De Avila, E. and Duncan, S.E. (1978) A few thoughts about language assessment: The LAU decision reconsidered. *Bilingual Education Paper Series, National Dissemination and Assessment Center* 1 (8).

Dean, C. (1999, December 3) Poor results exposed by poverty analysis. *Times Educational Supplement.*

DeFazio, A.J. (1997) Language awareness at The International High School. In L. Van Lier and D. Corson (eds) *Knowledge about Language. Vol. 6. Encyclopedia of Language and Education* (pp. 99–107). Dordrecht, The Netherlands: Kluwer Acadedmic Publishers, Inc.

Dei, G.S. (1996) *Anti-Racism Education: Theory and Practice.* Halifax: Fernwood Publishers.

Delpit, L. (1995) *Other People's Children: Cultural Conflict in the Classroom*. New York: The New Press.

Delpit, L. (1998) Ebonics and culturally responsive instruction. In T. Perry and L. Delpit (eds) *The Real Ebonics Debate* (pp. 17–26). Milwaukee, WI: Rethinking Schools.

Delpit, L.D. (1988) The silenced dialogue: Power and pedagogy in educating other people's children. *Harvard Educational Review* 58, 280–298.

Derewianka, B. (1997) National developments in the assessment of ESL students. In M.P. Breen, C. Barratt-Pugh, H. House, C. Hudson, T. Lumley and M. Rohl (eds) *Profiling ESL Children: How Teachers Interpret and Use National and State Assessment Frameworks* (Vol. 1, pp. 15–65). Canberra: Commonwealth of Australia.

DeVillar, R. and Faltis, C.J. (1994) Reconciling cultural diversity and quality schooling: Paradigmatic elements of a socioacademic framework. In R.A. DeVillar, C.J. Faltis and J. Cummins (eds) *Cultural Diversity in Schools: From Rhetoric to Practice* (pp. 1–22). Albany, NY: State University of New York Press.

DeVillar, R.A. and Faltis, C.J. (1991) *Computers and Cultural Diversity: Restructuring for School Success*. Albany, NY: SUNY Press.

Devlin, B. (1997) Links between first and second language instruction in Northern Territory bilingual programs: Evolving policies, theories and practice. In P. McKay, A. Davies, B. Devlin, J. Clayton, R. Oliver and S. Zammit (eds) *The Bilingual Interface Project Report* (pp. 75–90). Canberra City: Commonwealth of Australia.

DevTech Systems, Inc. (1996) *A Descriptive Study of the ESEA Title VII Educational Services Provided for Secondary School Limited English Proficient Students: Final Report*. National Clearinghouse for Bilingual Education.

Diaz, R.M. (1985) Bilingual cognitive development: Addressing three gaps in current research. *Child Development* 56, 1376–1388.

Diaz, R.M. and Klinger, C. (1991) Towards an explanatory model of the interaction between bilingualism and cognitive development. In E. Bialystok (ed.) *Language Processing in Bilingual Children* (pp. 167–192). Cambridge: Cambridge University Press.

Dicker, S. (1996) RTE Forum: Letters from readers. *Research in the Teaching of English* 30 (1), 373–376.

Dochy, F., Segers, M. and Buehl, M. M. (1999) The relation between assessment practices and outcomes of studies: The case of research on prior knowledge. *Review of Educational Research* 69 (2), 145–186.

Dolson, D. and Lindholm, K. (1995) World class education for children in California: A comparison of the two-way bilingual immersion and European Schools model. In T. Skutnabb-Kangas (ed.) *Multilingualism for All* (pp. 69–102). Lisse: Swets and Zeitlinger.

Donaldson, M. (1978) *Children's Minds*. Glasgow: Collins.

Douglas, D. (1998) Testing methods in context-based second language research. In L.F. Bachman and A.D. Cohen (eds) *Interfaces Between Second Language Acquisition and Language Testing Research* (pp. 141–155). Cambridge: Cambridge University Press.

Dressman, M. (1999) On the use and misuse of research evidence: Decoding two states' reading initiatives. *Reading Research Quarterly* 34 (3), 258–285.

Dunn, L. (1987) *Bilingual Hispanic Children on the US Mainland: A Review of Research on Their Cognitive, Linguistic, and Scholastic Development*. Circle Pines, MN: American Guidance Service.

Duquette, G. and Riopel, P. (eds) (1998) *L'education en Milieu Minoritaire et la Formation des Maîtres en Acadie et dans les Communautés Francophones du Canada*. Sudbury: Presses de l'Université Laurentienne.

Durgunoğlu, A.Y. (1998) Acquiring literacy in English and Spanish in the United States. In A.Y. Durgunoglu and L. Verhoeven (eds) *Literacy Development in a Multilingual Context: Cross-Cultural Perspectives* (pp. 135–145). Mahwah, NJ: Lawrence Erlbaum Associates.

Durgunoğlu, A.Y. and Verhoeven, L. (eds) (1998) *Literacy Development in a Multilingual Context: Cross-Cultural Perspectives*. Mahwah, NJ: Lawrence Erlbaum Associates.

Dutcher, N. (1995) *The Use of First and Second Languages in Education: A Review of International Experience*. Washington, DC: The World Bank.

Echevarria, J. and Graves, A. (1998) *Sheltered Content Instruction: Teaching English-Language Learners with Diverse Abilities*. Boston: Allyn and Bacon.

Edelsky, C. (1990) *With Literacy and Justice for All: Rethinking the Social in Language and Education*. London: The Falmer Press.

Edelsky, C., Hudelson, S., Flores, B., Barkin, F., Altweger, B. and Jilbert, K. (1983) Semilingualism and language deficit. *Applied Linguistics* 4 (1), 1–22.

Education Department of Western Australia (1994) *Supporting Linguistic and Cultural Diversity Through First Steps: The Highgate Project*. Perth: Education Department of Western Australia.

Education Quality and Accountability Office (1997) *Provincial Report on Achievement: English-Language Schools*. Toronto: Education Quality and Accountability Office.

Edwards, V. (1998) *The Power of Babel: Teaching and Learning in Multilingual Classrooms*. Stoke-on-Trent, England: Trentham Books.

El Paso Independent School District (1987) *Interim Report of the Five-Year Bilingual Education Pilot 1986–87 School Year*. El Paso: Office for Research and Evaluation.

Elley, W.B. (1991) Acquiring literacy in a second language: The effect of book-based programs. *Language Learning* 41, 375–411.

Elley, W. (1992) *How in the World do Students Read? IEA Study of Reading Literacy*. The Hague, Netherlands: The International Association for the Evaluation of Educational Achievement.

Elley, W.B. and Manghubai, F. (1983) The impact of reading on second language learning. *Reading Research Quarterly* 19, 53–67.

Engle, P. (1975) *The Use of the Vernacular Language in Education*. Washington, DC: Center for Applied Linguistics.

Escamilla, K. (1996) RTE Forum: Letters from readers. *Research in the Teaching of English* 30 (1), 371–373.

Faltis, C.J. and Hudelson, S.J. (1998) *Bilingual Education in Elementary and Secondary School Communities: Toward Understanding and Caring*. Boston: Allyn and Bacon.

Fern, V. (1995) Oyster school stands the test of time. *Bilingual Research Journal* 19 (3 and 4), 497–512.

Fielding, L.G. and Pearson, P.D. (1994) Reading comprehension: What works. *Educational Leadership* 51 (5), 62–68.

Fillmore, C.J. (1968) The case for case. In E. Bach and R. Harmes (eds) *Universals in Linguistic Theory*. New York: Holt.

Fishman, J. (1976) Bilingual education: What and why? In J.E. Alatis and K. Twaddell (eds) *English as a Second Language in Bilingual Education*. Washington, DC: TESOL.

Fitzgerald, J. (1995) English-as-a-second-language learners' cognitive reading processes: A review of research in the United States. *Review of Educational Research* 65, 145–190.

Fitzgerald, J. and Cummins, J. (1999) Bridging disciplines to critique a national agenda for language-minority children's schooling. *Reading Research Quarterly* 34 (3), 378–390.

Fordham, S. (1990) Racelessness as a factor in Black students' school success: Pragmatic strategy or pyrrhic victory? In N.M. Hidalgo, C.L. McDowell and E.V. Siddle (eds) *Facing Racism in Education* (pp. 232–262). Cambridge, MA: Harvard Educational Review.

Fordham, S. and Ogbu, J. (1985) Black students' school success: Coping with the burden of 'Acting White'. *The Urban Review* 18, 176–206.

Fradd, S. and Lee, O. (eds) (1998) *Creating Florida's Multilingual Global Work Force: Educational Policies and Practices for Students Learning English as a New Language*. Tallahassee, FL: Florida Department of Education.

Frederickson, J. (ed.) (1995) *Reclaiming Our Voices: Bilingual Education, Critical Pedagogy and Praxis*. Ontario, CA: California Association for Bilingual Education.

Frederickson, N. and Cline, T. (1990) *Curriculum Related Assessment with Bilingual Children: A Set of Working Papers*. London: University College London.

Freeman, D.E. and Freeman, Y.S. (1994) *Between Worlds: Access to Second Language Acquisition*. Portsmouth, NH: Heinemann.

Freeman, R.D. (1998) *Bilingual Education and Social Change*. Clevedon: Multilingual Matters.

Freeman, Y.S. and Freeman, D.E. (1998) *ESL/EFL Teaching: Principles for Success*. Portsmouth, NH: Heinemann.

Freire, P. (1970a) *Cultural Action for Freedom*. Cambridge, MA: Harvard Educational Review.

Freire, P. (1970b) *Pedagogy of the Oppressed*. New York: Continuum.

Freire, P. (1983) Banking education. In H. Giroux and D. Purpel (eds) *The Hidden Curriculum and Moral Education: Deception or Discovery?*. Berkeley, CA: McCutcheon Publishing Corporation.

Freire, P. (1985) *The Politics of Education*. South Hadley, MA: Bergin and Garvey.

Galambos, S.J. and Hakuta, K. (1988) Subject-specific and task-specific characteristics of metalinguistic awareness in bilingual children. *Applied Psycholinguistics* 9 (2), 141–162.

Gándara, P. (1999) *Review of Research on Instruction of Limited English Proficient Students: A Report to the California Legislature*. Santa Barbara, CA: University of California, Linguistic Minority Research Institute.

García, E. (1991) *Education of Linguistically and Culturally Diverse Students: Effective Instructional Practices* (Educational Practice Report 1). The National Center for Research on Cultural Diversity and Second Language Learning.

García, P. (1998) Educational neglect of LEP students under CA's statewide testing and reporting program (STAR). *NABE News* 22 (2), 29–30.

Genesee, F. (1979) Acquisition of reading skills in immersion programs. *Foreign Language Annals* 12, 71–77.

Genesee, F. and Lambert, W. (1983) Trilingual education for majority-language children. *Child Development* 54, 105–114.

Genesee, F., Lambert, W. and Tucker, G. (1977) An experiment in trilingual education. Unpublished report. McGill University.

Gérin-Lajoie, D., Labrie, N. and Wilson, D. (1995) *Etude Interpretative des Resultats Obtenues par les Elèves Franco-Ontariens et Franco-Ontariennes en Lecture et en Ecriture aux Tests de Niveaux Provincial et National*. Toronto: Centre de recherches en education franco-ontarienne, OISE.

Gersten, R. (1985) Structured immersion for language minority students: Results of a longitudinal evaluation. *Educational Evaluation and Policy Analysis* 7, 187–196.

Gersten, R. and Woodward, J. (1995) A longitudinal study of transitional and immersion bilingual education programs in one district. *The Elementary School Journal* 95 (3), 223–239.

Geva, E. and Wade-Wooley, L. (1998) Component processes in becoming English-Hebrew biliterate. In A.Y. Durgunoğlu and L. Verhoeven (eds) *Literacy Development in a Multilingual Context: Cross-Cultural Perspectives* (pp. 85–110). Mahwah, NJ: Lawrence Erlbaum Associates.

Gibbons, J. (1999) Factors in the development of literate register among minority language speakers. Paper presented at the AILA conference, Tokyo.

Gibbons, J. and Lascar, E. (1998) Operationalizing academic language proficiency in bilingualism research. *Journal of Multilingual and Multicultural Development* 19 (1), 40–50.

Gibbons, P. (1991) *Learning to Learn in a Second Language*. Newtown, Australia: Primary English Teaching Association.

Gibbons, P. (1995) *Learning a new register in a second language: The role of teacher/student talk* (Working Paper No. 1). University of Technology, Sydney.

Gibbons, P. (1998) Classroom talk and the learning of new registers in a second language. *Language and Education* 12 (2), 99–118.

Gibson, H., Small, A. and Mason, D. (1997) Deaf bilingual bicultural education. In J.

Cummins and D. Corson (eds) *Bilingual Education. Volume 5. Encyclopedia of Language and Education* (pp. 231–240). Dordrecht, The Netherlands: Kluwer Academic Publishers.

Gibson, M.A. (1997) Complicating the immigrant/involuntary minority typology. *Anthropology and Education Quarterly* 28 (3), 431–454.

Giroux, H.A. (1991) Series Introduction: Rethinking the pedagogy of voice, difference and cultural struggle. In C.E. Walsh *Pedagogy and the Struggle for Voice: Issues of Language, Power, and Schooling for Puerto Ricans* (pp. xv–xxvii). Toronto: OISE Press.

Giroux, H.A. (1993) *Living Dangerously: Multiculturalism and the Politics of Difference*. New York: Peter Lang.

Giroux, H.A. (1999) The war against cultural politics: Beyond conservative and neo-enlightenment left 'oppositions': A critique. In C.J. Ovando and P. McLaren (eds) *The Politics of Multiculturalism and Bilingual Education: Students and Teachers Caught in the Cross Fire* (pp. 22–49). Boston: McGraw Hill.

Glenn, C. and LaLyre, I. (1991) Integrated bilingual education in the USA. In K. Jaspaert and S. Kroon (eds) *Ethnic Minority Languages and Education* (pp. 37–55). Amsterdam: Swets and Zeitlinger.

Glenn, C.L. (1990) Introduction. In Office of Educational Equity, *Two-Way Integrated Bilingual Education* (pp. 5–6). Boston: Department of Education.

González, L.A. (1986) The effects of first language education on the second language and academic achievement of Mexican immigrant elementary school children in the United States. Doctoral dissertation, University of Illinois at Urbana-Champaign.

González, L. A. (1989) Native language education: The key to English literacy skills. In D.J. Bixler-Márquez, G.K. Green and J.L. Ornstein-Galicia (eds) *Mexican-American Spanish in its Societal and Cultural Contexts* (pp. 209–224). Brownsville: Pan American University.

Goodlad, J.I. (1984) *A Place Called School: Prospects for the Future*. New York: McGraw Hill.

Grabe, W. (1988) Reassessing the term 'interactive'. In P.L. Carrell, J. Devione and D.E. Eskey (eds) *Interactive Approaches to Second Language Reading* (pp. 56–70). Cambridge: Cambridge University Press.

Greene, J.P. (1997) A meta-analysis of the Rossell and Baker review of bilingual education research. *Bilingual Research Journal* 21 (2 and 3), 1–20.

Greene, J.P. (1998) *A Meta-Analysis of the Effectiveness of Bilingual Education*. Claremont, CA: The Tomas Rivera Policy Institute.

Grosjean, F. (1989) Neurolinguists beware! The bilingual is not two monolinguals in one person. *Brain and Language* 36, 3–15.

Grove, E. (1998) Review of 'Access: Issues in Language Test Design and Delivery'. *Australian Language Matters* 6 (3), 18–19.

Guerrero, M. D. (1997) Spanish academic language proficiency: The case of bilingual education teachers in the US. *Bilingual Research Journal* 21 (1).

Hakuta, K. (1986) *Mirror of Language: The Debate on Bilingualism*. New York: Basic Books.

Hakuta, K. (1998) Supplemental declaration of Kenji Hakuta. Legal declaration in Appeal of Proposition 227. Available at http://ourworld.compuserve.com/homepages/jwcrawford

Hakuta, K. (1999, August 1). SAT-9 scores and California's Proposition 227: Drawing legitimate inferences regarding its impact on performance of LEP students. *NABE News* 22 (8), 1-7. Available at: http://www.stanford.edu/~hakuta/SAT9.

Hakuta, K., Butler, Y.G. and Witt, D. (2000) *How Long Does It Take English Learners to Attain Proficiency?* Santa Barbara, CA: University of California Linguistic Minority Research Institute.

Hakuta, K. and Diaz, R.M. (1985) The relationship between degree of bilingualism and cognitive ability: A critical discussion and some new longitudinal data. In K.E. Nelson (ed.) *Children's Language* (Vol. V). Hillsdale NJ: Lawrence Erlbaum Associates.

Hall, D. (1995) *Assessing the Needs of Bilingual Pupils: Living in Two Languages*. London: David Fulton Publishers.

Hall, D. (1996) Differentiating the secondary curriculum. In T. Cline and N. Frederickson (eds) *Curriculum Related Assessment, Cummins and Bilingual Children* (pp. 53–75). Clevedon: Multilingual Matters.

Halliday, M.A.K. (1978) *Language as Social Semiotic*. Baltimore: University Park Press.

Halliday, M.A.K. and Hasan, R. (1989) *Language, Context and Text: Aspects of Language in a Social Semiotic Perspective*. Oxford: Oxford University Press.

Hansegard, N.E. (1972) *Tvasprakighet Eller Halvsprakighet?* Stockholm: Aldus Series 253.

Hardman, J. (1998) Literacy and bilingualism in a Cambodian community in the USA. In A.Y. Durgunoğlu and L. Verhoeven (eds) *Literacy Development in a Multilingual Context: Cross-Cultural Perspectives* (pp. 51–81). Mahwah, NJ: Lawrence Erlbaum Associates.

Harley, B., Allen, P., Cummins, J. and Swain, M. (1990) *The Development of Second Language Proficiency*. Cambridge: Cambridge University Press.

Harris, S. (1990) *Two Way Aboriginal Schooling: Education and Cultural Survival*. Canberra: Aboriginal Studies Press.

Harry, B. (1992) *Cultural Diversity, Families and the Special Education System*. New York: Teachers College Press.

Hassanpour, A., Skutnabb-Kangas, T. and Chyet, M. (1996) The non-education of Kurds: A Kurdish perspective. *International Review of Education* 42 (4), 367–379.

Hayes, C.W., Bahruth, R. and Kessler, C. (1991) *Literacy con Cariño: A Story of Migrant Children's Success*. Portsmouth, NH: Heinemann.

Heath, S.B. (1983) *Ways with Words*. Cambridge: Cambridge University Press.

Hébert, R. (1976) *Academic Achievement, Language of Instruction, and the Franco-Manitoban Student*. Winnipeg: Centre de Recherches, Collège Universitaire de Saint Boniface.

Heller, M. (1994) *Crosswords: Language, Education and Ethnicity in French Ontario*. Berlin: Mouton de Gruyter.

Heller, M. (1999) *Linguistic Minorities and Modernity: A Sociolinguistic Ethnography*. London: Longman.

Herdina, P. and Jessner, U. (2000) *A Dynamic Model of Multilingualism: Changing the Psycholinguistic Perspective*. Clevedon: Multilingual Matters.

Hernandez-Chavez, E., Burt, M. and Dulay, H. (1978) Language dominance and proficiency testing: Some general considerations. *NABE Journal* 3, 41–54.

Hiraoka, T. (1999, August) Learning new methods to swim in English ocean. *Asahi Evening News (Special Supplement)*, p. 3.

Hirsch, E.D.J. (1987) *Cultural Literacy: What Every American Needs to Know*. Boston: Houghton Mifflin Co.

Hornberger, N. (1989) Continua of biliteracy. *Review of Educational Research* 59 (3), 271–296.

Hornberger, N.H. (1991) Extending enrichment bilingual education: Revisiting typologies and redirecting policy. In O. García (ed.) *Bilingual Education: Focusschrift in Honor of Joshua A. Fishman* (pp. 215–234). Amsterdam: John Benjamins Publishing Company.

Hornberger, N.H. and Skilton-Sylvester, E. (2000) Revisiting the continua of biliteracy: International and critical perspectives. *Language and Education*.

Hornblower, M. (1998) No habla Español. *TIME* (January 26), 44.

Hulstijn, J.H. (1991) How is reading in a second language related to reading in a first language? In J.H. Hulstijn and J.F. Matter (eds) *Reading in Two Languages* (pp. 5–14). Amsterdam: AILA.

Hymes, D.H. (1971) Competence and performance in linguistic theory. In R. Huxley and E. Ingram (eds) *Language Acquisition: Models and Methods*. New York: Academic Press.

Igoa, C. (1995) *The Inner World of the Immigrant Child*. New York: St. Martin's Press.

Igoa, C. (1999) Language and psychological dimensions: The inner world of the immigrant child. Paper presented at the American Educational Research Association Conference, Montreal, Canada.

Jackson, M. (1999, May 28) Plan to delay tests for refugee pupils. *Times Educational Supplement*, p. 1.

Jalava, A. (1988) Nobody could see that I was a Finn. In T. Skuttnabb-Kangas and J. Cummins (eds) *Minority Education: From Shame to Struggle* (pp. 161–166). Clevedon: Multilingual Matters.

James, C. (1994) 'I don't want to talk about it': Silencing students in today's classrooms. *Orbit* 25, 26–29.

Jaspaert, K.L., G. (1989) Linguistic evaluation of Dutch as a third language. In M. Byram and Leman, J. (eds) *Bicultural and Trilingual Education* (pp. 30–56). Clevedon: Multilingual Matters.

Jasso, A. and Jasso, R. (1995) Critical pedagogy: Not a method, but a way of life. In J. Frederickson (ed.) *Reclaiming our Voices: Bilingual Education, Critical Pedagogy and Praxis* (pp. 253–259). Ontario, CA: California Association for Bilingual Education.

Jensen, A.R. (1969) How much can we boost IQ and scholastic achievement? *Harvard Educational Review* 39, 1–123.

Jitendra, A.K. and Rohena-Diaz, E. (1996) Language assessment of students who are linguistically diverse: Why a discrete approach is not the answer. *School Psychology Review* 25, 40–56.

Johnson, D.W. and Johnson, R.T. (1981) Effects of cooperative and individualistic learning experiences on interethnic interaction. *Journal of Educational Psychology* 73 (3), 444–449.

Johnson, R. and Supik, J.D. (1999, September) More students served in bilingual and ESL programs but more LEP students assigned to special education. *IDRA Newsletter*.

Johnson, R.K. (1997) The Hong Kong education system: Late immersion under stress. In R.K. Johnson and M. Swain (eds) *Immersion Education: International Perspectives* (pp. 171–189). Cambridge: Cambridge University Press.

Jones, A.R. (1998) *A Study of the Test of English for International Communication (TOEIC) Referenced to the Canadian Language Benchmarks (CLB)*. Mississauga, ON: Centre for Language Training and Assessment.

Kalantzis, M. and Cope, B. (1993) Histories of pedagogy, cultures of schooling. In B. Cope and M. Kalantzis (eds) *The Powers of Literacy: A Genre Approach to Teaching Writing* (pp. 38–62). London: The Falmer Press.

Kalantzis, M. and Cope, B. (1999) Multicultural education: Transforming the mainstream. In S. May (ed.) *Critical Multiculturalism: Rethinking Multicultural and Antiracist Education* (pp. 245–276). London: Falmer Press.

Kalantzis, M., Cope, B. and Slade, D. (1989) *Minority Languages and Dominant Culture: Issues of Education, Assessment and Social Equity*. Barcombe, England: The Falmer Press.

Kanno, Y. (in press) Bilingualism and identity: The stories of Japanese returnees. *International Journal of Bilingual Education and Bilingualism*.

Klesmer, H. (1994) Assessment and teacher perceptions of ESL student achievement. *English Quarterly* 26 (3), 8–11.

Koda, K. (1989) The effects of transferred vocabulary knowledge on the development of L2 reading proficiency. *Foreign Language Annals* 22, 529–540.

Kozulin, A. (1998) *Psychological Tools: A Sociocultural Approach to Education*. Cambridge, MA: Harvard University Press.

Krashen, S. (1993) *The Power of Reading*. Englewood, CO: Libraries Unlimited.

Krashen, S.D. (1996) *Under Attack: The Case Against Bilingual Education*. Culver City: Language Education Associates.

Krashen, S.D. (1999a) *Condemned Without a Trial: Bogus Arguments Against Bilingual Education*. Portsmouth, NH: Heinemann.

Krashen, S.D. (1999b) *Three Arguments Against Whole Language and Why They Are Wrong*. Portsmouth, NH: Heinemann.

Krashen, S.D. (1999c) Why Malherbe (1946) is NOT evidence against bilingual education. *NABE News* 22 (7), 25–26.

Krashen, S. (1999d) Training in phonemic awareness: Greater on tests of phonemic awareness. *Perceptual and Motor Skills* 89, 412–416.

Krashen, S. and Biber, D. (1988) *On Course: Bilingual Education's Success in California.* Sacramento: California Association for Bilingual Education.

Kristof, N.D. (1999, August 3) Low birth rate, rapid aging thwart technological gains. *Asahi Evening News*, pp. 1, 4.

LaCelle-Peterson, M.W. and Rivera, C. (1994) Is it real for all kids? A framework for equitable assessment policies for English language learners. *Harvard Educational Review* 64 (1), 55–75.

Ladson-Billings, G. (1995) Toward a theory of culturally relevant pedagogy. *American Educational Research Journal* 32, 465–491.

Lambert, W.E. and Tucker, G.R. (1972) *Bilingual Education of Children: The St. Lambert Experiment.* Rowley, MA: Newbury House.

Lantolf, J.P. and Frawley, W. (1988) Proficiency: understanding the construct. *Studies in Second Language Acquisition* 10 (2), 181–195.

Lasagabaster, D. (1998) The threshold hypothesis applied to three languages in contact at school. *International Journal of Bilingual Education and Bilingualism* 1 (2), 119–133.

Latino Link (2000) Bilingual Latinos earn more than those that speak English only. *Yahoo! News.* Available at: http://dailynews.yahoo.com/htx/ll/20000202/co/20000202002.html.

Laufer, B. and Nation, P. (1995) Vocabulary size and use: Lexical richness in L2 written production. *Applied Linguistics* 16 (3), 307–322.

Laufer, B. and Nation, P. (1999) A vocabulary-size test of controlled productive ability. *Language Testing* 16 (1), 33–51.

Lee, J.-W. and Schallert, D.L. (1997) The relative contribution of L2 language proficiency and L1 reading ability to L2 reading performance: A test of the threshold hypothesis in an EFL context. *TESOL Quarterly* 31, 713–739.

Legaretta, D. (1979) The effects of program models on language acquisition by Spanish speaking children. *TESOL Quarterly* 13, 521–534.

Leung, C. (1996) Context, content and language. In T. Cline and N. Frederickson (eds) *Curriculum Related Assessment, Cummins and Bilingual Children* (pp. 26–40). Clevedon: Multilingual Matters.

Li, C., Nuttall, R.L. and Zhao, S. (1999) The effects of writing Chinese characters on success on the water-level task. *Journal of Cross-Cultural Psychology* 30 (1), 91–105.

Lin, A. and Man, E. (1999) *English Language Critical Literature Review: First and/or Second Language as a Medium of Instruction.* Hong Kong. Hong Kong Standing Committee on Language Education and Research.

Lin, A.M.Y. (1997) Bilingual education in Hong Kong. In J. Cummins and D. Corson (eds) *Bilingual education. Vol. 5 Encyclopedia of Language and Education* (pp. 281–290). Dordrecht, The Netherlands: Kluwer Academic Publishers.

Lindholm, K. (1994, April) Standardized achievement tests vs. alternative assessment: Are results complementary or contradictory? Paper presented at the American Educational Research Association, New Orleans.

Lotherington, H., Ebert, S., Watanabe, T., Norng, S. and Ho-Dac, T. (1998) Biliteracy practices in suburban Melbourne. *Australian Language Matters* 6 (3), 3–4.

Lucas, T., Henze, R. and Donato, R. (1990) Promoting the success of Latino language-minority students: An exploratory study of six high schools. *Harvard Educational Review* 60, 315–340.

Lucas, T. and Katz, A. (1994) Reframing the debate: The roles of native languages in English-only programs for language minority students. *TESOL Quarterly* 28 (3), 537–562.

Lupul, M.R. (ed.) (1985) *Osvita: Ukrainian Bilingual Education.* Edmonton: Canadian Institute of Ukrainian Studies.

Lyon, J. (1996) *Becoming Bilingual: Language Acquisition in a Bilingual Community.* Clevedon: Multilingual Matters.

Macedo, D.P. (1993) Literacy for stupidification: The pedagogy of big lies. *Harvard Educational Review* 63, 183–207.

Macedo, D.P. (1994) *Literacies of Power: What Americans Are Not Allowed to Know.* Boulder, CO: Westview Press.

Mackay, R. (1992) Embarrassment in the classroom. In A. van Essen and E. Burkart (eds) *Homage to W.R. Lee: Essays in English as a Foreign or Second Language* (pp. 153–163). Berlin: Foris Publications.

MacMahon, B. (1992) *The Master.* Dublin: Poolbeg Press.

MacSwan, J. (1999) *A Minimalist Approach to Intrasentential Code Switching.* New York: Garland Publishing.

MacSwan, J. (2000) The threshold hypothesis, semilingualism, and other contributions to a deficit view of linguistic minorities. *Hispanic Journal of Behavioral Sciences* 22 (1), 3–45.

Maher, J.C. and Yashiro, K. (1995) *Multilingual Japan.* Clevedon: Multilingual Matters.

Mahshie, S. (1995) *Educating Deaf Children Bilingually: With Insights and Applications from Sweden and Denmark.* Washington, DC: Gallaudet University.

Malherbe, E.G. (1946) *The Bilingual School.* Johannesburg: Bilingual School Association.

Martin-Jones, M. and Bhatt, A. (1998) Literacies in the lives of young Gujerati speakers in Leicester. In A.Y. Durgunoğlu and L. Verhoeven (eds) *Literacy Development in a multilingual Context: Cross-Cultural Perspectives* (pp. 37–50). Mahwah, NJ: Lawrence Erlbaum Associates.

Martin-Jones, M. and Romaine, S. (1986) Semilingualism: A half-baked theory of communicative competence. *Applied Linguistics* 7, 26–38.

Mason, D. (1997) Response to Mayer and Wells: The answer should be affirmative. *Journal of Deaf Studies and Deaf Education* 2 (4), 277–282.

Matthews, P. (1997) *The Concise Oxford Dictionary of Linguistics.* Oxford: Oxford University Press.

May, S. (1994) *Making Multicultural Education Work.* Clevedon: Multilingual Matters.

May, S. (ed.) (1999) *Critical Multiculturalism: Rethinking Multicultural and Antiracist Education.* London: Falmer Press.

Mayer, C. and Wells, G. (1996) Can the linguistic interdependence theory support a bilingual–bicultural model of literacy education for deaf students? *Journal of Deaf Studies and Deaf Education* 1 (2), 93–107.

McCaffrey, J., McMurchy-Pilkington, C. and Dale, H. (1998) Teaching and learning issues in Maori medium education: Immersion plus one: An issues discussion paper for the Community Languages and ESOL conference, Palmerston North, September.

McCaleb, S.P. (1994) *Building Communities of Learners: A Collaboration among Teachers, Students, Families and Community.* New York: St. Martin's Press.

McGregor, C., Pitsiulak, P. and O'Donoghue, F. (1999, April) The hunger for professional learning in Nunavut schools. Paper presented at the American Educational Research Association conference, Montreal.

McKay, P. (1995) Developing ESL proficiency descriptions for the school context: The NLLIA ESL bandscales. In G. Brindley (ed.) *Language Assessment in Action.* Sydney: National Centre for English Language Teaching and Research, Macquarrie University.

McKay, S.L. and Wong, S.C. (1996) Multiple discourses, multiple identities: Investment and agency in second-language learning among Chinese adolescent immigrant students. *Harvard Educational Review* 66 (3), 577–608.

McLaren, P. (1994) *Life in Schools: An Introduction to Critical Pedagogy in the Foundations of Education (2nd edn).* White Plains, NY: Longman.

McLaren, P. and Muñoz, J. (1999) Contesting whiteness: Critical perspectives on the struggle for social justice. In C.J. Ovando and P. McLaren (eds) *The Politics of Multiculturalism and Bilingual Education: Students and Teachers Caught in the Cross Fire* (pp. 22–49). Boston: McGraw Hill.

McLaughlin, B. (1985) *Second-Language Acquisition in Childhood. Vol. 2: School-Age Children.* 2nd edn. Hillsdale, NJ: Lawrence Erlbaum Associates.

McNamara, B. E. (1998) *Learning Disabilities: Appropriate Practices for a Diverse Population.* Albany, NY: State University of New York Press.

McNamara, T. (1996) *Measuring Second Language Performance.* London: Longman.

McQuillan, J. (1998) *The Literacy Crisis: False Claims, Real Solutions.* Portsmouth, NH: Heinemann.

McQuillan, J. and Tse, L. (1996) Does research matter? An analysis of media opinion on bilingual education 1984–1994. *Bilingual Research Journal* 20 (1), 1–27.

McWilliam, N. (1998) *What's in a Word? Vocabulary Development in Multilingual Classrooms.* Stoke on Trent: Trentham Books.

Mercer, J. R. (1973) *Labelling the Mentally Retarded.* Los Angeles: University of California Press.

Merino, B. and Rumberger, R. (1999) Why ELD standards are needed for English learners. *University of California Linguistic Minority Research Institute Newsletter* 8 (3), 1.

Micklethwait, J. (2000, March 11-17). Survey: The United States. Oh, say, can you see? *The Economist* (insert, pp 1–18).

Miller, J.P. (1996) *The Holistic Curriculum.* Toronto: Ontario Institute for Studies in Education.

Mohan, B. (1986) *Language and Content.* Reading, MA: Addison-Wesley.

Mohanty, A.K. (1994) *Bilingualism in a Multilingual Society: Psychological and Pedagogical Implications.* Mysore: Central Institute of Indian Languages.

Moll, L.C., Amanti, C., Neff, D. and González, N. (1992) Funds of knowledge for teaching: Using a qualitative approach to connect homes and classrooms. *Theory into Practice* 31 (2), 132–141.

Moore, H. (1996) Telling what is real: Competing views in assessing English as a second language development. *Linguistics and Education* 8 (2), 189–228.

Moraes, M. (1996) *Bilingual Education: A Dialogue with the Bakhtin Circle.* Albany: State University of New York Press.

Morgan, B. (1998) *The ESL Classroom: Teaching, Critical Practice and Community Development.* Toronto: University of Toronto Press.

Morgan, B. (1999) Exploring critical citizenship in a community-based ESL program. Doctoral dissertation, University of Toronto, Toronto.

Morgan, G. (1996) An investigation into the achievement of African-Caribbean pupils. *Multicultural Teaching* 14 (2), 37–40.

Muñoz-Sandoval, A., Cummins, J., Alvarado, C.G. and Ruef, M.L. (1998) *Bilingual Verbal Ability Tests.* Itasca, IL: Riverside Publishing.

Nadeau, A. (1998) *California English Language Proficiency Assessment Project.* San Diego County Office of Education.

Nation, I.S.P. (1990) *Teaching and Learning Vocabulary.* Boston, MA: Heinle and Heinle Publishers.

National Clearinghouse for Bilingual Education (1997) *High Stakes Assessment: A Research Agenda for English Language Learners.* Washington, DC: National Clearinghouse for Bilingual Education.

Neuman, S.B. (1999) Books make a difference: A study of access to literacy. *Reading Research Quarterly* 34 (3), 286–311.

New London Group (1996) A pedagogy of multiliteracies: Designing social futures. *Harvard Educational Review* 66, 60–92.

New Standards (1995) *Performance Standards, English Language Arts, Mathematics, Science, and Applied Learning. Volumes 1, 2, and 3. Consultation Drafts.* Washington, DC: National Center for Education and the Economy.

Newman, D., Griffin, P. and Cole, M. (1989) *The Construction Zone: Working for Cognitive Change in School.* Cambridge: Cambridge University Press.

Nicoladis, E., Taylor, D.M., Lambert, W.E. and Cazabon, M. (1998) What two-way bilingual programmes reveal about the controversy surrounding race and intelligence. *International Journal of Bilingual Education and Bilingualism* 1 (2), 134–148.

Nieto, S. (1996) *Affirming Diversity: The Sociopolitical Context of Multicultural Education. 2nd edn.* White Plains, NY: Longman.

Nieto, S. (1999) *The Light in Their Eyes: Creating Multicultural Learning Communities.* New York: Teachers College Press.

Noonan, B., Colleaux, J. and Yackulic, R.A. (1997) Two approaches to beginning reading in early French immersion. *Canadian Modern Language Review* 53 (4), 729–742.

Norton, B. and Stewart, G. (1999) Accountability in language assessment of adult immigrants in Canada. *The Canadian Modern Language Review* 56 (2), 223–244.

Norton Peirce, B. (1992) Demystifying the TOEFL Reading Test. *TESOL Quarterly* 26 (4), 665–689.

Norton Peirce, B. and Stewart, G. (1997) The development of the Canadian Language Benchmarks Assessment. *TESL Canada Journal* 15 (1), 17–31.

Obondo, M.A. (1996) *From Trilingual to Bilinguals? A Study of the Social and Linguistic Consequences of Language Shift on a Group of Urban Luo Children in Kenya.* Stockholm: Centre for Research on Bilingualism, Stockholm University.

Obondo, M.A. (1997) Bilingual education in Africa: An overview. In J. Cummins and D. Corson (eds) *Bilingual education. Vol. 5. Encyclopedia of Language and Education* (pp. 25–32). Dordrecht, The Netherlands: Kluwer Academic Publishers.

Odani, S. (1999 (Summer)) Japan's baby bust: Young and old alike feeling the pinch. *Via: The Quarterly Onboard Magazine of the Airport Limousine* 24–25.

O'Donoghue, F. (1998) The hunger for professional learning in Nunavut schools. Doctoral dissertation, University of Toronto, Toronto.

Office of Educational Equity (1990) *Two-Way Integrated Bilingual Education.* Boston: Department of Education.

Ogbu, J. (1978) *Minority Education and Caste.* New York: Academic Press.

Ogbu, J.U. (1992) Understanding cultural diversity and learning. *Educational Researcher* 21 (8), 5–14 and 24.

Okazaki, T. (1999, August) Interrelationships between children's L2 acquisition, L1 maintenance, and interdependence. Paper presented at the AILA Congress, Tokyo.

Oller, J.W., Jr. (1979) *Language Tests at School: A Pragmatic Approach.* London: Longman.

Oller, J.W., Jr. (ed.) (1983) *Issues in Language Testing Research.* Rowley, MA: Newbury House.

Oller, J.W.J. (1997) Monoglottosis: What's wrong with the idea of the IQ meritocracy and its racy cousins? *Applied Linguistics* 18 (4), 467–507.

Olsen, L., Chang, H., De La Rosa Salazar, D., Leong, C., McCall Perez, Z., McClain, G. and Raffel, L. (1994) *The Unfinished Journey: Restructuring Schools in a Diverse Society.* San Francisco: California Tomorrow.

Olson, D.R. (1977) From utterance to text: The bias of language in speech and writing. *Harvard Educational Review* 47, 257–281.

Olson, D.R. (1994) *The World on Paper.* Cambridge: Cambridge University Press.

O'Malley, J.M. (1996) *Using Authentic Assessment in ESL Classrooms.* Glenview, IL: Scott Foresman.

O'Malley, J.M. and Pierce, L.V. (1996) *Authentic Assessment for English Language Learners: Practical Approaches for the K-12 Classroom.* Reading, MA: Addison-Wesley.

Ortiz, A.A. and Yates, J.R. (1983) Incidence of exceptionality among Hispanics: Implications for manpower planning. *NABE Journal* 7, 41–54.

Orwell, G. (1983) *The Penguin Complete Novels of George Orwell.* London: Penguin Books.

Ovando, C. and McLaren, P. (eds) (1999) *The Politics of Multiculturalism and Bilingual Education: Students and Teachers Caught in the Cross Fire.* Boston: McGraw Hill.

Ovando, C.J. and Collier, V.P. (1998) *Bilingual and ESL Classrooms: Teaching in Multicultural Contexts* (2nd edn). Boston: McGraw Hill.

Oyster Bilingual School (1999) *Local School Plan.* Washington, DC: Oyster Bilingual School.

Paribakht, T.S. and Wesche, M. (1997) Vocabulary enhancement activities and reading for meaning in second language vocabulary acquisition. In J. Coady and T. Huckin (eds)

Second Language Vocabulary Acquisition: A Rationale for Pedagogy. Cambridge: Cambridge University Press.

Patthey-Chavez, G.G., Clare, L. and Gallimore, R. (1995) *Creating a Community of Scholarship with Instructional Conversations in a Transitional Bilingual Classroom*. Santa Cruz: National Center for Research on Cultural Diversity and Second Language Learning.

Patthey-Chavez, G. and Goldenberg, C. (1995) Changing instructional discourse for changing students: The instructional conversation. In R. Macías and R. García Ramos (eds) *Changing Schools for Changing Students: An Anthology of Research on Language Minorities, Schools and Society* (pp. 205–230). Santa Barbara, CA: University of California Linguistic Minority Research Institute.

Paulston, C.B. (1982) *Swedish Research and Debate about Bilingualism*. Stockholm: Swedish National Board of Education.

Paulston, C.B. (1994) *Linguistic Minorities in Multicultural Settings*. Amsterdam/ Philadelphia: John Benjamins.

Payne, K.J. and Biddle, B.J. (1999) Poor school funding, child poverty, and mathematics achievement. *Educational Researcher* 28 (6), 4–13.

Peirce, B.N. (1995) Social identity, investment, and language learning. *TESOL Quarterly* 29 (1), 9–31.

Peña-Hughes, E. and Solís, J. (1980) *ABCs* (Unpublished report). McAllen Independent School District.

Pennycook, A. (1998) *English and the Discourses of Colonialism*. London: Routledge.

Pennycook, A. (ed.) (1999) *Critical Approaches to TESOL: Special Topic Issue of TESOL Quarterly* (Vol. 33 (3)). Washington, DC: TESOL.

Pérez, B. (1998a) Literacy, diversity, and programmatic responses. In B. Pérez (ed.) *Sociocultural Contexts of Language and Literacy* (pp. 3–20). Mahwah, NJ: Lawrence Erlbaum Associates.

Pérez, B. (1998b) Language, literacy, and biliteracy. In B. Pérez (ed.) *Sociocultural Contexts of Language and Literacy* (pp. 21–48). Mahwah, NJ: Lawrence Erlbaum Associates.

Pérez-Sélles, M. (2000) Quality bilingual programs yield high MCAS results. *NABE Newsletter* 21 (2), 1.

Peterson, B. (1994) Teaching for social justice: One teacher's journey. In B. Bigelow, L. Christensen, S. Karp, B. Miner and B. Peterson (eds) *Rethinking our Classrooms: Teaching for Equity and Justice* (pp. 30–38). Milwaukee, WI: Rethinking Schools.

Phillipson, R. (1992) *Linguistic Imperialism*. Oxford: Oxford University Press.

Phillipson, R. (1999) Voice in global English: Unheard chords in crystal loud and clear. *Applied Linguistics* 20 (2), 265–276.

Pike, L.W. (1979) An evaluation of alternative item formats for testing English as a foreign language. *TOEFL Research Reports No. 2*. Princeton, NJ: Educational Testing Service.

Poe, E.A. (1997/1842) The pit and the pendulum. In *Literature and Integrated Studies: American Literature* (pp. 253–264). Glenview, IL: ScottForesman.

Pogrow, S. (1999) Rejoinder: Consistent large gains and high levels of achievement are the best measures of program quality: Pogrow responds to Slavin. *Educational Researcher* 28 (8), 24–31.

Poplin, M. and Weeres, J. (1992) *Voices from the Inside: A Report on Schooling from Inside the Classroom*. Claremont, CA: The Institute for Education in Transformation at the Claremont Graduate School.

Porter, R.P. (1990) *Forked Tongue: The Politics of Bilingual Education*. New York: Basic Books.

Porter, R.P. (1998, May) The case against bilingual education. *Atlantic Monthly* 281 (5), 28–39.

Postlethwaite, T.N. and Ross, K.N. (1992) *Effective Schools in Reading: Implications for Educational Planners. An Exploratory Study*. The Hague: The International Association for the Evaluation of Educational Achievement.

Powell, A.B. and Frankenstein, M. (eds) (1997) *Ethnomathematics*. Albany, NY: State University of New York Press.

President's Commission on Foreign Languages and International Studies (1980) *Strength Through Wisdom: A Critique of US Capability*. Washington, DC: US Government Printing Office.

Qian, D.D. (1998) Depth of vocabulary knowledge: Assessing its role in adults' reading comprehension in English as a second language. Doctoral dissertation, University of Toronto, Toronto.

Qian, D.D. (1999) Assessing the roles of depth and breadth of vocabulary knowledge in reading comprehension. *The Canadian Modern Language Review* 56 (2), 282–307.

Quantz, R. and O'Connor, T. (1988) Writing critical ethnography: Dialogue, multivoicedness, and carnival in cultural texts. *Educational Theory* 38 (1), 95–109.

Ramírez, J.D. (1992) Executive summary. *Bilingual Research Journal* 16, 1–62.

Ramírez, J.D., Yuen, S.D. and Ramey, D.R. (1991) *Executive Summary: Final Report: Longitudinal Study of Structured English Immersion Strategy, Early-Exit and Late-Exit Transitional Bilingual Education Programs for Language-Minority Children* (Contract No. 300-87-0156). Washington, DC: US Department of Education.

Read, J. (1993) The development of a new measure of L2 vocabulary knowledge. *Language Testing* 10, 355–371.

Read, J. (1995, March) Validating the Word Associates Format as a measure of depth of vocabulary knowledge. Paper presented at the 17th Language Testing Research Colloquium, Long Beach, California.

Read, J. (1997) Assessing vocabulary in a second language. In C. Clapham and D. Corson (eds) *Language Testing and Assessment. Vol. 7. Encyclopedia of Language and Education.* (pp. 99–107). Dordrecht: Kluwer Academic Publishers.

Reid, E. and Reich, H. (1992) *Breaking the Boundaries: Migrant Workers' Children in the EC*. Clevedon: Multilingual Matters.

Reyes, M. (1992) Challenging venerable assumptions: Literacy instruction for linguistically different students. *Harvard Educational Review* 62, 427–446.

Ricciardelli, L.A. (1992) Bilingualism and cognitive development in relation to threshold theory. *Journal of Psycholinguistic Research* 21, 301–316.

Ricciardelli, L.A. (1993) An investigation of the cognitive development of Italian–English bilinguals and Italian monolinguals from Rome. *Journal of Multilingual and Multicultural Development* 14 (4), 345–346.

Riley, R.W. (2000) Excelencia para todos – Excellence for all. The progress of Hispanic education and the challenges of a new century. Remarks as prepared for delivery by US Secretary of Education, Richard W. Riley, Bell Multicultural High School, Washington, DC, March 15. Available at http://www.ed.gov/Speeches/03-2000/000315.html.

Rivera, C. (1984) *Language Proficiency and Academic Achievement*. Clevedon: Multilingual Matters.

Robson, A. (1995) The assessment of bilingual children. In M.K. Verma, K.P. Corrigan and S. Firth (eds) *Working with Bilingual Children* (pp. 28–47). Clevedon: Multilingual Matters.

Romaine, S. (1989) *Bilingualism*. Oxford: Oxford University Press.

Rossell, C.H. (1996) RTE Forum: Letters from readers. *Research in the Teaching of English* 30 (1), 376–385.

Rossell, C.H. (1998) Mystery on the bilingual express: A critique of the Thomas and Collier study. *READ Perspectives* 5 (2), 5–32.

Rossell, C.H. and Baker, K. (1996) The effectiveness of bilingual education. *Research in the Teaching of English* 30, 7–74.

Rossell, C.H. and Ross, J.M. (1986) The social science evidence on bilingual education. *Journal of Law and Education* 15, 385–418.

Ruiz, R. (1984) Orientations in language planning. *NABE Journal* 8, 15–34.

Samaniego, F. and Eubank, I. (in press) A statistical analysis of California's Case Study project in bilingual education. In R. Macias (ed.) *An Anthology of Recent Research on the*

Academic Performance of Linguistic Minority Children. Santa Barbara, CA: University of California Language Minority Research Institute.

Samway, K.D. and McKeon, D. (1999) *Myths and Realities: Best Practices for Language Minority Students.* Portsmouth, NH: Heinemann.

Sasaki, M. (1996) *Second Language Proficiency, Foreign Language Aptitude, and Intelligence: Quantitative and Qualitative Analyses.* New York: Peter Lang.

Saunders, W., O'Brien, G., Lennon, D. and McLean, J. (1999) *Successful Transition into Mainstream English: Effective Strategies for Studying Literature.* Santa Cruz, CA: Center for Research on Education, Diversity and Excellence.

Saunders, W.M. and Goldenberg, C. (1999) *The Effects of Instructional Conversations and Literature Logs on the Story Comprehension and Thematic Understanding of English Proficient and Limited English Proficient Students.* Santa Cruz: Center for Research on Education, Diversity and Excellence.

Schecter, S.R. and Bayley, R. (1998) Concurrence and complementarity: Mexican-background parents' decisions about language and schooling. *Journal for a Just and Caring Education* 4 (1), 47–64.

Schlesinger, A.J. (1991) *The Disuniting of America.* New York: W. W. Norton.

Schmitt, N. (1999) The relationship between TOEFL vocabulary items and meaning, association, collocation and word-class knowledge. *Language Testing* 16 (2), 189–216.

Shannon, S. (1995) The hegemony of English: A case study of one bilingual classroom as a site of resistance. *Linguistics and Education* 7, 175–200.

Shohamy, E. (1997) Second language assessment. In G.R. Tucker and D. Corson (eds) *Second Language Education: Vol. 4. Encyclopedia of Language and Education* (pp. 141–147). Dordrecht: Kluwer Academic Publishers.

Shohamy, E. (1999) Unity and diversity in language policy. Paper presented at the AILA conference, Tokyo, August.

Shohamy, E. (2000) *The Power of Tests: A Critical Perspective on the Uses and Consequences of Language Tests.* London: Longman.

Shor, I. (1992) *Empowering Education: Critical Teaching for Social Change.* Chicago: The University of Chicago Press.

Sierra, J. and Olaziregi, I. (1991) *EIFE 3. Influence of Factors on the Learning of Basque. Study of the Models A, B and D in Second Year Basic General Education.* Gasteiz: Central Publications Service of the Basque Country.

Sirotnik, K.A. (1983) What you see is what you get – consistency, persistency, and mediocrity in classrooms. *Harvard Educational Review* 53, 16–31.

Skourtou, E. (1995) Some notes about the relationship between bilingualism and literacy concerning the teaching of Greek as a second language. *European Journal of Intercultural Studies* 6 (2), 24–30.

Skutnabb-Kangas, T. (1979) *Language in the Process of Cultural Assimilation and Structural Incorporation of Linguistic Minorities.* Washington, DC: National Clearinghouse for Bilingual Education.

Skutnabb-Kangas, T. (1984) *Bilingualism or Not: The Education of Minoritites.* Clevedon: Multilingual Matters.

Skutnabb-Kangas, T. (1988) Resource power and autonomy through discourse in conflict: A Finnish migrant school strike in Sweden. In T. Skutnabb-Kangas and J. Cummins (eds) *Minority Education: From Shame to Struggle* (pp. 251–277). Clevedon: Multilingual Matters.

Skutnabb-Kangas, T. (ed.) (1995) *Multilingualism For All.* Lisse: Swets and Zeitlinger.

Skutnabb-Kangas, T. (2000) *Linguistic Genocide in Education – or Worldwide Diversity and Human Rights.* Mawah, NJ: Lawrence Erlbaum Associates.

Skutnabb-Kangas, T. and Toukomaa, P. (1976) *Teaching Migrant Children's Mother Tongue and Learning the Language of the Host Country in the Context of the Sociocultural Situation of the Migrant Family.* Helsinki: The Finnish National Commission for UNESCO.

Slavin, R. and Fashola, O.S. (1998) *Show me the Evidence! Proven and Promising Programs for American Schools*. Thousand Oaks, CA: Corwin Press.

Slavin, R.E., Madden, N.A., Dolan, L.J. and Wasik, B.A. (1996) *Every Child, Every School: Success for All*. Thousand Oaks, CA: Corwin Press.

Smith, P. (1999) Drawing new maps: A radical cartography of developmental disabilities. *Review of Educational Research* 69 (2), 117–144.

Snow, C.E., Cancino, H., De Temple, J. and Schley, S. (1991) Giving formal definitions: A linguistic or metalinguistic skill? In E. Bialystok (ed.) *Language Processing in Bilingual Children* (pp. 90–112). Cambridge: Cambridge University Press.

Snow, C.E. and Hoefnagel-Hohle, M. (1979) Individual differences in second-language ability: A factor-analytic study. *Language and Speech* 22 (2), 151–162.

Snow, D.E. and Hoefnagel-Höhle, M. (1978) The critical period for language acquisition: Evidence from second language learning. *Child Development* 49, 1114–1128.

Solomon, J. and Rhodes, N. (1996) Assessing academic language: Results of a survey. *TESOL Journal*, 5–8.

Solomon, J. and Rhodes, N.C. (1995) *Conceptualizing Academic Language*. Santa Cruz: National Center for Research on Cultural Diversity and Second Language Learning.

Soto, L.D. (1996) *Language, Culture, and Power: Bilingual Families and the Struggle for Quality Education*. New York: SUNY Press.

Spolsky, B. (1984) A note on the dangers of terminology innovation. In C. Rivera (ed.) *Language Proficiency and Academic Achievement* (pp. 41–43). Clevedon: Multilingual Matters.

Stedman, L. C. (1987) It's time we changed the effective schools formula. *Phi Delta Kappan* 69, 215–224.

Street, B. (1984) *Literacy in Theory and Practice*. New York: Cambridge University Press.

Street, B.V. (ed.) (1993) *Cross-Cultural Approaches to Literacy*. Cambridge: Cambridge University Press.

Stroud, C. (1978) The concept of semilingualism. *Working Papers*, 16, 153–172. Lund University, Department of General Linguistics.

Students for Cultural and Linguistic Democracy (1996) Reclaiming our voices. In C.E. Walsh (ed.) *Education Reform and Social Change: Multicultural Voices, Struggles, and Visions* (pp. 129–146). Mahwah, NJ: Lawrence Erlbaum Associates.

Stutz, T. (1999, November 4, 1999) Social conservatives, critics clash on phonics: Other states await Texas' decision on textbooks. *Dallas Morning News*, pp. 1A, 17A.

Swain, M. (1997) Collaborative dialogue: Its contribution to second language learning. *Revista Canaria de Estudios Ingleses* 34, 115–132.

Swain, M. and Lapkin, S. (1982) *Evaluating Bilingual Education*. Clevedon: Multilingual Matters.

Swain, M. and Lapkin, S. (1991) Heritage language children in an English–French bilingual program. *The Canadian Modern Language Review* 47 (4), 635–641.

Swain, M., Lapkin, S., Rowen, N. and Hart, D. (1991) The role of mother tongue literacy in third language learning. In S.P. Norris and L.M. Phillips (eds) *Foundations of Literacy Policy in Canada* (pp. 185–206). Calgary: Detselig Enterprises.

Teachers of English to Speakers of Other Languages Inc. (1997) *ESL Standards for Pre-K-12 Students*. Washington, DC: Teachers of English to Speakers of Other Languages Inc.

Terrazas, B. and and Students for Cultural and Linguistic Democracy (1995) Struggling for power and voice: A high school experience. In J. Frederickson (ed.) *Reclaiming Our Voices: Bilingual Education, Critical Pedagogy and Praxis* (pp. 279–310). Ontario, CA: California Association for Bilingual Education.

Thomas, W.P. and Collier, V. (1997) *School Effectiveness for Language Minority Students*. Washington, DC: National Clearinghouse for Bilingual Education.

Thompson, E. (1998) Introduction. In R. MacDougall (ed.) *The Emigrant's Guide to North America* (pp. vii–xxix). Toronto: Natural Heritage Books.

Tollefson, J. (1991) *Planning Language, Planning Inequality: Language Planning in the Community*. London: Longman.

Tompkins, J. (1998) *Teaching in a Cold and Windy Place: Change in an Inuit School*. Toronto: University of Toronto Press.

Traub, J. (1999, January 31). Bilingual barrier. *The New York Times Magazine*, pp. 32–35.

Troike, R. (1984) SCALP: Social and cultural aspects of language proficiency. In C. Rivera (ed.) *Language Proficiency and Academic Achievement*. Clevedon: Multilingual Matters.

Tse, L. (1999) Finding a place to be: Ethnic identity exploration of Asian Americans. *Adolescence* 34 (133), 122–138.

Ulibarri, D.M., Spencer, M. and Rivas, G. M. (1981) Language proficiency and academic achievement: A study of language proficiency tests and their relationship to school ratings as predictors of academic achievement. *NABE Journal* 5 (3), 47–80.

Umbel, V.M. and Oller, D.K. (1995) Developmental changes in receptive vocabulary in Hispanic bilingual school children. In B. Harley (ed.) *Lexical Issues in Language Learning* (pp. 59–80). Ann Arbor: Research Club in Language Learning.

Valdés, G. (1997) Dual-language immersion programs: A cautionary note concerning the education of language-minority students. *Harvard Education Review* 67 (3), 391–429.

Vásquez, O.A., Pease-Alvarez, L. and Shannon, S. M. (1994) *Pushing Boundaries: Language and Culture in a Mexicano Community*. New York: Cambridge University Press.

Verhallen, M. and Schoonen, R. (1998) Lexical knowledge in L1 and L2 of third and fifth graders. *Applied Linguistics* 19 (4), 452–470.

Verhoeven, L. (1991a) Acquistion of biliteracy. In J.H. Hulsijn and J.F. Matter (eds) *Reading in Two Languages* (pp. 61–74). Amsterdam: AILA.

Verhoeven, L. (1991b) Predicting minority children's bilingual proficiency: Child, family, and institutional factors. *Language Learning* 41, 205–233.

Verhoeven, L. (1994) Transfer in bilingual development: The linguistic interdependence hypothesis revisited. *Language Learning* 44, 381–415.

Verhoeven, L. and Aarts, R. (1998) Attaining functional literacy in the Netherlands. In A.Y. Durgunoğlu and L. Verhoeven (eds) *Literacy Development in a Multilingual Context: Cross-Cultural Perspectives* (pp. 111–134). Mahwah, NJ: Lawrence Erlbaum Associates.

Viadero, D. (1999, August 4) Research board urges broad approach to bilingual ed. *Education Week*, pp. 12.

Vincent, C. (1996) Singing to a star: The school meanings of second generation Salvadorean students. Doctoral dissertation, George Mason University, Fairfax, VA.

Vincent, D. (1997) The testing of reading in the mother tongue. In C. Clapham and D. Corson (eds) *Language Testing and Assessment. Vol. 7. Encyclopedia of Language and Education* (pp. 1–10). Dordrecht: Kluwer Academic Publishers.

Vygotsky, L. (1962) *Thought and Language*. Cambridge, MA: MIT Press.

Wagner, D. A. (1998) Putting second language first: Language and literacy learning in Morocco. In L. Verhoeven and A.Y. Durgunoglu (eds) *Literacy Development in a Multilingual Context* (pp. 169–183). Mahway, NJ: Lawrence Erlbaum Associates.

Wagner, S. (1991) *Analphabetisme de Minorité et Alphabetisme d'Affirmation Nationale à Propos de l'Ontario Français. Vol. I: Synthèse Theoretique et Historique*. Toronto: Ministère de l'Education.

Wald, B. (1984) A sociolinguistic perspective on Cummins' current framework for relating language proficiency to academic achievement. In C. Rivera (ed.) *Language Proficiency and Academic Achievement* (pp. 55–70). Clevedon: Multilingual Matters.

Walsh, C.E. (1991) *Pedagogy and the Struggle for Voice: Issues of Language, Power, and Schooling for Puerto Ricans*. Toronto: OISE Press.

Walsh, C.E. (ed.) (1996) *Education Reform and Social Change: Multicultural Voices, Struggles, and Visions*. Mahwah, NJ: Lawrence Erlbaum Associates.

Warschauer, M. (1999) *Electronic Literacies: Language, Culture, and Power in Online Education*. Mahwah, NJ: Lawrence Erlbaum Associates.

Watt, D.L.E. and Roessingh, H. (1994) Some you win, most you lose: Tracking ESL student drop out in high school (1988–1993). *English Quarterly* 26 (3), 5–7.

Wells, G. (1981) *Learning through Interaction: The Study of Language Development.* Cambridge: Cambridge University Press.

Wells, G. (1986) *The Meaning Makers.* Portsmouth, NH: Heinemann.

Wiley, T.G. (1996) *Literacy and Language Diversity in the United States.* Washington, DC: Center for Applied Linguistics and Delta Systems.

Williams, E. (1996) Reading in two languages at Year 5 in African primary schools. *Applied Linguistics* 17 (2), 183–209.

Willig, A.C. (1981/82) The effectiveness of bilingual education: Review of a report. *NABE Journal* 6, 1–19.

Willig, A.C. (1985) A meta-analysis of selected studies on the effectiveness of bilingual education. *Review of Educational Research* 55, 269–317.

Willis, P. (1977) *Learning to Labor: How Working Class Kids Get Working Class Jobs.* Lexington: D. C. Heath.

Wink, J. (2000) *Critical Pedagogy: Notes from the Real World. 2nd edn.* New York: Longman.

Wong Fillmore, L. (1990) Now or later? Issues related to the early education of minority group children. In C. Harris (ed.) *Children at Risk.* New York: Harcourt, Brace, Jovanovich.

Wong Fillmore, L. (1991) When learning a second language means losing the first. *Early Childhood Research Quarterly* 6, 323–346.

Wong Fillmore, L. (1992) Against our best interest: The attempt to sabotage bilingual education. In J. Crawford (ed.) *Language Loyalties: A Sourcebook on the Official English Controversy.* Chicago: University of Chicago Press.

Wong Fillmore, L. (1998) Supplemental declaration of Lily Wong Fillmore. Legal declaration in Appeal of Proposition 227. Available at: http://ourworld.compuserve.com/homepages/jwcrawford

Wong Fillmore, L. and Valadez, C. (1986) Teaching bilingual learners. In M.C. Wittrock (ed.) *Handbook of Research on Teaching* (pp. 648–685). New York: Macmillan.

Zanger, V.V. (1994) 'Not joined in': Intergroup relations and access to English literacy for Hispanic youth. In B.M. Ferdman, R.-M. Weber and A. Ramírez (eds) *Literacy Across Languages and Cultures* (pp. 171–198). Albany. SUNY Press.

Zehler, A.M., Hopstock, P.J., Fleischman, H.L. and Greniuk, C. (1994) *An Examination of Assessment of Limited English Proficient Students.* Arlington, VA: Development Associates Inc.

Subject Index

Academic achievement 29, 34-35, 37, 42, 52, 57, 85, 93, 97-100, 105, 108-110, 152, 166, 174, 189, 223, 226, 232, 240, 247, 255, 264, 270, 278, 282

Academic language proficiency 3, 7, 24, 35-37, 50, 54-111, 113, 126-7, 133-134, 136-138, 142, 162-163, 166, 173, 175, 190, 197, 203, 225, 273, 278

Additive bilingualism 7, 37-39, 100, 175, 182, 190-191, 193, 198

Africa 29, 186

African American students 1, 42, 218, 225, 248, 253, 277, 279

African Canadian students 52

African Caribbean students 51

American Sign Language (ASL) 29

Amigos program 21, 227-228, 231

Anglo-Saxon lexicon 76, 78-9, 127

Assessment 3, 13-17, 26, 30, 33-34, 36-37, 44-45, 47, 49, 53-54, 56-58, 76, 83-84, 91-92, 95, 103, 109-110, 112-168, 189, 199, 201, 203, 221, 227-9, 245, 251-252, 255, 259, 265, 270, 275

Assimilation 33, 41-42, 45-46, 50

Australia 29, 81-82, 97, 114, 130, 140, 142, 144-145, 151-153, 155, 157, 178, 271

'Banking' education 45, 47-48, 139, 257-258, 282

Basic interpersonal communicative skills (BICS) 3, 58-59, 65-66, 73-75, 85-111, 119, 199-200

Basque 38, 179, 202

Biliteracy 3, 20, 23, 25, 28, 95, 169-170, 178, 187, 190, 192-193, 198, 203, 210-216, 272-273

Burakumin students 12, 42

Cahuenga School 20, 228

California 14, 18-20, 26-27, 31-32, 35, 40, 50-51, 87-88, 94, 142, 148-150, 153, 174, 183, 195, 197-199, 208, 227, 239, 247-248, 264, 282

CALLA 270-271

Canada 4, 6, 13, 16, 20-21, 23, 29, 40-42, 51-52, 72, 114-118, 128, 138-139, 141, 145-146, 153-154, 170-171, 174, 180, 191-193, 202, 210-213, 234, 241, 250, 252

Coercive relations of power 4, 6-7, 31, 43-51, 54, 92, 95, 103, 105, 109-111, 169, 172, 192, 219, 229, 235, 244-246, 252-253, 269

Cognitive academic language proficiency (CALP) 3, 53-111, 119, 122, 126-127, 133, 138, 199-200

Cognitive demands 54, 59, 66, 68, 90, 98, 126, 137

Collaborative relations of power 31, 43-51, 229, 235, 239, 244, 246, 253, 269

Common underlying proficiency (CUP) 38, 182, 191

Communicative language testing 54, 121-123, 128, 134

Comprehensible input 24, 57, 83, 103, 139, 273-275

Contextual support 54, 59, 62, 66-72, 82-85, 90, 126, 136

Context embedded/context reduced continuum 59, 65-73, 81-83, 90, 114-115, 139, 145

Conversational language proficiency 3, 7, 15, 17, 24, 34-37, 39, 50, 53-111, 113, 124-128, 133, 136-137, 139, 153, 183-184, 196, 198-200, 203, 212, 226, 278

Cooperative learning 69, 217, 265, 267, 283

307